# CONTEMPORARY STATES OF EMERGENCY

# CONTEMPORARY STATES OF EMERGENCY

## The Politics of Military and
## Humanitarian Interventions

edited by

Didier Fassin and Mariella Pandolfi

ZONE BOOKS · NEW YORK

2013

ZONE BOOKS
1226 Prospect Avenue
Brooklyn, NY 11218

*First paperback edition*

Printed in the United States of America

Distributed by The MIT Press,
Cambridge, Massachusetts, and London, England


Library of Congress Cataloging-in-Publication Data

Contemporary states of emergency : the politics of military
and humanitarian interventions / edited by Didier Fassin and
Mariella Pandolfi.
     p.   cm.
  ISBN 978-1-935408-01-7
     1. Humanitarian intervention. 2. Humanitarian assistance.
3. Emergency management—International cooperation. 4. Disaster
relief—International cooperation. 5. Conflict management—
International cooperation. I. Fassin, Didier. II. Pandolfi, Mariella.

  JZ6369.C665 2010
  327.1′17—dc22

                                 2009040402

# Contents

# Introduction: Military and Humanitarian Government in the Age of Intervention

Didier Fassin and Mariella Pandolfi

> I am not insensible to the respectable sentiments of humanity which are invoked to support the case for intervention; but I also know that, of all things, the most cruel is a mistaken and useless interference.
> —*Letters by Historicus on Some Questions of International Law*, 1863

Earthquakes in Iran and Pakistan, tsunamis in Indonesia and Sri Lanka, mudslides in Venezuela and the Philippines, hurricanes in Honduras and Louisiana, floods in Burma and China, famine in Ethiopia and North Korea—the rhythm of life in contemporary societies is punctuated by disaster. Images of catastrophe form part of our everyday surroundings, evoking private and public responses of compassion and solidarity that prove more or less effective and prompting the mobilization of human and financial resources that development aid can no longer provide: the exodus of Bangladeshi refugees from India, the flight of the Vietnamese boat people, the genocide in Rwanda, the massacres in Darfur, the intifada in the Palestinian Occupied Territories, the civil wars in Somalia and Haiti, the ethnic oppression in Kosovo and West Timor. Political conflicts and their bloody consequences are similarly present in our media landscape, they, too, prompting surges of emotion and strategic calculations and calling for nongovernmental action and for military operations.

These two series of events—disasters and conflicts—are not as different as they might appear. While the former apparently result from natural phenomena and the latter from human confrontations, the boundary between the two remains porous. The 1983 famine in Ethiopia was the result of authoritarian policies and displacement of populations; the region of Aceh was both the worst hit by the tsunami in 2004 and the scene of long-standing conflict between the Indonesian armed forces and separatist groups; and the Burmese dictatorship prevented the rescue of the victims of the floods in Burma in 2008, its attitude contrasting with the Chinese government's decision to open the country to aid when faced with a similar disaster at the same time, keen as it was to show itself in a favorable light in the run-up to the Beijing Olympic Games. Above all, disasters and conflicts are now embedded in the same global logic of intervention, which rests on two fundamental elements: the temporality of emergency, which is used to justify a state of exception, and the conflation of the political and moral registers manifested in the realization of operations which are at once military and humanitarian. This book is devoted to that dual reality of contemporary interventionism: the generalization, at the international but also at the national level, of states of emergency and the institution of a military and humanitarian government as a mode of response to situations of disorder.

The principle of intervention, which has become normalized since the "right to intervene" has been asserted, constitutes an important political innovation of the late twentieth century, a break with the doctrine of sovereignty that had prevailed until then. Indeed, immediately after World War II, the UN Charter had stated that the new organization was based on the principle of the "sovereign equality" of its members (Article 2-1) and specifically proscribed intervention "in matters which are essentially within the domestic jurisdiction of any state" (Article 2-7), following a European legal tradition established at the time of the Treaty of Westphalia in 1648.[1] The response to conflict should be peaceful preventative action and, when conflict arises, mediation aimed at encouraging negotiation between the protagonists. Admittedly, decolonization put this doctrine to the test in the wars of liberation that established the sovereignty of colonized peoples and their right to self-determination in conflict with the sovereignty of colonizing states and with their logic of the fait accompli of conquest. However, with the creation of postcolonial sovereignties, independence brought a resolution of this tension. The Cold War also saw numerous military interventions, involving particularly the United States in Southeast Asia and Latin America, the Soviet Union in Eastern Europe and Central Asia, and their supporters in Central and Southern Africa, making respect for national sovereignty a relative concept, but essentially, these were classic conflicts between hegemonic powers that followed the mechanism of imperial wars. It might thus be tempting to think — and this is an interpretation frequently offered by those involved — that the fall of the Berlin Wall overturned this order because, on the one hand, the power relations were altered by the disappearance of one of the protagonists in the Cold War, and, on the other, the much heralded end of ideology gave way to a more consensual world of greater solidarity. However, rather than creating a new situation that called for interventionism of a kind previously unknown aimed at protecting populations, saving lives, and relieving suffering, the end of this conflict in fact reveals a paradigm that had been emerging over almost two decades.

From this point of view, India's military intervention aimed at ending the Pakistani Army's brutal repression of the people of East Pakistan, which eventually led to the birth of the independent state of Bangladesh in 1971, appears retrospectively as a turning point.[2] India justified its use of force on the grounds that it could not remain passive in the face of the massacres perpetrated by the Pakistanis, while, inversely, the position taken by the UN, which rejected any military action, was based on Article 2-7 of the UN Charter about domestic jurisdiction. In other words, while India championed the duty to intervene, the UN insisted on respect for sovereignty. The two logics, new and old, confronted one another and, in reality, if not in law, the new logic won out, since India, by entering into conflict with Pakistan, imposed humanitarian reason by force. The Security Council, divided along the lines of the Cold War, stuck to its official position, on which the society of states is based and which consists in preserving the international order at all costs. It could of course be objected that India's decision to intervene was also prompted by its interests in the region, its historical hostility toward neighboring Pakistan, and the massive influx of refugees into its territory, and that conversely, the UN failure to act was largely due to the geostrategic stakes involved in South Asia, influenced by the United States, which supported Pakistan against the Soviet Union, the traditional ally of India. Nevertheless, this moment marked a break in the dogma that had prevailed until then, and above all introduced a new discourse.

Moreover, the conflict between East and West Pakistan is emblematic not just as the first military operation clearly defined as humanitarian in aim, but also because it crystallized the Western world's realization that international regulatory bodies are powerless against the extreme violence of war. The nongovernmental organization MSF, Médecins Sans Frontières (Doctors Without Borders) was formed a few months after Bangladesh gained independence. It was founded by a group of former Red Cross members disappointed by their organization's silence during the Biafran war and shocked by the slaughter of the war in Pakistan. Some time later, the best-known of MSF's founders was to become the champion of the *droit d'ingérence*, the right to intervene, asserting the right of states to ignore the sovereignty of another state in the event of serious violation of humanitarian law.[3] Although this right is not recognized in international law — and still less the *devoir d'ingérence*, the duty to intervene, that some derive from it — Western countries have used it with increasing regularity to justify their interventions on the basis of

Security Council resolutions: in Iraqi Kurdistan in 1991 (Operation Steel, Resolution 688), in Somalia in 1992 (Operation Restore Hope, Resolution 794), and in Rwanda in 1994 (Operation Turquoise, Resolution 929), to cite only the first such instances. To sum up, then, during the 1970s and 1980s—thus, prior to the fall of the Berlin Wall—a new paradigm was gradually being put in place, a paradigm that asserted the right to intervene—or that at least allowed it to prevail over the respect of sovereignty—in the name of lives to be saved and populations to be protected. This paradigm is what we propose to call the "military and humanitarian government" of the world.[4]

Thus, contemporary interventionism is new in that it is legitimized in terms of a moral obligation, rather than a political principle—or more precisely (for morality has always had a place in the justification of war), it is new in that the politics of military intervention are now played out in the name of humanitarian morality. The old interventionism did indeed use moral arguments to determine whether there were grounds for intervening in defense of a weak state or to support a liberation movement, for example, but not in order to protect a population and save lives—it is this specific justification that is new and that is becoming normalized. We might take the example of Vaclav Havel (and Tony Blair) calling for "humanitarian intervention" in Kosovo in 1999, or George Bush (and, once again, Tony Blair) claiming "humanitarian assistance" as the primary objective of the invasion of Iraq in 2003.[5] A comparison of these two military operations—both conducted with Security Council backing—is doubly instructive. The parallel between them suggests a shift from legality toward legitimacy, or rather from a focus on international law to the invocation of the humanitarian argument. Not only does the protection of peoples take precedence over the sovereignty of states, but even the formalism of legal validation by the UN disappears (ironically bringing these cases closer to India's intervention in Bangladesh). Morality now justifies suspension of the rule of law. Yet the comparison also highlights the futility of many debates on the intentions and sincerity of the actors. In fact, the idealism of Havel, who saw the intervention in Kosovo as a victory for human rights over the nation-state, whose excesses he had experienced under the Communist empire, raises the same questions and produces the same consequences as the cynicism of Bush, who invoked defense of the Iraqi people and promised aid despite the fact that the intervention was strictly determined by economic and geostrategic interests (Tony Blair is certainly more difficult to place on this psychocognitive spectrum). In short, good faith is no redemption. Thus this dual observation of the situation in Kosovo and Iraq encourages a form of realism in the analysis of the stakes— and the consequences—of military interventions conducted today in the name of humanitarianism.[6] We cannot simply be satisfied with the supposed morality or the good faith claimed by actors. We need to grasp the new geography of conflicts and, with it, the new international political order.

Thus, humanitarian interventions could be seen as having replaced just wars. On one level, this shift is rhetorical. The debates around the decision to intervene in Kosovo or Iraq centered essentially on arguments that aimed to establish that these military operations were just or, for their opponents, unjust, and thus, they derived in some degree from the old paradigm. Not being founded in law, since they violated the sovereignty of states and were moreover not agreed to by a UN resolution, these operations needed an appearance of legitimacy in the eyes of the protagonists and above all in public opinion—a legitimacy easily conferred by the humanitarian argument. But the development of intervention as norm is more than rhetorical: It grows from a new assumption of self-evidence. Humanitarianism has become the justification for extralegal action.[7] In effect, the only higher reasons that can be set against international law are protecting populations at risk, saving the lives of those in danger, and relieving human suffering.[8] To return to the two series of crises cited above, we might say that the paradigm of disaster prevails over the paradigm of war. Intervention was used in Somalia, Bosnia, and East Timor at the moment when it appeared that thousands of people were being massacred or were in danger of dying in the same way that it was used in Honduras after Hurricane Mitch, in Iran after the earthquake, or in Sri Lanka after the tsunami. In the eyes of the actors, the urgency of the situation and the danger to victims—both of war and of disaster—justified the exception of intervention, which then needed no further justification, least of all in law.

In this operation, whereby the world's disorders, whether natural or human in origin, become equated, we can see a form of naturalization—or depoliticization—of war.[9] Indeed, the humanitarianization of intervention implies the neutralization of conflict situations. Now it is as if the only issue were aid to victims, as if the local context presented no historical peculiarities, as if military operations did not originate in the defense of the interests of the states conducting them. In the case of open conflict, this attempt at neutralization can succeed on only one condition: that there is a very wide gap between the forces involved, so that the military resources of the intervening powers are much greater than those of the belligerent countries. Thus, humanitarian intervention is still a law of the strongest—this is what makes it possible, for there is no question of intervening in Chechnya, Tibet, or even North Korea to protect populations at risk.

This relation of forces—and the realpolitik that, highly paradoxically, underlies military and humanitarian government—explains not only why local impulses toward resistance are discouraged, but also why the human cost of intervention is much lower for the intervening forces, even at the cost of placing the populations on whose behalf the intervention is supposedly undertaken in considerable danger: zero deaths among the NATO forces, compared with the five hundred civilians killed by the bombardment in Kosovo in 1999 and, by 2008, more than forty-five hundred deaths among the coalition troops compared with over a million mainly civilian deaths in Iraq since the invasion in 2003.[10] Given the need to ensure this imbalance between the actors involved, since the early 1990s and the emergence of humanitarian order, it has almost always been the United States and the countries of Western Europe that have intervened in this context, with or without the backing of the UN Security Council, in regions where economic and strategic issues are at stake. Conversely, the only operations undertaken by other states under the aegis of UN missions are those on the African continent in zones considered difficult to manage, such as Angola (the United Nations Angola Verification Mission, UNAVEM), Liberia (the United Nations Mission in Liberia, MINUL), Sierra Leone (the United Nations Observer Mission in Sierra Leone, MONUSIL) and the Democratic Republic of Congo (the UMONUC). Thus, power relations, but also logics of self-interest map a moral geography of the world, a map that reveals the global distribution of those who count, on the one hand, and those whose lives count, on the other.

Admittedly, the mixing of military and humanitarian action is regularly condemned by nongovernmental organizations, which proclaim their humanitarian aims and denounce military action as they intervene. MSF and Oxfam, in particular, reject any assimilation of their presence with the action of armed forces and usually make every effort to keep their distance, sometimes brutally, from international agencies such as the Office of the UN High Commissioner for Refugees, whose missions aimed at protecting populations, saving lives, and relieving suffering are close to their own, but, in the view of the NGOs, precisely too bound up with power plays between states. And it has to be recognized that the NATO bombardment in Kosovo is not equivalent to the actions of humanitarian organizations that cared for Albanian Kosovar refugees in the camps, nor the invasion of Iraq by coalition troops led by the United States to the dispatch of volunteers from the Red Cross and other associations who undertook to risk their lives to aid the people of Iraq. We need to be clear that the work of humanitarian organizations cannot be likened to the action of military forces. It is therefore important that analysis does not add to the confusion of categories that reigns on the ground by blurring the issues and by placing all actors and all logics on the same level. Moreover, this observation holds equally for each of the two sides that need to be distinguished here. Just as, on the military side, the intervention in Somalia and the intervention in Iraq do not follow from the same imperialist motivations on the part of the United States, similarly, on the humanitarian side, the position taken by MSF cannot be conflated with that of MDM, Médecins du Monde (Doctors of the World). Thus, sociological analysis needs to differentiate between actors and between their logics.

Nevertheless, as the attentive observer cannot fail to note, beyond the differences between humanitarian actors and the military that the aid organizations insistently highlight, the two sides come together on the same scene, in a reciprocal and asymmetrical dependency—the military increasingly calling on humanitarians to legitimize their interventions and the latter needing the former to ensure their safety. We know that the humanitarian organizations present in Rwanda at the time of the genocide found themselves powerless not only to act on behalf of the victims, but even to prevent the massacre of their own employees, and attempted to call for a military intervention, which came much too late. It is equally well known that MSF's report on the atrocities committed by the Serbs served to sanction the NATO air strikes in Kosovo, that a former president of MDM became the chairperson of Urgence Darfour, a French campaigning organization calling for military action against the Sudanese regime, and that a former French minister for humanitarian action, Bernard Kouchner, has defended the U.S. intervention in Iraq. Thus, humanitarian actors often justify military action precisely in the name of the humanitarian reason they embody. Furthermore, both military and the humanitarian actors share the temporality of emergency, both reject the sovereignty of states in the name of a higher moral order, and both are thus similarly engaged with extralegality and extraterritoriality, justified, in their view, by the legitimacy of their actions and the mobility of their sovereignty.[11]

In other words, in structural terms, military and humanitarian actors place themselves under the same law of exception. It is this reality that leads increasing numbers of belligerents, in some regions of the world, such as Afghanistan, Chechnya, Sri Lanka, and Sudan, to make no distinction between these actors, or at least to construe aid workers as characters among others on the war stage. Thus, kidnapping, assault, murder, and bombing become potential responses to this blurring of frontiers, though obviously incomprehensible and intolerable from the point of view of those who have come to bring aid to and express their solidarity with the victims of conflict.

What we seek to explore, then, in this book, beyond the range of contexts and the diversity of actors, is the state of exception that has progressively become established at the global level over the last two or three decades. This state of exception constitutes a sort of "no-man's land between public law and political fact, and between the juridical order and life"—in other words, a form of globalized biopolitics.[12] The state of exception thus forms the basis for a government that is at once military and humanitarian, resting on a logic of security and a logic of protection, on a law external to and superior to law, rooted as it is in the legitimacy of actions aimed at protecting life. This state of exception is inscribed in a temporality of emergency, which may become perennial through successive plans and missions, confirming the impossibility of reestablishing normal order, and in a spatiality of exclusion manifested in relief corridors and protected enclaves within territories that are no longer subject to a state monopoly of legitimate violence. The state of exception mobilizes technologies in the legal, epidemiological, and logistical fields, and even a form of technicality, which neutralizes political choices by reducing them to simple operational measures. Finally, the state of exception derives from a desire to intervene, and it increasingly appears that compassion for far-away suffering and its translation into the moral obligation to act has become one of the strongest political emotions in contemporary life.[13] We need only think of the impatience for action inspired by the images from Somalia and East Timor, the surge of generosity concerned with Ethiopia recently or Darfur today, or the world's agitation prior to the NATO air strikes in Kosovo and the coalition invasion of Iraq. It is clear that in these situations, we are outside the rationality of the politics of intervention. The states of emergency that we discuss in this book are always based on affective foundations, which may be distinguished from traditional war situations in that the passions brought into play are supposedly not nationalist, but are presented as universalist—or simply as humanist.

In the face of these profound transformations in the contemporary world and the false assumptions that generally underlie them (the assumption that emergencies, exceptions, and the need for intervention are self-evident), we believe that it is crucial for the social sciences to exercise their critical function—not in order to condemn any particular military operation or humanitarian rhetoric, this being the task of a form of political action that, as we have seen in both North America and Europe, has given rise to the biggest social mobilizations in Western societies in recent years, but in order to comprehend what such mobilizations leave unspoken or deliberately hide, to grasp their ambiguities and contradictions, to understand the bases of them and the stakes involved, and, in short, to make sense of a military and humanitarian government that is often imposed on us as if it went without saying. The collective reflection that we present here brings together anthropologists, sociologists, legal scholars, political scientists, philosophers, and also researchers who resist defining their work within disciplinary boundaries. Not all of the authors belong to the academic world, but all are engaged and involved in the public space in various ways, some of them even in the field of action. From a range of viewpoints and taking different paths, all consider their activity of inquiry, analysis, and writing to be related to an ethical and political responsibility.

This research began at a conference held in Montreal and at a seminar in Paris.[14] Over a period of five years, we continued our exchanges, refined our hypotheses, and recruited contributors to this book. During this period, the social transformations that we had glimpsed and to which we devoted our reflection became widely established: Military and humanitarian government continued to spread, even as the protests against it in the global public space became more open, stronger, and more collective. Fed by this recent history, the project thus evolved while retaining the same line of critical thought. All of the authors were concerned to knit together theoretical reflection, fieldwork, and a form of engagement with the world. We saw these three aspects as essential, whatever the different ways they were combined, depending on the discipline, the experience, and the authors' projects.

In the first part of the book, we focus on what might be called the foundations of the new military and humanitarian order: its philosophical, anthropological, and historical underpinnings.[15] Craig Calhoun reconstitutes the genealogy of the social imaginary of emergency since the wake-up call that the world received from the Lisbon earthquake and traces its links with the duty of charity, on the one hand, and the temptation of empire, on the other. Thus, the idea of the humanitarian gesture, as performed from Biafra to Darfur, has roots in a long history in the Western world. Adi Ophir extends this reflection, analyzing the process of "catastrophization" that operates in contemporary political thought and action. Adopting a notion used in cognitive psychology, he shows how objective phenomena and subjective interpretations are associated to produce the performative discourse on disaster. This discursive production has a range of consequences, but contributes in particular to the legitimization of a state of exception, as can be seen in Israel in the Palestinian Occupied Territories. Ugo Mattei then turns his attention to three contemporary figures of global capitalism: the rule of law, alternative dispute regulation, and the ideology of development. Each of these corresponds to a different way of managing problems and regulating failures in the system, respectively discrediting the alternatives to the dominant model, diverting demands for justice, and evading the causes of poverty. In this context, the state of emergency becomes an additional resource for legitimizing exploitation. Chowra Makaremi extends this investigation of global politics, examining the emergence of a new norm, that of human security, within international-development organizations, from the UN down. While this new register was initially concerned with meeting the basic needs of poor populations or the victims of conflict, its meaning has gradually shifted toward the arena of public order. Similarly, while this semantic slippage was first presented as grounding a peaceful approach to security issues, it rapidly became apparent that the notion of humanitarian intervention allowed for the reintroduction of the idea that military force is essential on the principle of the responsibility to protect. Finally, Vanessa Pupavac analyzes the origins of this alliance of humanitarian morality with political conservatism, expressions of which are still encountered today in the international arena. She traces a history from William Wilberforce, famous for his antislavery campaigning and hence seen as the father of British humanitarian thought, to E. F. Schumacher, whose work influenced contemporary humanitarian practices in Britain, particularly those of Oxfam—a history that helps to explain some of the current contradictions in actions in the developing world. Thus, we attempt to reveal the conditions of possibility—ideological, economic, juridical, and moral—of military and humanitarian intervention.

The second part of the book addresses the practical process of intervention in global situations on five continents. These case studies illustrate the diversity of contemporary forms of military and humanitarian intervention, but also the parallels between them. They examine both international operations in which states, interstate bodies, and nongovernmental organizations take action in countries faced with disaster or conflict and actions undertaken by governments to support their own people in situations of natural or human disaster. Remarkably, despite the manifest differences between these contexts, the same discourses of emergency and protection and the same mixing of military and humanitarian elements appear in each.[16] In this way, the figure of intervention acquires its broadest significance. Much more than monographs, these case studies thus offer a multi-sited reflection on the contemporary issues of military and humanitarian government. Mariella Pandolfi uses the study she conducted before, during, and after the NATO intervention in Kosovo to constitute this event as a paradigm of such states of permanent transition, which have proliferated in the last two decades in a series of military operations intended to restore order and preserve peace. Far from being accidental, these situations, of which the Balkans offers a definitive example, represent a structural component of intervention. The state of exception, announced as a temporary measure, becomes permanent. The suspension of sovereignty, promised to be of limited duration, lingers on. It is therefore crucial that analysts consider not only intervention, but also, and perhaps more importantly, the post-intervention context. Peter Redfield suggests a sort of counterpoint to the tragic picture of emergency promoted by both the media and the actors themselves. On the basis of a study conducted at the MSF's mission in Uganda, he reveals the everyday aspects of humanitarian activity and the uncertainty of the very notion of crisis in this context. In contrast to the romanticism of both volunteers and commentators, he shows the ambiguities of intervention that arise from saving lives and developing health care, necessities and contingencies, routines and exceptions. Paula Vásquez Lezama addresses a distinctive case in the form of the oxymoron "compassionate militarization." Following the natural disaster that resulted from the torrential rains in Venezuela in 1999, the government of Hugo Chávez declared a state of emergency in order to allow the army to intervene in the affected areas and save the populations in danger. This exception, which was broadly supported by Venezuelan society, nevertheless opened the way not only to the generalization of breaches of human rights in the initial period, but also subsequently to the normalization of a military order. In these conditions, the final gesture of the disaster victims, who, feeling abandoned by the authorities, crucified themselves in order to draw media attention to their situation, emerges as a humanitarian performance, staging the suffering of those excluded from the neo-Bolivarian revolution in the most spectacular way. Deirdre Howard-Wagner focuses on another case where a state of emergency was established to manage a population deemed to be at risk. Following the publication of a report demonstrating the scale of domestic violence and sexual abuse of children in the Aboriginal areas of Australia, Prime Minister John Howard's government decided in 2007 to send the army in to intervene. However, this incident was simply the latest in a long history of the social marginalization and racial stigmatization of indigenous populations. Here, too, the humanitarian argument was used to legitimize the government's police operation and the violation of the sovereignty of Aboriginal communities. Finally, Mary-Jo DelVecchio Good, Byron J. Good, and Jesse Grayman focus on the problems posed when humanitarian action takes place in a military context. The December 2004 tsunami, which resulted in an unprecedented natural disaster in Indonesia, affected populations that included some who were already subject to violence in the armed conflict between the government and resistance fighters. Aid operations, including the medical-psychological programs described by the authors, were thus embedded in a context of police monitoring by the government and compromises on the part of the NGO involved. Here, the conflict of sovereignty was played out between the government, the intervening organization, and the population concerned. The comparison of these five situations highlights the issues at stake in military and humanitarian intervention.

In the third part of the book, we attempt to go beyond the singularity of individual situations to take in the broader landscapes, both political and moral, created by military and humanitarian intervention. As we see it, the task is to understand the transformations, to analyze the stakes and the meaning, and to distinguish the logics and the actors in such interventions.[17] Adapting Joseph Conrad's metaphor, Didier Fassin proposes that we attempt to plumb the heart of humaneness—in other words, to grasp the tensions, contradictions, and even the aporias of humanitarian action conducted by nongovernmental organizations. While the moral reasoning behind such action is easily articulated—protecting populations, saving lives at risk, and relieving suffering—the concrete realization of missions challenges the principles of both intervention and neutrality. Choosing the side of the victims implies wittingly adopting a Manichean representation of conflicts that fails the test of the facts and that often leads to divisions between humanitarian actors themselves, in situations from Angola, to the Palestinian Occupied Territories, to Iraq. Alex de Waal offers a related analysis, tracing humanitarian interventionism from the 1992 operation in Somalia to the mobilization for Darfur since 2005. The enthusiasm that preceded the former, aimed at restoring peace in a country plunged into chaos and prey to famine, soon came up against the unexpected hostility of those to whom the military was attempting to bring humanitarian aid. However, examination of the desire for intervention arising from the latter situation suggests a failure to learn the lessons of previous experience and reveals that the same simplification of the issues, combined with the same whipping up of feelings, may lead to the same errors. Laurence McFalls attempts to make sense of what he calls the benevolent dictatorship of humanitarian government and the violence that accompanies it. In order to account for the ascendancy of humanitarian intervention as a paradigm of the contemporary world, he argues, the three Weberian forms of legitimacy need to be supplemented by a fourth—the therapeutic legitimacy used to justify exception. From the air strikes in Kosovo to the management of AIDS in Côte d'Ivoire, it is not only states, but also nongovernmental organizations that draw on this authority. Anne Orford returns to these various situations to unveil the relationship between the vulnerability of human lives and the power of states and their armies. All indications are that wars conducted to protect populations generally result in human losses that cannot be considered unforeseeable collateral effects, since they form part of the very logic of intervention. A range of judgments handed down by international courts of justice tends to confirm this fact while absolving the states concerned of their responsibility. In these circumstances, the covering up of the copy of Picasso's *Guernica* outside the UN Security Council chamber when Colin Powell spoke there to justify the U.S. intervention against Saddam Hussein can be seen as an ironic, but also premonitory harbinger of the hundreds of thousands of Iraqi civilian deaths. Finally, George E. Marcus considers the new place occupied by anthropologists in war contexts and more broadly in the domains of the military and humanitarianism. Whether as experts, reporters, or witnesses, the researchers, newly returned to these areas so long abandoned by the social sciences, also become themselves actors within them—not without ambiguity, since their concern to bear witness to violence and injustice often places them in objective competition with the aid workers. This ultimate irony underlines how important it is, in the study of the military and humanitarian government of the world on which we have embarked, not to avoid the difficulties and occasional impasses in our own critical work. Social scientists are themselves part of the contemporary landscape. They cannot evade their own responsibility. The knowledge they produce is not a truth outside the world: It is itself articulated with the political and moral issues they strive to bring to light.

When we began our collaborative study of contemporary states of emergency— a study that we had until then been conducting separately—the world had just experienced the attacks of September 11, 2001, the U.S. response against Afghanistan, and the invasion of Iraq by coalition forces. Threats against Iran were already beginning to be heard. The terrorist threat had inspired a Manichean representation of the world, divided between the Axis of Good and the Axis of Evil, by the U.S. government, which had used it to justify the introduction of antidemocratic measures such as the USA PATRIOT Act, standing for Uniting and Strengthening America by Providing Appropriate Tools Required to Intercept and Obstruct Terrorism Act (October 26, 2001) and the Military Order: Detention, Treatment, and Trial of Certain Non-citizens in the War Against Terrorism (November 13, 2001), and for the creation of extraterritorial zones outside the law, such as at Guantánamo Bay, Cuba, and Bagram Airbase in Afghanistan.

Thus, whereas the twentieth century had ended with the promise of a new international order, the twenty-first was beginning under the sway of violence and exception. In the theoretical simplifications that some ventured and that enjoyed unexpected public popularity, the "end of history" was replaced by the "clash of civilizations." At the same time, the memory of the failure of the peacekeeping operation in Somalia, the belated intervention following the Tutsi genocide in Rwanda, the abandoning of the enclave of Srebrenica to Serbian forces, the lethal air strikes in Kosovo—all events that had occurred within the previous ten years— was still fresh, while in Angola, Liberia, Sierra Leone, and the Democratic Republic of Congo, inaction in the face of massacres and atrocities seemed to indicate the international community's lack of interest in the troubles of the African continent, already afflicted by famine and AIDS. Countering traditional international law, the proliferation of conflict-related emergencies was thus bringing in a new juridico-political regime based on a principle of intervention theoretically underpinned by moral arguments, but heavily tempered by power stakes and vested interests. This state of the world in the early twenty-first century was marked by the triumph of interventionism, leading to a sort of state of permanent world war in which the United States, now the greatest military power, could even go so far as using humanitarian arguments to justify policing operations against its enemies.

In recalling this context—the normalization of exception, the generalization of intervention—we recall the state of intellectual necessity in which this book was conceived: the necessity to reflect on a state of the world in which military government and humanitarian government were together constructing a previously unseen political and moral order in which cynicism and ethics mingled and became indistinguishable. This world order and the extreme interventionism that characterizes it were of course linked to particular historical circumstances—the conjunction of international insecurity with an imperial ideology, the latter maintaining the former, and the arrogance of one side feeding the resentment of the other. The importance of the specific situation constituted by the Bush years and the political configuration that paved the way for aggressive alliances in Europe and elsewhere should certainly not be underestimated. Hence, we must similarly give due weight to the changes that may result from the election of Barak Obama as a new U.S. president less inclined to waging war, but also give weight to the emergence of a global recession that may mean that Western powers are in less of a hurry to become involved in costly interventions. However, the phenomena we are studying relate to profound juridico-political changes, and it is difficult to imagine that these will be radically challenged by changes in heads of state or by an economic crisis.

The norm of nonintervention, which formed the basis of international law for three and a half centuries, has been, if not replaced, at least displaced by the principle of intervention. Exception has become the rule: Walter Benjamin's well-known formula, "that the 'state of emergency' in which we live is not the exception but the rule,"[18] should be understood here as signaling not an indefinite extension of the state of exception, but rather the now indefinite extension of the possibility of it. This historic shift and the anthropological phenomena that can help to account for it—the ascendancy of the politics of life as a counterpoint to, but also a justification of power politics in the government of the world—define a new configuration of violence and the law that nevertheless links back to the oldest rule of intervention as expressed a century and a half ago by the *Times* columnist "Historicus" (the pen name of the British politician William Vernon Harcourt): "Intervention may be wise, may be right,—sometimes may even be necessary. But let us not deceive ourselves; intervention never has been, never will be, never can be short, simple, or peaceable."[19] Even dressed up in the cloak of humanitarian morality, intervention is always a military action—in other words, war.

*Translated by Rachel Gomme*

## NOTES

We are grateful to Michel Feher for his trust in our project, and we express our thanks, in the name of all the authors, to Bud Bynack for his remarkable copyediting and to Linda Garat for her attentive proofreading.

1   See the Charter of the United Nations, available on-line at http://www.un.org/en/documents/ charter/index.shtml (last accessed July 28, 2009), and Andreas Osiander, "Sovereignty, International Relations, and the Westphalian Myth," *International Organization* 55, no. 2 (Spring 2001): pp. 251–87.

2   This argument is put forward by Nicholas Wheeler in *Saving Strangers: Humanitarian Intervention in International Society* (Oxford: Oxford University Press, 2000), p. 71: "The significance of this case is that it was the first time in post-1945 international society that humanitarian claims were raised to justify the use of force." If we concur in taking the Indian episode as a sort of forerunner of the military-humanitarian era, it is particularly interesting in that it shows that, contrary to what is maintained by both supporters and opponents of the right to intervene, this principle may not be a Western invention imposed on the Third World.

3   Bernard Kouchner, cofounder of MSF and later of MDM, has championed the right to intervene, formulated by Bernard-Henri Lévy and theorized by Mario Bettati, since 1988. He described it as "emergency ethics," convincing the United Nations to recognize it in two resolutions of the General Assembly: Resolution 43/131 of 1998 on "humanitarian assistance to victims of natural disasters and similar emergency situations" and Resolution 45/100 of 1990, on the establishment of "relief corridors." See Sandrine Perrot, "Devoir et droit d'ingérence," available on-line at http://www.operationspaix.net/-Devoir-et-droit-d-ingerence (last accessed June 9, 2009).

4   We refer here to government not in the restricted sense of a state or interstate administration, but in the anthropological sense of a structure by which men and women are taken charge of and their behavior and the course of their lives acted upon, as understood by Michel Foucault in *Security, Territory, Population: Lectures at the Collège de France 1977–1978*, ed. Michel Senellart, trans. Graham Burchell (London: Palgrave Macmillan, 2007).

5   See Vaclav Havel, "Kosovo and the End of the Nation-State," *New York Review of Books*, 46, no. 10 (1999), available on-line (subscription required) at http://www.nybooks.com/articles/ article-preview?article_id=455; Marjorie Cohen, "The Myth of Humanitarian Intervention in Kosovo," in Alexsandar Jokic (ed.), *Lessons of Kosovo: The Dangers of Humanitarian Intervention* (Toronto: Broadview Press, 2003), p. 123; "Joint Statement by President Bush, Prime Minister Blair on Iraq's Future," April 8, 2003, available on-line at http://www.number10.gov. uk/Page3441 (last accessed June 9, 2009); and Kenneth Roth, "Setting the Standard: Justifying Humanitarian Intervention," *Harvard International Review*, 26, no. 1 (2004).

6   In this book, we prefer to maintain an explicit distinction between the two aspects of intervention—military and humanitarian—in contrast to a number of analysts, such as J.L. Holzgrefe in "The Humanitarian Intervention Debate," in J.L. Holzgrefe and Robert Keohane (eds.), *Humanitarian Intervention: Ethical, Legal and Political Debates* (Cambridge: Cambridge University Press 2003), pp. 15–52. Holzgrefe describes humanitarian intervention as "the threat or use of force across state borders by a state (or group of states) aimed at preventing or ending widespread and grave violations of the fundamental rights of individuals other than its own citizens, without the permission of the state within whose territory force is

applied." Because it adopts the arguments used to justify intervention, this definition tends to take them for granted, despite the fact that the boundary between policing and protecting, between military and humanitarian, is often unclear and porous, as we will see throughout this volume.

7   Significantly, in his analysis of the interventions in Kosovo and Iraq in "Words of War: Challenges to the Just War Theory," *Harvard International Review* 26, no. 1 (Spring 2004), Michael Walzer returns to the justifications he developed much earlier in *Just and Unjust Wars: A Moral Argument with Historical Illustrations* (New York: Basic Books, 1977), leading him to take a position in favor of military operations in the first case and against the military solution in the second. However, he adds: "It seems to me that it is easier to justify intervention on humanitarian than on liberation grounds, and that is the operative justification in Kosovo." Thus, interestingly, the humanitarian argument is now brought in to support the argument of justice.

8   A principle sanctioned by the World Summit of September 16, 2005, under the new denomination "responsibility to protect," or "R2P," in the UN jargon. See Mario Bettati, " Du droit d'ingérence à la responsabilité de protéger," *Outre-Terre* 3, no. 20 (2007): pp. 381–89.

9   We can see this as a depoliticization on the condition that we remain mindful of the caution offered by Paul Veyne, who points out, that the term "depoliticization" still risks being a normative judgment. See Paul Veyne, *Le pain et le cirque: Sociologie historique d'un pluralisme politique* (Paris: Seuil, 1976), p. 95. Here, our aim is simply to indicate the process by which historicity and conflictuality are displaced by urgency and compassion—for example, when humanitarian organizations equate the suffering of the Palestinians with that of the Israelis, neutralizing the specific reality of the occupation of the Palestinian territories and thus the asymmetry of the situation. See Didier Fassin, "La cause des victimes," *Les Temps Modernes* 59, no. 627 (2004): pp. 73–91.

10  On Kosovo, see the report by Human Rights Watch, "Civilian Deaths in the Nato Air Campaign," February 7, 2000, available on-line at http://www.hrw.org/legacy/reports/2000/nato and the comment by Kenneth Roth, the organization's executive director: "Once it made the decision to attack Yugoslavia, NATO should have done more to protect civilians. All too often, NATO targeting subjected the civilian population to unacceptable risks," Human Rights Watch, "New Figures on Civilian Deaths in Kosovo War," February 6, 2000, available on-line at http://www.hrw.org/en/news/2000/02/06/new-figures-civilian-deaths-kosovo-war (both last accessed June 11, 2009). On Iraq, see the study by the Johns Hopkins School of Public Health: Les Roberts, Riyadh Lafta, Richard Garfield, Jamal Khudhairi, and Gilbert Burnham, "Mortality after the Invasion of Iraq: A Cross-Sectional Cluster Sample Survey," *The Lancet* 368, no. 9545 (October 21, 2006): pp. 1421–28. The estimated death toll at that time was 654,000, 92 percent of which were violence related, and 31 percent of which were among coalition forces. The 2008 study by Opinion Research Business gives a comparable figure of 1,033,000 deaths (to a more recent date, hence over a longer period). These estimates contrast with the U.S. Army's silence: Their commander-in-chief, General Tommy Franks, stated: "We don't do body counts."

11  On the confusion between military and humanitarian action, see Didier Fassin, "Humanitarianism: A Nongovernmental Government," in Michel Feher, Gaëlle Krikorian, and Yates McKee (eds.), *Nongovernmental Politics* (New York: Zone Books, 2007), pp. 149–60. On the constitution of mobile sovereignties, see Mariella Pandolfi, "'Moral entrepreneurs,' souverainetés

mouvantes et barbelés: Le bio-politique dans les Balkans post-communistes," in Mariella Pandolfi and Marc Abélès (eds.), "Politiques: Jeux d'espaces," special issue, *Anthropologie et Sociétés* 26, no. 1 (2002).

12 We adopt here Giorgio Agamben's useful definition in *State of Exception*, trans. Kevin Attell (Chicago: University of Chicago Press, 2005), p. 1. The originality of Agamben's approach, in relation to the classic Schmittian view, which he also draws on, is his introduction of the question of life, following in this the analysis outlined by Walter Benjamin.

13 Luc Boltanski analyses this emotion very clearly in *Distant Suffering: Morality, Media and Politics* (Cambridge: Cambridge University Press, 1999), but does not draw out its political consequences. The first issue of MDM's journal, significantly entitled *Ingérences* — Interventions — which appeared in 1993, took the theme of "humanitarian desire." In a historical overview that, as we have seen, was an ideological construct, *Nouvel Observateur* journalist Jacques Julliard asserted notably that "humanitarianism is a new moral desire that replaces a political morality that died after the Cold War."

14 The international conference, Autour de l'intervention: Protagonistes, logiques, effets, was held at the University of Montreal and McGill University on October 23 to 25, 2003. Organized by Mariella Pandolfi, it brought together around thirty researchers and politicians. The research seminar, Political and Moral Anthropology, coordinated by Didier Fassin, ran from 2001 to 2005 at the École des Hautes Études en Sciences Sociales in Paris on the themes "Governing Populations, Producing Subjects" and "Moral Economy and Political Action." A large number of social scientists researching the crises of the contemporary world participated. Our common project came into being in these two spaces. At the conference and in the seminar, we met many of the authors and many others whose trace, we hope, the book retains.

15 Other useful references here include Michael Barnett and Thomas Weiss's chapter "Humanitarianism: A Brief History of the Present," in Michael Barnett and Thomas Weiss (eds.), *Humanitarianism in Question: Politics, Power, Ethics* (Ithaca, NY: Cornell University Press, 2008), pp. 1–48. However, our focus here is less on humanitarianism as such than on intervention, and hence on humanitarian exception as defined by Didier Fassin and Paula Vásquez in "Humanitarian Exception as the Rule: The Political Theology of the 1999 Tragedia in Venezuela," *American Ethnologist* 32, no. 3 (August 2005): pp. 389–405.

16 The juxtaposition of these cases, some of which concern the international order, while others relate to the national order, suggests that we could go beyond the generally accepted political-science reading of the contemporary tension between sovereignty and intervention. See, for example Stanley Hoffmann, *The Ethics and Politics of Humanitarian Intervention* (Notre Dame, IN: University of Notre Dame Press, 1996).

17 We might point here to David Keen's parallel attempt, in *Complex Emergencies* (Cambridge: Polity, 2008), to restore the complexity of contemporary wars in the face of the frequent simplifications offered by current accounts of them.

18 Walter Benjamin, "On the Concept of History," trans. Harry Zohn, in *Walter Benjamin: Selected Writings, Vol. 4, 1938–1940*, ed. Michael W. Jennings and Howard Eiland (Cambridge, MA: Harvard University Press, 2003), p. 392.

19 William Vernon Harcourt, *Letters by Historicus on Some Questions of International Law* (London: Macmillan and Co., 1863), pp. 46–47.

PART ONE: FOUNDATIONS

# The Idea of Emergency:
# Humanitarian Action and Global (Dis)Order

Craig Calhoun

The humanitarian emergency is an awkward symbol, simultaneously of moral purity and suffering, of altruistic global response, and of the utter failure of global institutions. The humanitarianism of response suggests a world united by common humanity; the emergencies themselves reveal a world divided by deep material inequality, by violent conflicts, and by illicit, exploitative trade.

Humanitarianism and humanitarian emergencies have assumed spectacular prominence in the last thirty years. It is partly because of housing built in floodplains and swept away by typhoons and tsunamis and, perhaps behind this, because of expanding global population and continuing poverty. And it is partly because of wars in which civilians have been targets of violence as well as "collateral damage," themselves in turn reflections of past colonialism, continually shifting global hegemonies, and sometimes new markets that make diamonds or drugs both stakes of some struggles and financing for others. But it is not clear that the last thirty years have seen more natural disasters, more deaths from wars, or simply more human suffering than earlier eras. There may be more floods with global warming, but less widespread famine. That bad things are happening is not, then, sufficient explanation for the prominence of humanitarian action or the growing emphasis on thinking in terms of humanitarian emergencies.

Both concepts, "humanitarian" and "emergency," are cultural constructs and reflections of structural changes. They come together to shape a way of understanding what is happening in the world, a social imaginary that is of dramatic material consequence. Behind the rise of the humanitarian emergency lie specific ways of thinking about how the world works and specific, if often implicit moral orientations. Humanitarianism flourishes as an ethical response to emergencies not just because bad things happen in the world, but also because many people have lost faith in both economic development and political struggle as ways of trying to

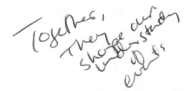

29

improve the human lot. Humanitarianism appeals to many who seek morally pure and immediately good ways of responding to suffering in the world. But of course, the world is in fact so complex that impurity and mediations are hard to escape. Recently, to the horror of many humanitarians invested in nonstate, purely ethical approaches to mitigating human suffering, the United States presented its invasion of Iraq as a "humanitarian intervention." And indeed, the notion of a humanitarian justification for wars has become widespread, although to the extent there is a field of humanitarian action, most of its leaders are set sharply against this notion. I focus here on that field, where war is a problem, and not a solution. But I will also try to show how hard it is to keep immediate ethical response sharply separate from entanglements in politics and development and indeed, in issues of security.

## THE EMERGENCY IMAGINARY

Think for a moment of Rwanda and Congo, Liberia and Sierra Leone, Colombia and Peru, Israel and Palestine, the former Yugoslavia, Afghanistan and Iraq, the December 2004 tsunami, the inundation of New Orleans by Hurricane Katrina, the deadly earthquake days later in Pakistan, the cyclones in Myanmar, and the earthquake in China. These are emergencies. They are also countries, conflicts, occasions, and events; they can be grasped in other ways. But on the evening news, they are emergencies.

"Emergency" is now the primary term for referring to catastrophes, conflicts, and settings for human suffering. It has rough cognates such as "disaster" and "crisis," with their half-hidden references to astrology and turning points. But the word "emergency" points to what happens without reference to agency, astral misalignments, or other causes or any specific outcomes. The emergency is a sudden, unpredictable event emerging against a background of ostensible normalcy, causing suffering or danger and demanding urgent response. Usage is usually secular. Use of the word focuses attention on the immediate event, and not on its causes. It calls for a humanitarian response, not political or economic analysis. The emergency has become a basic unit of global affairs, like the nation. "Darfur" is as much the name of an emergency as the name of a place.

What makes emergencies possible? Obviously, there are material conditions. Bad things happen: natural disasters, technological failures, wars, and other conflicts. But these are not the whole story. There is also a history. The Lisbon earthquake of 1755 was not an emergency in the same sense as the Asian tsunami of 2004 or the Sichuan earthquake of 2008. The difference lies not in the magnitude of suffering, but in several overlapping developments: a decline in the extent to which suffering itself and especially mass suffering is seen as inevitable, perhaps

30    CALHOUN

because divinely ordained; 350 years of development in international law, including Geneva Conventions and treaties about refugees; cultural transformation in the way humanity itself is understood and, with it, new public sympathy and concern for distant suffering; development of a massive new capacity to respond to distant suffering, much of which is rooted in infrastructural capacities created for war itself, as well as for economic activity, colonization, and political rule, but that also includes the development of organizations and institutions focused specifically on humanitarian action; and mass media that make possible a new immediacy of awareness of distant events and suffering.

The Lisbon earthquake was widely viewed as a divine act, perhaps of retribution or at least of warning. Such reckonings have not vanished, as evidenced by the actress Sharon Stone's suggestion that the Sichuan earthquake resulted from "bad karma" produced by the Chinese occupation of Tibet or the suggestions of some American evangelists that Hurricane Katrina was retribution for the tolerance of homosexuals in New Orleans. But if God is seen as a causal agent today, it is more often as an agent of salvation: "There but for the grace of God go I." Some combination of nature, technological failure, and human action is generally blamed for the events that cause emergencies. Where causality has a clearly identifiable human face, this may be seized as a focus of blame or of action to reduce suffering—as in the indictment of Sudan's General Omar al-Bashir, who certainly bears responsibility for his government's abuse of its power and its people—but for many humanitarians, that is beside the point. And for those seeking an explanation, focusing on an individual may distract from structural and systemic causes. Usually, however, international response focuses on the suffering itself, along with displacement and other results, and on what to do about it. And suffering is old, even though the humanitarian emergency is new. The humanitarian emergency is constituted, made available for a distinctive form of response, by a specific social imaginary.[1] This is circulated in the media, but also informs the work of UN agencies, nongovernmental organizations (NGOs), religious organizations, and other actors. The emergency imaginary has a substantial history, but usually feels natural, or at least modern.

The core features of the emergency imaginary come in two clusters. First, there are those concerned with emergencies themselves. Emergencies are understood to be sudden, unpredictable, brief, or at least very urgent, and exceptions to some sort of normal order. Second are those features related to humanitarian response: the idea of neutrality, the notion of humanity as a mass of individuals equally entitled to care, and a sense of ethical obligation based on common humanity, rather than on citizenship or any other specific loyalty.

Emergency thinking can appear well beyond the realm of humanitarian action. For example, a sudden financial upset — loss of liquidity in the market for mortgage-backed securities — appears as an emergency, an exception to stable market functioning that requires a response from central bankers or others concerned with financial order. Likewise, the buildup of troops on a neighbor's border or moves by "rogue states" to acquire nuclear capabilities may be interpreted as emergencies, and state responses may be expected.[2] Humanitarian emergencies typically become visible through refugees or the internally displaced, whose movements, perhaps accompanied by bodies beside the road, signal some upset of normal existence.

In all cases, there are usually early warnings, and at least some observers see enough long-term patterns to make emergencies predictable. Some financial analyst decried as a pessimist warns of pending market collapse; some public official decried as an alarmist warns of impending conflict; some UN observer dismissed as an overreacting do-gooder warns of killings, population movements, and hunger. The warnings may or may not be heeded. But what is crucial is that they do not really change the dominant sense of the emergency as something sudden that overtakes the country or region or world by surprise. This sense of suddenness and unpredictability is reinforced by the media, especially by television. The continuous stream of reporting on gradually worsening conditions is minimal and usually consigned to the back pages of newspapers and specialist magazines. It does not make the cut for headlines — let alone half-hour broadcast news programs. So when violence or vast numbers of people lining up at feeding stations do break through to garner airtime, they seem to have come almost from nowhere.

Yet we need to remind ourselves that this is the way in which we imagine — and thereby help constitute — emergencies, not simply an accurate description of their character. After all, the situation of displaced Palestinians is still termed an "emergency" after more than sixty years. The horrific emergency of the partition of India and Pakistan played out almost in slow motion over months and years, debated in the midst of the Indian independence movement, pressed and resisted in marches and meetings. Yet one of the first significant articles about the demographic impact of partition begins with the sentence "The advent of independence in the Indian subcontinent caught the experts by surprise."[3] And so it did, just as the end of the Cold War and the collapse of the Soviet Union caught the experts by surprise. As did the Ethiopian famine of 1984–85, though the Sahel drought had been growing more severe and the Ethiopian government more authoritarian for years. The 1984–85 emergency came at the end of a drought cycle that extended back into the 1960s. The revolutionary Ethiopian government, the Derg, had begun sharply to increase its exploitation of rural areas in the same period as its 1977–78 Red Terror. But then displacement from Ethiopia's villages became massive and interacted with drought to produce famine of "biblical proportions." And internal displacement combined with growing numbers of international refugees, especially those fleeing wars of national liberation in Eritrea and Tigray. So the world took note. And so it is in most emergencies. They are shocking. They feel sudden. But they are less sudden than they feel to those who learn about them only when they finally reach the evening news.

Both news and entertainment media circulate a flow of images that help to define humanitarian emergencies.[4] Men appear on tanks, crowd with guns and machetes into trucks, and lie in rows of dead bodies. Children appear with hands outstretched and often naked. Women appear lined up at feeding stations, holding babies, walking in long queues with bundles on their heads, or gathered around meager supplies. Scenes of physical devastation are prominent in pictures of natural disaster, while pictures of bodies figure more in conflict-related emergencies. Tents appear in rows suggesting the rationalization as well as the material support brought by the humanitarians. But though the pictures are "real," they also help construct an imagined picture, because they are selected from among tens of thousands available to newspaper and magazine editors and the marketers who prepare fundraising appeals for humanitarian organizations. And they are commonly selected in ways that conform to iconic templates and norms—not least about what men should be shown doing and women should be shown experiencing, of how to represent violence, suffering, and need.

The images are usually of strangers—not just people one happens not to know, but people paradigmatically distant. Anonymous sufferers stand against hard-to-place backdrops. There are commonly no symbols of national or other allegiances. Sometimes there are religious markings, but the images are remarkably interchangeable. They depict the state of emergency more than they depict particular places. And thus they are readily recognizable as emergency images when they appear in magazines or on television in Europe, America, or Japan. The photos produce sympathy, despite difference and distance.

Humanitarian action focuses paradigmatically on strangers. Refugees are the prototypical face of the emergency, strangers in their new lands as well as to those distant people who may try to send help. Humanitarian action deals with humanity at large, those to whom we have obligations precisely because they are human, not because we share some more specific civic solidarity with them. This is one of the reasons for impartiality and neutrality, basic features of the humanitarian stance. And humanitarian action addresses strangers who are suffering for reasons beyond their control—and in important senses, for reasons beyond the immediate focus of the humanitarian. Suffering means not only pain and death, but also loss of dignity and any other form of dehumanization. But there is a tendency for counting deaths and conversely lives saved to become the metric of action in humanitarian emergencies, reflecting a calculus of bare life, the minimum of human existence.[5] But this biological minimum is, perhaps, below the real minimum of the truly human, the capacity for speech and shaping social life.[6] It is a basic question where any specific response to emergencies falls along the continuum between dealing only in lives saved and nurturing the human capacity to create life together by building or rebuilding institutions.

Crucial to the emergency imaginary is a distinctive idea of the human. This is not unique to thinking about emergencies; it is part of a widespread modern understanding, especially, but not only Western. The category of the human seems self-evident and unproblematic as part of the background to thinking about emergencies and humanitarian response. But the category is not self-evident. In most usage, it involves thinking about humanity as a set of individuals and of individuals as equivalent to each other, all deserving of moral recognition. This is a historically distinctive, mainly modern way of thinking. To imagine human beings in the abstract, as it were, in their mere humanity, disembedded from kinship, religion, nationality, and other webs of identity and relationship is not universal. Replacing ties among people with a notion of equivalence among strangers is linked not only to ethical universalism, though, but also to the notion of "bare life," and to the administrative gaze of states, and to thinking in terms of populations.[7]

That the global media deal so substantially in images, not only in analyses, adds to the capacity to nurture sympathy—though this of course has a modern history not uniquely dependent on visual images, but also on shifting sensibilities and foci of imagination. The instant global circulation of images makes distant suffering seem immediate; it appears in real time as a simultaneous part of our reality. Of course, the ubiquity of images is not always a spur to action. It can encourage us simply to treat emergencies, however ironically, as a background constant of our global condition. The images can breed "compassion fatigue," as well as action. Nonetheless, they are deployed not just by news media, but also by NGOs seeking to raise money, and they do seem to attract attention. On balance, they add impetus to humanitarian responses.

But it is not imagery alone that makes action seem mandatory. It is crucial also that effective action seems possible. It was not comparably possible when the Lisbon earthquake struck. There was charity through the Catholic Church and some aid came from England. But it took weeks, even months, to arrive. Charity was mostly in the form of alms for survivors, not an attempt to change the survival rate. The aid from abroad was help in reconstruction, as much as an attempt to ease suffering. But of course, there was also profiteering (hardly unknown today) and a particularly severe version of blaming victims in that era of Inquisition.

Voltaire's famous portrayal in *Candide* takes the earthquake as an opportunity to demonstrate man's inhumanity to man. Still, there was sympathy—and shock. Modern sensibilities were already developing in 1755. But the actual capability to act on such sensibilities was limited. The capacity to respond is provided by new transportation and communications technologies, by the sheer wealth of the more developed world, and by the range of organizations that have been created to deliver services on a global scale. The capacity to act at a distance is demonstrated daily by markets and military operations. It not only enables people to put good intentions into material practice. It encourages people to think in terms of an emergency imaginary that suggests not only that there are sudden, unpredictable events that cause massive suffering, but also that urgent response is mandatory.

## CHARITY

An older ideal of charity informs the newer emergency imaginary. Both general norms of mitigating human suffering and norms of the honorable conduct of war are ancient and widespread. For the most part, the idea of charity, as the saying suggests, "begins at home." That is, it is about care for the poor within a community. But charity is sometimes extended to strangers. Consider the biblical parable of the Good Samaritan: members of the sufferer's own group refuse to help, but an outsider does. Christianity has particularly notable injunctions to a kind of cosmopolitan charity, rooted in love of God and God's love for all people. Various injunctions to charity in other religions also open up a wider potential reach, for example the Islamic notions of *zakat* and *sadaqa*, which suggest different kinds of virtuous behavior—an obligation to give for the glory of God, or simply because it is commanded, which is different from a considerate or sympathetic response to suffering. But—again for the most part, since it is hard to generalize about such ideas on a global scale—charity is a norm about individual action in giving, whether care, or food, or money. Only sometimes is it extended into the development of institutions such as charitable hospitals. And only inconsistently is it linked to the idea of a universal ethics.

Charity is typically seen as a moral way to relate to people who suffer, but not necessarily as a way to end suffering. Here, again, there are sayings to make the point, such as "The poor shall always be with us." Charity is often embedded in more hierarchical understandings of humanity, as part of the obligations those with resources and standing owe to those without. It constitutes a relationship of dependency, not of equivalence. This is one reason both Enlightenment and Romantic thinkers often decried it, seeing it as damaging to human dignity.

Charity was transformed by humanitarianism in the modern era, especially

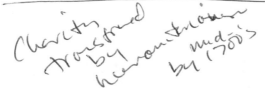

from the mid-1700s—the very time of the Lisbon Earthquake—on. The great example of this was the antislavery movement, which in turn strengthened and reinforced the trend. Largely organized in religious terms, this drew on a transformation within parts of Protestantism. From a focus on the internal rectitude and purity of religious communities, evangelicalism brought a new outward orientation. It addressed a world of strangers as potential converts. It saw slavery not simply as a personal issue for slave owners, but as a national sin. And it combined a more traditional charitable orientation with a new humanitarian emphasis. A prominent image of the antislavery movement showed an African in chains with the motto "Am I not a man and a brother?" In this, there is an assertion both of the new logic of human equivalence and of an older religious notion of connection—brotherhood. At its outset, the antislavery movement (among Europeans and Americans, as distinct from among slaves) was primarily a matter of charity, of the moral rectitude of those who would give slaves their freedom and end the scourge of the slave trade. But increasingly, charity mingled with a new logic of rights, an insistence on freedom as a human entitlement.

Religion figured prominently as well in the 1863 founding of the Red Cross and the more general movement for humane treatment of those injured in war. Britain's Florence Nightingale (who came from a prominent Christian abolitionist family) and the Swiss evangelical Henri Dunant both drew on religious motivations and arguments as well as on religious symbolism in seeking to provide care for those who suffered. This was especially important at a time when civilian armies became more common and inflicted massive civilian casualties and suffering.

From the religious traditions of its roots, humanitarianism drew an ideal of witnessing. This meant being in solidarity with those who suffered, even when their suffering could not be ended. The International Committee of the Red Cross provided life-saving medical assistance when it could, but it is important to note that much of its early work focused on mitigating the suffering of the dying. Medical care was rudimentary. But dying was not instant. And in addition to water and clean bandages, nurses helped the dying write home, pray, and achieve what in the middle of the nineteenth century was praised as a "good death." This was bound up with confession and faith. But the idea of extending care to the injured and dying was embraceable on more secular grounds, as well. And it extended after death. America's Clara Barton, the "Angel of the Battlefield," who would go on to found the American Red Cross, was active in enumerating the dead, notifying families, and securing proper burial. At one point she employed forty-two headboard carvers.

Witnessing also meant helping to make suffering manifest to the world—and the ideal remains an important theme in humanitarian organizations such as MSF, Médecins Sans Frontières (Doctors Without Borders) today. This did not mean that there was no message for political leaders. Publicized suffering could be an implicit accusation. Nonetheless, the founders of the Red Cross sought to reduce suffering through politically neutral means. In an era of revolutionary politics, the changes they sought and the services they provided were conceived as nonpartisan. By the time of the Franco-Prussian War, the International Committee of the Red Cross provided its care under a flag of neutrality. This flag, of course, appropriated a Christian religious symbol. Care—charity—was provided not only out of religious motivation, but also on the basis of a religious understanding of what common humanity meant beyond national identities.[8]

In a context such as World War I, this sort of humanitarianism was distinct from campaigning for peace. In the first place, humanitarianism focused on the direct expression of God's love—or human conscience—through care for the suffering. One could also be a humanitarian in this sense without passing judgment on the justice of a war, whereas the pacifist condemned the military conflict itself. Charitable humanitarians pursued the mitigation of suffering, rather than the transformation of institutions.

The same sort of distinction would separate humanitarian action from human rights activism in the second half of the twentieth century. Though humanitarianism drew on some of the same sources as advocacy for human rights—notably the notion of common humanity—the theme of neutrality separated the two. The human rights movement sought to universalize the rights of citizens and insisted that these are not gifts, but entitlements. It was also more secular than humanitarianism. But even the notion of human rights implied rights that obtain before politics, in humanity as such, even if it requires state action to secure them.

Political neutrality did not, of course, mean religious neutrality. Religion figured importantly in the motives of individuals who responded to the suffering of strangers, and it helped to give meaning to their struggles. It also helped to provide organizational purpose and practical structures. Not only did religious communities raise money for humanitarian action, its development overlapped that of religious missionary work. This was not always or only proselytizing—though it often was. It included hospitals that ministered without regard to the patient's faith, as well as schools and orphanages in which particular faiths were taught.

But an important feature of missionary work is precisely that it is undertaken in order to reach people outside the community of the faith and commonly outside the national community. Needy humanity is its typical object. This makes it different from religious work undertaken primarily to serve coreligionists. Of course, some religious charities did—and some still do—seek primarily to serve members of their own faith. But in a certain basic sense, these are less humanitarian than those that seek to serve humanity at large.

*Care central as distinct for addressing causes of suffering* [handwritten annotation in top margin]

Ideas of charity continue to inform humanitarian action. Not only does providing care remain central, as distinct from seeking to address the causes of suffering, bring peace, or pursue development. Charity also underwrites an exemption of humanitarian action from the usual utilitarian calculus of efficiency and the modernist reckoning of success. This dimension of humanitarianism is different from that centered more on progress, which we will consider in a moment. An ideal of charity is linked to an important dimension of particularism in the humanitarian project. Each suffering person is individually its object. There is no calculus by which to compare two hours spent with one dying patient and two hours spent giving antibiotics quickly to twenty. Faced with the enormity of suffering in emergencies, humanitarians are torn between the more particularistic ministry that eases some suffering and acknowledges that it cannot end all and the more universalistic, but instrumental attempt to budget resources and refine procedures to achieve maximum effect.

## IMPERIALISM

Missionary work was, of course, closely related to colonialism and imperialism. And these same sources have been influential in the genealogy of humanitarianism. To start with, imperialist ventures occasioned an important rethinking of the category of the human.

The famous Valladolid debate of 1550–51 was especially intellectually serious and influential, but not totally unique in the story of European struggles to decide how to think of non-Western peoples and in particular indigenous inhabitants of the New World. At Valladolid, the Dominican friar, Bartolomé de las Casas and the secular priest Juan Ginés de Sepúlveda, presented opposing arguments that remain instructive. Both drew on Aristotle, Aquinas, and the humanist tradition—thus, on relatively mainstream theology—but where Las Casas saw Amerindians as free men in the natural order, Sepúlveda saw them as natural slaves. The material issue was how the Indians would be treated, but behind it lay the question not of their humanity, but of the nature of humanness. For Las Casas, whose arguments carried the debate and swayed the Spanish king, at least in the abstract, humans are theologically equivalent bearers of souls. This idea of humanity as a series of conceptually equivalent individuals increasingly influenced modern thinking, including eventually the conception of human rights. And of course, even in this early incarnation, these issues were not narrowly theological alone. The king supported Las Casas's position partly because it strengthened central state power, while colonial landowners more often supported Sepúlveda's idea of natural slavery, which suggested that their exploitation of the indigenous population could proceed with greater autonomy.[9] Las Casas's perspective was informed by that of Francisco de Vitoria and the School of Salamanca, which had pursued not only the development of natural rights theory, but also of an economic analysis that encouraged new degrees of commercialization based on private property. This reinforced the notion of the equivalently entitled human individual, the potential bearer of property as well as of a soul. Nascent humanitarian thought thus could underwrite simultaneously new forms of commercial organization resistant to slavery and direct criticism of slavery as morally repugnant. The terms in which it did so were consonant with the broad modern reliance on the idea of ideally autonomous and conceptually equivalent individuals.

More generally, missionaries and other humanitarians often called attention to abuses of colonized peoples—both indigenous people and transported slaves. Sometimes the abusers were directly the colonial powers, sometimes they were landowners and others whom the missionaries wanted the colonial powers to restrain. At the same time, though, humanitarian ideas appeared also as part of the rationale for colonialism. Humanitarianism was often part of the "civilization" that colonial powers sought to bring to the peoples they conquered.

The "civilizing" powers brought education and medical care, as well as spiritual services to the colonies. These missions contributed to the development of a "welfarist" notion of human flourishing that was also gaining ground in Europe and that helped to underpin new doctrines of state legitimacy in which kings ruled in order to make the lives of their subjects better. But while "conversion" most directly informed the spiritual work of missionaries, it was not absent from their more material projects and those of the colonial powers. The *mission civilisatrice* sought to convert "wild" natives into better people and the prisoners of unfortunate traditions and superstitions into modern, rational human beings. Europeans commonly saw non-Western others the way Enlightenment philosophers saw backwardly superstitious Catholics.

Evidence of the barbarity and backwardness of others was put forward in support of the argument that they would benefit from European rule—at least if Europeans lived up to their moral responsibilities. If non-Western people were savages, their savagery was reflected in inhumane treatment of other people. European projects of improving the natives were often played out in controversies over women's bodies. Colonial civilizers sought to save women from *sati*, foot binding, and other traditional practices. As Partha Chatterjee has shown, this encouraged anticolonial nationalists to claim women and traditional gender practices as particularly important to their national cultures.[10] The link to contemporary human rights debates over female genital mutilation should not be missed—or to why "helpless women and children" figure so prominently in stereotypical images of emergencies.

More generally, the notion that the natives could not govern themselves was a vital legitimation for colonial rule. Europeans chose not to look at larger geopolitical factors that weakened political structures so much as to assume these were simply backward. Where there was fighting among the natives or where seemingly cruel and inhumane practices were prevalent, so much more did it appear that European rule would be beneficial. This sort of rationale remains prominent into the twenty-first century, of course, underwriting various neoimperial ventures, including the American invasion of Iraq. It also underpins the idea of humanitarian intervention—particularly the idea that one might use military force abroad to achieve humanitarian objectives. The military is more and more actively involved in humanitarian action, even where regime change is not the goal, partly because of the effectiveness of military logistics, partly to provide security where humanitarian neutrality is no longer effective.

Colonial projects were often exploitative, of course, but they were also efforts to stabilize and administer regions marked by conflicts and disruptions. While ideologically, colonial powers ascribed the disorder to the backwardness of local populations, in fact, such conditions were often as much the result of earlier Western "explorations" and armed trading projects. It was, after all, the East India Company, not the British state more directly, that launched the colonial engagement in India. And throughout the world, a variety of less centrally organized ventures paved the way for colonial rule: conquests motivated by the search for gold; plantations displacing local farmers or hunters, exploiting local or imported labor, and producing specialized export crops on land that once fed local populations; and shipping, in which each voyage was a capitalist venture with the ship's captain trying to secure his own profits, as well as returns on the investments of merchants. While sometimes colonial administrations were directly exploitative, often they sought to keep the peace and manage "public" affairs while private businesses undertook their commercial, extractive, or productive activities. In other words, colonial states were not entirely unlike states in general—but with much farther-flung domains and without the notion that those ruled were fellow nationals.

Colonial rule helped to occasion the growth of managerial professions such as public health, as well as the development of public statistics and disciplines such as anthropology. Colonial governments were also pioneers of disaster response, even while they helped to create the disasters. Disasters in the colonial era were not only nightmares for the local populations, they were managerial problems for colonial states. Crises had to be managed by colonial rulers relatively directly, without the range of NGOs and international agencies that exist today to do similar work. Famines and epidemics were prominent as colonial challenges, perhaps most famously the global influenza epidemic of 1918–19 and the famines in Bengal in the early 1770s and again in 1943, after Britain lost Burma to the Japanese.

Humanitarian action was generally contained within the relations of single metropole to its colonial possessions. It was not generically global or oriented toward all of humanity at large. It was also productive of the kind of "population thinking" invoked by Foucault in his accounts of state formation more generally.[11] One result was that colonial powers were typically much more systematic in collecting statistics and monitoring the effectiveness of their work than later humanitarian actors. This reflected the dominance of practical administration, rather than moral expression in their work. But modern humanitarians, too, are increasingly called on to adopt a managerial orientation.

Centrally, colonial projects shaped a "First World" consciousness. They divided the world into actors and those acted upon. This was not merely a European phenomenon. It extended to the United States and in varying degrees to other colonial and imperial powers, as, for example, when the Japanese supported antifoot-binding movements in colonized Taiwan. The division was almost always racially marked. It was usually organized in terms of a progressive view of history, emphasizing the march of civilization. If India and China were at least recognized as having other (allegedly inferior, but competitive) civilizations, others—especially Africans—were typically seen as outside of progressive history except when incorporated by Europe.[12] They were especially in need of the European *mission civilisatrice*; they were objects of action more than its subjects. This remains an uncomfortable feature of humanitarian action.[13]

Humanitarian action is sometimes described as the nice face of a new colonialism. This is mainly an accusation made from outside humanitarian movements, but those who carry out humanitarian relief sometimes worry that there is a grain of truth in it. Those who work by entirely civilian means are especially anguished by humanitarian interventions that use force to try to end emergencies or violent regimes. And there are even proposals to divide the world into "humanitarian spheres of influence," which would give certain world powers the responsibility to intervene in emergencies in their regions.[14] But even where militaries are not involved, humanitarian action has a managerial orientation, minimizing the threats that displaced populations pose to the otherwise smooth operation of global economies. Effective humanitarian action may reduce population flows that threaten the population welfare of richer countries or it may reassure those anxious about immigration generally that they are nonetheless responding to human needs. Of course, humanitarian action is not merely managerial—it is also moral. But, like missionary activity and the *mission civilisatrice*, the moral message is double-edged.

## PROGRESS

In the nineteenth century, the idea of humanitarianism was deeply bound up with that of progress. It was not just colonial subjects who were to be improved, but humanity in general. Through reform of poor relief, education, prisons, mental hospitals, and a host of other institutions, humanitarians sought indefinite improvement in the human condition. As Thomas Haskell writes, "An unprecedented wave of humanitarian reform sentiment swept through the societies of Western Europe, England, and North America in the hundred years following 1750."[15] Ending slavery was, as we saw, one instance. Projects such as the founding of the Red Cross also participated in this broader sense of humanitarianism, as well as in the narrower one of emergency response. But it was not just suffering from war that beckoned to humanitarians. It was any suffering that seemed avoidable.

Humanitarianism took root in the modern world not only as a response to war or to "emergencies," but also as part of an effort to remake the world so that it would better serve the interests of humanity. This reflected a variety of different changes in social order, ethics, and cognition. It reflected the rise of modern industry, the development of modern states, and the early achievements of modern science and technology, all of which encouraged the notion that human action could be mobilized to transform conditions long taken as inevitable.[16] It reflected a new value placed on everyday life that enabled people to weigh "the good" in the well-being of ordinary people, and not only extraordinary achievements or spiritual values pointing beyond this world.[17] It reflected a new sense of the interconnection of actions, including actions at a substantial distance from each other, that may have been rooted in capitalism and colonialism, but that encouraged not only self-interested response, but also new understandings of responsibility.[18]

Advances in caring for the unfortunate were seen as evidence of advances in civilization. Of course, so, too, was development, understood initially as a package of economic, political, cultural, and social factors—not simply as economic growth—and pursued by socialists as well as capitalists. Advances in development were expected to reduce the frequency and intensity of emergencies.

This sort of thinking was in tension with the notion that "The poor shall always be with us" that informed traditional thinking about charity. Increasingly, poverty was viewed as a solvable social problem. The same went for emergencies—effective forecasting, planning, and administration should reduce them. Epidemics were the model for the nineteenth century, to be managed effectively in the short term and eliminated in the long term by sanitation and science. The new humanitarianism was largely secular. Even when motivations and conceptual frameworks were religious, it was firmly oriented toward this-worldly improvements and results measurable in human time. It is no accident that Florence Nightingale was a pioneer of the use of statistics as well as of nursing care. Humanitarianism became associated with advancing human welfare. There was change in what seemed possible, as well as in values and evaluations. Enlightenment, the Industrial Revolution, science, technology, and the modern state all combined to make effective action on humanity seem possible.

Evolutionary theory gave an intellectual underpinning to this project, though as often as it was rooted in the work of Darwin, it was amalgamated to a general expectation of progress. Metaphors of maturation were prominent, alongside the notion of selection. The ideal of civilization was still basic. But the broad faith in and pursuit of progress guided efforts to reform all sorts of social institutions and especially to reform the lives of the poor and the weak. Efforts to save lives in emergencies were drawn into this agenda. Of course, the altruistic idea of softening the roughness of the human condition was not uncontroversial. For Social Darwinists, it suggested action counter to the struggle for survival that drives evolution. And some humanitarians embraced the idea of improvement in the species in versions that now seem unsavory, such as eugenics.

Lester Frank Ward, a polymathic geologist who became the first president of the American Sociological Society (later changed to Association in an era of acronyms), caught the spirit of putting knowledge to work as well as something of the distinctive modernity of the project:

It must be admitted that humanitarian institutions have done far less good than either juridical or ethical institutions. The sentiment [of humanity] is of relatively recent origin…it exists to an appreciable degree in only a minute fraction of the most enlightened populations. It is rarely directed with judgment…the institutions established to support it are for the most part poorly supported, badly managed, and often founded on a total misconception of human nature and of the true mode of attaining the end in view.[19]

The end in view, as much for Ward's version of evolutionism as for Benthamite utilitarianism, was improvement of the human condition. And indeed, as the Benthamite parentage suggests, humanitarian reform throughout the nineteenth century was partly a project of rationalization. Even where ills could not entirely be ended, at least not immediately, efforts to mitigate them could be made more orderly and subjected to more goal-directed action, not merely sentimental charity. As a reviewer wrote of Jane Addams, the pioneering sociologist and social worker who founded Hull House, famous for finding Christ in every person, even the drunk or destitute, her essays "breathe in every sentence the spirit of rationalized humanity."[20]

Humanitarianism thus joined with colonial and domestic state projects and the rise of corporate capitalism in adopting a more managerial orientation. Managerial rationalization was applied to colonies, students in school, urban planning, welfare relief, factories, prisons, armies, the unemployed, and eventually refugee camps. In the process, it helped to give rise to social science. The managerial orientation involved trying to apply knowledge to problems—whether raising factory productivity, or eradicating yellow fever, or assimilating immigrants, or developing the logistical capacity to supply aid in emergencies. This was as true of those who sought uplift and social change as of those who sought simply to protect property or power. What started as a broad engagement of the new middle class in social reform during the nineteenth century had become, by the twentieth, a set of increasingly specialized projects, each with attendant fields of academic and practical expertise. For example, the founder of Columbia University's Sociology Department, Franklin H. Giddings, had wide scientific ambitions and was a pioneer of the idea of scientific sociology, but was brought there to occupy a chair created to improve the administration of charities.

Philanthropy was to become more scientific, as Andrew Carnegie would famously put it. Private organizations would take on public purposes, putting wealth gained in capitalist enterprises to work improving the lot of humanity at large. Behind the modern foundation lay a history of religious organizations, from monasteries to overseas missions. A similar history issued in the modern nongovernmental organization. For many, civil society was rethought not as a realm of social connection per se, but as "the voluntary sector" in which people empowered by possession of wealth would act (or hire agents to act) to advance humanity and alleviate ills. For two hundred years, the notion of acting directly outside the state has coexisted with that of demanding more or better state action. The welfare state was a product of this history as much as was the NGO. But the welfare state was (at least in part) the achievement of a struggle in which ordinary people demanded—through unions, churches, and social movements—that their needs be better met. The NGO and scientific philanthropy were more often top-down efforts in which money and expertise empowered some to act for—or on—others.

Most of this work was organized internally in individual countries. But it also grew in colonies and in missionary work that cut across colonial and national boundaries. Organizations had been formed to assist refugees since the wars of the Protestant Reformation and were formed anew in connection with different wars, revolutionary struggles, and efforts to support fleeing slaves. Refugees became the focus of a global emergency response in the 1930s, and indeed, it is from this point on that the association of refugees and emergencies became consistent.

Humanitarian action, as it has developed since World War II and especially since the 1970s, represents both continuity with this tradition and a break within it. There is continuity in the continued proliferation of organizations, from the International Rescue Committee, through a range of religious groups and NGOs, to the United Nations and the Bretton Woods organizations. While some would focus on development as a means to improve the human condition, many would focus on immediately alleviating human suffering. There is continuity in the mobilization of ever more people to work on behalf of humanity at large and other people at long distances. And there is continuity in a managerial orientation—still sometimes in conflict with more immediately moral commitments. Humanitarians today are called on to devise quantitative measures of "reductions in excess mortality." Funders demand evidence of cost effectiveness, often using bureaucratic tools such as "logical framework analysis" (LogFrame, for short), devised initially to run military organizations, though organizations like MSF still speak in terms of volunteers. Entrants into the field increasingly come from specialized master's degree programs and expect to pursue a professional career. Organizations undertake efforts to set and maintain "standards." Manuals of best practices are produced, with guidance not just on how many liters of water are required for each person (by sex), but on how to conduct triage. And of course, humanitarian action depends not simply on moral commitment, but on massive logistical capacities—to move food, medicine, and other supplies around the world to regions with few roads and many dangers.

However, if management and operations reveal continuity with the history of pursuing progress, humanitarianism today is more sharply distinguished in its purpose. Most projects for improving the human condition were directly political and/or economic and associated with long-term agendas. But humanitarianism has come to center more clearly on alleviating emergencies. The term "humanitarian" now is reserved for actions free from longer-term political or economic entanglements, actions deemed right in themselves, the necessary moral response to emergencies. It is something good to do without waiting for progress, even if you have doubts that progress will ever come. The emergency has become definitive because it is understood to pose immediate moral demands that override other considerations.

## EMERGENCIES AS EXCEPTIONS

In the emergency imaginary, emergencies arise as exceptions to otherwise normal social conditions—stable governments, tolerance between ethnic groups, the availability and distribution of food supplies. Whether they involve tsunamis and earthquakes beyond human control, desertification resulting from human degradation of land and water supplies, or conflicts manifestly made by mortals, they appear as exceptions to the normal. Wars are exceptions to peace. Wars that affect civilians on a massive scale are exceptions to wars contained within "normal" military boundaries. Genocide, new wars, and terrorist tactics that directly target civilians or blur the distinction between combatants and noncombatants are understood commonly as the results of "breakdowns" in local social relations — exceptions — rather than as the recurrent products of global markets for diamonds, drugs, and weapons that transform local disputes and alliances.

Of course, aid workers on the ground often know that more is involved and are often aware that immediate emergencies have histories. Agencies struggling to feed refugees in Sudan today remember that there have been refugees there before; those trying to help victims of fighting in the Democratic Republic of Congo are well aware that fighting has flared in the region before; and certainly, the repetitive character of floods in Southeast Asia has not escaped either state officials or international relief organizations, and these work to stockpile food and other supplies locally. Nonetheless, the very idea of the emergency emphasizes the immediacy of each occurrence and derives a significant part of its capacity to command attention and mobilize resources from this sense of immediacy.

The media reinforce this understanding on a broad scale. A sense of immediacy is definitive for funding programs by governments and charitable organizations alike. It drives direct-mail advertising. Likewise, many are recruited to work in the field by the sense of guarantee that their work will help people directly — not only if economic development eventually takes place or if politicians finally make peace. Nonetheless, the emergency depends on the normal: the peaceful, the calm, the planned, the smoothly flowing. It gains its conceptual clarity from contrast.

International and global affairs have long been constructed in terms of two core principles. First, the primary units of analysis — and of power, stability, and interest — are nation-states. These may enter into relationships — alliances, balances of power, rivalries — but they are the units. Second, there exist a range of flows across these nation-states that meet or obstruct their interests, challenge their power, and call for their action. The flows may be of goods, or people, or ideas, or even diseases. The nation-states are clearly concerned to control their borders, but usually also seek to maximize the benefits and minimize the costs of flows across them — not simply to close them.

The system of states and flows works in an orderly fashion in an ideal realm of theory, and to some extent, at least some of the time, this is matched by reality. But one need not detail the world wars, massive population displacements, or great depressions of the twentieth century to grasp that the phrase "global order" often borders on the oxymoronic. Still, for all the upsets, the language of global order has survived. It is even carried forward today into hopes for a new cosmo-politan order to replace the order of nation-states. Order is the realm of nomo-thetic generality; exceptions are idiographic particulars. Order is normal; disorder is exceptional, no matter how frequent.

Of course, the opposition between a more or less predictable system of state relationships and flows and the putatively unpredictable eruptions of emergencies in the conception of global order is deeply ideological. It clearly reflects interests favored by the existing order and the specific power relations constitutive of that order. Carl Schmitt famously incorporated the capacity to declare a state of excep-tion into his concept of sovereignty—and the lineage of this idea stretches back at least to Machiavelli. Drawing on the work of Jacques Derrida and Walter Benja-min, Giorgio Agamben has turned this idea on its head to ask whether in an era of sovereignty taken to an abusive extreme, we live always in a state of exception.[21] But the exception is not simply the sovereign declaration. It is also the notion of emergency itself, not only because it is the counterpart to the very idea of order, but also because it carries a demand for action.

Arguments in favor of military intervention have sometimes been made in similar terms. At various points in the nineteenth century, European powers did intervene on more or less humanitarian grounds to try to manage crises created by the decline of the Ottoman Empire, foreshadowing debates about humanitar-ian intervention today, though they did not act to prevent the genocidal violence against Armenians. The Holocaust and World War II are ambiguous, but formative cases for modern humanitarianism. The Holocaust did not produce the emergency response that later generations came to think it should have and so stands as an exemplary case of failure, although the mobilization in support of refugees was more successful, if still very imperfect. The war itself was organized mainly as an interstate conflict, and emergency response was mostly assimilated to the older approaches by states, colonial powers, and the Red Cross. But it produced civilian death and devastation on a new scale, leading to increased calls of "Never again."

The International Rescue Committee grew out of the International Relief Asso-ciation active in the 1930s. And in due course, the United Nations was formed and added agencies with their own emergency mandates. But it was the postwar pro-cesses of decolonization and national liberation and struggles to draw new political boundaries that created the occasion for a specific focus on humanitarian emergen-cies. Postwar Europe faced emergencies, as well as general need for reconstruction, exacerbated by the division of the West from the East. But it was the partition of Palestine that created Israel and the partition of India attendant on the creation of Pakistan that produced the most powerful exemplars. Despite the upheavals, development remained the dominant global agenda—interpreted, to be sure, in different ways by socialist and capitalist powers, but embraced by both. The ideal of sovereign nation-states, each developing greater prosperity, greater democracy, and greater standing in the community of nations was compelling. It dominated not only the perspective of rich countries on their own success and the chances for others, but the hopes associated with independence in most former colonies. Emergencies were mostly understood as setbacks on the path of development.

The failed Biafran struggle for independence and the combination of a war of liberation and a devastating cyclone in Bangladesh were not only famous instances of emergencies, but paradigmatic in their refraction through Western and global media. George Harrison's Concert for Bangladesh was the first in a series of massive celebrity benefits now associated with emergencies. The history of neutral humanitarian assistance to those suffering in war has been harnessed to a variety of new circumstances, a process that continues as environmental degradation and climate change figure more and more in occasioning emergencies, including many, such as the crisis in Darfur, that also involve politics and armed conflict. Thus, the term "complex humanitarian emergency" was coined in the 1970s, with the primary example of Mozambique in mind. It referred to emergencies created by displacements of people and other collateral suffering occasioned by armed conflict in which sides and territories were unclear, and in which the primary parties were not (or at least not all) recognizable states. The implication of the term was that previous humanitarian emergencies were simpler. In any case, it was harder to fit such conflicts into a narrative of development. But they could still be contrasted with a somewhat vague image of the normal and treated as exceptions.

The notion of keeping the humanitarian and the military sharply distinct has come under enormous stress. It is perhaps a lost cause.[22] In the context of the breakup of Yugoslavia and of the Central African wars and genocides, it seemed to many that military interventions must be seen as necessary humanitarian responses to certain sorts of emergencies.[23] Even those who sought to keep the work of humanitarian assistance "neutral" found this increasingly difficult, partly because they could not avoid working with armies or in zones controlled by one or another party to the combat. And at the same time, campaigners for human rights were commonly unsympathetic to arguments that humanitarian assistance requires neutrality.

Arguments for "nonconsensual humanitarian interventions" come in two kinds. One, for which the invasion of Iraq stands as an extreme example, is that governments are so abusive of citizens that humanitarian goals will be advanced by regime change. This is closer to human rights argumentation, but draws on aspects of the idea of humanitarian progress. The other, used in arguing for implementing humanitarian assistance against the will of the Myanmar government after Cyclone

Nargis, is more that aid must be delivered and that government preferences are more or less beside the point. This is much more in synch with humanitarian argumentation generally, though it can also be made readily in human rights terms. In general, humanitarian response to emergencies has focused on the alleviation of suffering by nonmilitary means, precisely because military action necessarily has meant entanglement in longer-term political problems. Medical care, by contrast, could be understood as always right in itself, though here, too, questions would arise, notably in Rwanda, where doctors worried they were patching up *genocidaires* who would return to killing.

The desire for direct engagement and moral purity is not entirely new. On the contrary, the field of humanitarian response to emergencies entered a phase of dramatic growth amid the waning of 1960s-era protest politics. Many of the early protagonists were activists from the left who grew disillusioned with more conventional programs for political and economic change. Humanitarianism was in a sense a way to retain the emotional urgency of 1960s politics, but in a form not dependent on any political party, movement, or state. The theme of witness drawn from Catholicism and previous charity work was helpful in this regard. Humanitarians could bear witness against evil and express solidarity with those who suffered without a broader analysis of causes or a program for political-economic change. This made it easier to maintain the sense of immediate, affective engagement that had been important to 1960s radicalism. It also provided an escape from the endless ideological arguments and the jockeying for advantage that undercut coalitions and collective action and from the corrupting influences of political power. In the wake of '68, many former activists found it all too evident how often self-interested ambition had been combined with seemingly altruistic political activism, even if the activists were able to misrecognize their own ambitions as something purer. Direct action in witnessing and solidarity with horrendous suffering reduced the time lag between intention and result that had allowed for ulterior motives to become dominant. Or so it seemed.

The gap between intention and result opens up the classic Platonic-Aristotelian distinction that Max Weber integrated into modern social theory as the difference between value-rationality (*Wertrationalität*) and instrumental rationality (*Zweckrationalität*). But if instrumentality seemed to many humanitarians of the 1970s colder, less immediate, and more open to corruption, it was also the realm of causal analysis, planning, and the assessment of effects. And one of the stories of humanitarian response to emergencies since the 1970s has been tension between value-rational immediacy and the need to think instrumentally, a need introduced by funders, by the imperatives of organizational life, and by triage on a larger scale: the challenge of deciding where to expend scarce resources. Resources remained scarce, despite (or perhaps partly because) of an explosive growth in humanitarian responses to emergencies. There were new refugee flows, famines, conflicts, and sometimes genocides through the 1970s and 1980s: the Vietnamese Boat People, the Cambodian mass murders, the fighting in the former Portuguese colonies in Africa, and a series of catastrophes in the Horn of Africa linked to both conflict and climate. Then, the end of the Cold War helped make for yet another wave of conflicts by simultaneously destabilizing alliances and leaving the world awash in cheap arms. The 1990s saw an enormous proliferation of conflicts and refugee movements, often dozens at a time in different parts of the world.

During this period, a variety of new organizations entered the previously small and relatively close-knit field of emergency relief. This had grown dramatically in the 1970s and then expanded yet again in the 1990s. Some organizations were entirely new, while others were long-standing development organizations that added emergency relief projects to their portfolios. Change at the UN is symptomatic. Though the founding mission of the UN was peace, and this remained prominent, the mission of most of the UN agencies created in its first forty years was development. But from the 1990s on, response to emergencies became more and more prominent in the work of the UN, not least because development became increasingly the domain of the Bretton Woods organizations. Eventually, special appeals, largely for emergency response, came to generate larger amounts than the core UN budget. The Office for the Coordination of Humanitarian Affairs was set up not just because there were so many emergencies, but because there were so many different organizations working in emergency relief, seeking funds from the same donors, and trying to take slightly different messages to the same public. In the field as a whole, an effort to set standards for effective work gained more and more attention (notably with the Sphere Project initiatives seeking a Humanitarian Charter, as well as minimum standards in disaster response).

Alongside the codification of best practices, a variety of professional training programs have been developed. And inside humanitarian organizations, formal reporting and assessment practices are more prominent. In a world dominated by moral concerns for suffering and still recruiting its new entrants largely on this basis, a variety of instrumental concerns structure daily practices. These include simply sustaining organizations through fundraising, internal management, and media relations. They also include trying to rationalize the necessary choices—where to work or how much to invest in what kinds of logistical or medical capacities. Even where the goal is only better informing necessary decisions about where to invest scarce resources, the result is to highlight the tension between the tacit particularism of an ethic that values care as right in itself and the comparative calculi of greater or lesser goods.

*instrumentalizat of moral action*

This instrumentalization of moral action is frustrating to some in the field, but much more worrying is instrumentalization of another kind. Humanitarian organizations themselves are often perceived as instruments of foreign policy by donor governments. And even where no single state dominates the work of an organization, there are expectations about the management of emergencies that transcend the logic of simple charity or palliative care for those in immediate need.

It is conceivable that instrumentalization in each of these two senses, along with the wave of new entrants, will spell the end of the humanitarian field of emergency response as it came to be conceived over a longish history and as it flourished especially in the four decades after 1968. Humanitarianism or response to emergencies became a "field" by virtue of establishing boundaries, hierarchies of value, a space of positions, and competition for standing. MSF represented a kind of ideal for many others in the field, able to resist both political influence and the potentially corrupting influence of donor demands, especially from state donors. MSF ranked high in a hierarchy where distinction accrued to those acting with the most clearly moral purpose, altruistically, amid danger. It was known as the organization that would go where others would not.[24] This meant that MSF could refuse funds that might tie it down; others were more dependent on the vicissitudes of fund-raising and donor demands. MSF benefitted from a reputational capital specific to the humanitarian field, centered on the extent, immediacy, and neutrality of service to those who suffered.

And of course, there was a similar hierarchy in the reputations of individuals as they moved among organizations, working in emergencies around the world, accumulating experiences like medals. The field developed a set of practices and styles to be taught to new entrants, organizations and individuals alike. If they were initially informal and taught in practical contexts (and in late-night review sessions at makeshift bars), they became increasingly codified. They became the subjects of academic articles and courses. More influentially, they became objects of the humanitarian reform movement, which set out to professionalize the field, raise its standards, and develop norms.

Indeed, humanitarians have long felt a need to police the boundary of their field. Their first term of reference is "neutrality." Humanitarians do not take sides. They do not advocate for one army to win the war, for one government against another, or even for human rights. This is not only a matter of clarity of purpose or of sticking to the moral for its own sake. It is also a practical consideration. Neutrality is the basis for access; it is the basis for the notion that no one should shoot at those flying the red cross or red crescent, delivering medical assistance or food. This is one reason why the growing role of militaries in providing humanitarian assistance is so troubling. And as that suggests, the ideal of neutrality is becoming harder to sustain. When military interventions are made in the name of human rights or human welfare, this undermines the very idea that the humanitarian response to emergencies can be distinctive.

The boundary with human rights advocacy is even more problematic, but follows similar principles. Many humanitarian groups reject human rights advocacy as too political.[25] This means not just that there is a politics behind the human rights arguments, but rather that the human rights field is oriented toward lobbying campaigns, getting treaties signed, and otherwise working directly with and on states. Humanitarians, by contrast, avoid states. This is one reason for strong emphasis on the notion of "autonomy" for the NGOs working in the area, though in fact, such autonomy is often much more illusive than its frequent invocation implies. They tend to see states as the sources of problems far more than of solutions. They often work in situations of state failure, though they often find themselves creating substitutes for states, for example as they work to maintain order in refugee camps. Humanitarians also argue that danger is increased and access reduced by human rights organizations that move into delivery of humanitarian services.

The second term of reference in humanitarians' definition of their own field is "urgency." Humanitarians respond immediately to acute need. They are thus at the opposite end of a continuum from development assistance that tries to address long-term issues of poverty or disempowerment—even though humanitarians would acknowledge that these make people vulnerable to emergencies. While the theme of neutrality has to do with the autonomy of the humanitarian field from politics, that of urgency has to do with autonomy from the economy. This is not autonomy from material conditions and constraints; it is autonomy from the pursuit of solutions by means of economic transformation. Advocates for development against other forms of aid often cite the adage that if you give someone a fish, you feed them for a day, but if you teach them to fish, you enable them to feed themselves for life. Humanitarians are unabashedly in the fish-for-a-day business. They stress that someone who dies today will not learn to fish tomorrow.

The theme of urgency is closely coupled with that of direct action. Humanitarianism is defined by action, not consequences, and especially by action directly delivered through human contact on-site. This is part of what creates the constant tension with instrumentalization. In Weber's Aristotelian terminology, the dominant ethos of humanitarian action, value rationality, is focused on doing what is good in itself, not what is good for some other purpose.[26] Yet there are increasing demands for attention to the longer-term implications of humanitarian action and hence for the application of instrumental rationality. Which humanitarian practices, for example, best promote the "early recovery" of suffering regions? How should emergency relief give way to development assistance? Can humanitarian care be provided in ways that encourage respect for human rights? Can the situation of women be improved in lasting ways, taking the very disruption of the humanitarian emergency as an occasion for remaking culture?[27]

It is easiest to maintain the focus on value-rational action in the field, on-site in the middle of the emergency and much harder back at headquarters. In the field, while working directly to ease suffering, moral purpose is embodied in the suffering subjects served and in the work itself. This gives meaning to the long hours; it gives a kind of fullness to the days and to life.[28] To be sure, there must be triage, and it can be heartbreaking. There is burnout, and this is a young people's line of work—in that, not unlike activism. But the experience of hard work directly oriented toward doing good and toward doing good for people one can see directly is what sustains many in humanitarian action. It is not an experience one can easily maintain at all hours. Even in the field, bureaucratic work, logistical snafus, and frustrating negotiations with other organizations intrude. But like *communitas*, the sense of intense sharing and unity evoked in Victor Turner's accounts of ritual, emotionally meaningful direct action can be recurrent enough to pull one through the more routine structures and conflicts.[29] This is much less true sitting in an office in New York or London. Indeed, this sense of direct moral action is distinctively absent from much of the work necessarily done in the headquarters of humanitarian organizations. It is not that people do not think they are doing the right thing, but that "rightness" is embedded in procedures, statistics, and long-range planning—and often in worse: bureaucratic turf struggles, questions of conscience about what funding to take, and resentments over who got promoted. Yet, of course, the work doesn't get done without funding, logistics, and procedures.

## CONCLUSION

The idea of humanitarian action continues aspects of ancient traditions of charity. These are reworked in varying degrees, with more emphasis on witnessing and often on enhancing the rationality and effectiveness of value-rational action. From the history of European imperialism on, humanitarianism has drawn on an orientation toward saving, if not necessarily civilizing, the world. This combines often with the project of governing the ungovernable, though few humanitarians would embrace the managerial aspect of their work quite so unambiguously. The Enlightenment and the nineteenth-century idealization of progress has also influenced modern humanitarianism. This is particularly true where it is closest to human rights work and most engaged in the notion of seeking solutions, rather than only mitigating suffering. The field is divided along a continuum from those who would care for and witness to suffering, to those who would try to end humanitarian emergencies.

But though all these dimensions of genealogy remain formative, the project of humanitarianism that has flourished especially since World War II is also distinct. What most gives it separate identity is the idea of emergency—both simply in the sense of urgency and in the deeper sense that this underwrites an exception to all sorts of other rules and projects that can be deferred to more normal times or other sorts of actors. Humanitarianism is thus kept distinct from several other projects. It is not the long-term agenda of economic development. It is not the promotion of democracy. It is not advocacy for human rights. It is the focus on immediate response suggested by the emergency imaginary, with its emphasis on apparently sudden, unpredictable, and short-term explosions of suffering. And it is sustained by the experience—or at least the hope—of altruistic work, of work embedded in direct moral purpose. But the whole field of humanitarian action is also shaped by professionalization, the effort to achieve standards, and the growth of organizations devoted to humanitarian action, but embedded in a larger field where issues of development, democracy, and other sorts of progress also contend. In addition, it is proving increasingly hard to keep emergency response distinct from military operations, including wars justified as humanitarian ventures.

The emergency that draws people and resources into humanitarian action is a creature of globalization, but also of a particular moment in the history of global-ization. It can be imagined as such because media exist to see its effects in nearly real time, because an ideological framework exists to frame a sense of connection to those suffering at a distance, and because organizational capacities exist that make it possible to take effective action. At one level, this is a massive moral achievement, a capacity to care for strangers in a radically new way. At another level, it is a construction of events in various places—Biafra, Bangladesh, Rwanda, or Darfur—that comes not from those places, but from the cosmopolitan centers of the Global North. The painful events of conflict, floods, and famine are not false. They are grinding dimensions of everyday life, and sometimes they rapidly become much worse. But the emergency imaginary frames these events not as they look to locals, but as they appear to cosmopolitans. Emergencies are crises from the point of view of the cosmopolis. The attention of the "international community"—the newspaper accounts, the TV news, the donors, and the agencies—is on the efforts of outsiders to help, to minister to strangers. Too often, the story seems to be: Moral white people come from the rich world to care for those in backward, remote places.

The efforts of humanitarian relief workers are remarkable and noble. It takes nothing away from the significance of their labors to say, however, that they are fraught with tensions. Indeed, humanitarian workers are a highly self-critical group, constantly struggling with the contradictions of their work. And most recognize, moreover, something that the media accounts leave out. International aid workers are not the source of most care provided in emergencies. Most comes from neighbors, family, friends, and in general simply those who live at the scene. The cosmopolitan experts in disaster can play an important role. But it is important to remember that the story is not only about them. It is just that they are usually the only ones able to speak. And conversely, one of the most distinctive features of the emergency imaginary as it circulates in the global media is that it renders those who suffer in emergencies as voiceless masses.

"Emergency" thus is a way of grasping problematic events, a way of imagining them that emphasizes their apparent unpredictability, abnormality, and brevity and that carries the corollary that response—intervention—is necessary. For some, the intervention may be only care: paradigmatically, food, medicine, and shelter. Close to this end of the continuum one may add witnessing, something short of a political response, yet more than a turning away from the evils that occasion the emergency. For others, though, the international emergency both can be and should be managed. One should use the best practices, methods, and technologies to alleviate as much suffering as possible—and perhaps also to alleviate as much threat to global order as possible. But the managerial response to an emergency focuses on restoring the existing order, not on changing it. And the more agendas for long-term change are incorporated into emergency response, the less it is distinguished by immediacy or escape from competing agendas and complex moral judgments. The construction of emergencies as exceptions to normal order and of humanitarianism as the special action they demand underwrites a sort of suspension of other concerns. Thus, there are responses that seek to mitigate harm (such as sending food), institutions that share costs (such as insurance), and "preparedness" efforts to make future responses better. But transforming the global order—say, by making it more egalitarian as a way of limiting future suffering—is not on the manager's agenda. And if it is on the witness's agenda, it is embraced without much optimism that major change can be achieved very soon.

## NOTES

I have benefitted from comments by audiences at NYU, Yale, Manchester, the American University of Cairo, the University of California at San Diego, and the American Sociological Association, insights from discussions with many professionals in humanitarian action, and especially from Pamela DeLargy of the UN Population Fund.

1   On the idea of social imaginaries, see Charles Taylor, *Modern Social Imaginaries* (Durham, NC: Duke University Press, 2004) and the introduction by Dilip Gaonkar and various contributions to the special issue "New Social Imaginaries," *Public Culture* 14, no. 1 (2002). For more on the history of the social imaginary of the humanitarian emergency, see Craig Calhoun, "A World of Emergencies: Fear, Intervention, and the Limits of Cosmopolitan Order," The thirty-fifth Sorokin Lecture, *Canadian Review of Sociology and Anthropology* 41, no. 4 (November 2004): pp. 373–95.

2   Although there were efforts to provide relief to victims of natural disasters and conflicts in the nineteenth and early twentieth centuries, the notion of emergency was used mostly to refer to market crises, governmental collapses, and actual or threatened wars—the sorts of things that led to declarations of a state of emergency and sometimes to the suspension of normal laws or operating procedures.

3   Kingsley Davis, "India and Pakistan: The Demography of Partition," *Pacific Affairs* 22, no. 3 (1949): pp. 254–64.

4   As Luc Boltanski has argued, in an important sense, the global image of humanitarianism is about neither the suffering nor the NGOs seeking to relieve it, but the media itself. See Luc Boltanski, *Distant Suffering: Morality, Media, and Politics* (Cambridge: Cambridge University Press, 1999).

5   See Giorgio Agamben, *Homo Sacer: Sovereign Power and Bare Life*, trans. Daniel Heller-Roazen (Stanford, CA: Stanford University Press, 1998).

6   Compare Hannah Arendt, *The Human Condition* (Chicago: University of Chicago Press, 1958).

7   James Scott, *Seeing Like a State: How Certain Schemes to Improve the Human Condition Have Failed* (New Haven, CT: Yale University Press, 1998). "Population thinking" is a concern spread through a variety of Michel Foucault's texts and lectures from the 1970s onward. See Michel Foucault, *Résumé des cours, 1970–1982* (Paris: Julliard, 1989) for a sampling. See also the helpful review article by Bruce Curtis, "Foucault on Governmentality and Population: The Impossible Discovery," *Canadian Journal of Sociology* 27, no. 4 (Fall 2002): pp. 505–53.

8   Initially, this was a clearly Christian understanding of common humanity. But it is significant that the Red Cross could fairly readily be complemented by the Red Crescent and eventually by an idea of religion as such offering a basis for recognizing common humanity behind the divisions of nations or even civilizations.

9   Among the first sociological generalizations about emergencies (or "catastrophes," as they were termed) is that response would typically centralize social power. The argument was offered by Herbert Spencer in *Principles of Sociology*, 3 vols. (1876–96; Westport, CT: Greenwood Press, 1975) and affirmed by William Graham Sumner, Emile Durkheim, and others including Pitirim A. Sorokin, "Impoverishment and the Expansion of Governmental Control," *The American Journal of Sociology* 32, no. 2 (September 1926): pp. 206–16, and *Man and Society in Calamity: The Effects of War, Revolution, Famine, Pestilence upon Human Mind, Behavior, Social Organization and Cultural Life* (New York: Dutton 1942).

10   Partha Chatterjee, *Nationalist Thought and the Colonial World: A Derivative Discourse?* (Atlantic Highlands, NJ: Zed Books, 1986).

11   Foucault, *Résumé des cours, 1970–1982*.

12   See Eric Wolf's classic account in *Europe and the People without History* (Berkeley: University of California Press, 1982).

13   While the mass media portrayal of humanitarian action is overwhelmingly positive, even

celebratory, reflections by those who have worked in humanitarian relief are commonly self-critical and sometimes agonized. See for, example, David Kennedy, *The Dark Sides of Virtue: Reassessing International Humanitarianism* (Princeton, NJ: Princeton University Press, 2004); Fiona Terry, *Condemned to Repeat?: The Paradox of Humanitarian Action* (Ithaca: NY: Cornell University Press, 2002), and Kenneth Cain, Heidi Postlewait, and Andrew Thomson, *Emergency Sex (and Other Desperate Measures): True Stories from a War Zone* (London: Ebury, 2004).

14    See, for example, Gary J. Bass, *Freedom's Battle: The Origins of Humanitarian Intervention* (New York: Knopf, 2008).

15    Thomas L. Haskell, "Capitalism and the Origins of the Humanitarian Sensibility," pts. 1 and 2, *American Historical Review* 90, no. 2 (1985): pp. 339–61 and no. 3 (1985): pp. 547–66. See also Shelby T. McCloy, *The Humanitarian Movement in Eighteenth-Century France* (Lexington, KY: University of Kentucky Press, 1957).

16    For two contrasting treatments, see Robert A. Nisbet, *History of the Idea of Progress* (New York: Basic Books, 1980) and Christopher Lasch, *The True and Only Heaven* (New York: Norton, 1991).

17    See Charles Taylor, *Sources of the Self* (Cambridge, MA: Harvard University Press, 1989).

18    See Haskell, "Capitalism and the Origins of the Humanitarian Sensibility."

19    Lester F. Ward, "Mind as a Social Factor," *Mind* 9, no. 36 (1884): pp. 563–73.

20    Stanton Coit, "Review of *Philanthropy and Social Progress*, by Miss Jane Addams, Robert A. Woods, Father J.O.S. Huntington, Professor Franklin H. Giddings, and Bernard Bosanquet (New York: Crowell, 1892)," *International Journal of Ethics* 4, no. 2 (January 1894): pp. 241–46.

21    Carl Schmitt, *The Concept of the Political*, trans. George Schwab (Chicago, University of Chicago Press, 1996); Giorgio Agamben, *State of Exception*, trans. Kevin Attell (Chicago: University of Chicago Press, 2004). Agamben would stress the normalization of the state of exception inherent in, for example, the USA PATRIOT Act (the Uniting and Strengthening America by Providing Appropriate Tools Required to Intercept and Obstruct Terrorism Act of 2001) passed by the Bush administration to grant it special powers to combat terrorism and other threats to the U.S. population. I want to emphasize a different aspect, suggesting that we do not grasp the exception adequately simply in its declaration, as a constituting act of will, the point of connection between law and violent force. We need to inquire also into the ways an emergency imaginary makes action appear necessary, but also circumscribes the sorts of action that are necessary: emergency response, for example, or preparedness for future emergencies, rather than change to the system of "order" itself.

22    Especially since the invasion of Iraq, the issue of entanglement with the military has become a crucial theme in discussions of "crises of humanitarianism." See Michael Ignatieff, *The Lesser Evil: Political Ethics in an Age of Terror* (Princeton, NJ: Princeton University Press, 2004); David Rieff, *A Bed for the Night: Humanitarianism in Crisis* (New York: Simon and Schuster, 2003); Stephen John Stedman and Fred Tanner (eds.), *Refugee Manipulation: War, Politics, and the Abuse of Human Suffering* (Washington, D.C.: Brookings Institute, 2003); Terry, *Condemned to Repeat?*; and Kennedy, *The Dark Sides of Virtue*.

23    Arguments for military intervention are by no means confined to left-liberals (or erstwhile left-liberals), but it was novel for left-liberals to be among the most active advocates of military intervention. Arguments were often rooted in a humanitarian agenda, and the Rwandan genocide became a symbol of the implications of failure to act. For many, "action"

clearly meant military action to stop the genocide after its onset, rather than other kinds of actions initiated much earlier. For various sides in this debate, see Seyom Brown, *The Illusion of Control: Force and Foreign Policy in the 21st Century* (Washington, D.C.: Brookings Institution Press, 2003); Mark R. Duffield, *Global Governance and the New Wars: The Merging of Development and Security* (New York: Zed Books, 2001); Martha Finnemore, *The Purpose of Intervention: Changing Beliefs of the Use of Force* (Ithaca, NY: Cornell University Press, 2003); Samantha Power, *A Problem from Hell: America in the Age of Genocide* (New York: Basic Books, 2002); and Nicholas J. Wheeler, *Saving Strangers: Humanitarian Intervention in International Society* (Oxford: Oxford University Press, 2000). Michael Barnett, in *Eyewitness to a Genocide: The United Nations and Rwanda* (Ithaca, NY: Cornell University Press, 2002), addresses the role of the UN in Rwanda. Among the journalistic reports that focused attention on the absence of intervention in Rwanda, see Philip Gourevitch, *We Wish to Inform You that Tomorrow We Will Be Killed with Our Families: Stories on Rwanda* (London: Picador, 1999); and Linda Melvern, *A People Betrayed: The Role of the West in Rwanda's Genocide* (New York: Zed Books, 2000). Alan Kuperman, in *The Limits of Intervention: Genocide in Rwanda* (Washington, D.C.: Brookings Institution Press, 2001), makes the case that successful intervention in Rwanda after the killing had started was more or less "logistically" impossible. Gary J. Bass situates his support for military intervention within an account of its imperial history in *Freedom's Battle: The Origins of Humanitarian Intervention* (New York: Knopf, 2008).

24  Dan Bartolotti, *Hope in Hell: Inside the World of Doctors without Borders* (Buffalo, NY: Firefly Books, 2006), p. 13.

25  See David Rieff, *A Bed for the Night* (New York: Simon and Schuster, 2003), for a strongly argued case against both combining humanitarian action with human rights advocacy and believing that human rights advocacy has in fact generated very much progress. His foil for this argument is often Michael Ignatieff, who in *The Lesser Evil* presents humanitarianism and human rights together as part of a "revolution in moral concern."

26  Max Weber, *Economy and Society* (Berkeley: University of California Press, 1968). See, for example, vol. 1, p. 21.

27  See, for example, the *Inter-Agency Standing Committee (IASC) Guidelines on Mental Health and Psychosocial Support in Emergency Settings* (Geneva: IASC, 2007) in which the mandate to "protect" psychological and social well-being shades into the effort to "promote" it in lasting ways.

28  See Charles Taylor, *A Secular Age* (Cambridge, MA: Harvard University Press, 2007) on the notion of "fullness" as a way of inhabiting the world, an experience in which a person's entire surrounding is imbued with meaning and perhaps moral significance, not reduced to the distanced relationships of scientific observation or instrumental use. Part of the appeal of humanitarian work in the field, despite its hardships, is that it offers a chance to experience this fullness, even in a secular age.

29  See Victor Turner, *The Ritual Process: Structure and Anti-Structure* (Chicago: Aldine, 1969).

# The Politics of Catastrophization:
# Emergency and Exception

Adi Ophir

The main thrust of my argument is to provide a conceptual framework for under-standing "emergency" in terms free from the discourse of sovereignty and its legal implications and in a way that still holds open a certain, limited place for the sover-eign decision on the exception. While I am joining here scholars such as Ann Stoler, who insists on "degrees of sovereignty,"[1] and Thomas Aleinikoff, who speaks about sovereignty's "semblances,"[2] the theoretical context of my argument is different from theirs: It is an attempt to construe a political theory of man-made disasters and use man-made disasters as a viewpoint from which it becomes possible— in fact, necessary—to revise some of political theory's basic concepts. The immedi-ate political context of this project and its initial motivation has been an attempt to provide a comparative-theoretical perspective on the recent catastrophization of the Occupied Palestinian Territories and on the Gaza Strip, in particular.

## A TWO-TIER CONCEPT OF CATASTROPHIZATION

The neologism "catastrophization" is a common, technical term in cognitive psy-chology and psychiatry. It designates an "anxiety disorder" in which one interprets "a specific, mildly negative event as having global and negative implications for one's view of the self and/or one's future." [3] For the psychologist or psychiatrist, catastrophe lies in the eyes of the beholder. Catastrophization is a "cognitive bias" in which some event that "in reality is merely inconvenient or uncomfortable" is magnified into something "terrible, awful, and unbearable."[4] Individuals who are "high in social anxiety" tend "to interpret positive social events in a negative way and to catastrophize in response to unambiguous, mildly negative social events."[5] Those who tend to catastrophize are inclined to overgeneralize risk-related factors and to exaggerate the chances of the worst possible thing happening.

Cognitive psychologists seem quite confident in their ability to distinguish their patients' distorted sense of reality from their own sober evaluation of what is really dangerous. They may believe that catastrophe is in the eyes of the beholder, but sometimes catastrophes do happen, and a sober understanding of reality must overcome an opposite cognitive bias — the tendency to deny this possibility. Taking the possibility of real catastrophes into account, one may say that "catastrophization" is a disorder, indeed, but of the world, not of the mind, in which "specific, mildly negative events" generate — gradually or abruptly — other events with "global and negative implications for one's self, one's world, and one's future."[6]

I would like to call these events or states of affairs by the name "evils." Evils — always in the plural — involve suffering and losses, humiliation and scarcity, deprivation and neglect. For the cognitive psychologist, catastrophization designates a "subjective" attitude: One is panicked, helplessly, by the misconceived prospect of a coming avalanche of evils that one is going to suffer. For the historian or political theorist, the humanitarian expert or the journalist, catastrophization can also mean the processes that bring about that very avalanche of evils that injure entire populations. "Objective" catastrophization is the sudden or gradual rise in evils' quantity, quality, frequency, span of distribution, and durability — in short, a rise in "the volume of evils" and the accompanying decline in the availability and effectiveness of means of protection, healing, and restoration. Catastrophization is a process in which natural and man-made forces and factors work together to create devastating effects on a large population.

A brief note about the distinction between man-made and natural factors is in place here. In extreme, rare cases, actual, objective catastrophization may be generated by unknown natural forces and go completely unnoticed until a full-fledged disaster takes place. Such a state of affairs is almost as abstracted from the contemporary human world as the state of nature. Some human agency is usually involved in the process of catastrophization, to a certain degree, at least, either by contributing to the production and distribution of an avalanche of evils or by contributing to its mitigation. In late modernity, it has become quite obvious that both the rise in the volume of evils and the decline in the efficiency of evils' mitigation are socially and politically mediated.[7] Women and men have become capable of tracing processes of catastrophization, forecasting disasters, anticipating and mitigating much of their negative effects, providing extensive assistance to the victims so as to prevent further deterioration of their situation, and helping them restore their ruptured lifeworld. At the same time, women and men have become capable of catastrophizing entire regions, in fact the whole globe. In late modernity, there are no more natural disasters, because catastrophization is always socially and politically mediated.[8]

Processes of catastrophization may advance more or less rapidly, more or less abruptly, with changing frequencies; they may expand or contract, have accumulated effects that lead to a crash or take the form of a sudden blast with dissipating effects. But there is a difference between catastrophization and catastrophe. The latter is not simply a process that takes place in and expands over time and space, but rather an event that transforms both time and space. A catastrophe is an event in the strong sense of this term. Catastrophes are large-scale or megadisasters that affect multitudes or entire populations and leave their marks on many people's space and time.[9] Space is marked by the deterritorialization of a whole region and then by a reterritorialization of a special zone within it, a zone of disaster. This is the area where former orders crumble, normal expectations become meaningless, the self-evident dimension of everyday life is lost, and where, amid ruins of all kinds, the survivors experience a dramatic reduction in their ability to move and to communicate.

Time is marked by a clear and painful differentiation of a terrible present from a relatively peaceful past, before it all happened, and from a future one longs for, when it will all be over. In the catastrophic present, people still remember a past in which sheer survival was not the issue and often recall the moment or event in which their lives were shattered, and they cannot think about a different condition without imagining a certain leap into the future. However, it is not only the content of the lived experience that was or would be radically different before or after the event. The nature of time itself changes. Durations, sequences, repetitions, the empty moments of waiting, the intervals between one happening and another—all these are transformed during the time of catastrophe and will be recovered only gradually, if at all, when a new normalcy will be established.

The rupture in lived time and experienced space is not merely subjective. It has an objective dimension, because it is the condition within which the many survivors experience their space and time, and this condition has clear objective manifestations. In space, the disaster zone may be isolated, disconnected, access to it may be limited or forbidden, the ways out may be blocked; in time, the pace of events may be greatly accelerated, or just the opposite—for hours or days, nothing happens, and waiting itself is so tormenting that it becomes part of the catastrophe.

Catastrophization is different. It is a process, not a cataclysmic event that ruptures space and time. The pace of the process may be slow, and only some of its manifestations may be perceived. In fact, the process may be imperceptible and not be experienced at all. What matters in catastrophization is the steady and significant rise in the presence, quantity, and effect of evils—the volume of evils—and the decline in the means for protection and relief. Without an intervention that would counter it, the simultaneous intensification of the destructive forces, together with the increase in people's vulnerability and exposure to these forces, might cause a total collapse or disintegration of the lived environment. Catastrophization is a process in which catastrophe is imminent. However, what is imminent has not happened yet. This suspended moment of catastrophe, which catastrophization implies, this interval that makes possible both moral urgency and political manipulation, will be the focus of my analysis.

The "volume" of evils, of exposure and vulnerability, makes sense only in relation to a certain more or less defined population. Disasters happen in and to cities, communities, whole regions; catastrophization occurs within and across populations and regions. The city can be considered as the true subject and hero of a disaster, as was the case in late medieval and early modern plagues, but in order to follow the plague and understand its catastrophizing effect, one must have a notion of the city's population, its normal pattern of death and burial, the distribution of disease and deaths across neighborhoods, and so on.[10] Populations and regions need not exist prior to the catastrophizing process; they may instead be defined by this process. (Think, for example, about potential carriers of HIV, actual carriers of HIV, and those who have already developed symptoms of AIDS.) The population defined by catastrophization is the medium of the catastrophizing process. The quantification of evils that catastrophization implies must have a defined realm of reference in which more and less dramatic changes in the pattern of evils' production and distribution may be observed, quantified, and measured. Some way to observe and measure events in a multitude must be assumed, and this is precisely what the notion of population has made possible. While catastrophes may happen to communities, cities, or, more abstractly, to multitudes, catastrophization, in the way I propose to employ the concept, is a process that can be conceived and articulated only in relation to populations. It presupposes the notion of population and is one way to account for the condition of a given population. And since "population" belongs to and presupposes a certain discourse of governmentality,[11] catastrophization, too, must be thought of as part of such a discourse.

Governmentality introduces two different connotations here—more precisely, two different planes of reality. The first is catastrophization as an object of concern or interest for anyone whose task is to govern people, things, and territories, especially by means of those processes that take place by and through means and acts of government, or due to the withdrawal of or failure to provide such means. The second is catastrophization as a process that is made to appear, take shape, and assume its specific spatiotemporal dimensions by and through a discourse of governmentality that articulates an order of evils as imminently catastrophic.[12] Hence, catastrophization is always "governmental," and as such, it subsists in two distinct planes that are neither reducible to nor separable from each other and whose specific interrelations vary across periods, types of regime, and geopolitical circumstances.

The first plane is the plane of actual or "objective," environmental, political, economic, and bodily processes in which nature has been entirely socialized and in which organized human activity can appear as devastating as the forces of nature.[13] This is the plane in which human beings and (socialized) nature, in concert or separately, cause multiple deaths, endemic violence, massive dislocation, severe shortage and deprivation, the deterioration of health services and hygienic conditions, the desolation of entire regions, and the destruction of the fabric of life of numerous people.

The second plane is "discursive." The classification of evils into processes, events, and state of affairs — the distinctions, for example, between accidents, a structured failure of systems, and the intentional and systematic production of evils, or between scarcity, malnutrition, famine and starvation, the assessment of deterioration in living conditions, the definition of events as "humanitarian emergencies," "catastrophes," or "natural disasters" — all these are effects of a discourse of governmentality, but they are also discursive means of catastrophization. They designate objects to be observed, described, measured and analyzed, predicted, and interfered with by and through a certain discourse, and they all result from applying certain rules of "object formation" in that discourse. These are the discursive means through which the catastrophizing process assumes its objective status.[14] It is only through this mise en discours of the catastrophizing process that "emergency claims" or "emergency statements" can be pronounced in response to that process.[15]

By replacing the subjective bias of the overly anxious person with the discursively constructed concern of rational persons whose task or vocation is to warn others of a coming catastrophe or to manipulate its unfolding, we have replaced a sterile opposition (between objective and subjective catastrophization) with a fruitful, that is, dialectical opposition between actual and discursive catastrophization, conceived as two aspects of an intersubjective, socially constructed experience. Psychological catastrophization presupposes, as we have seen, a clear distinction between an adequate, objective sense of reality and a subjective, distorted one. The dual nature of "governmental catastrophization" implies a somewhat similar distinction between actual processes and their discursive articulation. However, the discursive is neither subjective nor necessarily a distorted representation of the real; it is rather the condition for the possibility of its observable appearance and conceptual configuration. At the same time, discursive catastrophization may become part of the actual processes that determine the way a catastrophe is unfolding and takes shape or is anticipated, mitigated, and sometimes even prevented.

Governmental catastrophization may take place simultaneously on these two planes, the actual and the discursive, but even on the rare occasions when this happens, there is always a gap between the two. Often, discourse records what nature, governments, and other powerful human agents have caused or have failed to do, and traces their policies and actions in the debris they have left behind. Less often—and yet this is something we have learned to expect from a functioning system of government—some discursive catastrophization precedes the actual processes and enables (or pretends to enable) preparedness and mitigation. This, for example, is the case with earthquake preparedness in places where earthquakes strike often enough.[16]

The gap between the two planes is not simply temporal. Planned policies and sporadic acts carried out by state apparatuses, economic firms, and other bodies governing people, things, and territories may bring about, more or less gradually, more or less systematically, a series of devastating effects that affect large populations. But the same effects may also be the result of failing—purposefully or inadvertently—to take specific actions that might have prevented the catastrophe or have mitigated its impact. In both cases, the objective processes might go unnoticed and be misunderstood and misrepresented. Then the accumulative effect of the widespread production of evils is not accounted for, disasters are not inscribed into public memory, their victims simply disappear without a trace, and some recognized devastating effects are explained away as soon as they are recorded. Discursive catastrophization is the more or less systematic response to— or preemption of—unacknowledged or disavowed actual catastrophization. It is the effort to articulate "humanitarian conditions" that can be inspected, followed, and explained, become objects of a continuous gaze, and be spaced out in charts and tables. The deterioration of these conditions can be measured and compared, and "the verge of humanitarian catastrophe" can be delineated and declared.

Catastrophization in this sense is a way to describe a state of affairs so as to make what has been a "tolerable" or "normal" situation seem too dangerous or intolerable, to arouse moral and political reactions, and to mobilize assistance. The described process, which has been naturalized or normalized before now, appears as either exceptional or as bearing potentially exceptional consequences. An imaginary threshold that separates a state of disaster or the happening of catastrophe from protracted disastrous conditions is invoked. It might have already been crossed, with or without notice, it may be declared as imminent and too close, but in any case, by the very fact that it has been stated, invoking the crossing of this imaginary threshold is an appeal for an exceptional response.

The situation is still more complicated, however. Because it is embedded in various governmental mechanisms, discursive catastrophization often structures the discourse of governmentality and imposes its focal point of attention. This attention may be classified, in a rather simplified way and regardless of the different sources of objective catastrophization, into three distinct temporal axes and modes of presence of disaster.

Disaster lies in the future. Discursive catastrophization seeks to anticipate it and to contribute to preparedness for the coming disaster. This may include natural disasters such as earthquakes and floods, but also the anticipation and portrayal—realistic, exaggerated, or imaginary—of the imminent danger posed by an enemy whose intention and actions are not simply negative, but threaten the very existence of the group, the state, or the ruling power.

Disaster is unfolding. Discursive catastrophization seeks to trace its patterns of expansion and to help contain it and mitigate its effects.

Disaster is protracted and is not perceived or experienced as such. Discursive catastrophization seeks to draw attention to the protracted deterioration in the living conditions of a given population, in a given area, to articulate this deterioration as a potentially catastrophic process, and to cope with its results.

This typology of discursive catastrophization is indifferent to either the viciousness or the sources of destruction. It is instead attentive to its advance, pace, accumulation, and fluctuation and more concretely to the moment when the threshold of catastrophe is crossed. Discursive catastrophization offers a perspective on human evils from which atrocities, wars, massive dislocations, plagues, or earthquakes seem equally relevant and the justifications for the actions or failure to act that have brought them about appear almost equally irrelevant, for what is crucial is to understand the way these different sources affect and exacerbate each other and how they may be subdued.

In a similar vein, objective catastrophization has to be analyzed independently. The mode of presence of disaster is not telling in this context. More important are the different sources, mechanisms, and processes involved in the production of the catastrophic conditions. A possible classification might distinguish between natural, ecological, economic, and technological sources and might insist on the fact that each of these sources is always already political, as well, and that each embodies discursive catastrophization. However, it would be a mistake to assume that discursive catastrophization always works to counter actual processes of catastrophization. Discursive catastrophization may play at least three different roles in actual catastrophizing processes.

Discursive catastrophization may legitimize the political generation of a catastrophe and mobilize people to take part in it. Discursive catastrophization also is often perceived as part of a concerted effort to mitigate the effect of an unfolding catastrophe and to reallocate some of the risks that it involves. Finally, discursive catastrophization may contribute to the suspension of an impending catastrophe by promoting the monitoring of the sources of risks and the indices of deteriorating well-being. The first two of these roles are quite trivial and straightforward, and I will discuss them only briefly. The third role, the suspension of an impending catastrophe, is more ambiguous and calls for more careful consideration.

**LEGITIMIZATION** By portraying the enemy—be it a state, a nation, a class, or any other group of people, their land, or their property—as agents of potential catastrophe, catastrophizing discourse contributes to the political acceptance and even naturalization of catastrophic measures employed in order to crush the disastrous agents, be they the enemy state, its country, or its population. Thus, for example, race discourse may catastrophize the presence of the racialized other and legitimize a political decision to unleash massive forces of destruction or to naturalize genocidal policies, mobilizing the threatened population to kill everyone in its midst who has come to symbolize and incarnate the imminent danger. As we know well, a similar role may be played today by the discourse of security: The security of one group might appear as a sufficient reason for the elimination of another. Once a group is associated with an imminent catastrophe that threatens another group, the very presence of members of that group, let alone anything they may do or have done, is perceived as part of a catastrophizing process that must be stopped by all means, even at a cost of creating disastrous conditions for the carriers of risk.

**THE MITIGATION AND REALLOCATION OF RISKS** When disaster is threatening, unfolding as a cataclysmic event, or lingering as a chronic deterioration, the threshold of catastrophe is "a call to arms" for anyone who can help; it designates a new set of priorities and reshuffles resources accordingly. Discursive catastrophization is mobilized to "decatastrophize" a state of affairs by alerts, preparedness, containment, and mitigation. And yet, demarcating the threshold often means a more or less systematic, more or less purposeful neglect and abandonment of those still living at a distance from the imaginary line and who are now "out of focus," outside the area threatened or hit by disaster.

**SUSPENSION** When catastrophization becomes a set of governmental policies, a measured and restrained means of governance, the presence of an imaginary, ghostlike threshold of catastrophe often becomes a warning sign for the forces that use catastrophization as a means of governance. These forces should not cross the imaginary line, lest they lose the legitimization of those who support them or lest they have to take the burden of responsibility for the population they have abandoned. They catastrophize, but they wish to keep the catastrophe itself in suspension, not removing its threat or its causes, and at the same time not letting something that may be grasped as a catastrophe happen, either. Hence, this case — which I call "catastrophic suspension" — is of particular interest, because it creates the condition for collaboration between the actual catastrophizing forces and the agents of catatrophizing discourse that seemingly oppose them. Both parties share an interest in drawing the line between the "normal" and the catastrophic and keeping the existence of the impending catastrophe at a distance. In addition, production of disastrous conditions in a given area, for a given population, is often motivated by and goes hand in hand with a special care for others who are not part of the targeted population or the stricken zone and whose well-being and security (are said to) necessitate the governmental implementation of catastrophic policies. The concern for those whose well-being is (said to be) at stake shifts attention away from the area that discourse seeks to catastrophize and prevents one from grasping and conceiving the causes of the real conditions there.

While actual catastrophization is a process with one clear direction — from relatively normal conditions to catastrophic ones — discursive catastrophization may go in two opposite directions and may do so simultaneously: creating a catastrophe and mitigating its effects. But it may also go in no direction at all, helping to keep catastrophe in suspension, collaborating, purposefully or not, with the forces that have operationalized catastrophization and using it as measured, calculated, and controlled means of governance. A paradigmatic example of this latter state of affairs is Israel's rule in the Occupied Palestinian Territories, where controlled catastrophization has been consistently employed by the Israeli authorities since October 2000.[17] This strategy has not met much objection or dissent from the Israeli public, due in part to a legitimizing discourse that catastrophizes the Hamas government by associating it with suicide terror, on the one hand, and with the deadly threats of Hezbollah and Iran, on the other, by presenting Iran as a satanic enemy determined to destroy Israel. The rockets fired by the various Palestinian militias are thus interpreted not as a form of guerilla warfare and acts of resistance to the Israeli occupation, but as the spearhead of those forces determined to bring about the complete destruction of the state of Israel, a second Jewish Holocaust. These assertions — true or false, it does not matter — play a significant role in producing the catastrophization of Gaza.

## THE THRESHOLD AND THE EXCEPTION

Discursive catastrophization should be further examined. First, it should be clearly distinguished from the act of giving an account of a catastrophe whose existence has already been established. When one counts bodies in the immediate aftermath of a hurricane, the unfolding of which everyone could have watched (for example, Hurricane Katrina), tells stories from the death camps, or collects the testimonies of the genocide's survivors (for example, in Rwanda), one does not catastrophize, but rather describes a given catastrophe. In such cases, the catastrophe has already been established as a fact and as a more or less defined object of discourse, something to be observed and accounted for, explained and commemorated. One does not have to establish that a catastrophe is really taking place, or has taken place, or is soon to take place, but, assuming that this has been the case, one describes and analyzes what has happened or is happening, questions its causes, or tries to comprehend the experiences it has produced.[18] Establishing the fact that a catastrophe is actually taking place or that it did or is about to take place is precisely what is at stake in discursive catastrophization. In other words, discursive catastrophization is a formation of discourse in which the occurrence of a catastrophe is always problematized. Part of this problematization is concerned with the occurrence itself: Must there be an event, clearly distinguished in time and space, in order for a catastrophe to take place?

Usually, such a problematization is involved even in the most dramatic event of devastation, an event that multitudes of people experience as a rupture of their shared and personal time, as a shattering of their shared lifeworld and private selves, and as a brutal deterritorialization and reterritorialization of their shared space. However, at the extremes, catastrophization and catastrophe might be rigorously separated. At the extremes, there are no catastrophes, only silent, objective processes of catastrophization, on the one hand, and loquacious discursive catastrophization of objective processes, on the other hand. At one extremity, catastrophe is reduced to nothing because it is a matter of the experience of victims whose disappearance has left no trace and survivors who have been silenced. At the other extremity, catastrophization is a purely discursive matter with no corresponding subjective experiences. A catastrophe that is not constituted as an object of any discourse is what one may call the perfect disaster, which, like the perfect crime, would take place without leaving a trace. It may well be that the Nazi elite dreamed of such a perfect disaster when they contemplated "the final solution" to "the Jewish problem."[19] In the inverse situation, discourse and the experienced event are no less kept apart, discursive catastrophization produces no corresponding experience, and the disastrous effects may be no less "perfect."

Discursive catastrophization takes place today in several partly related, partly overlapping discursive fields. It comes in reports and testimonies composed by individuals or commissioned by local and international humanitarian organizations, human rights groups, governmental and nongovernmental commissions of inquiry, journalists, and other men and women of conscience and goodwill.[20] The history of this genre goes back at least to the Crimean War,[21] it includes European imperialism since then, and it has also accompanied almost any significant "natural" disaster in the twentieth century. But after World War II, and especially since the 1980s, with the dramatic growth in the presence of nongovernmental organizations that followed the end of the Cold War, "the retreat of the political," and the mediatization of politics, a clear change in the quantity, quality, and variety of the catastrophizing literature can be observed. The reports have become more elaborated; more factors have been documented, measured, and analyzed; statistics has become the lingua franca of these reports; more risk factors have been identified and analyzed; and experts and expertise of all kinds have contributed to the professionalization and depoliticization of discursive catastrophization, while new groups have been defined as "populations in danger."[22]

The reports vary in precision and scope, depth of analysis, the use of technical tools drawn from the social sciences, and the language of presentation. There are more and less politicized experts who take more and less reflexive and critical positions, looking at catastrophic processes from wider or narrower perspective. But common to most of them is a certain sense of moral urgency, which is often lacking from reports of the same kind concerning the socioeconomic conditions of deprived populations in "normal" situations. Sometimes only the rhetoric of urgency remains, while the detailed analysis is assumed, but left inexplicit. Often acute cases of massacres, famine, dislocation, and epidemic are placed alongside "milder" cases, which show similar symptoms, but spread at lower pace and on a smaller scale. Catastrophization here serves two different purposes: the portrayal of a series of related events or states of affairs as a large-scale disaster that demands an urgent response and the portrayal of relatively unrelated events as expression of a single, identified cause or problem whose cumulative effect demands a no less urgent response.

A quick comparison between two publications of the humanitarian organization MSF, Médecins Sans Frontières (Doctors Without Borders) may illustrate this double sense of urgency and, by implication, of discursive catastrophization. In the introduction to the first report of *Populations in Danger*, published by the French branch of MSF in 1992, Rony Brauman wrote that the authors had "chosen critical situations" in reference to a "scale of severity of crises." They thus limited their analysis to the "ten cases that appeared to be the most tragic in the past year."[23]

By contrast, five years later, the American branch of MSF started publishing an annual list, *Top 10 Underreported Humanitarian Stories*, with short reports on each "humanitarian story." In it, it is not "critical situations" located at the acute end of a "scale of severity" that are the focus. Instead, it is the sheer accumulation of numbers that come from across the entire globe that assumes the figure of catastrophe, and it does so only through and within the realm of the humanitarian discourse. The report for 2006 records violent clashes that forced one hundred thousand people to flee from their homes in the previous year in the Central Republic of Africa, alongside violent clashes in central India that forced fifty thousand people to leave their homes during the last twenty-five years, an average of two thousand per year, 2 percent of the dislocation in Central Africa.[24] Even more significant is the attempt to portray tuberculosis as a major humanitarian crisis that every year claims the life of two million people all over the globe. The problem, the report claims, is the lack of adequate drugs to cure the disease, the lack of attention to this disease in the pharmaceutical industry, and "not seeing the necessary urgency to tackle the disease." The sense of urgency is a pure effect of the accumulation of cases in the charts of the humanitarian organizations. Although some regions and some kinds of populations are more conspicuously hit by tuberculosis, the report does not cite any event, dramatic or otherwise, and does not mention even the quiet spread of an epidemic.

Even if no one would ever actually experience a situation as a catastrophe, discursive catastrophization thus may articulate the accumulation of evils as a disaster and produce the emergency statements that call people to respond. This discursive effect may be the most important feature of catastrophization: to determine that intangible moment, the crossing of a line that should change one's attitude from ignorance and indifference to careful, interested attention, from interested attention to action, or from acting at a distance to actual intervention. This is the moment when one hears that "something (or something else) must be done." When the threshold is crossed, a true exception has been created.

It is therefore not by accident that the term "humanitarian emergency" has replaced "catastrophe" as a more appropriate description for such a situation. "Humanitarian emergency" may designate what happens when the threshold of catastrophization is crossed. But it may also designate a state of alert that must be declared when deteriorating conditions bring a region or a population too close to the threshold. When a sovereign declares an emergency, it means, among other things, declaring a state of alert and calling for special preparedness in order to face an existential threat. Many humanitarian organizations have adopted the same language and tend to declare an emergency as a state of alert in order to avert the coming of the catastrophe itself. Sometimes they declare a "humanitarian emergency alert," that is, an alert regarding an emergent emergency.[25] Thresholds multiply; for an alert to be declared, a certain threshold has to be crossed, just as for an actual emergency. The difference between the two is not well defined, and it changes from one organization to another and from one situation to another.

A legally, politically, or governmentally declared state of exception, like the humanitarian alert, is meant to avert or preempt a true state of exception. But the threshold—of the emergency or the catastrophe—is never given; it is never a fait accompli, and the ambiguity problematizes any attempt to take it as such. Whether it is announced as a line that has been crossed or as an approaching turning point, it also appears or is pronounced as an imperative: "Something must be done," either in order not to cross it or in order to cross back, to "decatastrophize" a catastrophic situation. An "indistinction" between fact and norm, similar to the indistinction between "a situation of fact" and "a situation of right" that Agamben ascribes to the state of exception declared by a sovereign,[26] here finds a clear expression outside the logic of sovereignty, and this is true even if the appeal to "do something" is addressed to a sovereign. The very existence of nongovernmental agents of discursive catastrophization make it clear that no sovereign can claim today a monopoly over the exception.[27] Seen from the humanitarian perspective, an emergency does not refer to any authority, but to the human condition as such, that is, to the condition of living or surviving as humans. In a humanitarian emergency, it is the human condition itself that becomes exceptional. In fact, it is then that the unbearable human condition emerges.

For all these reasons, it has appeared absolutely necessary to operationalize emergencies. A systematic attempt to "regulate" the discourse of catastrophization, establish objective guidelines for discursive catastrophization, and determine the threshold of catastrophe in a way that would be appropriate for a variety of crises all over the world was part of an ambitious endeavor of a group of scholars working at or with the UN University in Helsinki. Raimo Väyrynen, a key figure in the group, proposed a way to "operationalize" what the group termed "Complex Humanitarian Emergencies" (CHEs). A humanitarian emergency is a "multidimensional...social crisis in which large numbers of people unequally die and suffer from war, displacement, hunger, and disease owing to human-made and natural disasters." It becomes complex when more than one of these types of evils coexist and exacerbate each other. A CHE is indifferent to the sources of evils and includes all their types, from war to genocide, from epidemics to famine. However, each one of the four types of evil is operationalized independently,[28] and thus CHEs can also be measured and compared. The four types of evils of which a CHE consists (warfare or violence, dislocation, famine, and disease) are easy to measure: warfare by the number of deaths that can be ascribed to it; dislocation by the number of refugees; hunger by children underweight; and disease by child mortality.[29] But the classification of CHEs into types and the assessment of their severity are based on the coexistence of several types of evils.[30] A CHE is declared to be acute when the numbers are high enough in all four categories. When only three categories are involved, a CHE is "serious," and it becomes merely "violent" when it consists of two categories only, one of which is usually war.[31]

Throughout the attempt to operationalize emergencies, one question keeps recurring: "Whether the rate of [the emergency's] destruction must accelerate and pass a certain threshold before it qualifies as a crisis, or should drawn-out disasters, whose costs accumulate only over a period of time, also be included in the definition?"[32] The solution proposed is typically ambiguous: On the one hand, a distinction should be made between protracted and accelerated emergencies, while on the other hand, one should keep in mind that acceleration itself is subject to change. Thus, "emergencies can move from one category of intensity to another," and hence a protracted disaster may suddenly accelerate, cross the line, and become a fully complex humanitarian emergency.[33]

The threshold is ambiguous on at least three accounts: first, because it is not clear where exactly the line should be drawn—even the choice of a unit of measurement (a state or a region) for determining some possible standards is questionable.[34] Second, the threshold is ambiguous because the line may be crossed at any given moment due to accumulation or acceleration.[35] Third, it is ambiguous because it is never certain whether identifying, determining, or declaring the threshold is a matter of recognizing a fact or of fulfilling a duty. This ambiguity is structural, and it inheres the efforts of operationalization.

The attempt to operationalize emergencies does not (and is not meant to) determine a threshold of catastrophes; rather, it only determines conventional ways to problematize such a demarcation. To operationalize means to determine what one should monitor, count, and take into account in order to frame the question of the threshold and make possible an informed decision on the threshold, which is nothing but the governmental form of the sovereign decision on the exception. But this governmental decision also deconstructs the very structure of sovereignty, its coherence and monopolistic claims, because it is a decision given to or made by a variety of governmental and nongovernmental agents such as humanitarian experts and activists, agents that are still involved in governmentality.

It is important to operationalize emergencies—this is the basic assumption of Väyrynen and his colleagues—and the reason is obvious. The humanitarian emergencies are not those declared by a sovereign, but those imposed upon him and those created because sovereign power has shrunk or collapsed altogether, and when they happen, they unfold as ungovernable situations, populations, and territories. To operationalize emergencies is a first step and a condition for the reintegration of the territory and the population in the emergency zone into a governable realm. Whether the governing authorities are old or new, state authorities, international, intergovernmental authorities, or international nongovernmental entities matters less than making the zone of emergency governable again.[36] Hence, CIA analysts and independent humanitarian experts may find themselves linked together in the tables and charts drawn by emergency experts,[37] exchanging information and insights through their conceptual scheme and form of discourse. They share an interest in making emergency zones governable in order to save lives (the humanitarians) or maintain a certain world order (the state agents). They all assume the uncertain, indeterminable threshold of catastrophe as the moment in which a true exception to the rules (of a political order or of a lifeworld) has been created in or can be ascribed to a given region in relation to a given population. They all assume that when such an exception is established, an urgent need for justification and exceptional action would emerge. A license is given and an appeal is made to individuals and authorities to go out of their way. When a political sovereign declares a state of emergency, he merely interprets this situation within a legal-political framework and extends his authority accordingly. However, this interpretation is neither primary nor necessary.

From this perspective, war may appear as a means of actual catastrophization—one among others. Identifying or declaring the enemy appear as an effect of catastrophization, and the very concept of the enemy presupposes catastrophization as a special power on the use of which the sovereign might claim a monopoly that he does not really have. Instead, a dangerous virus, environmental pollution, or illegal immigrants may be declared to be the enemy by experts and concerned citizens, and the threshold of catastrophe may be drawn and redrawn by many social actors. This threshold is a scene of contest, struggle, and dissent, and the claims of a sovereign power, however they are pronounced, are neither primary nor constitutive of this scene. In other words, in a world like ours, the sovereign is not the sole author of the exception, and his word on it is not the last one, although the claim to be such a sole author and to have the last word may be a good way to characterize sovereignty as a special kind of political claim.

Moreover, it is important to emphasize that it is not only the case that the sovereign has no monopoly over the interpretation of the exception, but also that his interpretation presupposes the catastrophization of the exception. The sovereign decision on the exception, in the sense given to it by Carl Schmitt, assumes and implies the real possibility of a catastrophe.[38] When a sovereign declares an emergency, he presumably responds to the fact that a true exception has taken place or might soon take place—or at least this is how the state of exception is presented to the public.[39] The imminent danger of a catastrophe is an implicit part of the deliberation and the ruling on the exception, as well as of its legitimization. In this sense, a sovereign decision on the exception is simply an authorized form of catastrophization and one of its earliest expressions. Although this authorized form claims to be independent of any governmental or ideological discourse, it is at this moment that it stretches its legitimacy and exposes itself to severe disobedience, as well as to the competition of governmental or ideological discourses that claim authority over catastrophization. Thus, the notion of "complex humanitarian emergency" is a recent attempt to stabilize a field of action that has become rather hectic by introducing professional standards for dealing with catastrophes and operationalizing the exception.

The legal category of the exception is by no means the best perspective from which to understand catastrophization. It is the other way around: Declaring a state of emergency has always presupposed some sense of catastrophization—false, imaginary, virtual, sincere, or realistic—and should be understood in its context. In today's globalized political order—and this may be one of its novelties—only a power that has given up any kind of legitimacy and therefore has become indistinguishable from the use of sheer force may give up any pretext of catastrophization when declaring a state of emergency. Whenever power is not indifferent to its legitimization, some kind of catastrophization is presupposed by the sovereign decision on the exception. Hence, the changing discursive conditions of catastrophization, including the inevitable conflict of interpretations regarding the threshold of catastrophe, both precede the sovereign decision and immediately follow it, undermining its claim for spontaneity, determination, and conclusiveness. That emergency has become such a prevalent concept in contemporary political and critical theory is not a sign for the return or persistence of sovereignty. It is instead an expression of the fact that sovereigns have lost their alleged monopoly over catastrophization and that the emergency can no longer be restricted to the realm of law. The partial and limited or full and straightforward suspension of the law is just one form that a response to catastrophization may take. Similarly, the state is not the only agent threatened with catastrophe or to whom a catastrophic power is ascribed. These are populations that are at risk, but that at the same time pose the risk.

It has always been the task of an enlightened, politically aware public to call the bluff of false catastrophization and to oppose power when it rules by manipulating fears and anxieties. Today, when catastrophization has its experts, when these experts inhabit a whole cultural field (in Bourdieu's sense of this term)[40] where heterodoxy regularly contests orthodoxy, and when power inheres in that field, and does not only confront it from the outside, the task of knowledgeable citizens and responsible officials and bureaucrats has become less risky, perhaps, but much more complicated. They have to distinguish among the various psychological, humanitarian, and legal-political meanings of catastrophization and make sure that neither their government nor their experts (pretend to) suffer from the severe "cognitive bias" and "anxiety disorder" that psychiatrists ascribe to catastrophization.

In contemporary strong states,[41] when governments catastrophize, their discourse is often followed by decisions on exceptional measures, while the sovereign decision on the exception is usually followed by a series of governmental catastrophizing acts. Facing catastrophization, sovereign and biopolitical apparatuses in strong states must work in concert and be completely integrated at this moment.[42] The whole population should be realigned according to the coming danger. Populations at risk and populations considered as risky should be defined, targeted, monitored, segregated, and more closely controlled. The sovereign decision on the exception, if it has ever been anything more than a hypothetical or imaginary moment in the theory of sovereignty, is now translated into and replaced by numerous local bureaucratic decisions on the exception, and the threshold of catastrophe is redrawn from all directions in various contexts of governance and domination, aid, relief, and subjugation by governmental and nongovernmental agencies alike. These different actors compete and struggle over the definition of the exception, the threshold of catastrophe, the nature of objective catastrophization, and the validity of discursive catastrophization. The existence of "degrees of sovereignty" that has always characterized empires, according to Ann Stoler,[43] thus characterizes the everyday life of any contemporary strong state and is only most conspicuous in states with imperial tendencies.

Catastrophization has become a more or less distinct branch of biopolitics that differs from more common and less dramatic political struggles and biopolitical practices due to its special concern with the moment of the exception. The "true exception" implied by the ghostly presence of the threshold of catastrophe both authorizes and calls upon governments and citizens alike to act in unusual ways. These may vary from evacuation to war, from deportation to the establishment of refugee camps, from targeted killings to heroic sacrifices. They may include dramatic changes in public and private allocations of resources, breaking contracts and alliances and making new ones, crossing borders, or ignoring them altogether. A formal suspension of the law may precede or accompany such actions, but certainly, this is not always the case. Exceptionality is much wider than the suspension of the law. What is common to all these forms is their temporary nature, or more precisely, the fact that they are proposed and declared as temporary, ad hoc responses to an emergency.[44] They are meant (or presented) as temporary interjections and interventions in cases where the social order has collapsed or is about to collapse, and they are supposed to take place as part of an interim regime that should facilitate the restoration of an old order or the constitution of a new one. Decentered, fragmented, and always contested as these moments of exceptionality are, they may still end up forming a clear pattern, leaving the impression of a clear policy, expressing a recognizable principle of governance. Moreover, in zones of emergency, such principles may be more clearly recognizable or more decisively at work than in the zones of normalcy.[45]

If one insists on a Schmittian reading of this situation, one would have to say that the sovereign is he who freezes a turbulent field of catastrophization, draws clearly the catastrophic threshold, imposes an unambiguous meaning on conflicting and confusing signs, and determines a direction and a mode of response to the emergency. No such sovereign exists, however, and catastrophization has become one domain among many where this becomes plainly visible. The Bush administration's response to the attack on the World Trade Center has been nothing but a series of catastrophizing acts. But there has been not a single moment since 9/11 when any of these acts went uncontested. Not one of them has been implemented without being transformed or at least affected by a lively field of catastrophization in which many, from the Pope to Osama bin Laden, from the highest generals to petty bureaucrats, from experts on terrorism to experts on hunger and malnutrition, and from loyal citizens to lawless immigrants, have had a say. The relatively successful attempt of the U.S. president to extract from this situation a recognition of his claim to be the ultimate catastrophizing authority and to use it in order to extend and enhance the effectiveness of some of the administration's biopolitical technologies should not mislead us to underestimate the power of all other agents in the field, where numerous local, partial, little quasi-sovereigns constantly decide on exceptions. And yet this plurality may yield a result that, without being the outcome of any single decision, could seem like an expression of a certain more or less coherent policy or of the shared interests of certain players in the field.[46]

I started by indicating that the broader context of this discussion is an attempt to construct a political theory of disaster. It is worth noting that in the history of political theory, disaster, whether man-made or natural, was often conceived as part of the circumstances in which power operates or one of the consequences of its operation, but in both cases, it was conceived as external to power. Hannah Arendt may have been the first to offer an analysis of catastrophization as a constitutive element of power. The two forms of power she studied in the *Origins of Totalitarianism*, imperialism and totalitarianism, may be construed as two phases in the "interiorization" of disaster within the realm of power. What has been presented here can be conceived as a new phase in the same process that characterizes a posttotalitarian, postcolonial world. This, I think, is the epistemological condition of the contemporary notion of emergency. It is within this framework that one should understand the humanitarian, security-related, and legal aspects of emergency and grasp the way in which these different aspects are differentiated without ever being truly dissociated. This is also the context for understanding the double meaning of emergency, that is, as a response to discursive catastrophization, on the one hand, and as a way to create or accelerate the condition of actual catastrophization, on the other.

The collaboration between the forces that mitigate disasters and those capable of or actually producing them is not a result of a neoliberal ideology of professionals or of the tendency of humanitarian organizations to depoliticize violent crises and man-made disasters, ignore their "root causes," or channel the energy of their professionals and volunteers from politics to medicine and other caring professions. More generally, the professionalization of the aid industry or the fact that it has become an industry and as such is now exposed to economic forces like any other market enterprise are not enough to explain this collaboration. The fault—if it is a fault at all—lies with catastrophization as a special domain of governmentality, or rather with the two tiers and double-edged structure of this special domain.

## ON THE VERGE OF HUMANITARIAN CATASTROPHE

I have distinguished above three ways in which discursive catastrophization may be involved in the actual production of catastrophes: legitimization, mitigation, and suspension. The third way, I have said, is characteristic of some contemporary zones of emergency, of which the Israeli rule in the Occupied Palestinian Territories since the second intifada may serve as a clear example. Let me look briefly at this case and draw from it some general conclusions.

The Israeli government responded to the Palestinian uprising with excessive violence, the generous and indiscriminate use of live ammunition, and the extensive destruction of houses, land, and property.[47] It was not physical violence, however, but spatial disintegration and fragmentation that emerged as the main technology of domination and control that Israel used in order to contain and suppress the Palestinian resistance and to stop a stream of suicide attacks in Israeli cities west of the Green Line, the de facto post-1948 border of Israel. The effect of the new regime of movement on the Palestinian population was enormous. The situation further deteriorated when Israel responded aggressively to a terrorist attack (in Hotel Park in Netanya on Passover eve 2002), reconquered several Palestinian towns, crushed the security apparatuses of the Palestinian Authority, and dismantled many other institutions of the Palestinian government in Operation Defensive Shield. The Israeli Defense Forces resumed the massive demolition of Palestinian houses in order to create "clean" areas and to punish families of suspects in terrorist activity, and thousands of Palestinians became homeless. Soon there appeared the first reports that catastrophized the conditions in the Occupied Palestinian Territories. They tried to ring the alarm bells, using rhetoric of urgency that had not been used before. First came the Bertini Report, which insisted on the fact that "the growing humanitarian crisis" is "man-made" and listed several "indicators" for the crisis: an increase in malnutrition, deteriorating health, and the exhaustion of coping mechanisms.[48] The report cited a survey made by scholars from Johns Hopkins University that found a "substantial increase in the number of malnourished children over the past two years, with 22.5 percent of children under five suffering from acute (9.3 percent) or chronic (13.2 percent) malnutrition," with much higher rates in Gaza than in the West Bank.[49]

These numbers were then cited and recycled by a few other reports that added information about unemployment, poverty, and health conditions and that started to analyze their causes. Jean Ziegler, the special rapporteur on the right to food to the UN secretary general, wrote in October 2003 that "the Occupied Palestinian Territories (OPT) are on the verge of humanitarian catastrophe" and specified the Gaza Strip again as facing "a distinct humanitarian emergency in regard to... malnutrition," the level of which had increased so much that it became "equivalent to levels found in poor sub-Saharan countries."[50] Ziegler's report was viciously criticized by the Israeli government, which, with some help from the American administration, forced the secretary general to refrain from adopting the report as an official UN document. The Israeli officials did not contest the figures, only the ascription of responsibility. In regard to their pressure, Ziegler said: "My mandate is precise: the respect of the right to both solid and liquid food. That is my only concern. I saw a horrifying humanitarian disaster which worsens because of the occupation. I have carried my mandate to the letter; I have reported drastic deterioration of the dietary situation of the Palestinian population and the reasons for its being."[51] Similar expressions of catastrophization may be found in later reports. For example, John Dugard, special rapporteur of the Commission on Human Rights, stated clearly: "There is a humanitarian crisis in the West Bank and Gaza. It is not the result of a natural disaster. Instead, it is a crisis imposed by a powerful State on its neighbor."[52]

My point is not to claim that the situation in the Gaza Strip did not deteriorate significantly after April 2002, but that discursive catastrophization followed the objective catastrophization, made some aspects of it visible, observable, and accountable, articulated them, and endowed them with its specific figure. The figure was neither that of a natural disaster nor that of a "complex humanitarian emergency"—the accumulated numbers of dislocated people, victims of violence, and the rate of malnutrition were too low for that—but rather that of a threshold. Ziegler was the most explicit: "The Occupied Palestinian Territories (OPT) are on the verge of humanitarian catastrophe." He also suggested that this "fact"—or rather, this way to perceive the situation—was not entirely foreign to the Israeli authorities: "The Israeli authorities recognized that there was a humanitarian crisis in the Occupied Palestinian Territories. They did not dispute the statistics of increasing malnutrition and poverty of the Palestinians."[53] Despite recurring obstacles on the provision of aid by the United Nations Relief and Works Agency (UNRWA), the U.S. Agency for International Development (USAID), and other international organizations, Israel remained committed to preventing the Occupied Territories from crossing the dangerous, imaginary threshold. "There will be no famine in Palestine," Israeli representatives kept reiterating as Israeli authorities kept frequent local shortages from turning into a famine. The authorities also took pride in the fact that UNRWA had added iron to the flour it distributes in the Occupied Palestinian Territories in order to fight malnutrition, thus maintaining the Palestinians at the threshold without letting them cross it.[54]

Israeli authorities were quick to adopt a humanitarian discourse and share it with the humanitarian organizations. "In the protocol of every operation, the first thing mentioned after security matters is the humanitarian issue.... When an operation starts, we gather the representatives of the humanitarian organizations active in the area and, as long as the operation continues, we coordinate their mode of action in the area.[55] Clearly, the army officers recognize the phenomena of catastrophization, and they are even ready to observe it through the conceptual lens of the humanitarian discourse and admit that the new regime of movement and other measures taken by the ruling apparatus are the causes of catastrophization. They hardly dispute the statistics, as Ziegler reported, and see the humanitarian crisis as "regrettable, but inevitable, consequence of security measures that were necessary to prevent attacks on Israelis."[56] And yet, at the same time, denying reports that find, for example, "a growing evidence that declining income amongst Palestinians are a primary cause of acute and chronic malnutrition in young children...Israeli officials have argued that '[n]o one is starving in the Gaza Strip and the West Bank.'"[57] "There will be no famine in Palestine, no famine in Palestine," told a chorus of IDF "humanitarian officers" to Ariella Azoulay, in her documentary short film *The Food Chain* (2003).

This is a consistent Israeli policy. It has not changed with the "disengagement," when Israel has pretended to end the occupation of the Gaza Strip and dismissed its responsibility and obligations as the occupying power, and it only has become more blatant and explicit since the Hamas won the election in Gaza and took effective control of the Palestinian government there in June 2006. The strip is encircled and enclosed as a camp. Almost all its supplies come through the Gaza Strip's gates, which are fully controlled by Israel, and the opening of these gates for men and commodities is recognized by everyone as a humanitarian issue of utter importance, one that is constantly on the agenda at every new round of talks or violence. Though Israel often interrupts the provision of basic food by UNRWA and other NGOs, it never does so for more than a few days. Similar "punitive measures," such as electricity shutdowns and blockage of gasoline deliveries, are also used in a limited and restrained fashion without ever cutting off the supply of these resources completely. Israel could produce famine in Gaza by imposing complete isolation, and it could add to the chaotic situation by cutting off electricity for good, but such measures are plainly not part of the Israeli repertoire. Catastrophization seems to have clear limits in Gaza.

Note, however, that what is considered as an unacceptable humanitarian condition has changed dramatically over the years, together with the means to intervene and stop the accumulation of evils. In the late 1980s, during the first intifada, any local curfew that lasted more than a week was a matter of much concern among Israelis and foreign humanitarians alike. In 2007, many weeks of cordons and closures that disrupt the lives of hundreds of thousands have become the rule, while emergencies are quite rare. Before the Oslo Accords, there were hardly any NGOs to share the burden with Israel, and UNRWA mostly served the population of the refugee camps, with only 10 percent of its budget going to direct distribution of food and almost none of it to families outside the refugee camps. In 2008, no fewer than ten organizations distributed food in the Occupied Territories, UNRWA served more than half of the population, including thousands of families outside the camps, and most of its budget went to food assistance and emergency cash assistance.[58] And yet at the same time, a threshold of a "real," full-fledged catastrophe was still hovering, and everyone was—or pretended to be—concerned about it, committed to not letting it be crossed.

Israel has knowingly contributed to the catastrophization of the Occupied Palestinian Territories, especially through the new regime of movement established since 2000, and it has consistently refused to change its policies in order to ameliorate the Palestinian living conditions. The systematic destruction of the Palestinian social fabric and the reduction of the Palestinian economy to sub-Saharan standards are seen as a fair price that Palestinians have to pay for the security of Israelis. The occasional "humanitarian gestures" the government is willing to offer remain symbolic and would never compromise the draconian administrative-military rule of Palestinian space and movement. In other words, the Israeli government is completely aware of its contribution to the catastrophizing process and would do nothing to cope with its root causes. And yet, the same government pretends that it would go out of its way, if necessary, to avoid crossing the threshold of catastrophe.

Thus, for example, when Hamas took over full control of the Gaza Strip in June 2006, the Israeli government had another opportunity to prove its commitment to the survival of Gazans. The major humanitarian organizations working in the region published emergency reports soon after the event, expecting full closure of the strip and calculating for how long existing supplies of basic food and medication would last.[59] Yet the Israeli government was quick to respond to the crisis, allowing the trucks of UNRWA, The World Food Programme, and the frozen vaccines sent by the United Nations Children's Fund (UNICEF) to enter Gaza, despite the fact that these organizations had to coordinate their activity with the boycotted Hamas government without the mediation of the "legitimate" forces of President Mahmud Abbas. While starvation was prevented, blockade of the gates to the transport of other goods continued and became the rule, rather than the exception, causing severe damage to the faltering Gazan economy.[60] This economy has been made ever more dependent on international donations, on the one hand, and on the willingness of the Israeli government to open the gates every once in a while so as to put the catastrophe on hold, on the other.

Opening the gates is all Israel has to do on its own in order to prevent famine in the Gaza Strip. A number of humanitarian organizations, UN agencies, special delegates of the European Union, and other diplomats readily place themselves as a buffer between the catastrophizing machinery of the occupation and the catastrophe itself. They help Israel suspend "the real" catastrophe while catastophizing the Occupied Palestinian Territories. The suspension itself has become part of the machinery of catastrophization, and the suspended catastrophe has become an essential element in the machinery of the Israeli rule.[61]

Placing the catastrophization of the Occupied Palestinian Territories in a wider context, one may note that the "catastrophic suspension" is neither a result of the military operation or economic policies of a strong state such as Israel nor the effect of weak, disintegrating state apparatus such as that of the Palestinian Authority, which give in to the violence of rebels and paramilitary forces. Catastrophic suspension is the result of the withdrawal of some legal and biopolitical apparatuses of the strong state from a given territory and population, which is accompanied by the excessive presence and activity of military and police forces of the Israeli state in ways that prevent other governing agents from governing effectively the evacuated zone. Myriad regional and international forces are drawn into the zone of emergency that the dominating power has brought to the verge of catastrophe, but their presence only enhances the sovereignty of the strong state. The three moments of power that characterize catastrophic suspension — withdrawal of legal and biopolitical apparatuses; coercive, violent prevention of the emergence of alternative modes of governance; and the acceptance of occasional humanitarian interventions in exceptional cases—are all expressions of decisions and policies of a strong state.

A different, more prevalent pattern may be identified in other zones of emergency, especially in territories controlled by weak states, that is, where a strong state has collapsed or has never been established. In these areas, state apparatuses do not withdraw; rather, they have disintegrated or have never been strong enough to exercise full sovereignty over their territory and population. Catastrophization in areas where states are weak is "nongovernmental" in the full sense of the word. Nonstate forces, tribal warlords, and paramilitary groups that spread destruction may rely on the mechanism of the state, but only partly, to the extent that they can seize it from the outside and use it for the purpose of destruction. Political power in this model has to be accounted for in regional more than national or centralized terms and is characterized by a rhizomatic, rather than a hierarchical structure. The decentering of power goes hand in hand with the interiorization of catastrophe within the rhizomatic realm of power, which may be described as a deconstructed and inverted imperialism—deconstructed, because it lives off the ruins and debris of the long-withdrawn empire and the collapse of the fragile state structure that the empire left behind, inverted, because it is driven by the expansion of scarcity and usually not directly by the expansion of capital.

The gains of the devastating forces in many contemporary zones of emergency are not to be measured in terms of relative positions in a global capitalist market and not even in terms of the opportunities opened for players in that market, but in terms of the capacity of the different authorities to continue the subjugation and destruction of their own populations.[62] This means that the rhythm of catastrophization, its naturalization, and its frequent tendency to turn protracted disasters into cataclysmic catastrophes do not necessarily respond to foreign investments and interventions in the economic system and that they will not come to a halt without a radical change in the way power is structured.

## CONCLUSION

We may speak, then, of at least two distinct models of political catastrophization in contemporary zones of emergency. The first, catastrophic suspension, is associated with strong states and characterized by a partial withdrawal of state apparatuses and the intensification of security-related apparatuses, the intensive problematization of the threshold of catastrophe, and systemic, unavoidable collaboration between the ruling power and the humanitarians and other professionals of catastrophization. The other model, nongovernmental catastrophization, is associated with weak states and characterized by the collapse of state apparatuses, the naturalization of political catastrophization, and an ad hoc, contingent collaboration between local authorities of all kinds and the humanitarians.[63] In the first model, "a real state of emergency" is an always present ghost; in the second, ghostlike forces create and maintain it.[64]

## NOTES

The first version of this paper was presented at the conference Zones of Emergency held at the Van Leer Jerusalem Foundation in June 2007. This paper is the result of lively discussions I have conducted over the last few years with Ariella Azoulay, Michal Givoni, and Tal Arbel on the notions of catastrophe, emergency, and sovereignty. I am indebted to them all, but unfortunately cannot share with them responsibility for any of the faults that still prevail in my text.

1    Ann L. Stoler, "On Degrees of Imperial Sovereignty," *Public Culture* 18, no. 1 (Winter 2006): pp. 125–46.

2    Thomas Alexander Aleinikoff, *Semblances of Sovereignty: The Constitution, the State, and American Citizenship* (Cambridge, MA: Harvard University Press 2002).

3    Lusia Stopa and David M. Clark, "Social Phobia and Interpretation of Social Events," *Behaviour Research and Therapy* 38, no. 3 (2000): pp. 273–83. Similar definitions abound in the professional literature.

4    Mark Dombeck, "Cognitive Restructuring," available on-line at http.//www.mentalhelp.net/poc/view_doc.php?type=doc&id=9350 (last accessed January 11, 2009).

5    Stephanos Ph. Vassilopoulos, "Interpretation and Judgmental Biases in Socially Anxious and Nonanxious Individuals," *Behavioral and Cognitive Psychotherapy* 34, no. 2 (April 2006): pp. 243–54.

6    Stopa and Clark, "Social Phobia and Interpretation of Social Events."

7    This was already clear to Rousseau in the middle of the eighteenth century. In a famous letter to Voltaire responding to his poem on the earthquake in Lisbon, Rousseau says that even earthquakes are thus mediated: "Nature did not construct twenty thousand houses of six to seven stories there, and…if the inhabitants of this great city had been more equally spread out and more lightly lodged, the damage would have been much less, and perhaps of no account. All of them would have fled at the first disturbance, and the next day they would have been seen twenty leagues from there, as gay as if nothing had happened." "Rousseau's Letter to Voltaire on Optimism," in Roger D. Masters and Christopher Kelly (eds.), *The Collected Writings of Rousseau*, vol. 3 (Hanover, NH: Published for Dartmouth College by the University Press of New England, 1992), p. 110.

8    It is not only the proliferation of "complex emergencies" since the late 1980s that accounts for the obliteration of the distinction between the natural and the man-made, as some observers suggested, but more generally the thorough socialization (and hence politicization) of the natural environment of humans. For the emphasis on "complex emergencies" see, for example, *Definitions of Emergencies*, Document Presented to the Executive Board of the World Food

Programme, available on-line at http://www.reliefweb.int/rw/lib.nsf/db900SID/HMYT-6QDQ5K/$FILE/wfp-definition-feb2005.pdf?OpenElement (last accessed January 11, 2009).

9   Personal disasters, that is, events that affect one or a few individuals, will not be considered here.

10  A perfect example may be found in the opening pages of Daniel Defoe's *The Journal of the Plague Year* (1722).

11  Michel Foucault, *Security, Territory, Population: Lectures at the Collège de France, 1977–1978*, ed. Michel Senellart, trans. Graham Burchell (New York: Palgrave Macmillan, 2007), esp. lectures 3 and 4.

12  It is important to distinguish here between a discourse of governmentality in the Foucauldian sense and governmental and nongovernmental bodies and agencies. Both types of bodies practice a discourse of governmentality.

13  This is a recurring theme in Hannah Arendt's *The Origins of Totalitarianism* (1951; Harcourt Brace and Company, 1973), for example, pp. 186–97.

14  I assume here Foucault's discussion of the formation of objects as part of an order of discourse. See Michel Foucault, *The Archaeology of Knowledge* (New York: Pantheon Books 1972), pt. 2, ch. 3.

15  For "emergency statements" and its distinction from "horror statements," see Ariella Azoulay, *The Civil Contract of Photography* (New York: Zone Books, 2008), ch. 4. My text owes this book and its author much more than a passing footnote can express.

16  See, for example, the fascinating reports and suggestions made by the California Seismic Safety Commission in its *Progress Report for the California Earthquake Loss Reduction Plan* (Sacramento: State of California, December 2003). Because estimation of the next major earthquake is based on statistics of past events, and not on the existence of warning signs, the gap between discursive and objective catastrophization is the clearest in this case. More complicated is the case of the discourse on global warming, for example, where relatively few cases of loss can be reported at the moment, and they are really marginal in relation to the cataclysm everyone expects, and yet warning signs abound. See, for example, *Climate Change and Human Security*, published by Radix, April 15, 2007, available on-line at http://www.radixonline.org/cchs.html (last accessed January 13, 2009). A different case is that of catastrophization based on the demonization of an enemy, which may meet all the criteria of the psychological disorder, except that it is publicly amplified and politically orchestrated.

17  Thinking about this case has inspired my whole analysis of catastrophization. Ariella Azoulay has started looking into the management of the threshold of disaster in Gaza in her film *The Food Chain*. See also Azoulay Ariella and Adi Ophir, "On the Verge of Catastrophe," a paper presented in the conference The Politics of Humanitarianism in the Occupied Territories, The Van Leer Jerusalem Institute, April 2004; Ariella Azoulay and Adi Ophir, "The Monster's Tail," in Michael Sorkin (ed.), *Against the Wall* (New York: The New Press, 2005); Ariella Azoulay and Adi Ophir, *This Regime Which Is Not One* (Tel Aviv: Resling 2008) [in Hebrew], pp. 297–311.

18  This, for example, is Arendt's position in *The Origins of Totalitarianism*. The point is not to establish that "administrative massacres" of hundreds of thousands in colonial Africa or the concentration camps and the death industry in Europe were catastrophic, but to understand why the production of catastrophes was necessary for the totalitarian regimes and a possible means of governance for imperialism. See Adi Ophir, "Arendt's Theory Of Man-Made Disaster," *Insights*, forthcoming.

19  Long before Claude Lanzmann's *Shoa* and independently of Theodor Adorno's famous last
    chapter of *Negative Dialectics*, Hannah Arendt understood this aspect of totalitarian power
    and its catastrophes. See *The Origins of Totalitarianism*, pp. 433–37. She came to this under-
    standing almost in passing, while discussing the secret police and the element of secrecy in
    totalitarian regimes. (*Ibid.*, esp. pp. 419–37). Following Arendt's insights and observations, we
    may say that what brought totalitarian disasters to near perfection was not the sheer number
    of victims or the vast magnitude of the destruction they left behind, but their tendency to
    destroy the event of disaster itself and rule out the possibility of testimony. Extermination
    was meant to bring to an end not only the lives of so many, but also the irretrievable loss
    that their death had created. After the catastrophe, there were to have been left no people
    who could mourn and commemorate and then use their memories as a basis from which to
    begin something new. Destruction becomes perfect when even the ruins and remnants are
    destroyed, so that no recordable event could be reconstructed and no life, no action, can
    spring out of the ashes. Totalitarian regimes did not produce a truly perfect political disaster,
    after all, precisely because they failed to wipe out the traces of the disasters for which they
    were responsible.

20  If there is one thing that clearly distinguishes contemporary catastrophes—the so-called
    "natural disasters," as well as political catastrophes, conflicts, military occupations, colonial
    wars, civil wars, and everything included under the term "humanitarian emergencies"—from
    their predecessors, it is the abundance of this kind of literature.

21  See, for example, Alexander Tulloch, *The Crimean Commission and the Chelsea Board* (Lon-
    don: Harrison 1857); Hugh Small, *Florence Nightingale: Avenging Angel* (New York: St. Mar-
    tin's Press 1998), ch. 4.

22  This is the name of an annual report published since 1992 by Médecins Sans Frontières, *Popu-
    lations en danger* (Paris: Hachette, 1992). It may be described as an established venue and
    forum of catastrophization.

23  Médecins Sans Frontières, *Population en danger*, p. 8 (my translation).

24  The report is available on-line at http://www.msf.org/msfinternational/invoke.cfm?objectid=
    06616F5A-5056-AA77-6CE49B621A0C195D&component=toolkit.report&method=full_html (last
    accessed January 13, 2009).

25  For example, one can find in this statement issued by *The Charity Navigator: Your Guide to
    Intelligent Giving* in February 2006: "Humanitarian Emergency Alert: Kenyan Food Crisis."
    The statement opens with a typical description of a given situation: "The people of Kenya,
    where over 50 percent of the population already lives in poverty and where life expec-
    tancy is only 47 years, are now facing a potential famine due to drought. The government
    of Kenya estimates that upwards of 3.5 million are at risk from the worsening food crisis. 50
    percent poverty is not a reason for alert, in Kenya, but the prospect of a new food crisis is
    a reason to turn the bells on." Available on-line at http://www.charitynavigator.org/index.
    cfm?bay=content.view&cpid=386 (last accessed January 13, 2008).

26  Giorgio Agamben, *Homo Sacer: Sovereign Power and Bare Life*, trans. Daniel Heller-Roazen
    (Stanford, CA: Stanford University Press 1998), pp. 18–29.

27  I have developed this argument in "The Sovereign, The Humanitarian, and the Terrorist," in
    Michel Feher (ed.), *Nongovernmental Politics* (New York: Zone Books, 2007).

28  Raimo Väyrynen, "Complex Humanitarian Emergencies: Concepts and Issues," in E. Wayne
    Nafziger, Raimo Väyrynen, and Frances Stewart (eds.), *War, Hunger, and Displacement: The*

*Origins of Humanitarian Emergencies* (Oxford: Oxford University Press, 2000), pp. 60–72.

29  *Ibid.*, p. 49.

30  In addition to the basic measurements, some other indicators of an emergency are also considered. Thus, for example, the number of human rights violations can be "used to operationalize an emergency by setting country-specific minimum standards." *Ibid.*, p. 59.

31  *Ibid.*, pp. 72–80; Jeni Klugman, *Social and Economic Policies to Prevent Complex Humanitarian Emergencies—Lessons from Experience*, United Nations University, World Institute for Development Economics Research (Helsinki: Wider, 1999).

32  Väyrynen, "Complex Humanitarian Emergencies," p. 55.

33  *Ibid.*

34  *Ibid.*, p. 72.

35  For a discussion of the flexible and explicitly unstable notion of emergency, which obviously implies the unstable threshold of catastrophe, see Michal Givoni, "The Advent of the Emergency: Political Theory and Humanitarian Expertise," paper presented at the workshop Zones of Emergency, The Van Leer Jerusalem Institute, June 2007.

36  Sometimes governability is not only a matter of the target population, but of accountability at home. It is necessary, states a 2005 report of the World Food Programme, to "strike a balance between allowing flexibility to respond quickly to varying crisis situations and providing accountability to donors for the allocation of emergency food aid." *Definitions of Emergencies*; see n.7 above. The definition of emergency should therefore be flexible enough so as to determine the threshold of catastrophe—and the moment of intervention—in a way that would allow the introduction of domestic considerations into the evaluation of the disaster-stricken area.

37  For example, in E. Wayne Nafziger, Frances Stewart, and Raimo Väyrynen, eds., *War, Hunger, and Displacement: The Origins of Humanitarian Emergencies* (Oxford: Oxford University Press, 2000).

38  Carl Schmitt: "The exception, which is not codified in the existing legal order, can at best be characterized as a case of extreme peril, a danger to the existence of the state or the like." *Political Theology* (Cambridge, MA: The MIT Press, 1985), p. 6.

39  A good example came recently from Pakistan, whose then president, Pervez Musharraf, defended his decision to impose emergency rule by insisting that he was only "acting to curb extremism," which put in danger "Pakistan's sovereignty," and to suppress "a judiciary that had paralyzed its government." BBC World Service, November 3, 2007. It does not matter how sincere such statements are.

40  See, for example, Pascal Dauvin, Johanna Siméant, and the Collectif d'Analyse de l'Humanitaire International (CAHIER), *Le travail humanitaire: Les acteurs des ONG, du siège du terrain* (Paris: Presses de Sciences Po, 2002), esp. chs. 3–5; Philippe Ryfman, *La question humanitaire: Histoire, problematique, acteurs et enjeux de l'aide humanitaire internationale* (Paris: Ellipses, 1999), pp. 142–49.

41  A quick note on the distinction between weak and strong states should be introduced here: A strong state is not necessarily a state that intervenes in all areas of life, but a system of power that has the capacity of such interventions and their further expansion. The withdrawal of state apparatuses from the economy, for example, should be conceived as a form of contraction in the Kabbalistic sense of this word. The state has contracted, but it is fully capable of expanding back into the space it has evacuated. Weak states are incapable of doing that.

They do not intervene because they do not have means or capacity for intervention. Thus, the difference between a strong and a weak state is a difference in capabilities and potentiality. The weak state cannot operate, efficiently or at all, the state apparatuses that the strong state decides to withdraw or to put on hold. The privatization of the welfare state and the dismantling of some of its apparatuses that provide a safety net to weakened sectors of the population do not reflect the weakening of the state as long as the course can be reversed and the state can take control of the spheres it has abandoned.

42  I assume here the Foucauldian distinction between these two apparatuses. See, for example, Michel Foucault, *Society Must Be Defended: Lectures at the Collège de France, 1975–76*, ed. Mauro Bertani, trans. David Macey (New York: Picador 2003), ch. 2.

43  Stoler, "On Degrees of Imperial Sovereignty."

44  Technological and industrial regulations and new patterns of consumption called for in the face of global warming are exceptions to this rule, because the catastrophe will remain imminent for a long time, even if all the necessary measures are taken.

45  Israel may supply a good example: Separation along national lines is the organizing principle of the Israeli regime. The zone of emergency in the Occupied Territories is where this principle becomes most visible and where experimentation with new forms for the expression and implementation of this principle takes place.

46  This is not the case in Iraq, I think, but has certainly been the case in the Occupied Territories. Something similar may be said about situations and contexts as different as the Ukrainian government's dealing with the aftermath of Chernobyl, the American administration's response to Katrina, and the Colombian government's response to the paramilitary challenge.

47  The facts were reported by almost every human rights organization working in the Occupied Territories. See, for example, B'Tselem, *On Human Rights in the Occupied Territories: Al-Aqsa Intifada*, June 2001, available on-line at http://www.btselem.org/Download/200106_Issue7_Eng.pdf (last accessed January 15, 2009).

48  Ms. Catherine Bertini, Personal Humanitarian Envoy of the Secretary-General, *Mission Report 11–19 August, 2002*, available on-line at http://www.reliefweb.int/library/documents/2002/un-opt-19aug.pdf (last accessed July 17, 2009).

49  *Ibid.*, para. 54. According to this survey 13.2 percent of children in Gaza suffered from "acute malnutrition, more than three times the rate in the West Bank (4.3 percent) and the rate of chronic malnourishment in Gaza (17.5 percent) was five times higher than in the West Bank (3.5 percent)."

50  *Economic, Social and Cultural Rights: The Right to Food*, [unofficial] Report by the Special Rapporteur, Jean Ziegler, The United Nation, Advanced Edited Copy, October 2003, available on-line at http://www.unhchr.ch/pdf/chr60/10add2AV.pdf (last accessed January 15, 2009).

51  Quoted in Silvia Cattori, "Wonderful Jean Ziegler," September 25, 2003, available on-line at http://www.silviacattori.net/article246.html (last accessed January 15, 2009).

52  John Dugard, *Question of the Violation of Human Rights in the Occupied Arab Territories, including Palestine*, Report of the Special Rapporteur of the Commission on Human Rights submitted on September 8, 2003, available on-line via a search at http://www.unhchr.ch/huridocda/huridoca.nsf (last accessed January 15, 2009). Similar expressions may be found in, for example, the *Amnesty International: Report 2003* (London: Amnesty International Publications, 2003), or a special report, "Development Assistance and the Palestinian Occupied Territory" published by the International Development Committee of the British House

of Commons on February 5, 2004, excerpts of which are available in the *Journal of Palestine Studies* 33, no. 3 (2004): pp. 157–63.

53 *Economic, Social and Cultural Rights: The Right to Food*, ch. 3, para. 38, p. 14.

54 Israeli Defense Forces humanitarian officers and UNRWA officer Richard Cook, interviewed by Ariella Azoulay in her documentary Food Chain (2003).

55 Lieutenant Colonel Orly Malka, speaking with Ariella Azoulay, *The Food Chain* (2003).

56 *Economic, Social and Cultural Rights: The Right to Food*, ch. 3, para. 38, p. 14.

57 *Amnesty International: Report 2003*, pp. 53–54.

58 UNRWA Emergency Appeal, 2007, available on-line at http://www.un.org/unrwa/emergency/appeals/2008-appeal.pdf (last accessed January 19, 2009).

59 See, for example, The United Nations Humanitarian Coordinator for the Occupied Palestinian Territories, Office for the Coordination of Humanitarian Affairs, *Gaza Humanitarian Situation Report, 20 June 2007*, available on-line at http://www.ochaopt.org/documents/Gaza_sit_rep_20_June_2007.pdf (last accessed January 19, 2009).

60 The average daily income in Gaza is $2.10, and almost two-thirds of the population are now dependent on food distribution. The report *Border Closures: "Effect on Private Sector in Gaza,"* prepared by the Palestine Trade Center and the Palestinian Federation of Industries, July 12, 2007, and available on-line at http://www.paltrade.org/cms/images/enpublications/PSCC%20presentation%202007.07.pdf (last accessed January 19, 2009) estimates that more than thirteen hundred containers of imported goods were stuck at the Israeli freight terminals and warehouses during the first month after Hamas took power, while the total losses of sales of undeliverable goods was $16 million.

61 Suspension is a basic structure of the Israeli regime of occupation. The forty-year-long suspension of a final decision on the status of the Occupied Territories and their Palestinian inhabitants has played a crucial role in the Jewish colonization of the territories and has helped develop the system of separations that characterizes the occupation today and that is being implemented legally, economically, and spatially. On suspension as a mechanism of governance and domination in the Occupied Palestinian Territories see Azoulay and Ophir, "On the Verge of Catastrophe"; Azoulay and Ophir, "The Monster's Tail"; and Azoulay and Ophir, *This Regime Which Is Not One*.

62 Väyrynen expresses the same idea from a different perspective: "The spread of digital capitalism has created an economy where the prosperity of society depends on intellectual and social capital rather than on material resources. These forms of capital cannot be conquered by military means, but only destroyed by them." *War, Hunger, and Displacement: The Origins of Humanitarian Emergencies*, p. 45.

63 This distinction does not pretend to be exhaustive or inclusive. It is meant as a preliminary attempt to map and classify contemporary zones of emergency. My assumption is that other models would be found to be relatively marginal. I also assume that in some areas, one may find an interesting fusion of the two models. This may be the case when a weak state still governs a certain area effectively and exercises catastrophic suspension there while other areas are exposed to the devastating impact of nongovernmental forces.

64 "Ghostlike" is a metaphor frequently used by victims who describe the paramilitary groups and extralegal death squads that have ruined their lives. It is not only their nightly visits that make them appear as phantoms, however, but also the fact that there is no clear governmental body that they embody and no clear body politic that they represent.

# Emergency-Based Predatory Capitalism:
# The Rule of Law, Alternative Dispute Resolution, and Development

Ugo Mattei

In a state of emergency, ordinary political life is suspended. To exit from a state of emergency by curing its causes or addressing its consequences is the "target" constructed as being in the interest of everybody and as the end that everybody must pursue. In a state of emergency, no critique is acceptable, and there is no place for a loyal opposition. Everybody must be on board in pursuit of the target. The state of emergency thus is a desirable condition for power. It is a highly effective way to avoid opposition—perhaps the only effective way in a pluralist political scenario such as a parliamentary democracy or the unstructured global political arena. Thus, the state of emergency is a stabilizing political strategy, a true foundation of "predatory capitalism," which is how I define the realized form of the current system of global production. In turn, predatory capitalism requires and develops ideological apparatuses to sustain it. A state of emergency thus serves as false consciousness. A thick ideological layer constructs as in the interest of everybody what is in fact a project of domination of the powerful few over the powerless many. In this project, the law serves a double purpose as at the same time a coercive and an ideological apparatus of domination—a stick and a carrot.

This essay explores current global developments in which general states of emergency are "invented" or "exaggerated" to sustain legal transformations that, while presented as being in the interest of everybody, cover projects of domination.[1] From the perspective of the law, we will discuss three instances.

The first is the rule of law, which is presented as an objectively desirable device of governance, while in fact, it functions as a predatory device to privatize the public domain. The invented emergency is in this case the lack of the rule of law, which denies legal legitimacy and respectability to any alternative to the Western vision of legality. Thus, an emergency is created to introduce the rule of law in societies lacking this benefit of civilization.

89

The second is alternative dispute resolution (ADR), which is always presented as a cure for the emergency created by the so-called "litigation explosion," a spectacularly exaggerated condition of adjudication in current times. Grounded in this state of emergency, ADR systematically favors the stronger economic and political interests against the weaker ones while at the same time effectively taming social dissent and silencing the demand for justice. The emergency here is the impossibility of delivering ordinary public access to justice and the consequent beneficial nature of any kind of private alternative.

The final instance is the ideology of development, an entirely abstract and thus invented ideology presented by the dominant media and by an apologetic chorus of academics as the ultimate target in a progressive evolutionary process. Development promises happiness and well-being to poor countries while in fact functioning as a strategy of political and economic intervention. Thus, the ideology of development, indisputable in every emergency, serves the interests of strong political actors seeking to plunder the underdeveloped. The emergency here is seen as the prevalence of poverty, an idea organized around capitalist-generated consumer needs, while development, rather than being blamed as responsible for many of the policies generating poverty, is in fact presented as the only cure for it.

My arguments do not address any particular legal system. Rather, they discuss global legal transformations produced in different geographical and political settings by the hegemonic corporate forces of predatory capitalism. The impact of such forces can be variable across geographical space, and its predatory success depends on the strengths of the complex aggregate of resisting forces. Nevertheless, what we will encounter here are trends that are clearly visible in most areas of the world.

## THE RULE OF LAW

It is hard to imagine another expression of Anglo-American political discourse, that is as well known and prestigious at the global level as "the rule of law." There is debate as to the exact date when the term was coined, but there is agreement as to the place where it was born: glorious England, maybe from the era of the Magna Carta or maybe some centuries later in the famous *Fuller's Case* (1607–1608), in which the legendary judge Sir Edward Coke argued that "the king in his own person cannot adjudge any case" because the common law, as a system of "artificial reason and judgment," had been built up over centuries and could be understood only by those who had carefully studied it. The king lacked the knowledge that was the basis of judicial legitimacy. Centuries later, an icon of English constitutional law, Albert V. Dicey, condemned the traditional Continental (Napoleonic) state administration as irreparably authoritarian because it lacked "the rule of law": On the Continent, unlike in the Anglo-American world, the ordinary judiciary has very limited jurisdiction over state powers. The U.S. Constitutional experience provided a fundamental boost to the prestige of the rule of law. Specifically, in *The Federalist Papers* (in particular in Madison's Number 10 and Hamilton's Number 23), the rule of law was conceived as the only way to guarantee political stability in a society characterized by inequalities and in which wealthy landowners were in the minority and had to be defended against the majority of the population who did not own property. The rule of law, which entrusts to courts possessed of legal wisdom the protection of private property, remained an essential institutional guarantee for property owners in the post-Revolutionary American constitutional order destined to gain its current worldwide hegemony.

With such a celebrated chorus presenting the rule of law as the ideal solution to every abuse of political power, it is almost impossible to find someone willing to argue against a political system based on such a sacred idea, despite its clearly conservative origins as the protector of the privileges of a landed aristocracy. This is like arguing against a "fair" legal system, an "efficient" economic system, or a "tasty" meal. In short, "the rule of law" is the kind of idea that everybody places on a sacred pedestal, protected and defended on almost every side. This is a truly "bipartisan" notion and is held sacred by conservatives and liberals alike (paradoxically, since the latter are supposedly more devoted to change than to the preservation of the status quo), an icon as much to the English constitutional monarchy as to the heirs of the American Revolution. Some years ago, Niall Ferguson, a Scottish historian whose political views were very close to the "Third Way" of Tony Blair and Bill Clinton, published a book, *Empire*,[2] with the same title as the controversial essay written by Michael Hardt and Antonio Negri.[3] The central thesis was that English imperial expansion most certainly produced mischief in the form of wars, genocide, plunder and deportation, but that it also benefited its victims by providing them with an invaluable legacy: the rule of law, which he claims is capable of transforming a traditional system of government, a system (such as prevailed in India) that otherwise would have developed according to an Eastern autocratic tyranny, into a modern democracy.

There is never a high-level international meeting in which "the rule of law" does not become the concept that brings everyone to agreement. For example, in July 2005, at the closing of the G8 Summit meeting in London, Tony Blair—still shaken by the terrorist attacks in the city of few days earlier—nevertheless presented his "Plan for Africa" and promised (in the context of general commotion and approval) that debt forgiveness would depend solely on the African's willingness to develop "the rule of law."[4] Two years later, the promise of debt cancellation still existed only on paper, but to make up for this, the G8 Summit meeting organized an important conference specifically dedicated to the rule of law. And what other concept has the ability to lead to a consensus between Hillary Clinton and Condoleezza Rice, two of the most powerful women in the world, in the middle of an electoral campaign? If you look through one of the recent issues of the *Berkeley Journal of International Law*, you will find the response.[5] Both spoke about the rule of law in a seminar organized by the powerful American Bar Association. I crossed out the names and circulated the two papers among the students in one of my seminars at Hastings Law School. I asked them to figure out who wrote which piece, and it proved to be impossible for the students to distinguish between the two papers, because each reported exactly the same trite point of view.

At the end of the 1990s, Puntland, in far northeastern Somalia, was trying to strengthen a situation of relative peace in a zone left out of the massacres that followed the Operation Restore Hope intervention by the U.S.-led United Task Force in 1992–93 to attempt to guarantee the delivery of humanitarian aid. The region requested United Nations financing for the reconstruction of a parliamentary building for a political meeting between traditional leaders. They did not receive any funds for reconstruction, but in its place obtained the participation of a handsomely paid international team of experts who were mandated to supervise the respect for the rule of law in the "transitory constitution" that the Somalis were trying to negotiate.[6] This proved to be difficult to achieve, because Somali political culture is based on agreed-upon solutions reached through constant negotiations between groups. In fact, the rule of law, as its purely Western history demonstrates, is nothing more than a model in which the decision-making power in microconflicts is principally assigned to a professional jurist legitimated by his or her legal-technical knowledge. Therefore, who is to settle a dispute is neither a subject that is endowed with religious, moral-philosophical, or traditional legitimation, as is the case with the Islamic judge (*qāḍī*), nor does it involve a politician (as in the case of socialist systems) who could appeal, in many cases, to some degree of democratic legitimization. It is easy to see, at this point, the main reasons according to which the professional culture of jurists, under the guise of upholding "the rule of law," expropriates much of the decision-making power belonging to the religious and political authorities.

The rule of law is in fact one of the malleable notions in which everyone can see the values in which he or she believes. Thus, the World Bank, by following the teachings of a University of Chicago guru, imposes the rule of law as part of the "structural adjustment" necessary as the condition for granting loans. By doing this, the World Bank secures foreign investments as a form of private property based on the sanctity of contracts. Similarly, when a young volunteer endowed with good intentions—and who we can easily imagine is of liberal political opinions—takes part in a program for the enhancement of the rule of law financed by an American university, an NGO, or a government (there are many of these programs, for example, the ones that Italy finances in Afghanistan or that Canada underwrites in Mali), he or she reads into the rule of law the protection of fundamental human rights and believes that the development of the rule of law might really be useful for the protection of some oppressed minority.[7]

Between these two fundamental ideas of the rule of law—the protection of property rights and the protection of human rights—there is a historical antinomy. There is certainly the rule of law in the first sense in a system such as Alberto Fujimori's Peru, Augusto Pinochet's Chile, or Horacio Serpa Uribe's Colombia in their acceptance of investment guarantees, protection for property rights, and the sanctity of contracts. From the same perspective, Evo Morales's Bolivia, Hugo Chavez's Venezuela, and Fidel Castro's Cuba are generally considered to lack the rule of law, since foreign investors are put under very strict controls and sometimes exposed to the risk of nationalization, to the point that conservatives would like to ban these countries from the community of civilized nations.

From the point of view of human rights, according to the other meaning of the term "the rule of law," one can certainly find many systems (including the last three mentioned) where fundamental human rights (shelter, sanitation, education, and so on) are very much protected, while property rights are not, because private property and contractual freedom suffer severe limitations in the public interest. As a historical example, think of Salvador Allende's Chile, but also of many European social democracies, beginning with the Scandinavian countries. As Naomi Klein claims, and as many others before her have claimed, respect for the rule of law in the first sense, respect for private property, is incompatible with the respect for the rule of law in the second sense, respect for the effectiveness of human rights, since developing fundamental human rights cannot avoid the redistribution of resources, something that is incompatible with the intangibility of property and of contracts.[8] But this obvious conflict is hidden by the use of a common denominator, "the rule of law."

It is worth repeating that whatever sense of the term we choose, the meaning of "the rule of law" finds its roots in the deepest self-consciousness of Western civilization. It is certainly remote from non-Western political experiences. The "Orientalism" that altogether dominates Western political discourse feeds on the perception of the "other" (the non-Western) as lacking "the rule of law" and therefore lacking "law" itself, and consequently the basis of human rights. This discourse rejects the idea that the legal profession is just one of the ways in which conflicts can be governed in a complex society. It perhaps may be a "better" technical instrument, but certainly is not a more legitimate one from a democratic perspective, since jurists lack democratic legitimacy. From this perspective, the narrative around the legal history of people considered "without history" is false beyond all limits.[9] According to the Orientalist account, certain Islamic countries have known the rule of law thanks only to the efforts of legal modernization at the beginning of the twentieth century, while many others are still in the darkness of *sharia*. In the same vein, Latin American countries should thank the colonizers and Saint Ignatius Loyola. African countries, after rejecting colonization and the legal benefits described by Ferguson, had to wait until the fall of the Berlin Wall, after which the international financial institutions have been allowed to intervene in their legal systems, which are not seen any longer as political entities, but as simple infrastructures of their economic systems. Finally, China, it is said, incrementally and cautiously, was able to understand the importance of the rule of law after a long history in which it underwent a transition from Confucian antiformalism to Maoist antilegalism. In this account, even Russia needs to be helped to open her eyes and acknowledge the continuity, despite the Revolution, between Czarist autocracy, the horrors of historical Communism, and Putin's revanchistic personalism. They all lack the rule of law, a gap that only Western corporate capitalism can help to fill.[10] They all have to solve their "legal emergency" before they can be admitted as fully respected and reliable members of the "family of civilized nations."

## ALTERNATIVE DISPUTE RESOLUTION

In the previous section, I tried to demonstrate how the rule of law, as a legal notion and political scheme that is largely embraced by both the political right and by liberals, shows a hidden, dark, imperialist side that is difficult to discern due to the ambiguous semantic politics of the term. A structurally similar phenomenon involves the notion of alternative dispute resolution (ADR), which is exalted both by the right and by liberals as a solution to the problems of access to justice.[11]

It should be noted that in many Western countries, including the two that I have been specifically studying, Italy and the United States, justice is scarcely available to those that do not have sufficient financial resources and considerable patience. In fact, the costs involved in the justice process are quite significant, accompanied by epic waiting times. In many cases, it requires years to receive a judgment, even in the case of a simple dispute arising out of a contractual default, a divorce, a termination of employment, or a car accident. In most industrialized countries, investment in the public justice system did not follow the growth in needs for adjudication in progressively more complex settings. Beginning in the

1980s, many countries reduced investment in access to justice as part of a general-ized dismantling of the welfare state. Even in this sector, the mantra of privatiza-tion promised miracles to cure "the litigation explosion." The exponential increase in lawsuits being filed and brought before courts of justice was thus taken to be an objective condition causing problems for justice. A heavy case load, rather than insufficient public investment, could be singled out as the structural incapacity of the public justice system to render timely decisions. Despite empirical studies (the most notable being those of the U.S. legal sociologist Marc Galanter) that have demonstrated that the "litigation explosion" is a phenomenon largely exaggerated, if not completely invented, the assumption that we need an emergency cure for it remains dominant.[12]

An impressive ideological mechanism was put in place at the end of the 1970s, creating a favorable climate for any alternative that promised to reduce the burden on the courts: ADR. Such a mechanism, a real industry featuring a newly organized profession of "mediators," new academic chairs and departments, and a boom-ing academic and popular literature, supports and at the same time hides inter-ests having very little to do with the proclaimed desirable goals of ADR: to be an instrument to make justice available and accessible to everyone. In fact, judicial delay encourages strong corporate interests to choose arbitration as an alterna-tive to litigation, a private (confidential) solution praised by the dominant legal cultures as a major cultural and technical advancement. Of course, such enthu-siastic judgments concerning arbitration are not completely unbiased, given the elite status of the judicial profession, academia, and practicing attorneys who are involved in civil arbitration (above all, but not exclusively, in dealing with interna-tional questions), obtaining, as they do from such private alternatives to ordinary litigation, a most important source of their income.[13]

It should therefore be easy, from a critical standpoint, to understand the forces that have progressively contributed to enlarging the spheres of arbitration, let alone the various forms of legislation and transnational organizations that place this private alternative solution on an incrementally favorable light. The latter include the Convention on the Recognition and Enforcement of Foreign Arbitral Awards, established under UN auspices in 1958, the UN Commission on Interna-tional Trade Law (UNCITRAL), established by the UN General Assembly in 1966, the Principles of International Commercial Contracts prepared in 2004 under the aus-pices of the International Institute for the Unification of Private Law, also known as UNIDROIT, an independent, intergovernmental organization based in Rome, and so on. Paradoxically, because of the political-cultural forces supporting it, arbitra-tion in fact makes the ordinary judicial process increasingly inaccessible, despite the political and cultural rhetoric that celebrates it as a solution to the problem of access to justice. Arbitration is in fact nothing more than a simple form of private justice, more agile, more efficient, and of course much more expensive than the ordinary forms of justice. The ADR industry manages to render its adjudication increasingly impermeable to the ordinary jurisdictional challenges that operate by way of scholarly judicial and legislative interventions, to the point that this form of ADR becomes independent and completely self-sufficient, thus serving the interests of the wealthy class that can enjoy its own "law." This fact is not new in the Western legal experience. The old tradition of the *lex mercatoria*, a system of customs and practices enforced through merchant courts, was highly developed as early as the fourteenth century and unfolded unchallenged until the early twentieth century, when the great Swiss legislator Eugen Huber began to stress its political incompatibility with the idea of equality before the law.

The success of privatized justice thus is not much different from the success in the package-delivery field of an express courier service such as DHL. It is more convenient and more efficient than the public postal service for those without budgetary constraints. Moreover, through arbitration, merchants once again can be sovereigns of their own law, the new *lex mercatoria*, and reconquer the status of "more equal than others" that as a class they had lost at the beginning of the twentieth century. This new law, as a judicially viable alternative, carries its own potentially distinctive values, which "the industry" succeeds in describing as perfectly compatible with, if not more advanced than, the ordinary laws of the land. Thus the idea of a special law serving the interests of the "class" of "merchants" is being reintroduced.

The risks of privatized justice, however, are very acute. As is invariably the case when efficiency is used as a legitimating device, the "haves" come out ahead. Typically, on current arbitration panels, local as well as international, two private judges (most often professors or famous attorneys) are appointed by the parties and de facto serve as quasi-advocates concerned with preserving their professional relationship with the lawyers who have appointed them. The third private judge, serving as the president, is nominated either by the parties in agreement or by some third party. The president, himself a private professional, is at high risk for being influenced by the interests of the most powerful party, because doing so can provide more potential future lucrative opportunities to serve as a private arbitrator.[14]

If at first glance the success of arbitration as a form of ADR seems to be merely that of a simple and desirable alternative for the upper class, in truth, this produces significant mischief for the ordinary person (*quivis de populo*) and more generally damages the idea of legality within a pluralist society. In the first place, what emerges is a particular system of governance under which any social class powerful enough is entitled to its own particularized law, as if unity were not a value in society and as if efficiency and the survival of the fittest were themselves the only justification for the law. In addition, the blooming of forms of ADR allowing the affluent part of society to access its own privatized law produces the ulterior degradation of the ordinary judicial system, which is systematically despised by the cultural industry that sustains ADR and which is eventually abandoned by everyone who can afford to do so. In fact, if all the best professionals are employed in the very lucrative business of arbitration and strongly encourage its use by their wealthy clients, it becomes evident that the ordinary system increasingly worsens. This is just what has happened in the United States with public schools, compared with private ones.

But the risks to which arbitration exposes the legal conquests of the twentieth century, which at least formally produced equality between the social classes and as a result of which merchants could not invoke a sovereign law different from what applied to all other citizens, pale in comparison with those created by mediation, the second form of ADR and one more recent introduction. Here, too, you find the same rhetorical basis, the need to confront the "litigation explosion." However, while in arbitration, the idea persists of a solution to controversies based on notions of right and wrong established by legal professionals on the basis of neutral verifications of the entitlements of the parties, an idea that is deeply rooted in the Western legal tradition, mediation constructs a radically different form of justice. Indeed, the dispute in mediation is not decided by a third party—a judge or an arbitrator—on the basis of "objective" findings of right and wrong. On the contrary, in mediation, the parties come together to reach an "alternative" solution by seeking a reasonable compromise. This process is quite often aided by a facilitator who is experienced more in psychology than in the law. Notions of right and wrong disappear. What remains are cases that are adjudicated on the basis of an idea of reasonableness conceived in terms of a social model of the "good person," someone who is submissive, integrated, not idiosyncratic, and who does not create "problems." In mediation, the "harmony ideology" prevails (to use the title of the classic volume of Laura Nader),[15] and the party who is praised is the one who is willing and able to concede (under pressure from the mediator) at least some of his or her rights for an objectively favorable compromise. Those who seek to assert their rights are quite often seen as impulsive, rebellious, and potentially subversive. The result is the "medicalization" of the process, as the mediator becomes like a therapist facilitating consent and thus helping a deviant person (who still retains his or her rights) to achieve harmony with society.

In colonial Africa, traditionally weak social actors (for example, women) who sought adjudication in the modern courts established by the colonial powers were turned down and sent to seek "traditional justice" in the form of mediation, which was considered by the colonizers to be better adapted to tame people with more rebellious dispositions. During the Meiji period in Japan, and frequently today, the idea of citizens seeking to assert an individual *right* (a term that has only recently been added to the Japanese dictionary) was considered a subversive concept that rendered people incapable of conforming to collective norms and accepting traditional mediation.[16] In modern-day China, in order to eliminate the trend toward the assertion of individual rights—a consequence of an increasingly more professionalized judicial system—the state invoked a return to Confucian harmony.[17] Since the second half of the 1970s, during the tenure of Chief Justice Warren E. Burger at the United States Supreme Court, mediation in the United States became a powerful industry of social consensus and of the production of harmony. Despite speaking a language that is largely foreign to the American ideal of rights and the tradition of dissent, the mediation industry has been fueled by the creations of university chairs and masters programs in vocational training and has led to numerous published volumes and organized conferences dedicated to this approach. The mediation industry offers to reasonable ("harmonious") persons a model of dispute resolution promoted for its capacity to reduce stress and save money. This rhetoric is powerful. The benefits of such a model are obvious and evident to everyone: Why create congestion in the courts, expend money and resources, and wait for years for adjudication on rights issues when there is a perfectly reasonable solution that is immediately at hand?

But the dangers of the mediation model in an individualistic culture such as that of the West are frightening.[18] Mediation is obligatory in many instances in the United States. If the parties do not accept mediation to settle their dispute, they may not have access to the courts. In family law cases, for example, the parties must try court-ordered professional mediation before they are given access to resolution within the court. This is true in a number of other different fields. The biggest risks of ADR as a model of decision making that structurally favors the strongest party or entity lie in the disparity in power between the husband and the wife, the boss and the worker, the corporation and the consumer, the weaker state and the more powerful state (as in international mediations on water disputes that grant jurisdiction to the International Court of Justice). If mediation fails to reach a settlement, the blame is placed on the party that caused the failed attempt by refusing an offer or discontinuing the mediation, demonstrating this party's irrationality, rather than on the party who originally violated the other party's rights. This is how blame gets attributed to the abused wife who does not succumb to mediation to settle a child-support or spousal-support case because she never wants to see the abusive husband again, the consumer who does not accept a settlement offered by a corporation, the worker who insists that his or her right that was violated be restored and respected, instead of accepting a "reasonable" compromise that quite possibly the boss and the trade union have agreed upon, and the weaker state that does not accept a border compromise.

Until the end of the 1970s, the ideal that everybody should have his or her day in court was pursued in Western cultures by means of expensive welfare programs. For example, free public defenders were provided to low-income defendants, and the state provided other forms of subsidies to increase access to justice. In Germany and Sweden, these services reached the maximum levels of civilization, but more or less effectively were pursued as an ideal everywhere.[19] The demise of the welfare state has produced a decline in the ideal of access to justice for all—the same fate that has happened to access to education, health care, and other services. The irresistible development of ADR thus must be understood in connection with the demise of the welfare state. Ideological hostility to the welfare state, first in the United States and then all over the world, coincides with a new, postmodern phenomenon. As a response to the access to justice problem, the ADR industry promised a huge saving in welfare funds. The access problem was to be solved by denying it exists, with the extra advantage that the nonconformist man or woman loses the right to have a court rule on their case and perhaps can be cured of their unreasonableness and dissent.

## DEVELOPMENT

Among the flexible terms, empty of a precise meaning but fuelled by uncritical positive connotations, "development" also deserves some comments. Like the notions of the rule of law and alternative dispute resolution, this concept occupies an important place in the ideological tool kit that supports predatory global capitalism. The variations that make the term "development" vague are historical and geographical and can best be traced by glancing at the transformations of the international financial institution that carries development in its social charter: the World Bank Group.

In 1944, in the famous context of the Bretton Woods agreements, the allied powers appeared to follow the enlightened (and later betrayed) advice of Lord Keynes in attempting to create a formula of international financial governance capable of stabilizing the world that they would inherit from imminent victory in World War II. In this framework, the International Bank of Reconstruction and Development (IBRD) was established. The IBRD was the first institution of the World Bank Group, and the term "development" is inscribed in its name and charter. As it is well known, in addition to the World Bank, the Bretton Woods agreements also gave life to the International Monetary Fund (IMF), an institution that sponsors development even for states that are already developed. The international political climate was already showing the beginnings of an extremely tense competition with the still-allied Soviet bloc, which explains, much more than the official historical account, even the U.S. bombing of Hiroshima as crucial for the capitalist bloc to obtain strategic positioning in the confrontation with the Soviet Union.[20]

"Development" remains in the chartered name of the second institution of the World Bank Group, the International Development Association (IDA), which in 1980, at the beginning of the decade that would "end" the Cold War, engaged in the practice of loaning money to the "poorest countries"—the poorest of the poor. The IDA attempts to produce a consensus, something that Antonio Gramsci teaches us is essential to any project of hegemony. At the same time, it institutionalized the Reagan-Thatcherian logic in which solidarity within the society must be circumscribed as much as possible.

For the entire phase of formal decolonization (1961, with its emancipation of seventeen African colonies, is known as the "Year of Africa"), which was surely one of the most important civilizing consequences of the Cold War, (the other being the development of the welfare state as a pacifying device within Western capitalism), the promise of development came to be utilized by both imperialist blocs to exercise renewed influence on the newly independent states that entered into the assembly of the sovereign nations. For desperately poor countries, left in dire poverty by the colonizers, (the French literally took the light bulbs from the African public offices with them), it was absolutely unavoidable to knock at the doors of the international financial institutions to obtain the indispensable liquidity to prevent immediate collapse. So the World Bank, with lower interest rates compared with those of private banks, basked in its glory for quite some time. The number of member states progressively grew until it reached its current 185, and the promise of development secured a fundamental role even in the politics of the new postcolonial leaderships—as much in the kleptocratic ones as in the respectable ones. Development truly became a "bipartisan" idea in the deepest sense of the term, even tempting leaders with the prestige of Jawaharlal Nehru in India, Julius Nyerere in Tanzania, and Fidel Castro and Che Guevara in Cuba.

It did not take a lot of time before the poor countries understood that they had placed themselves in the hands of a usurious international financial system. The double oil crisis of the 1970s filled the vaults of private banks with appalling quantities of petrodollars that were offered at first priority to the most corrupt elites of the Third Word at relatively low interest rates, bringing poor countries into ever-increasing indebtedness to finance their luxury-import economies, and the absurd standards of living of the urbanized ruling elites. For a time, a price increase in raw materials, which were produced in great part in poor countries, contributed to the mirage of development, a dream from which poor countries soon abruptly woke. By the mid-1980s, the project of development had to confront the sudden fall in the international prices of agricultural products and a rapid increase in interest rates due to the risk of default. It then became apparent that the indebtedness of poor countries had become unsustainable.

At that point, the Bretton Woods institutions took the gloves off and revealed the merciless capitalist reality hidden behind international organizations so prestigious as to be structurally connected to the United Nations. In reality, beyond posing as public-minded international organizations, the World Bank and the IMF display the governance model of a private corporation, in which whoever invests the most money is who commands and in which the short-term interests of shareholders dominate. It follows that, despite the presence in these organizations of numerous other member states, the reins of command are solidly in the hands of the United States and of the developed states that control a huge block of the votes. Exactly like a company that, in order to avoid default by its debtors, puts them under controlled administration, the international financial institutions in effect put the indebted states into receivership. In order to service their debt, they are forced to hand over their political sovereignty to the lenders. In Mali, for example, the office of the IMF is located in the same building as the Ministry of Economics. Structural Adjustment Plans (SAPs) are required for obtaining any other financing, whether from the World Bank, the IMF, or even the private sector.[21] The SAPs were grounded in the Reagan-era rhetoric according to which, if you see a man who is hungry, do not give him a fish but teach him how to fish— and loan him the rod.

Not surprisingly, all this ends up in the fundamental recipe for the privatization of the entire public sector so that it can be bought "at cost" by the global corporations. The structural adjustment of the economy consisted in fact of the simultaneous introduction of the following points. First, let markets freely determine prices while reducing or eliminating all state controls. Second, transfer all resources held by the state to the private sector. Third, reduce the budget of the state as much as possible. And fourth, reform the courts and the bureaucracy in such a way as to facilitate the development of the private sector. These four fundamental points are spelled out in the financing contracts in a series of detailed prescriptions that the assisted states must implement into law: the abolition of minimum wages, the abolition of food subsidies, the abolition of cost-reduction programs for housing rents, the reduction of work-safety standards and environmental standards, and the obligation to contract out public services such as transportation, education, health care, and pensions to the private sector.

Naturally, such an assault on the political and judicial sovereignty of the member states would not have been possible without the global process of depoliticizing the law that coincided with the end of the Cold War. To be sure, the separation of law from politics long has been a strategy for the legitimization of power in the West, perhaps the most defining element of our highly professionalized legal tradition. Nevertheless, a new level of sophistication in this strategy has been reached with the construction of law as a technology, a remarkable trait of the postmodern condition in the law. In fact, the intimate relationship between law and politics has been exposed by a variety of realist, sociological, and critical schools of thought originating in Germany, France, Italy, and the United States since the beginning of the twentieth century.[22] Consequently, for the entire period between Yalta and the fall of the Berlin Wall, intervention in Third World legal systems was taboo on the part of the World Bank and the IMF so as not to affect the delicate political equilibrium between the blocs. (It is still expressly forbidden by Article IV, section 10 of the constitutive agreement of the IBRD: "Political Activity Prohibited.") Only at the end of the 1980s, then increasingly aggressively until today, in the name of development and of law as a technology of governance capable of fostering it, did the World Bank and the IMF become legal-judicial (and therefore political) actors in the processes of globalization. The World Bank not only contractually bound the states to structural adjustments, but sponsored studies, conferences, projects, and research centers devoted to the law, development, and its legal-economic analysis, thus playing a pivotal role in the production of the thick ideology of technological progress that today dominates global discourse about the law. The abdication of political sovereignty on the part of the indebted state thus becomes a natural consequence of any "efficient" system of global governance that ostensibly serves the purpose of reconstructing the economy of a state, but that in fact allows its plunder by the global corporations that indirectly own the "owners" of the World Bank.[23] As anyone who does not wish to bury his or her head in the sand knows, the neoliberal prescriptions implemented in the name of development, in particular privatization, have produced and are producing terrible social disasters everywhere, not only on the periphery, but also in the center. These prescriptions mercilessly strike at the weakest and increase repression, often contracted out, in order to suffocate every last hope of revolt and every attempt at emancipation.[24]

Confronted since the Seattle protests of 1999 with widespread, rampant opposition to structural adjustment, the World Bank has revamped the old, never-suppressed, and well-tested development ideology, enriching the term "development" with the expression "sustainable" or "equitable." This is how SAPs became Comprehensive Development Frameworks (CDFs). Nevertheless, this has not changed in the least the simplistic vision of an evolutionary, unilinear, and necessary social progress based on technocratic legality whose "impact" is measurable in terms of the growth of the gross national product.[25] However, in subaltern contexts, the development ideology that seems very much to contaminate the discourses of all of our acclaimed technocrats, of our presentable politicians, and of our careerist and elitist academics begins to be frontally challenged by the first symptoms of a renewed awakening of the global conscience. In the words of Vincent Tucker, an African scholar:

> Development is the process whereby other peoples are dominated and their destinies are shaped according to an essentially Western way of conceiving and perceiving the world. The development discourse is part of an imperial process whereby other peoples are appropriated and turned into objects. It is an essential part of the process whereby the "developed" countries manage, control and even create the Third World economically, politically, sociologically and culturally. It is a process whereby the lives of some peoples, their plans, their hopes, their imaginations, are shaped by others who frequently share neither their lifestyles, nor their hopes, nor their values. The real nature of this process is disguised by a discourse that portrays development as a necessary and desirable process, as human destiny itself.[26]

The rhetoric of development today, like Frankenstein's creation, escapes the control of its creator. It alienates not only the "underdeveloped" states, but also "us." Transformed into a faithful ideology of the predatory logic of privatization and therefore intellectually sponsored, as in the rule of law or ADR, by the strong powers and by the corporate media, today, development is mere deeply bipartisan propaganda in the hands of the winners in the processes of global transformation. In its name, what triumphs is the hubris of the Tower of Babel, the delirium of omnipotence, a triumph of quantity over quality, a psychosis for which the saving of half an hour on a train trip justifies any and all environmental destruction. The rhetoric of development blindly drags us through the logic of the very short period, determined by corporate three-month reports to the shareholders, in which triumphs in the plunder and squandering of natural resources are not seen as destruction and waste, but as constant, desirable, necessary, and infinite growth and progress.[27]

## CONCLUSION

Civilization today does not need bipartisan institutional ideologies uncritically accepted as the only way to exit from an undesirable emergency, be it the lack of democracy and of the rule of law, the litigation explosion and alternative dispute resolution, or poverty and the deficit of development. Such emergencies are most often invented, and such bipartisan ideas hide projects of hegemony, subjugation, and the domination of weaker social actors within the attempt to lure them into these traps. They are functions of predatory capitalism. What civilization needs, on the contrary, is a return of critique and dissent, exactly the opposite of bipartisan agreement. What it needs is a cosmopolitan, highly revolutionary political program capable of recuperating the public sector, political sovereignty, the communal gathering of hope and resources, the quality of life as opposed to the quantity of material wealth, a more equitable size of the slices of the cake—maybe smaller, but tastier for everyone—and care for future generations, as opposed to the brutal selfishness of current individual materialism. If we are not able to succeed together to create this different world, our destiny will be to continue to work as consumers in shopping malls (for how long?), reassured by the trite formulas repeated by the corrupted, if not outright racist pundits,[28] constantly blaming on the victims their Western-produced underdevelopment. Very soon, but perhaps too late, we will wake up understanding the tragic consequences of our own moral underdevelopment. Perhaps it will then be too late to exit the only real emergency: the predatory assault on our planet.

## NOTES

1   On the spectacular aspects of legal capitalism, see Ugo Mattei, "A Theory of Imperial Law: A Study on U.S. Hegemony and the Latin Resistance," *Indiana Journal of Global Legal Studies* 10, no. 1 (2003), also published in *Global Jurist Frontiers* 3, no. 2 (2003), available on-line at http://www.bepress.com/gj/frontiers/vol3/iss2/art1/ (subscription required).

2   Niall Ferguson, *Empire: The Rise and Demise of the British World and the Lessons for Global Power* (New York: Basic Books, 2003).

3   Michael Hardt and Antonio Negri, *Empire* (Cambridge, MA: Harvard University Press, 2001).

4   Commission for Africa, *Our Common Interest: Report of the Commission for Africa* (New York: Penguin Books, 2005).

5   See "International Rule of Law Symposium," *Berkeley Journal of International Law* 25, no. 1 (2007).

6   See Ugo Mattei, "Foreign-Inspired Courts as Agencies of Peace in Troubled Societies," *Global Jurist Topics* 2, no. 1 (2002), available on-line at http://www.bepress.com/gj/topics/vol2/iss1/art1 (requires subscription).

7   A similar point is made in Nicolas Guilhot, *The Democracy Makers: Human Rights and International Order* (New York: Columbia University Press, 2005).

8   Naomi Klein, *The Shock Doctrine: The Rise of Disaster Capitalism* (New York: Metropolitan Books, 2007).

9   The term is borrowed from the classic Eric Wolf, *Europe and the People without History* (Berkeley: University of California Press, 1984).

10  In general on such accounts, see Teemu Ruskola, "Legal Orientalism," *Michigan Law Review* 101, no. 1 (October 2002): p. 179

11  See, in general, Laura Nader, *The Life of the Law: Anthropological Projects* (Berkeley: University of California Press, 2002).

12  See Marc Galanter, "The Day After the Litigation Explosion," *Maryland Law Review* 46, no. 3 (1986).

13  See Yves Dezalay and Bryant G. Garth, *Dealing in Virtue: International Commercial Arbitration and the Construction of a Transnational Legal Order* (Chicago: University of Chicago Press, 1996).

14  See Per Henrik Lindblom, "La risoluzione alternativa delle controversie: L' oppio del sistema giuridico?" in Vincenzo Varano (ed.), *L'Altra giustizia* (Milan: Giuffrè, 2007), p. 219.

15  Laura Nader, *Harmony Ideology: Justice and Control in a Zapotec Mountain Village* (Stanford, CA: Stanford University Press, 1990).

16  See Eric Feldman, *The Ritual of Rights in Japan* (Cambridge: Cambridge University Press, 2003).

17  See Ugo Mattei and Laura Nader, *Plunder*: When the Rule of Law Is Illegal (Hoboken, NJ: Blackwell, 2008).

18  See Elisabetta Grande, "Alternative Dispute Resolution, Africa and the Structure of Law and Power: The Horn in Context," *Journal of African Law* 43, no. 1 (1999): pp. 63–70.

19  See Ugo Mattei, "Access to Justice. A Renewed Global Issue?" in Katharina Boele Woelki and Sjef Van Erp (eds.), *General Reports of the XVII Congress of the International Academy of Comparative Law* (Brussels: Bruylant, 2007), pp. 383–408.

20  See Jacques R. Pauwels, *The Myth of the Good War* (Toronto: James Lorimer and Co., 2002).

21  See Giles Mohan, Ed Brown, Bob Milward, and Alfred B. Zack-Williams, *Structural Adjustment: Theory, Practice and Impacts* (London: Routledge, 2000).

22  See Duncan Kennedy, "Two Globalizations of Law and Legal Thought: 1850–1968," *Suffolk University Law Review* 36 (2003).

23  See Mattei and Nader, *Plunder*.

24  See Klein, *The Shock Doctrine*. For data on the growth of privatized repression, see Elisabetta Grande, *Il terzo strike: La prigione in America* (Palermo: Sellerio, 2007).

25  See Luca Pes, "Disciplinary Boundaries in Approaching African Development," *Global Jurist Advances* 7, no. 3, available on-line at http://www.bepress.com/gj/vol7/iss3/art6 (subscription required).

26  Vincent Tucker, "The Myth of Development: A Critique of Eurocentric Discourse," in Ronaldo Munck and Denis O'Hearne (eds.), *Critical Development Theory: Contributions to a New Paradigm* (London: Zed Books, 1999), p. 1. See also Serge Latouche, *Survivre au développement* (Paris: Mille et Une Nuits, 2004).

27  See Thomas Friedman, *The World is Flat: A Brief History of the Twenty-First Century* (New York: Farrar, Straus, and Giroux, 2005).

28  See Guy Debord, *Comments on the Society of the Spectacle*, trans. Malcolm Imrie (London: Verso Books, 1990).

# Utopias of Power: From Human Security to the Responsibility to Protect

Chowra Makaremi

> Recently, a new concept—human security—has received attention. This is a people-centered approach that is concerned not so much with weapons as with basic human dignity...human security includes safety from chronic threats such as hunger, disease, and repression, as well as protection from sudden and harmful disruptions in the patterns of daily life.
> —Ingvar Carlsson, Commission on Global Governance, *Our Global Neighbourhood*

In the last two decades, a normative frame has emerged that determines the approach to situations of state failure and that sets new priorities for intervention: a nonmilitary vision of security that displaces the processes of securitization into the social, economic, and physical environment—into "the patterns of daily life." The discourse of human security is a discourse of intervention that focuses on individuals and populations. But it also applies to a set of techniques and a program of action implying various actors, state, international, private, and civil society, and several fields of activity, from military-humanitarian interventions to the negotiation of international treaties. Originating in the world of practitioners and international institutions in the mid-1990s, the idea and definitions of human security have been explored in well-funded research programs and by an academic community of policy advisors for agencies and states.[1] However, social-science researchers who are not engaged in these networks of global governance seem unconcerned by and even ambivalent toward the blooming of the paradigm. Although for a long time now the idea of human security has interested only those convinced by its mandate, the large amount of writings and international programs dedicated to human security make it a rich source of analysis. Why, for example, is there a reformulation of needs and rights in terms of security? How can we (re)think the political relation that is at the heart of any process of securitization? How do human security projects frame techniques of population management in situations of emergencies? How does the redefinition of security and emergency play within existing power relations at stake in situations of foreign interventions?

Despite the earlier lack of concern, for the last few years, critical studies have been exploring the ethico-political shift that is building new paradigms of action in the post–World War world.[2] In what follows, I will examine the genesis of this concept of human security and its development within institutions as attempts to redefine security have shifted from the idea of "human development" originally concerned with "basic needs" to norms and techniques of humanitarian actions, military doctrines, and, finally, the legalization of interventions in the name of a "responsibility to protect." While acclaimed as a demilitarized approach to security, the concept of human security has been remilitarized in humanitarian interventions, promoting notions of emergency and safety as moral grounds for political action. This legacy introduces the idea of human security as a practice of government in response to the narrative of global chaos.

## SECURITIZING THE PATTERNS OF DAILY LIFE

Since the 1990s, questions of environment, identity, crime, and welfare have been reframed in terms of "security."[3] A turning point in this process was the introduction of a new word in the 1994 *Human Development Report*, redefining security as "humane" and broadening the use of the concept from exclusive military threats to economic, social, and environmental threats. Promoted by economists Amartya Sen and Mahbub ul Haq, the report is an annual evaluation chronicling the overall world progress as well as state-by-state situations of "human development" since 1990 within the UN Development Programme. The inventor of the paradigm, Mahbub ul Haq, insisted that "the emerging concept of human security forces a new morality on all of us through a perception of common threats to our very survival."[4] Why did the redefinition of security originate in an institution of economic development—and a peripheral agency, at that,[5] and how did this new concept of global security originate within the project of "developing humans"?[6]

The answer is that the concept of human security began as a rhetorical, strategic promotion of development approaches through the process of securitization. Securitization takes place when an "issue is presented as an existential threat,"[7] that is, as an emergency. Conversely, attempts by policy makers and analysts to label a problem as a security issue necessarily require a political strategy that "frames the issue either as a special kind of politics or above politics," a strategy "requiring emergency measures and justifying actions outside the normal bounds of political procedure."[8] Those who theorize these mechanisms seem critical of an actual broadening of security issues, arguing that it is not advisable to think in terms of securitization in various fields and at various levels of socioeconomic life, since this strategy indeed suspends the normal processes of politics.[9] However, those concerned with human development see securitization not as an issue of politics and the suspension of normal political procedures, but as an issue of socioeconomic engineering and measurement.

The index of such a measurement appears in a report coordinated by the UN Development Programme: the Human Development Index. This development-centered ranking of the wealth of nations is intended to replace the gross domestic product as a measure of economic achievement by a combination of wealth and new indexes quantifying the "qualities of life" of the population—life expectancy at birth and the literacy rate.[10] The "agreeable fact that these determinants of a person's good *are* measurable and comparable...irrespective of what a person's conception of her good happens to be,"[11] and the claim that once measured, they can be maximized and secured, made possible not just new approaches to universal, human, development, but a new concept of human security. The universal threats that define the new paradigm of security are "hunger, disease, and repression," building a continuum between decontextualized biological and political dimensions that together establish the patterns of daily life. Behind these new approaches lies the long-standing dream of liberal political economy: to secure life, choices, and opportunities, through an adequate management of risks and contingencies.[12] This new ethical objectivism, based on indexes and figures, naturalizes what until then was contained within the political sphere. It then frees the notion of securitization from the political questions involved in the exercise of power, and ultimately, the exercise of force. The previous system had delimited the instrumental use of security to a circle of political decision makers, the military, paramilitary organizations, the police, militias, and so on. From a risk-management perspective, this ambiguous reversal in the use and connotation of security sees power relations and social formations as other forces that—whether successfully or inadequately mastered—can determine life or death. As the following Borges-like definition puts it: "In the final analysis, human security is a child who did not die, a disease that did not spread, a job that was not cut, an ethnic tension that did not explode in violence, a dissident who was not silenced."[13]

Translated into actions and projects, however, this concept of human security has resulted in imperatives of protection, care, and emergency. In practice, over the last decade, the project of "developing humans" has supported the normalization of interventions and opened the floor to a new doctrine of interventionism in the UN Security Council.

## "FREEDOM FROM WANT" AND, FOREMOST, "FREEDOM FROM FEAR"

The Plenary Meeting of the United Nations General Assembly on September 15, 2005, declared: "We recognize that all individuals, in particular vulnerable people, are entitled to freedom from fear and freedom from want, with an equal opportunity to enjoy all their rights and fully develop their human potential. To this end, we commit ourselves to discussing and defining the notion of human security in the General Assembly."[14]

The complex expressions "freedom from fear" and "freedom from want," which mix ideas of rights, law, and emotions, mobilizing a universal theory of human agency, come from the "four essential freedoms" enumerated by President Franklin D. Roosevelt in the State of the Union Address he delivered on January 6, 1941 to convince the Congress to commit the country to entry into World War II.[15] The context was a political analysis of world dangers:

> Armed defense of democratic existence is now being gallantly waged in four continents. If that defense fails, all the population and all the resources of Europe and Asia, Africa and Australia will be dominated by conquerors. And let us remember that the total of those populations in those four continents, the total of those populations and their resources greatly exceeds the sum total of the population and the resources of the whole of the Western Hemisphere—yes, many times over.[16]

This reformulation of the world situation acknowledges the extraordinary amount of alien (non-Western) populations and resources as the shifting battlefront of international relations. The introduction of these two new freedoms also assumes a project of emancipation from those "universal" emotions, fear and want, considered as the catalysts of political disorders and orders.[17] Introduced into the preamble of the 1948 UN Declaration of Human Rights, freedom from fear and freedom from want have become the aim of the new paradigm of human security, which is used to manage violence through intervention in the post–Cold-War era—a continuation of the moralized, view of peace by war that characterized Roosevelt's original use of the term.

Of the two, it appears that a concern for achieving freedom from fear is prevailing as the notion of human security evolves. Following the rupture of several states in civil conflicts and the defeat of UN-led humanitarian interventions in Somalia, after difficulties in Bosnia, and failure in Rwanda, the context of the late 1990s marked the narrowing of human security from holistic and development programs to a concern for safety and protection from violence. While UN police operations stumbled (the interventionist being treated as another party to decentralized conflicts), principles of human security were reinvested in an effort to conceptualize a discursive and operational apparatus of civil-military intervention.[18] In the UN arena, the idea prevailed that a reform should "allow the Security Council to authorize action in situations within countries, but only if the security of people is so severely violated as to require an international response on humanitarian grounds."[19] At the same time, state powers such as Japan, Norway, Canada, and, more recently, the European Union, became interested in human security as a possible program of foreign policy. It may seem contradictory that states would support a people-centered redefinition of security. The notion, however, turned out to be a useful and flexible tool to manage new conditions of sovereignty in the global context.

Canada, particularly, and the then minister of foreign affairs, Lloyd Axworthy, constantly advocated in favor of the concept of human security throughout his mandate as a nonpermanent member and president of the UN Security Council, which, at that time, adopted several resolutions on the protection of civilians and vulnerable groups during armed conflicts.[20] Following that, the Canadian minister of foreign affairs took the lead in negotiating an international agreement for banning land mines. After the initial failure of this project at the UN, a "coalition of like-minded" states,[21] supported by the lobbying and counsel of powerful Western NGOs, negotiated the 1997 Convention on the Prohibition of the Use, Stockpiling, Production and Transfer of Anti-Personnel Mines and on Their Destruction. "The Ottawa Convention," as it is called, has been praised and offered as an example of the application of a human-security "global agenda."[22] The banning of land mines is an exemplary human-security project, "providing an alternative source of security to that associated with geopolitics"[23] in an international agreement to eradicate threatening weapons—an agreement that substantial land-mine producers such as the United States refused to sign.

The Ottawa Convention is exemplary in that it avoids engagement with the issues of war and conflict themselves, but still focuses on warfare. It is concerned with the effects of a weapon on individuals—civilians. Its concern for land-mine injuries is a paradigmatic case of the human-security approach, focusing on the long-term and human-dimension of the effects of conflicts on populations—how wars deprive individuals of a part of their vital or core being and how this deprivation disables people. Moreover, the unforeseen, accidental nature of land-mine injuries and their relationship to everyday activities and places (cultivating fields, traveling, playing around the house) give an idea of what insecurity may mean at the level of daily life. Thus, land-mine injuries dramatically illustrate how people need to be secured in their basic, physical integrity so that their daily lives also remain intact.

The shift in favor of freedom from fear brings two consequences when applied: a temporal frame of action focused on emergencies and on the present, and a spatial frame focused on physical integrity. This instrumental use radically changed the meaning of the notion of human security as it was being largely diffused in policy papers and agendas. Specifically, it absorbed the original, development approach into the conceptual framework of human security. The definition of human security as physical safety was strengthened and put forward as a practical line of action that could be taken by states. In a policy statement by then minister of foreign affairs, Lloyd Axworthy, entitled *Human Security: Safety for People in a Changing World*, Canada thus proposed to make "safety for people" the principal object of its statecraft.[24] In the same vein, he advocated "grounding the human security agenda in sound fact—for example, knowledge of the pathology of small weapons, the health impact of conflicts, etc."[25] Later, the call for a doctrine of human security in the European Union would build on this narrow definition of safety, as opposed to vague, holistic, and development-oriented approaches. In 2005, the Barcelona Study Group, a collection group of influential academics and experts commissioned to develop a common policy on foreign and military affairs for the EU proposed what was called the Human Security Doctrine for Europe. The project relied on an operational definition of human security based on the "identification of a narrower core of human security threats." "Genocide, large-scale torture, inhuman and degrading treatment, disappearances, slavery, crimes against humanity and war crimes...come under this category. Violations of the right to food, health and housing, even grave and massive ones, are not commonly recognized as belonging to this category, although some authors would make a case for these as 'survival rights.'" Instead, it claimed, "a narrower category of situations that become intolerably insecure, as outlined above, could be one of the criteria for deciding to deploy operational capacities."[26]

The focus on safety as protection against an all-encompassing idea of violence redefines the subject of security through mechanisms of abstraction and decontextualization. This, however, does not entail a shift between generous ideas and the necessity for focused action in the name of efficiency. Since the modern origins of the concept of human security, indeed, mechanisms of abstraction have been at play, be they UN Development Programme's "thresholds" of destitution or the UN's normative protection of vulnerable "categories of humanity."[27] The EU conception of human security, however, goes one step further by abstracting from the concept of security "food, health, and housing"—the concrete elements of the pattern of daily life that was the raison d'être of the original paradigm shift to the focus on human security within the UN Development Programme—in favor of protection from violence and "freedom from fear." Building on the tradition that it leaves out, the narrowing process contrasts life in its vital functions and the social life of individuals, choosing to focus on the former. The threshold process opens the path to a separation between a bodily person (the "core" of our being, in human security literature) and the everyday life of the body—a peripheral life that is now excluded from the scope of protection.

The definition of human security as freedom from fear leads precisely to defining "a narrower category of situations that become intolerably insecure" as "one of the criteria for deciding to deploy operational capacities."[28] From Roosevelt, to the Barcelona Study Group, to Axworthy, the freedom-from-fear approach has rested on an ambiguity. On the one hand is a pacifist call for "a world-wide reduction of armaments to such a point and in such a thorough fashion that no nation will be in a position to commit an act of physical aggression."[29] The Ottawa process for banning land mines and Axworthy's engagement for the reduction of small arms follow this emphasis on disarmament.[30] Mary Kaldor, the head of the Barcelona Study Group, was also a founding member of European Nuclear Disarmament and author of the first statistics on the arms trade at the Stockholm International Peace Research Institute.[31] However, on the other hand, until world disarmament happens, the duty of those who call for reducing and eradicating weapons is said to be to use them appropriately through "military intervention for human protection purposes."[32] This expression means that humanitarian intervention involves the use of military force to provide assistance to people whose political, economic, and social conditions are untenable. This ambiguity in the concept of the freedom from fear reverses the paradigm of security that was first defined by its nonmilitary focus and emphasis on demilitarization and converts it into a redefinition of security achieved by military means.

This remilitarization of humanitarian ethics and standards of securing lives carries with it a wide range of private and civil-society actors, mechanisms of subcontracting, and norm-building processes that affect populations worldwide. It has therefore reconfigured the conditions of possibility of state sovereignty in the context of globalization. Celebrating a global approach to human security, indeed, is not antithetical to patriotic values, as Axworthy shows: "We have never been more self-confident about our place in the world.... This is perhaps because the human security agenda is one that promotes Canadian interests while projecting Canadian values."[33] However, the discourse of human security, with its rhetoric of a world in disorder and its valorization of the protection of human life by military interventions, if necessary, erodes the concept of state sovereignty in the name of enforcing humanitarian standards of safety wherever necessary. As the last decade and more in Kosovo have shown,[34] the concept of human security puts into question norms of sovereignty and reopens a wide range of possibilities in the political organization of populations and lands, from occupied territories to independent states, by means of several forms of tutelage and presence, be they military or not, legal or not.

## THE HUMAN SECURITY NETWORK

Since 2000, the concept of human security had framed a "foreign policy ethics" for Western democracies that are evaluating "how to restore the usefulness of their armed forces in a world redefined by the United States over the skies [sic] of Kosovo and Afghanistan."[35] Particularly, Canada, as well as the European Union, have embodied the institutional concept in coordinated humanitarian and military operations in areas defined by emergencies. More than a mere ethical slogan for interventionist foreign policies, the paradigm has been based on two principal ideas: first, a globalized vision of security in which the safety of the populations of others and their resources is the guarantee of one's own national security and consequently the management of global disorder as a goal of national self-interest.

The idea of justifying one's concern for the security of others in this way acquired a new dimension after September 11, 2001 and the reconfiguration of security discourses. "The whole point of a human security approach is that Europeans cannot be secure while others in the world live in severe insecurity. National borders are no longer the dividing line between security and insecurity: insecurity gets exported," Marlies Glasius and Mary Kaldor declare.[36] The case of post-2001 Afghanistan sheds a light on this globalization of the idea of national security. After 2001, analysts and scholars put forward the idea that the Taliban is the product of the camps established by the UN High Commissioner for Refugees for Afghans in Pakistan.[37] Adherents to the Taliban, it was argued, are mainly produced by an incomplete humanitarian management of the forced displacements of the last decades. Their individual and physical insecurity, their poverty, the destruction of social frameworks, and the lack of psychological care made them a threat to regional and global security.[38] The call for humanitarian action brought together concern for the care of victims and a traditional security approach to conflicts around the idea of a win-win situation: The securitization of the victims' basic needs is also the guarantee of the security of Western states.[39] Humanitarian intervention, as a political process, thus becomes a pact of security anchored in the bodies of aid beneficiaries. Indeed, the 1994 *Human Development Report* organizes the paradigm of human security in seven dimensions of security—environmental, economic, political, community, personal, sanitary, alimentary—in an onionlike structure, drawing layers of security inward towards the individuals who are supposed to anchor the process.

The "merging of development and security,"[40] as Mark Duffield calls it, introduces a broader, globalized view of human security, while development programs are integrated within the programs of humanitarian intervention, including projects such as demining, converting poppy cultivation into "the cultivation of legal" crops, and "reconstructing" the area of Kandahar.[41] In undertaking these programs, the Canadian International Development Agency Program—the first of the aid donors in Afghanistan—has lost the relative autonomy it used to have in terms of its development agenda.[42] Since 2001, development, indeed, became one of the three pillars of the government of Canada's "integrated intervention" in Afghanistan, labeled as "Protecting Canadians: Rebuilding Afghanistan."[43] In fact, because of the situation in the field, the Canadian International Development Agency mainly financed humanitarian aid, distributed by Canadian soldiers in an attempt to "win hearts and minds." Populations in need of care and control thus stand at the core of the security network. This apparatus translates all dimensions of life in terms of security and, at the same time, fuses together issues of development, the military, and humanitarian assistance in one and the same process, phrased in terms of human security.

The process of redefining our ideas of war and peace in this way and of bringing about new configurations of life in the name of human security has developed as an answer to how Western democracies should address the threat of global disorder that is bursting existing frameworks such as traditional ideological oppositions, existing assumptions about the conduct of wars, established international agreements on the conduct of hostilities, and so on.[44] In the last decade, Mary Kaldor has become one of the most acclaimed theorists of "new wars" understood in this way.[45] She has argued, in particular, that since the end of the Cold War, there has been a reconfiguration of warfare—and more broadly, a reconfiguration of the relationship between violence and the political. While analyzing the politics of wars and the "globalized war economy" using the examples of Bosnia-Herzegovia and Nagorny-Karabakh in the Caucasus, Kaldor echoes other analysts of conflict management in pointing out the "ruptures" in the modes and forms of violence.[46] Despite disagreements and differences in nuance, such analysts commonly share the vision of incipient chaos and the causal assumptions illustrated by Robert D. Kaplan's colorful title in an article published in the *Atlantic Monthly*: "The Coming Anarchy: How Scarcity, Crime, Overpopulation, Tribalism and Disease Are Rapidly Destroying the Fabric of Our Planet."[47] The disorder occurring in several parts of the world is said to be marked by an economy of war based on pillage and by an "extreme" form of globalization: translational, informal, illegal networks, remittances, and the diversion of humanitarian aid. "The new type of warfare is a predatory social condition," Kaldor writes in *New and Old Wars*,[48] that not only damages the zones of conflict, but also contaminates neighboring areas, spreading refugees, identity-based politics, and trafficking. It creates "bad neighborhoods," clusters of disorders in world society and the global economy, such as the Balkans, Caucasus, the Horn of Africa, and the Middle East. The human-security doctrine will build on this idea while referring to conflicts as 'black holes' generating many of the new sources of insecurity…that spread across borders and are increasingly difficult to contain."[49] The new wars are said to be marked by two forms of violence: the genocidal violence of states adopting exclusive, ethnic definitions of national belonging and citizenship and a free, generalized violence derived—at best—from older forms of identity politics. This quite unintelligible violence is marked by anomie, as well as by a withdrawal of violence from the political realm to reappear elsewhere, in apolitical forms of violence—Kaldor's core argument. Another important result of such disorder is a change in warfare, which becomes unrestrained, technologically archaic, and barbaric.[50] In the end, like many analysts of "global chaos," Kaldor advocates a "civilizing process" of cosmopolitan law enforcement (that is, an international law for individuals) and, finally, the use of force that resembles that employed by the police.

This way of thinking posits the idea of human security as a practice of government in response to the discourse of global chaos. It follows that such a response is not about instituting order, but about *Managing Global Chaos*, as the title of a book by Chester C. Crocker and Fen O. Hampson forthrightly puts it.[51] Within these perspectives, the shift from political order to the management of disorder becomes a shift in the technology of government, a shift advocated as a way to cope with "new wars" and to gain control over "moving power systems."[52] Evolving modes of intervention under the banner of human security have come to depend on the notion of policing violence.

## POLICING VIOLENCE AS A TECHNIQUE OF GOVERNMENT

In the last several years, Canadian peace operations, that is, operations undertaken under a UN peacekeeping mandate or within a—usually NATO-led—"coalition of the willing," have deployed police officers in addition to traditional military forces, a policy for which Canada claims "leadership."[53] The use of police as peacekeepers in war-torn areas illuminates how the securitization process is imagined under the paradigm of human security. It defines intervention as a combination of several strategies: the coercive exercise of force ("executive policing"), the humanitarian securitization of lives ("assisting aid and humanitarian assistance"), the normalization of social relationships, by a "neutral" third party ("monitoring and investigation of human rights violations"), and the normative implementation of political organization ("institutional capacity building," lending "support to electoral process," "security sector reform").[54] The model inspired the EU Human Security Doctrine, which sought new practices of intervention to address the principal issue in the use of force: the "dangerous disjunction between traditional security instruments and actual security needs."[55] The report thus proposed a "Human Security Response Force," composed of fifteen thousand men and women, of whom at least one-third would be civilian (police, human rights monitors, development and humanitarian specialists, administrators, and so on). The force would be drawn from troops and civilians already made available by member states as well as a proposed Human Security Volunteer Service composed of volunteer students and personnel from NGOs, and private corporations.[56] Intervention in the name of human security thus merges military and civilian agents, with the focus of the intervention being the government of populations. In this sense, it confirms what already is taking place in the management of zones of disorder: the coengagement of international and state-based public forces and elements of the private sector—be they NGOs, experts working on short-term contracts, private military companies, or private security companies—through mechanisms of funding, subcontracting, and lobbying.[57] In the Canadian military-development program in Afghanistan, for instance, the state development agency finances a large number of private NGOs and is a donor to international agencies for humanitarian relief.[58] At the same time, the military subcontracts with private companies to provide security, logistics, and training for the Afghan administration and police forces.[59] The rise of this private-public and civilian-military complex marks the emergence of new modes of warfare—another version of Kaldor's new wars—that fit the rationale of global governance.[60] The human-security doctrine solidifies and gives a frame to ad hoc practices of population management inherited from the evolution of capitalist economics and public policies in the West.

The emphasis on humanitarian ethics and concern for the survival of populations reconfigure the strategies of crisis management as a technique of government. The issue now facing human-security intervention is how to adapt the use of force to a situation where lives matter. The imposition of control has to target forms of political violence expressed in terms of systems of flows, decentralization, and the blurring of the difference between civilians and combatants, all while not being "very destructive" in terms of human lives.[61] This operates in a specific economy of power, one that valorizes sparing both the use of force and the taking of lives by trying to control and influence actions in a more intimate way.

In the end, the idea of policing violence focuses on flows: Securitization is concerned with deactivating the dangerous movement effects that break out from zones of insecurity.[62] A multiplicity of dangerous situations and potential threats takes the place of concrete risks and namable foes. This reconfiguration implies the need for police activity and efforts to monitor uncontrolled movements spreading from "black holes" and "bad neighborhoods." For example, Canada is a frequent "safe third country" of destination for Haitians leaving Haiti, and it welcomes a large migrant community from this country. Not surprisingly, then, Haiti is the main receiver of Canadian International Development Agency Program development programs after Afghanistan. These programs are oriented toward good governance, fighting corruption, and restoring the rule of law—although one may argue that the economic, agrarian, and environmental situation in Haiti should require more development-oriented aid policies. However, Canadian International Development Agency Program programs are said to be part of an "integrated approach,"[63] and they coordinate with the interventions of the Canadian police (the National Defense and the Royal Canadian Mounted Police) within the frame of the UN Stabilization Mission.[64]

## LEGALIZING AND LEGITIMATING INTERVENTIONS

This humanitarian interventionism is now undergoing a process of legalization within the UN Security Council in the name of the "responsibility to protect."[65] UN Security Council Resolution 1674, passed in April 2006, is a final segment of the curve in the impressive trajectory of the development of the concept of human security in the last decades, from the peripheral UN Development Programme to the very core of the UN institution. The resolution definitively associates the concept of human security with the humanitarian norm of action. By means of the Human Development Index, the idea of human security is derived from the constitution, or rather the recognition, of the global human population as a subject of knowledge and biopower. This initial shift toward population(s) as the means and end of government is what initiates a redefinition of interventions and their justification within the legacy of the human security concept, reframed via the indefinite and polysemic idea of "responsibility." The overall argument follows former Secretary-General Annan's reflection on sovereignty and intervention:[66] The sovereignty of states and their legitimacy to be granted sovereignty in a "collective security" system is rooted in their responsibility to their populations: the state now is the "servant of its people, and not vice versa."[67] If states do not prove responsible to their population, that is, if they fail to provide for their human security,[68] then the "international community" has the responsibility to free this population from its irresponsible governors through an intervention. As the title of one of Annan's books, *We the Peoples: The Role of the United Nations in the*

*21st Century*, shows, the argument of responsibility takes root in the shift toward a "people-centered" paradigm of government. As Michel Foucault noted, in this paradigm, with "the emergence of the problematic of population…population will appear above all as the final end of government. What can the end of government be? Certainly not just to govern, but to improve the condition of the population, to increase its wealth, its longevity, and its health."[69]

While legitimating interventions, the project of human security also made their legalization technically possible. Security Council Resolution 1674 is put into practice by including the threat to civilians in a conflict as a "threat to collective security" under Chapter VII of the UN Charter: threats under Chapter VII of the charter authorize the use of force.[70] The inclusion of "civilians and protected persons" in the scope of "international peace and security" is in fact the outcome of a number of resolutions during the last decade in favor of specific groups within several conflicts.[71] They refer, indeed, to one of the programs of human security: seeking protection for "vulnerable" categories of people.[72]

While achieving collective security has been the founding narrative of world society since 1945, human security is nonetheless changing this narrative in such a way that some agents remain, while new ones appear and others disappear. The concept of a responsibility to protect is an answer to and redefinition of the "right of humanitarian intervention" that emerged in the 1990s with a humanistic vision of humanitarian action. The history of the norm is charged with a legal utopianism: the aspiration to transcend governments in the name of the common good of humanity.[73] In the field, however, this state of mind encounters the actions and goals of military interventionists and the organization of new humanitarian-military apparatuses. Far from norm building and the legal debates, the apparatuses of humanitarian intervention open a space where the concrete consequences of the discourse of human security develop, as the Canadian programs in Afghanistan show. As the responsibility to protect, the doctrine of human security reemerges on the path opened up by the security machineries in operation for more than a decade. In the case of interventions, the development of a technical and strategic apparatus in the name of human security has been a turning point, activating in return an institutional process of legalization. In the process, the humanitarian imaginary and the passionate discourses of the "duty to intervene" have been lost.

## CONCLUSION

The development of the concept of human security leads from offices dedicated to development and the elimination of poverty to the core of the power and the central Security Council. Laid out in programs and speeches, its itinerary is entangled with utopianism. The demilitarized, people-centered idea of security was first proposed as a "practical utopianism."[74] The founding fathers of the concept of human security within the human development school then led the battle for what was labeled a New International Economic Order in the 1970s.[75] The "right to intervene" also was built on the short-lived utopian vision of creating "humanitarian corridors" that would serve the good of the people above the interests of the states. Finally, doctrinal attempts to bridge the gap between legality, legitimacy, and the idea of responsibility turned to the Enlightenment's cosmopolitan perspective on governance and its unified history of humankind:[76] "Basically, it is the cosmopolitan alternative, but [we] thought the term rather intellectual, hence 'human security,'" Mary Kaldor and Alan Johnson write in *New Wars and Human Security*,[77] and the utopianism of the notion is a rather ambiguous one. This ambiguity, however, may be what makes the difference between a totalizing ideology, and the "open," "invisible" ideology that is human security as a horizon of thought printed "in our heads."[78]

That perspective on governance can be seen in a little-known treatise published by Émeric Crucé in 1623, *Le nouveau Cynée, ou discours d'état*. Before the Peace of Westphalia in 1648 imposed its own solution in the form of the modern nation-state, Crucé dreamed of an alternative to wars and violence. Building precociously on the idea of united humanity ("Distant places and separated houses do not weaken the sameness of blood"),[79] Crucé conceived peace not as the mere absence of war, but as a positive program based on freedom of movement and commerce, concerned with feeding the poor, regulating systems of justice, and stabilizing currencies. This ideal would be achieved through an early version of the modern United Nations, a permanent international council in the city of Venice under the collegial direction of monarchs from all religions and all civilizations. This universal vision of humanity, however, excluded "cannibals and savages," whom Crucé proposed to offer as a target to military men so as to divert them from war among themselves. Today's "cosmopolitan alternative" strangely echoes this ambiguous utopia by stating that "armies which were originally maintained for the defense of borders have been used for peace-keeping operations outside, and sometimes far away from, those borders." These are seen as "somehow relevant and useful operations, whether to serve humanitarian goals or to keep the armed forces fit."[80] This vision of "far away" violence also recalls the controversial statement of the barbaric nature of the "new wars," their archaism, and their irrational explosions of violence, conceived as *anomia* and as a withdrawal from the political.

The contemporary "zoning" of humanitarian emergencies and states of violence—the identification of conflict zones, safe humanitarian zones, International Zones—recaptures the ambiguity of the concept of human security in political actuality through a multilevel process of securitization. On the one hand, it implies narratives of global chaos and consequently mechanisms of management through military and humanitarian interventions. On the other, it involves techniques of care and the engineering of minimum standards for the survival of populations.[81] These build on mechanisms of separation at different levels and the threshold and onion-shaped definition of individuals as those whose "core" needs to be secured. While being put forward as a doctrine, a paradigm, or a buzzword, "human security" is the point of conjunction of these practices. It is a "strategical thinking of crises,"[82] anchored in the safety of an "individual" who is the empty place of the political subject. While presenting the world both as an integrated globe and as a space pierced by zones and "black holes" of chaos, the concept of human security engages power relations in a complex play of inclusion and exclusion in which the greatest difficulty remains to think what is outside. This may relate to the "inclusive," "centrifugal" dimension of security mechanisms,[83] which work in terms of regulation and circulation. Or else it may lie in the genesis of the program itself: In 1947, Theodor Adorno and Max Horkheimer used the idea of "freedom from fear" to name "the project of modernity," as they phrased it:[84] "Man imagines himself free from fear when there is no longer anything unknown. That determines the course [of] enlightenment.... Nothing at all may remain outside, because the mere idea of outsideness is the very source of fear."

## NOTES

1   Among these research programs are the Program on Humanitarian Policy and Conflict Research at the Harvard School of Public Health, the Centre for Research on Inequality, Human Security and Ethnicity at Oxford University, and the Canadian Consortium on Human Security (CCHS) based at the University of British Columbia.

2   See especially the studies of Mark Duffield on Western interventionists' practices and the merging of security and development as a new regime of government: Mark R. Duffield, *Global Governance and the New Wars: The Merging of Development and Security* (London: Zed Books, 2001), and "Securing Humans in a Dangerous World," *International Politics* 43, no. 1 (February 2006): pp. 1–23. See also Michael Dillon and Julian Reid, "Global Liberal Governance: Biopolitics, Security and War," *Millennium: Journal of International Studies* 30, no. 1 (2001): pp. 41–66; Vivienne Jabri, "War, Security and the Liberal State," *Security Dialogue* 37, no. 1 (2006): pp. 47–64.

3   Kenneth Booth, "Security in Anarchy: Utopian Realism in Theory and Practice," *International Affairs* 67, no. 3 (1991): pp. 527–45; Barry Buzan, *People, States and Fear: An Agenda for International Security Studies in the Post–Cold War Era*, 2nd ed. (London: Longmans, 1991).

4    Mahbub ul Haq, *Reflections on Human Development: How the Focus of Development Econom-ics Shifted From National Income Accounting to People-Centered Policies, Told by One of the Chief Architects of the New Paradigm* (New York: Oxford University Press, 1995), p. 116.

5    The United Nations Development Programme belongs to UN "programs and funds," which are third-rank institutional agencies working under "principal organs" such as the Security Council and "specialized institutions" such as the Criminal Penal Court. It directly depends on the General Assembly and the Economic and Social Council, which, since the end of the Cold War, have been less influential in the UN decision-making process, where the Security Council prevails. And the United Nations Development Programme is concerned with devel-opment, a field that has become marginal since the failure of the political and economic aspi-rations of the Third World countries in the late 1970s, giving way, in the last two last decades, to a logics of security upheld by the Security Council.

6    Mark R. Duffield, "Getting Savages to Fight Barbarians: Development, Security and the Colo-nial Present," *Conflict, Security & Development* 5, no. 2 (2005). pp. 141–59.

7    Barry Buzan, Ole Waever, and Jaap de Wilde, *Security: A New Framework for Analysis* (Boul-der, CO: Lynne Rienner, 1998), p. 23.

8    *Ibid.*, pp. 23–24.

9    Ole Waever, "Securitization and Desecuritization," in Ronnie L. Lipschutz (ed.), *On Security* (New York: Columbia University Press, 1995), pp. 46–87.

10   Ul Haq, *Reflections on Human Development*.

11   Partha Dasgupta, *An Inquiry into Well-Being and Destitution* (Oxford: Clarendon Press, 1993), p. 6.

12   Michel Foucault, *Security, Territory, Population: Lectures at the Collège de France, 1977–1978*, ed. Michel Senellart, trans. Graham Burchell (New York: Picador, 2009).

13   United Nations Development Programme, "New Dimensions of Human Security," *Human Development Report 1994* (New York: Oxford University Press, 1994), p. 22.

14   United Nations, "Resolution Adopted by the General Assembly: 2005 World Summit Out-come," A/RES60/1, para. 143, available on-line at http://www.unglobalcompact.org/docs/about_the_gc/government_support/A-RES-60-1_.pdf (last accessed June 14, 2009).

15   "The third is freedom from want, which, translated into world terms, means economic under-standings which will secure to every nation a healthy peacetime life for its inhabitants—everywhere in the world. The fourth is freedom from fear, which, translated into world terms, means a world-wide reduction of armaments to such a point and in such a thorough fashion that no nation will be in a position to commit an act of physical aggression against any neigh-bor—anywhere in the world." Franklin D. Roosevelt, "The Four Freedoms," Address to Con-gress January 6, 1941, *Congressional Record* 87, pt. 1, pp. 44–47.

16   *Ibid.*

17   Thomas Hobbes's *Leviathan* (1651) is famous for its account of fear and envy. In order to achieve political tranquility, humans replace fear of each other with fear of the state. "Fear stabilizes subjectivity and this makes the Commonwealth possible," as William Sokol-off puts it in "Politics and Anxiety in Thomas Hobbes's Leviathan," *Theory & Event* 5, no. 1 (2001), available on-line at http://muse.jhu.edu/login?uri=/journals/theory_and_event/v005/5.1sokoloff.html (last accessed October 12, 2009). The political function of these emo-tions is also central to Kant's idea of "unsocial sociability." For Kant, the inclination to fear and to want is a catalyst of political societies and therefore the condition of progress:

"Thanks be to Nature, then, for the incompatibility, for heartless competitive vanity, for the insatiable desire to possess and to rule! Without them, all the excellent natural capacities of humanity would forever sleep, undeveloped." Immanuel Kant, "Idea for a Universal History from a Cosmopolitan Point of View" (1784), in Immanuel Kant, *On History*, ed. Lewis White Beck, trans. Lewis White Beck, Robert E. Anchor, and Emil L. Fackenheim (Indianapolis: Bobbs-Merrill, 1963), pp. 11–26.

18    Boutros Boutros-Ghali, *An Agenda for Peace: Preventive Diplomacy, Peacemaking and Peace-keeping* (New York: United Nations Department of Public Information, 1992); and *An Agenda for Peace* (New York: United Nations Department of Public Information, 1995).

19    Ingvar Carlsson, Commission on Global Governance, *Our Global Neighbourhood* (Oxford: Oxford University Press, 1995), p. 181.

20    The resolutions included UN Security Council Resolution 1261 (1999), On the Children and Armed Conflict; UN Security Council Resolution 1325 (2000), On the Special Needs and Human Rights of Women and Children in Conflict Situations; and UN Security Council Resolution 1612 (2005), On the Use of Child Soldiers.

21    Fen O. Hampson et al., "Promoting the Safety of Peoples: Banning Anti-Personnel Landmines," in Fen O. Hampson et al. (eds.), *Madness in the Multitude: Human Security and World Disorder* (Toronto: Oxford University Press, 2002), p. 82.

22    Rolland Paris, "Human Security: Paradigm Shift or Hot Air?" *International Security* 26, no. 2 (2001): pp. 87–102; Michael Small, "The Human Security Network," in Robert Grant McRae and Don Hubert (eds.), *Human Security and the New Diplomacy: Protecting People, Promoting Peace* (Montreal: McGill-Queen's Press, 2001), pp. 231–35; Gary King and Christopher L.J. Murray, "Rethinking Human Security," *Political Science Quarterly* 116, no. 4 (2001–2002): pp. 585–610.

23    Robert Falk, "Humane Governance for the World: Reviving the Quest," *Review of International Political Economy* 7, no. 2 (2000): p. 324.

24    Lloyd Axworthy, *Human Security: Safety for People in a Changing World* (Ottawa: Department of Foreign Affairs and International Trade Government of Canada, 1999), pp. 5–6.

25    Lloyd Axworthy, "A New Scientific Field and Policy Lens," *Security Dialogue* 35, no. 3 (2004): p. 349.

26    Marlies Glasius and Mary Kaldor, "A Human Security Doctrine for Europe," in Marlies Glasius and Mary Kaldor (eds.), *A Human Security Doctrine for Europe: Projects, Principles, Practicalities* (London: Routledge, 2005), p. 7.

27    S. Neil MacFarlane and Yuen Foong-Khong, *Human Security and the UN: A Critical History*, UN Intellectual History Project (Bloomington: Indiana University Press, 2006). This tendency is illustrated by the protective norm building within the UN for specific groups, such as the Convention on the Rights of the Child (1989) or the Convention on the Rights of Persons with Disabilities (2007).

28    Glasius and Kaldor, "A Human Security Doctrine for Europe," p. 8.

29    Roosevelt, The "Four Freedoms."

30    Hampson et al., "Promoting the Safety of Peoples: Banning Anti-Personnel Landmines," pp. 80–97.

31    Mary Kaldor and Alan Johnson, *New Wars and Human Security: An Interview with Mary Kaldor* (London: Foreign Policy Centre, 2007).

32    International Commission on Intervention and State Sovereignty, *The Responsibility to Protect*,

ch. 7, available on-line at http://www.iciss.ca/report2-en.asp (last accessed June 16, 2009).

33  Lloyd Axworthy, "Notes for an Address by the Honourable Lloyd Axworthy Minister of Foreign Affairs to the Canadian Commission for UNESCO Annual General Assembly," Ottawa,
March 26, 1999, available on-line at http://w01.international.gc.ca/minpub/Publication.aspx
?isRedirect=True&publication_id=374953&docnumber=99/25&language=E (last accessed June
17, 2009).

34  Mariella Pandolfi, "'Moral entrepreneurs,' souverainetés mouvantes et barbelés: Le bio-
politique dans les Balkans post-communistes," in Mariella Pandolfi and Marc Abélès (eds.),
"Politiques: Jeux d'espaces," special issue, *Anthropologie et Sociétés* 26, no. 1 (2002); "Laboratory of Intervention: The Humanitarian Governance of the Postcommunist Balkan Territories," in Mary-Jo DelVecchio Good, Sandra Teresa Hyde, Sarah Pinto, and Byron J. Good
(eds.), *Postcolonial Disorders* (Berkeley: University of California Press, 2008), pp. 157–86.

35  David Chandler "Rhetoric without Responsibility: The Attraction of 'Ethical' Foreign Policy,"
*British Journal of Politics and International Relations* 5, no. 3 (August 2003): pp. 295–316;
Aaron Karp, "Small Arms: Back to the Future," *Brown Journal of World Affairs* 9, no. 1 (Spring
2002): p. 184.

36  Glasius and Kaldor, "A Human Security Doctrine for Europe," p. 10.

37  See Arthur C. Helton, "Rescuing the Refugees," *Foreign Affairs* 81, no. 2 (March/April 2002):
pp. 71–82 and *The Price of Indifference: Refugees and Humanitarian Action in the New Cen-
tury* (Oxford: Oxford University Press, 2002); Ahmed Rashid, *Taliban: Islam, Oil, and the New
Great Game in Central Asia* (New Haven, CT: Yale University Press, 2000); Suzanne Schmeidl,
"(Human) Security Dilemmas: Long-Term Implications of the Afghan Refugee Crisis," *Third
World Quarterly* 23, no. 1 (2002): pp. 7–29.

38  Schmeidl, "(Human) Security Dilemmas."

39  Helton, *The Price of Indifference*; Schmeidl, "(Human) Security Dilemmas."

40  Duffield, *Global Governance and the New Wars*, p. 15.

41  The zone is "securitized" by the Canadian army within the NATO mission.

42  Pierre Beaudet, "L'interventionnisme humanitaire canadienne, entre l'instrumentalisation et
le soutien aux populations en détresse," *Géostratégiques*, "Les O.N.G.," no. 16 (May 2007):
p. 127.

43  Government of Canada, "Protecting Canadians: Rebuilding Afghanistan," available on-line at
http://www.afghanistan.gc.ca/canada-afghanistan/approach-approche/index.aspx?menu_
id=1&menu=L (last accessed August 11, 2009).

44  Mariella Pandolfi and Chowra Makaremi, "La sécurité humaine," *Parachute*, no. 124 (October
2006), "Violence Unlimited," issue, pp. 143–48. After hosting the Barcelona Study Group, the
city of Barcelona organized a permanent exhibition called From War to Human Security, under
direction of Mary Kaldor, promoting the idea of human security as what reconfigures and
replaces "peace" in our complex world. Kaldor and Johnson, *New Wars and Human Security.*

45  Mary Kaldor, *New and Old Wars: Organized Violence in a Global Era* (1999; Stanford, CA:
Stanford University Press, 2007).

46  Hans Magnus Enzensberger, *Civil Wars: From L.A. to Bosnia* (New York: Free Press, 1994);
Paul Collier, "Doing Well out of War: An Economic Perspective," in Mats Berdal and David
Malone (eds.), *Greed and Grievance: Economic Agendas of Civil Wars* (Boulder, CO: Lynne
Rienner, 2002), pp. 91–111.

47  Robert D. Kaplan, "The Coming Anarchy: How Scarcity, Crime, Overpopulation, Tribalism and

Disease are Rapidly Destroying the Fabric of our Planet," *Atlantic Monthly* (February 1994): pp. 44–76.

48  Kaldor, *New and Old Wars*, p. 116.

49  Glasius and Kaldor, "A Human Security Doctrine for Europe," p. 6.

50  Some who have taken an anthropological perspective have opposed this widespread conception of new violence as archaic and anomic, pointing out that modes of violence anchored in different cultural traditions, although incomprehensible to external observers, can be meaningful as ways to assign perpetrators a place in the world. See Arjun Appadurai, "Dead Certainty: Ethnic Violence in the Era of Globalization," *Public Culture* 10, no. 2 (Winter 1998): pp. 225–47; Roland Marchal and Christine Messiant, *Les chemins de la guerre et de la paix: Fins de conflit en Afrique orientale et australe* (Paris: Karthala, 1997).

51  Chester C. Crocker and Fen O. Hampson with Pamela Aall, *Managing Global Chaos: Sources of and Responses to International Conflict* (Washington, D.C.: United States Institute of Peace Press, 1996).

52  Alain Joxe, *Empire of Disorder* (New York: Semiotext(e), 2002), p. 161.

53  Government of Canada, "International Peace Operations Branch," available on-line at http://www.rcmp-grc.gc.ca/po-mp/index-eng.htm#cont (last accessed August 11, 2009).

54  *Ibid.*

55  Glasius and Kaldor, "A Human Security Doctrine for Europe," p. 4.

56  The Study Group on Europe's Security Capabilities: A Human Security Doctrine for Europe, "Executive Summary," *The Barcelona Report Presented to EU High Representative for Common Foreign and Security Policy Javier Solana Barcelona*, September 15, 2004, available on-line at http://www.ongd.lu/article.php3?id_article=588 (last accessed June 22, 2009).

57  See Duffield, *Global Governance and the New Wars* and "Getting Savages to Fight Barbarians."

58  See the list of development projects funded by the Canadian International Development Agency: Government of Canada, "Protecting Canadians: Rebuilding Afghanistan," Development Projects, available on-line at http://www.afghanistan.gc.ca/canada-afghanistan/projects-projets/dev.aspx (last accessed August 11, 2009).

59  Agency Coordinating Body for Afghan Relief (ACBAR), "ACBAR Report on Private Security Companies," Kabul, September 16, 2004.

60  Duffield, *Global Governance and the New Wars*, p. 45. Of the nine members of the Barcelona Study Group, five are researchers at the London School of Economics Centre for the Study of Global Governance.

61  Glasius and Kaldor, "A Human Security Doctrine for Europe," p. 5.

62  Dillon and Reid, "Global Liberal Governance."

63  Canadian International Development Agency, "Haiti" (2008), available on-line at http://www.acdi-cida.gc.ca/CIDAWEB/acdicida.nsf/En/JUD-12912349-NLX (last accessed June 22, 2009).

64  Royal Canadian Mounted Police, *International Peace Operations — 2006–2008 Biennial Review*, (Ottawa: R.C.M.P., 2008), p. 24.

65  UN Security Council Resolution 1674, S/RES/1674, 2006, available on-line at http://daccessdds.un.org/doc/UNDOC/GEN/N06/331/99/PDF/N0633199.pdf?OpenElement (last accessed June 22, 2009) and based on the International Commission on Intervention and State Sovereignty's text, *The Responsibility to Protect* (ICISS, 2001), launched by then Canadian foreign minister Lloyd Axworthy.

66  Kofi Annan, "The Prospects for Human Security and Intervention in the Next Century," UN Press Release, September 20, 1999.

67  *Ibid*.

68  International Commission on Intervention and State Sovereignty, *The Responsibility to Protect*, p. 13.

69  Foucault, *Security, Territory, Population*, p. 105.

70  After a number of well-intended "condemnations" and "affirmations," para. 26 of UN Security Council Resolution 1674 notes that "the deliberate targeting of civilians and other protected persons…in situations of armed conflict, may constitute a threat to international peace and security."

71  Glasius and Kaldor, "A Human Security Doctrine for Europe," p. 7.

72  "The protection of children," "women in war," and "the protection of displaced persons" mobilize UN programs and commissions through several specialized agencies (the United Nations Children's Fund, the Office of the UN High Commissioner for Refugees, the Office for the Coordination of Humanitarian Affairs) and related networks of NGOs.

73  Bernard Kouchner, *Ce que je crois* (Paris: Grasset, 2005); Mario Bettati, *Le droit d'ingérence: Mutation de l'ordre international* (Paris: Odile Jacob, 1996).

74  Booth, "Security in Anarchy."

75  The economic and legal struggles in the 1970s of what was then called the "Third World" to reform the UN toward the goal of producing a New International Economic Order (NIEO) were launched in 1973 by the Algerian summit conference of the nonaligned countries, aimed at equalizing the terms of trade and reforming world economic institutions. (These ideas were developed further in Mahbub ul Haq, *The Poverty Curtain* [New York: Columbia University Press, 1976]). The NIEO initiative has been enthusiastically accompanied by practical action on the part of intellectuals such as Mario Bettati, the legal expert and future architect of the "humanitarian right to intervene" in the 1990s, and Mahbub ul Haq, author of the term "human security." See Mahbub ul Haq, "The Third World Challenge: Negotiating the Future," *Foreign Affairs* 59, no. 2 (Winter 1980–81), available on-line at http://www.foreignaffairs.com/articles/34588/mahbub-ul-haq/the-third-world-challenge-negotiating-the-future (last accessed October 12, 2009); and Mario Bettati, "La réforme de l'ONU pour l'instauration d'un nouvel ordre économique international," *Politique Étrangère* 41, no. 4 (1976): pp. 385–98. Being dedicated to development, the UN Development Programme was on the forefront of these debates in the 1970s. The initiative lost momentum after a decade of fruitless negotiations.

76  Anthony Pagden, "The Genesis of 'Governance' and Enlightenment Conceptions of the Cosmopolitan World Order," *International Social Science Journal* 50, no. 155 (March 1998): pp. 7–16.

77  Kaldor and Johnson, *New Wars and Human Security*.

78  Claude Lefort, *Les formes de l'histoire: essais d'anthropologie politique* (Paris: Gallimard, 1978).

79  "La distance des lieux, la séparation des domiciles n'amoindrit point la proximité du sang," Emeric Crucé, *Le nouveau Cynée, ou discours d'état: Représentant les occasions et moyens d'établir une paix générale et liberté du commerce par tout le monde*, ed. Alain Fenet and Astrid Guillaume (1623; Rennes: Presses Universitaires de Rennes, 2004), p. 82, available in English as Emeric Crucé, *The New Cineas*, trans. C. Frederick Farrell, Jr. and Edith R. Farrell (New York: Garland, 1972).

80  Glasius and Kaldor, "A Human Security Doctrine for the Europe," p. 5.

81  Such techniques are applied through the World Food Organization and the UN High Commission for Refugees programs, as well as in the World Bank's "fight against poverty."

82  Mariella Pandolfi, "La scena contemporanea: Paradossi etici e politici," in Matilde Callari Galli, Giovanna Guerzoni, and Bruno Riccio (eds.), *Culture e conflitto* (Rimini: Guaraldi Editore, 2005), pp. 43–61.

83  Foucault, *Security, Territory, Population*, p. 45.

84  Max Horkheimer and Theodor Adorno, *Dialectic of Enlightenment*, trans. John Cumming (1947; New York: Herder and Herder, 1989), p. 16.

# Between Compassion and Conservatism:
# A Genealogy of Humanitarian Sensibilities

Vanessa Pupavac

Gordon Brown's 2008 article in the *Daily Telegraph*, "We Must Defend the Union," on the state of the United Kingdom, singled out the Make Poverty History campaign as one of the ways people express their common values today.[1] The British government wanted to make a statement about national values, but had been struggling to identify shared values as belief in national institutions has declined. Humanitarianism thus came to the fore in official policies to promote a sense of Britishness, from annual charitable appeals such as Comic Relief, to British military recruitment campaigns, to citizenship education.

Accordingly, humanitarian concerns have received growing attention in both the formal and informal school curriculum and beyond. The teaching of geography has been heavily revised over the last decade to reflect British humanitarian concerns,[2] while teachers have been directed by the Department of Children, Schools and Families and the Department of International Development to curriculum materials prepared by aid organizations, such as Oxfam's *Education for Global Citizenship: A Guide for Schools*. Individual schools regularly sponsor charitable appeals. One popular charitable event directed at children is the annual appeal of the BBC children's program Blue Peter. It has been broadcast for fifty years and is one of the primary introductions British children have to humanitarianism through its documentary reports and annual appeals. The annual appeal alternates each year between domestic and overseas causes and is often adopted by schools. British schools in 2007 were busy commemorating the bicentennial of the 1807 Slave Trade Act, as were Blue Peter and other television programs. Yet while the bicentennial was widely officially marked, interest in the simultaneous fiftieth anniversary of Ghanaian independence was muted and received little attention. The impulse to remember British abolition of the slave trade rather than Ghanaian independence indicates the contemporary character of British humanitarian sensibilities and how they are distinct from democratic sentiments.

The birth of modern British humanitarianism is bound up with the antislavery movement. Indeed Britain's best-known abolitionist, William Wilberforce, is credited with establishing the character of British humanitarian sensibilities, and his legacy continues to be feted in Britain.[3] An examination of the bicentennial of the Slave Trade Act 1807 is therefore a convenient way to take stock of Britain's humanitarianism as a major international donor power. This essay critically reviews Wilberforce's humanitarian philosophy two hundred years ago and identifies common themes it shares with present-day British aid philosophy.

The charitable ideal has been linked to reciprocal duties within a community and of hospitality toward strangers. Humanitarianism based on mutual relations and interests or facing strong political pressures from the population has a different character from one with a narrow social basis. British humanitarianism's character has been influenced by middle-class reform circles and their relations to society. Tensions have existed historically within British humanitarianism between its radical humanist strands and more conservative antihumanist strands. On the one hand, British humanitarianism attempted to carve out a space where our common humanity would be recognized beyond international, political, or social divisions. Its aspirations to affirm our common humanity, however partial, temporary, and inadequate in practice, signified a yearning to transcend existing historical conditions domestically and internationally. This impulse is seen in Oxfam's origins during World War II, when it sought to provide relief to starving people in Nazi-occupied Greece, recognizing a common humanity transcending wartime divisions.[4] On the other hand, British humanitarianism historically was entangled with British imperial expansion and expressed conservative fears of radical political change and the role of the masses following the French Revolution.

Development aid has enjoyed a more progressive reputation than emergency relief, but my analysis here, which is focused on British development thinking, suggests that present British humanitarianism leans toward Wilberforce's conservative humanitarian tradition. In identifying philosophical continuities, I am not arguing that British humanitarianism is inevitably tainted by the original sins of its conception. But its prominence in public life in various periods has coincided with the contraction of social concern and progressive politics, rather than with their straightforward expansion. Its present conservative character, notwithstanding its radical self-perception, is influenced by the demise of progressive politics and a disconnect from a popular social basis.

## WILBERFORCE'S CONTRADICTORY HUMANITARIAN TRADITION

William Wilberforce was undoubtedly a key figure behind the 1807 Slave Trade Act and the 1834 Abolition of Slavery Act. He was also a leading British philanthropist in other causes, including criminal-justice reform and the plight of child workers. He is credited with helping establish dozens of charities, including the Society for Betterment of the Poor (1787) and the Society for the Prevention of Cruelty to Animals (1824), as well as major evangelical Christian organizations such as the Church Missionary Society (now the Church Mission Society) (1799) and the British and Foreign Bible Society (now the Bible Society) (1804).[5] Wilberforce's philanthropic exertions were praised for ushering in "the better hour," in the poet William Cowper's much-quoted phrase.

Wilberforce, as Britain's most celebrated abolitionist, shows how British humanitarians could be opposed to progressive politics, tolerate vast social inequalities, and treat the problems faced by the population in terms of law and order. Wilberforce supported the Corn Laws, which imposed duty on imported corn to protect British agricultural interests, even though they supported high bread prices and exacerbated hunger among the population. He was actively involved in political repression, helping draft draconian legislation to outlaw trade unions and radical political parties. He also supported the authorities in opposing a public inquiry into the 1819 Peterloo Massacre, when cavalry soldiers charged a peaceful demonstration calling for parliamentary reform and repeal of the Corn Laws, and he supported repressive measures against the demonstrators, including the suspension of habeas corpus. In addition, he pursued the arrest and prosecution of political activists through his Society for the Suppression of Vice and Encouragement of Religion.[6] Radical writings such as William Hazlitt's 1825 *Spirit of the Age* associated Wilberforce with the forces of reaction, not with progressive politics.[7] So judging the humanitarian Wilberforce as politically illiberal is not being anachronistic, but rather is to judge him by the politics of his day, contrary to his glowing representation during successive British antislavery anniversaries.

How could Wilberforce, identified with emancipating slaves, be actively involved in denying political rights to the majority of his population? Wilberforce's contradictions reflected the postrevolutionary reaction to the French Revolution among the expanding middle classes and evangelical circles in Britain and their retreat from radical, democratic politics. In this vein, Wilberforce singled out suppression of the slave trade and reform of social manners as his two life goals and omitted eradicating poverty and social inequalities from his core concerns.[8] Wilberforce's *A Practical View of Christianity* had wide influence on the British philanthropic circles of his day and shows his primary concern with spiritual poverty, rather than material poverty.[9] Wilberforce, seeing humanity as essentially sinful, attributed Britain's state of crisis to the parlous state of religion and to weak public and personal morality. His abolitionism involved a spiritual concern for religious salvation, both for a slave-owning society and for the slaves themselves, uniting his causes of abolition and social morality. He saw slavery as an unnatural immoral system, but believed that slaves had to be educated for (moral) freedom, just as the population domestically had first to be educated before expanding the franchise. Consequently, he advocated the gradual emancipation of slaves, believing that immediate emancipation "would be productive of universal anarchy and distress," just as an expanded franchise would be domestically. This humanitarian concern for moral salvation, with its evangelical roots, carried through in British overseas missionary work. Meanwhile, Wilberforce saw the existence of social hierarchies and poverty as natural conditions and followed Malthusian ideas treating impoverishment as caused by overpopulation and excess. He condemned a culture asserting material self-interests, promoted a sense of austere public-spiritedness, and feared that the spread of material wealth to the middle and lower classes was corrupting social morals.

But while Wilberforce sincerely believed the poor to be closer than their affluent betters to a state of grace, his religious consolation offered cold comfort to a population suffering pauperization. Wilberforce's paternalistic, antimaterialist model of spiritual betterment inevitably had an apologetic air when he expected the population to reconcile themselves to social inequalities and when he suppressed their political activities. His religious philosophy sat rather too comfortably with conservative, post-Revolutionary politics—as did abolitionism for a class that was learning to exploit free labor. Antislavery has been critically analyzed in this period of political repression and rapid industrialization as a residual progressive cause among former progressive members of the middle classes now fearful of radical political change. Abolitionism answered the psychic needs of mill owners, giving them a sense of moral purpose, although they may have been otherwise hardened to the immediate suffering around them. The radical writer William Cobbett, also a contradictory figure, observed in 1824 about the evangelical leadership: "Rail they do…against the West Indian slave-holders; but not a word do you ever hear from them against the slave-holders in Lancashire and in Ireland. On the contrary, they are continually telling the people here that they ought to thank the Lord."[10]

Analyzing Wilberforce's mix of moral evangelism, paternalism, and antidemocratic politics also helps explain how British humanitarianism became entangled with British imperial expansion. For many, imperial rule was an extension of the moral and social responsibilities of a paternalistic domestic order. Wilberforce's gradualist abolitionism was later echoed in British colonial policy, which was based on the belief that colonial trusteeship was necessary before national self-determination could occur. Further links may be drawn between Wilberforce's fears of commerce's corrupting influence and British colonial and postcolonial development fears of modernization corrupting populations. British aid organizations are heavily influenced by a moral, antimaterialist critique of society that echoes Wilberforce's humanitarian philosophy, but they consciously eschew a missionary role, despite historically evolving out of overseas missionary work. Even organizations such as Christian Aid or the Catholic Agency for Overseas Development, whose names proclaim their religious links, emphasize the secular, ecumenical character of their aid work. This feature contrasts with the U.S. aid sector, which is more overtly religious and involved in missionary work, although not necessarily as antimaterialist.[11] I will focus here on the antimaterialist strain in British development thinking.

## BRITISH HUMANITARIANISM'S ROMANTIC SUBJECTS

Wilberforce's evangelical denunciation of commerce's corrupting influence reinvokes the long Western cultural trope of the pastoral against the sinful city. Earlier pastoral idylls were commonly only literary conventions, but the Industrial Revolution sharpened their cultural significance in Britain. Romantic critiques of industrialization by writers such as the Brontës, Wordsworth, and other writers resonated widely. Moreover, just as writers were turning to nature for solace from the miseries of the city, the wealthy were fleeing from urban squalor and social disturbances to the suburbs or the depopulated countryside.

Social critiques commonly portrayed rural innocence destroyed by urban exploitation. Fearful of industrialization's social consequences, some middle-class reformers considered nonindustrial rural social models. The British Victorian Arts and Crafts and Pre-Raphaelite movements looked nostalgically back to an idealized, premodern Middle Ages in revulsion against modern urban society. They wanted to maintain rural labor and revive the handicrafts against the dominance of mechanized work. Major strands of modern British culture defined themselves against mass urban-industrial society. The literary critics F.R. Leavis and Denys Thompson outlined a modest, harmonious, and simple rural life, anticipating the basic-needs approach of international development: "They satisfied their human needs, in terms of the natural environment; and the things they made....together with their relations with one another constituted a human environment, and a subtlety of adjustment and adaptation, as right and inevitable."[12]

But the power of such Romantic primitivism risked undermining, rather than advancing social concern. Cultural critiques expressed Romantic preferences for simple rural folk and ambiguity over working-class betterment, sometimes openly deploring the working classes for vulgarity and philistine consumption. John Carey's *The Intellectuals and the Masses* has critically documented British intellectual prejudices against working people for their tinned food and cheap entertainment. Carey's study observes that when intellectuals merge the masses back into an innocent pastoral world, the masses are redeemed, but also eliminated as subjects.[13] The masses cannot exist in a preindustrial idyll. Here, intellectuals displayed, in the writer George Eliot's words, "sensibilities of taste," rather than rational, humane sensibilities.[14] Some British intellectuals ended up following Nietzsche's antihumanism and rejected humanitarianism in favor of aesthetics, along with their rejection of industrial society.[15]

Romantic conservatism was restrained domestically in the face of the social demands from the working classes during much of the nineteenth and twentieth centuries. Romantic portrayals of organic, preindustrial communities were treated skeptically by social scientists. The cultural critic Raymond Williams argued fifty years ago that "it is foolish and dangerous to exclude from so called organic society the penury, the petty tyranny, the disease and mortality, the ignorance and frustrated intelligence which are also among its ingredients."[16] Writers such as George Eliot, Elizabeth Gaskell, and Thomas Hardy remained conscious of the difficulties experienced by the rural poor and the attractions of the town, despite the urban miseries they documented.

Anti-industrial ideas were not taken up as viable social models by British mass political movements in the nineteenth and twentieth centuries. Post–World War II British progressive politics affirmed the common man in political slogans such as "homes fit for heroes." Official policies endorsed the need for the provision of universal material welfare, from council houses to unemployment payments. If British social critics remained concerned about the population's moral improvement, they recognized the importance of their material improvements. Accordingly, Richard Hoggart's classic *The Uses of Literacy* asserted how material achievements open up social and moral possibilities:

> They wanted these goods and services not out of a greed for possession, a desire to lay their hands on the glittering products of a technical society, but because the lack of them made it very difficult to live what they called a "decent" life, because without them life was a hard and constant fight simply to "keep your head above water" spiritually as well as economically. Thus with a better place to wash in and better equipment, it would have been possible to keep the family as clean as they felt "proper." We no longer hear about the sheer stink of a working-class crowd. A real progress was clearly possible and was a worthwhile aim.[17]

The postwar ideals of the common man and social altruism have been elaborated on by Richard Titmus,[18] who studied the significance of blood donorship and transfusion services. His book *The Gift Relationship* outlines how altruism toward strangers could be realized in modern society by blood donations. Blood transfusion is premised on our common humanity and the equivalence between people. The gift of blood affirms our common humanity and our common human needs. The donation of blood involves an individual donor's altruism, his or her belief in the altruism of strangers toward strangers and a sense of potentially being one of the strangers in need.

Although the cultural studies of Hoggart, Williams, and others challenged accounts romanticizing the preindustrial past, while sociological accounts such as Titmus's pointed out how modern urban society could be underpinned by a strong sense of social commitment, a lament for the decline of rural life and the rise of mass urban society persisted with the older landed gentry or the upper middle classes. In the mid-twentieth century, for example, *The English Village* and *The Survival of the English Countryside*, by Victor Bonham-Carter, an early conservationis who helped found the Soil Association, deplored the commercialization of farming and the demise of rural ways of life. These ideas were also more likely to persist in the charitable sector, which was dominated by the upper middle classes, than in the postwar welfare-state sector.

In important respects, current British aid organizations also evolved in reaction against industrial society. Their philosophy has historically accorded more with Bonham-Carter's aversion to modern industrialization than with Hoggart's affirmation of its benefits for ordinary people. They have been inclined to idealize authentic traditional peasant communities as counterposed to an inauthentic, corrupting industrial society. Anti-industrial sentiments have followed anthropological thinking, which also informed colonial administration. Anthropology, of all the disciplines, has probably most exuded a Romantic primitivism. Anthropologists often have expressed alarm at how contact with modernity destabilizes the societies they research. Modernity's destabilizing impact on traditional societies also disturbed colonial administrators and shaped colonial thinking on development which sought to deter nationalist movements.[19] British colonial advisers feared that the European presence undermined the traditional ways of life of subject populations. They singled out coercive military rule, urbanization, and unregulated exploitative extraction industries as fostering alienated, rootless, mobile "deracinated" populations. Indirect rule or native administration was to mediate the disturbing European presence and reinforce the authority of rurally based tribal leaders against the influence of the emerging modern, urbanized, politicized, nationalist leaders. Native administration was accompanied by education policies seeking to limit modern influences, including knowledge of European languages. Colonial advisers recommended the promotion of primary schooling in native languages with a curriculum emphasizing training in relevant skills, rather than in European languages, and deemphasizing academic attainment. Such cultural idealizations of developing countries as premodern societies persisted after national independence. The British in India were overwhelmingly attracted to Gandhi's spiritual, harmonious, traditional vision, rather than to Nehru's vision of a modernizing state, as Ruth Prawer Jhabvala's novels wryly portray.

Indeed, one of the attractions of colonial service or postindependence voluntary service for Bonham-Carter's readership was to escape from mass urban society.[20] Humanitarian work in the developing world offered the possibility of retaining a world of servants and of receiving deference no longer possible at home for a former colonial class who found it difficult to reconcile themselves to postwar British egalitarianism.[21] British aid work drew upon colonial administrative experience as well as upon the sentiments of a younger generation of postindependence aid workers inspired by feelings of international solidarity with national independence struggles. Yet there was an element of escape from disappointed political activism at home to more exotic, less accountable activism abroad when the post-1968 counterculture rejected the Western industrial masses for the Romantic ideal of the premodern rural peasant. Romantic antimaterialism consolidated in the British aid sector as national struggles internationally and the working class domestically receded as political forces.

### E. F. SCHUMACHER'S ANTIMATERIALIST AID PHILOSOPHY

E. F. Schumacher's 1970s classic *Small Is Beautiful* is considered the bible of the British development community. Schumacher's transformation from the chief economist of Britain's heavy coal industry to a leading advocate of nonindustrial development illustrates the retreat of British social-reform circles from an engagement with mass industrial society. Schumacher identified himself with the English socialist tradition, particularly its strong moral sense, which brought him closer to Wilberforce. His spiritual asceticism and concerns over consumerism remarkably echo Wilberforce's evangelical philanthropy, although they appear to be politically different at first sight.

Wilberforce and Schumacher may be defined as pessimistic humanists, mistrusting a humanity unchecked by God and emphasizing the prevalence of human depravity.[22] Godless man, Schumacher believed, is a Machiavellian immoral figure driven by hubris, power, and greed. Religious awe, respect for nature, and humility have to be cultivated for social peace. Schumacher commended Buddhism for its altruism and for seeing "the essence of civilization not in the multiplication of wants but in the purification of human character."[23] Both Schumacher and Wilberforce saw the spread of prosperity as corrupting and sought a spiritual, nonmaterialist model of social improvement, understanding social happiness in terms of spiritual well-being. Schumacher, while impressed by Marx's writing, intensely disliked his materialism, atheism, and class hostility. He considered that publicly owned industries cultivate a public-service ethos, but that they struggle to influence their own workforce, let alone wider society, against a culture of greed. His philosophical influences shifted from economic and socialist writings to spiritual writings and figures such as Gandhi and Ivan Illich.

Over the decades, Schumacher gradually became less worried about the standard of living in industrial societies than about the quality of culture.[24] He attacked working-class materialism and criticized aspirations to industrialize the developing world as cultivating the wrong values. He shared Wilberforce's Malthusian ideas about population limits and wanted to moderate human needs. But an even worse prospect for Schumacher was that humanity might be able to overcome natural limits and become limitless. If humanity escaped nature's limits, he feared, materialism would be allowed free reign. He preferred technologically simple, local solutions, such as assisting villagers to build their own village pumps, rather than solutions employing industrial mechanization to reduce labor. His work on intermediate technology led him to make links with organizations such as the Soil Association, highlighted above. He worried that foreign aid makes people "poorer by giving them Western tastes."[25] He preferred nonmaterial aid to material aid, arguing that "a gift of knowledge is infinitely preferable to a gift of material things.... The gift of material goods makes people dependent, but the gift of knowledge makes them free."[26]

Oxfam's interest in Schumacher's ideas is documented in Ben Whitaker's informative history of the organization, *A Bridge of People*. Oxfam criticized the thinking underlying existing projects of international development for conflating growth with development and for seeing development primarily in material terms. Instead, it advanced a moral understanding of development: "The truly un- or underdeveloped human being" is someone who knows that "other people are starving or dying from preventable cause and fails to do what he can to rectify this."[27]

## BRITISH HUMANITARIANISM'S POLITICAL CONSERVATISM

While Wilberforce and Schumacher wanted to offer a spiritual model of wellbeing, it is worth recalling the political context in which their philosophies developed. Wilberforce's call for humility and acceptance of poverty appeared at a time of impoverishment and the suppression of social demands. Schumacher's *Small Is Beautiful*'s focus on basic needs was attractive to developing populations suffering from poverty, but a political vision limiting them to basic needs represented a curb on their aspirations. Schumacher's denunciation of materialism appeared when developing countries were flexing their new political authority internationally and seeking to renegotiate their international economic positions, as in the 1974 UN Declaration on a New International Economic Order or OPEC's successful renegotiation of oil prices with the West. Domestically, the 1970s in Britain were a decade of trade-union militancy, with workers demanding higher material living standards. Schumacher enjoyed good relations with the National Union of Miners for his defense of the coal industry against the threats posed by the increasing use of oil and nuclear energy.[28] But his antimaterialist philosophy clashed with British workers' material demands, expressed, for example in the 1972 and 1974 miners' strikes. Moreover, the vogue for his ideas coincided with the breakup of the postwar Keynesian welfare consensus by the 1974 Labour government that was exploited by the Conservative government of the 1980s, which adopted policies incrementally attacking working-class organizations and living standards. Both Wilberforce and Schumacher therefore opposed contemporary social demands and embodied conservative, elite political perspectives.

Schumacher failed to consider how his ideas might have a politically apologetic character when local, low-technological subsistence farming approaches became prescriptions for developing countries, delegitimizing material aspirations beyond basic needs and legitimizing much backbreaking manual work in the developing world, conditions that earlier development models hoped to overcome. Schumacher condemned repetitive industrial labor, but his approach Romanticized unmechanized rural labor and other nonindustrial livelihoods and failed to acknowledge their boring, repetitive aspects—agricultural "shovelling, shovelling, shovelling," to borrow his words on industrial work.[29] Simultaneously, nonindustrial models, with their "Teach a man to fish," slogan assumed that the majority of people in the developing world wanted only to be fishermen or farmers. How did Schumacher's model meet the ambitions of the potential Schumachers in the developing world, who aspired to a life outside agriculture? Schumacher did not have an adequate answer. His failure, like Wilberforce's, was linked to his belief that the poor are spiritually superior to the affluent, ideas he shared with Mother Teresa, another influence on British humanitarianism. The controversial nature of his nonmaterial, spiritual model of well-being became apparent, for example, when he praised separate development in South Africa.[30]

The British aid sector's embrace of Schumacher's antimaterialist philosophy for both developing countries and industrial countries distanced it from contemporary

British working-class activism. Whitaker's history notes Oxfam's long-standing concern about being a predominantly middle-class organization lacking a solid basis in the working classes.[31] Oxfam failed to win over nonacademic industrial Oxford, even as it saw itself as part of the global village—an indicatively pastoral analogy. Consider Oxfam's antimaterialist opposition to the strong labor militancy associated with the Oxford Cowley car plant. Car workers were among the most militant and highest-paid industrial workers in Britain, including Cowley's approximately twenty-two thousand workers in the early 1970s. Government attacks on trade-union militancy singled out Cowley workers for disrupting the economy and exacerbating economic crisis.[32] Their official and unofficial strike actions achieved significant wage increases and raised living standards, but their activism also encompassed international solidarity with political movements elsewhere, from Chile to Vietnam. Conversely, Oxfam headquarters a few miles away was discussing how its staff should embrace wage restraint and adopt simpler lifestyles as a model for the rest of British society.[33] Oxfam's How the Rich Should Live project envisaged eliminating poverty by reducing personal consumption in the industrial world, a model at odds with local car workers' demands. Retrospectively, Oxfam's proposals for personal sacrifice effectively complemented official austerity measures in the 1980s attacking trade-union militancy and imposing wage restraints. Ironically, Oxfam moved headquarters in 2003 to a business park located on the site of the former car plant.

Antimaterialist thinking has become more established than when Whitaker wrote his history of Oxfam three decades ago. The Department for International Development and British aid organizations endorsed the World Bank's *Voices of the Poor* 2000 report. The World Bank report—significantly for a financial institution— proposed well-being, rather than wealth as the goal of development. Echoing Wilberforce's and Schumacher's philosophies, the report declared that "wealth and wellbeing are seen as different, and even contradictory."[34] Repeatedly, the report emphasized the nonmaterial needs of the poor, defining well-being and ill-being in psychological terms, as "states of mind and being. Wellbeing has a psychological and spiritual dimension as a mental state of harmony, happiness and peace of mind." The report concluded that substantial material advancement is unnecessary to well-being and that small improvements make a big difference to the poor. Yet careful analysis of the background documents suggests that the poor interviewed in the World Bank research were more concerned about their material wants than the report represented.[35]

Low horizons of material well-being also characterize recent British humanitarian campaigns such as Make Poverty History, as well as *altermondialisme*, or antiglobalization thinking. British humanitarian thinking severs the links between well-being, social justice, and material advancement in developing countries. Too often, British humanitarianism (and broader antiglobalization movements) romanticized the lives of the rural poor—precisely what Hoggart and Williams warned against. Condemnation of modern consumer society neglects how major material improvements have mattered for the well-being and dignity of the working classes. People in the industrial world now do less backbreaking work and overall spend less time working, if education and retirement are taken into account. Moreover, condemnations of consumerism may express elite sensibilities of taste against the rest of the population, rather than humanitarian sensibilities, as George Eliot also warned and as I highlight below.

## PESSIMISTIC HUMANITARIANISM

Humanitarianism spectacularly came to prominence in the 1985 Live Aid concert for the Ethiopian famine—the year that the government defeated the twelve-month miners' strike and the remnants of the British working-class political movement. British humanitarianism became burdened with unfulfilled hopes for justice and peace as progressive political visions contracted, but was also shaped by shrinking political visions and pessimism about humanity.[36] Political disorientation sharpened British humanitarianism's long-observed swings between hubris and despair over its mission.[37]

The demise of progressive politics encouraged a diminished view of citizens and their moral, social capacity. Political and cultural elites slipped into jaundiced views of the population, no longer having to take into account the working classes organized as a class speaking for itself. Social distance can encompass nostalgia, just as earlier distance unfavorably contrasted the urban and the rural laboring classes. Michael Collins's *The Likes of Us* documents cultural prejudices against the white working classes and their sense of being neglected, findings echoed in a 2008 BBC national survey.[38] Titmus's *The Gift Relationship*, informed by democratic ideals of the common man and communal trust, assumed people's altruism. In contrast, official regulations on adult volunteers and major charities such as the National Society for the Prevention of Cruelty to Children approach every adult as a potential abuser.[39] Cultural disenchantment carried over into humanitarian sensibilities. Characteristically, artist Peter Howson's degraded view of the common man as expressed in his British paintings continued in his Bosnian paintings, when he was appointed official British war artist in Bosnia.

A degraded view of ordinary people came through the representation of history in the bicentennial celebration of the 1807 Slave Trade Act. National self-congratulatory accounts of abolition have long been challenged by studies analyzing international rivalries, national economic interests, and imperial expansion, factors well beyond humanitarian concerns.[40] But both grand national narratives and critical social, political, and economic analysis are being displaced by micronarratives inclined to present history as a series of human-rights abuses, giving little sense of historical development.[41] From the school curriculum to media reporting and humanitarian appeals, accounts are infused with morality tales stressing victims' personal feelings and perpetrators' behavior.[42] In this vein, the bicentennial put forward a narrative of whites' racial oppression and enslavement of blacks, challenged by a brave minority of enlightened souls. The simplistic narrative of perpetrators and victims maintained Wilberforce's reputation as a political progressive while ignoring the active agency of slaves in Haiti or how most of the British population was disenfranchised during Wilberforce's lifetime.[43] The dominant narrative implicitly revised the history of slavery as a system supported by the British population. Ignoring the political suppression of ordinary people, the current narrative echoes Wilberforce's paternalism in presupposing that humanitarianism requires interventions by an enlightened elite against an unenlightened mass. Contemporary British humanitarianism thus appears somewhat estranged from ordinary people, and its advocates seek not just to reform others, but to reform their own domestic population.[44]

## RAISING AWARENESS

Present-day humanitarian campaigning in Great Britain appears to lack confidence in people's humanitarian sensibilities or capacity to be active in public life, despite continuing donations from citizens and despite the fact that public sensibilities toward the Ethiopian famine, for example, were more quickly awakened than the professional sensibilities of aid agencies in the field.[45] Consequently, both official and nongovernmental campaigns increasingly have tried to connect with the population through the schools—a paternalistic, undemocratic form of political education and indoctrination.[46]

Consequently, as well, much humanitarian advocacy work is devoted to raising people's awareness. Campaigns to raise awareness about a wide range of issues have proliferated, as is reflected in an Awareness Campaigns Register compiled to assist the public relations industry, which lists over seven hundred national awareness campaigns. This focus on raising awareness has evolved from therapeutic theories of empowerment. Many British awareness campaigns are linked to health concerns, but therapeutic concepts have caught on in humanitarian advocacy, as well. Proliferating awareness-raising campaigns suggest cultural concern with one's own or others' sensibilities and echo Wilberforce's evangelical concern to reform social manners and personal conduct, albeit in secular, therapeutic language. Pre-occupation with cultivating a sensitive personality is underscored by the frequent use of the shorthand phrase "raising awareness" without always tacking on the specific cause.

A fascinating study of "ribbon culture" has researched the cultural meaning and etiquette of ribbon or wristband wearing as a fashion statement representing awareness and empathy without having to understand the causes.[47] Sarah Moore's analysis of self-expression displacing social understanding suggests how humanitarian awareness-raising campaigns may actually represent a contraction of social concerns, not their expansion. Tellingly, the original 1985 Live Aid concert wanted to raise money to "feed the world," whereas the 2005 Live 8 concert was about raising our awareness of poverty. And promotion of the Make Poverty History white band sometimes reads like fashion-magazine tips. Consider this advice on the Make Poverty History Web site: "You can wear the white band in any way you like—as a wristband, an armband, a headband, or a lapel badge."[48]

Awareness-raising initiatives may fall into conspicuous ethical display as they draw attention to the person thereby representing a narcissistic turn. The Million Faces photographic petition to control arms, which invites people to submit photos of themselves, as opposed to the customary signatures, epitomizes this self-display. Participants are advised: "Faces aren't just there to look pretty—use yours to show your support for Control Arms" and "Do your best 'my face is going to make a difference' face and snap."[49] Such campaigning flatters participants and imbues acts of self-publicity with moral meaning. Oxfam UK's Generation Why proposed "Do what you love doing—just change the world while you're doing it,"[50] promoting minimalist involvement with minimal inconvenience as politically significant.

## ETHICAL CONSUMPTION AND SENSIBILITIES OF TASTE

Concomitantly, an emphasis on personal ethics has grown as progressive collective politics has declined and social change has come to be understood essentially as the sum of individual actions. Much advocacy in Britain relates to ethical consumption as a core aspect of ethical living and as a site of social action. Ethical consumption developed from the boycotts of South African goods, which became the dominant manifestation of political opposition to apartheid among liberals in Britain. This focus has been reinforced as aid organizations such as Christian Aid and Oxfam and national figures such as the archbishop of Canterbury, Rowan Williams, have taken up climate change and concentrated on people's lifestyles in industrialized societies as problems. Oxfam's Unwrapped program, for example, offers donation gifts such as goats for farmers, and women's livelihood programs, including an alternative humanitarian wedding-gift list, as an ethical alternative to buying and giving unwanted consumer presents. Individual projects come together through the annual Fairtrade Fortnight, which is helping institutionalize ethical consumption norms.

Ethical tourism also has grown, accompanied by Fair Trade Travel logos and Responsible Tourism Awards and other initiatives.[51] British aid organizations have begun promoting their own ethical tourism schemes, such as Oxfam's Global Challenges, alongside their reports criticizing mass tourism's impact on developing countries and the environment.[52] Ethical tourism is particularly targeted at the growing British "gap year" market of young people travelling after graduating from school or the university.[53]

Ethical sensibilities also are affecting British retail. The student organization People and Planet has put much of its campaigning energies into this area, focusing recently on the High Street clothing retailer Primark: "We have chosen to target PRIMARK because of its influence on UK retail practices, in particular its power in driving down prices and fuelling demand for 'fast fashion.'"[54] Ethical campaigns rightly note that industry self-regulation is slow to improve poor working conditions and that significant changes require social pressure. In response to such pressure, major retailers are offering customers ethical consumption through selected sales linked to fair trade, ethical and environmental sourcing, or charitable donations. Thus, the supermarket chain Sainsbury's informs customers: "Our Values Make Us Different." Marks & Spencer and Oxfam are coordinating a scheme where anybody donating old M&S clothes to Oxfam will get an M&S £5 voucher. Topshop is currently selling African print dresses with the proceeds going toward funding children's projects in Ghana.

This focus on the consumer emphasizes redistributing consumption, rather than transforming production and redistributing wealth to advance the living standards of all globally. Not surprisingly, paradoxes exist in focusing on consumption as a form of political social action and personal ethics.[55] Those most likely to be concerned about ethical consumption are among the wealthier social groups with higher rates of consumption. Shopping as social action fits, rather than necessarily opposes, a consumer outlook in which it is difficult to conceive of action beyond consumption. Moreover, ethical consumption may represent a form of conspicuous ethical consumption. Affluent consumers may demonstrate their superior discernment, compared with that of the masses, by means of their organic diets, expensive foreign travel to novel destinations, and specially sourced authentic fair-trade and ecological goods. In addition, ethical attacks on mass consumerism uncomfortably echo earlier elite attacks on the masses, moral sensibilities blurring with sensibilities of taste.[56] Predominantly middle-class campaigners targeting retailers selling cheap, mass-produced clothes subconsciously mix elitist and moralistic judgments about the masses and their consumption patterns. Such impressions are reinforced by how ethical judgments complement official policies and cultural judgments, which question the population's personal tastes and relationships. Consider Oxfam's poster in the London tubes in 2008: "Obesity levels rising while two-thirds of the world go hungry." This simplistic connection implicitly appeals to tacit class prejudices and blames hunger in the developing world on the masses overeating in Britain—obesity in Britain is associated with the least powerful low-income groups—rather than furthering understanding of the causes of poverty in Britain or the developing world.

There appears to be little room for the urban masses in the contemporary British humanitarian vision, again echoing the earlier vision of British cultural elites. This is perhaps unsurprising, given the humanitiarian aid sector's continuing failure to broaden the social profile of its staffs.[57] Indicative of the demographical narrowness of the ethical campaigners is Oxfam's Why Generation advice on the best ethical careers. A respondent observed that its list failed to include nonprofessional work: "What about people who sweep the streets, unblock the drains, empty dustbins etc.?"[58] Ironically, a British aid organization claiming to be part of a global community should envy the diverse ethnic and social profile of customers and staff in the average Primark store, including lower-income groups, working-class whites, and migrants sending remittances and cheap consumer goods to their families.

Activism organized around consumption in an unequal world logically attributes more agency to higher socioeconomic groups who enjoy higher consumption patterns, as opposed to lower socioeconomic groups on lower wages and with lower standards of living. Social pressure arising from a narrower social basis has a character different from a mass political movement concerned with raising workers' standards of living and working conditions. Tensions exist between concern for workers' rights and living standards and concern for limiting mass consumption. People and Planet's 2007 campaign against Primark demanded that the company ensure that those producing their goods receive "a living wage."[59] A living wage involves social determinations of what constitutes a decent standard of living and the affordability of the goods and services that are socially expected. Today's campaigns targeting cheap, mass-produced goods forget the social significance of the mass production of cheap clothing historically for working-class dignity and the realization of a living wage.[60] Even where aid reports note the sense of shame expressed by the poor who cannot afford decent clothes or shoes, as the World Bank's *Voices of the Poor*,[61] they nevertheless marginalize material questions and the positive social good of producing cheap goods as part of ensuring living wages globally.

Industry self-regulation and moral campaigns have historically been slow to transform the material conditions of the poor. The cause of climate change is giving moral legitimacy to this reluctance. Ethical-consumer campaigns challenge multinational corporations, but they are prepared to lower the material living standards of populations among industrialized populations and to contain the material aspirations of people in the developing world beyond basic needs. Following Schumacher, finding solutions to poverty and environmental problems that allow humanity to have higher consumption patterns globally appears morally repugnant, even if achievable. Aid organizations have tied solutions to climate change to their antimaterialist development philosophy. Christian Aid's recent reports on climate change invoke the global poor against the lifestyles of industrial countries and want to codify a framework that obliges industrial countries to "adopt lower-impact lifestyles" and developing countries to serve the basic needs of the poor.[62] Their models of what constitutes basic needs consciously oppose the inhuman assumptions of earlier ecological writing, which brutally regarded famines and disasters as nature's way of dealing with overpopulation, but their antimaterialist philosophy implies limiting social mobility, rather than advancing the material position of the masses globally.

Just as British humanitarian sensibilities disapprove of mass consumption domestically, they fear developing populations' aspirations to material prosperity and access to modern consumer products. They express revulsion at the Chinese or Indians adopting postindustrial countries' material standards of living, from cars, to refrigerators, to air conditioners. British cultural preferences persist for an austere Buddhist China or an India of Gandhian spiritualism and self-denial. Ethical consumption may ignore the costs for the masses domestically and globally, just as Wilberforce's support for the Corn Laws ignored the costs for the poor of his day. But if developing countries are not industrialized and are limited to basic needs, they will remain ever vulnerable to emergencies and indefinitely entangled in dependent relationships with donor powers. Meanwhile, environmentalism may legitimize new forms of protectionism, excluding competition from farmers in the developing countries in the name of saving the planet.[63]

## CONCLUSION

Two centuries ago, Wilberforce's humanitarianism helped abolish slavery, but denied the political and social rights of humanity. British humanitarianism today wants to promote social and environmental justice, but is wary of emancipating humans from nature. A current Oxfam advertising slogan is the neat "Be Humankind." Nevertheless, aid organizations are becoming planet-centered and have decentered humanity. The shift was symbolized by the change of name of the British student organization from Third World First to People and Planet in the 1990s.

At the heart of humanitarianism is or should be the humanist impulse to recognize a common humanity transcending political, social, and cultural divisions. This impulse was evident in the founding of organizations such as Oxfam. Transcending difference, the humanitarian ideal points to the gap between present conditions and the human potential to create a flourishing life and enriched relationships for all. Humanitarianism at its best symbolizes hope replete with meaning: the nobility of the human spirit and the promise of its triumph over inhuman conditions. A nonhuman-centered humanitarianism is an oxymoron. We have already witnessed the dangers of humanitarianism forgetting to treat people as ends in themselves. Twenty years ago, the aid sector was slow to recognize the Ethiopian famine because humanitarian organizations were wedded to their development vision. In the 1990s, it withdrew aid to Hutu refugees because it prejudged them as genocides en masse.[64] These stark examples warn how professional humanitarianism may become insensitive to human suffering and even deny groups humanitarian consideration. Tellingly, Malthusian population concerns have resurfaced in humanitarian circles. Contemporary British humanitarianism is infused with profoundly antihumanist, antiprogressive sensibilities leading to policies eschewing human emancipation for human bondage to a natural order. A posthuman humanitarianism risks denying compassion today and the promise of a better future for humanity.

## NOTES

1    Gordon Brown, "We Must Defend the Union," Daily Telegraph, March 25, 2008.
2    Alex Standish, *Global Perspectives in the Geography Curriculum: Reviewing the Moral Case for Geography* (London: Routledge, 2008).
3    E. P. Thompson, *The Making of the English Working Class* (Harmondsworth, UK: Penguin, 1968); and Rowan Williams, "Down with Godless Government," *The Sunday Times*, Times Online, April 22, 2007, available at http://www.timesonline.co.uk/tol/comment/columnists/guest_contributors/article1687465.ece (last accessed June 22, 2009).
4    Ben Whitaker, *A Bridge of People: A Personal View of Oxfam's First Forty Years* (London: Heinemann, 1983).
5    Kevin Belmonte, *William Wilberforce: A Hero for Humanity* (Grand Rapids, MI: Zondervan, 2007); William Hague, *William Wilberforce: The Life of the Great Anti-Slave Trade Campaigner* (London: HarperPress, 2007); John Pollock, *Wilberforce* (London: Constable, 1977); The Wilberforce Central Web site, http://www.wilberforcecentral.org/wfc/Wilberforce (last accessed June 22, 2009).

6  Hague, *William Wilberforce*, pp. 250–56 and 440–46; Adam Hochschild, *Bury the Chains: The British Struggle to Abolish Slavery* (Basingstoke, UK: Pan Books, 2005); Thompson, *The Making of the English Working Class*, pp. 112–13 and 141.

7  William Hazlitt, *Spirit of the Age, or Contemporary Portraits* (London: Collins, 1969); Robert Hind, "William Wilberforce and the Perceptions of British People," *Historical Research* 60, no. 143 (October 1987): pp. 321–35; Thompson, *The Making of the English Working Class*.

8  A.A. Green "'Was British Emancipation a Success?: The Abolitionist Perspective," in David Richardson (ed.), *Abolition and Its Aftermath: The Historical Context, 1790–1916* (London: Frank Cass, 1985), pp. 183–202.

9  William Wilberforce, *A Practical View of the Prevailing Religious System of Professed Christians, in the Higher and Middle Classes in This Country, Contrasted with Real Christianity*, 6th ed. (1798) London: Century Collections Online, Gale Group available on-line at http://galenet.galegroup.com/servlet/ECCO (password required).

10  Thompson, *The Making of the English Working Class*, pp. 160 and 434.

11  Julie Hearn, "The 'Invisible NGO': US Evangelical Missions in Kenya," *Journal of Religion in Africa* 32, no. 1 (2002): pp. 32–60.

12  Raymond Williams, *Culture and Society 1780–1950* (Harmondsworth, UK: Penguin, 1961), pp. 37 and 252.

13  John Carey, *The Intellectuals and the Masses: Pride and Prejudice among the Literary Intelligentsia, 1880–1939* (London: Faber and Faber, 1992), pp. 44–45.

14  George Eliot, *Felix Holt, the Radical* (London: Penguin, 1995), pp. 121–22.

15  Carey, *The Intellectuals and the Masses*, pp. 12–17.

16  Williams, *Culture and Society*, p. 253.

17  Richard Hoggart, *The Uses of Literacy* (Harmondsworth, UK: Penguin, 1958), p. 172.

18  Richard Titmus, *The Gift Relationship: From Human Blood to Social Policy* (Harmondsworth, UK: Penguin, 1970).

19  Mark R. Duffield, *Development, Security and Unending War: Governing the World of Peoples* (Cambridge: Polity, 2007).

20  J.M. Lee, *Colonial Development and Good Government* (Oxford: Clarendon Press, 1967).

21  David Cannadine, *Ornamentalism: How the British Saw Their Empire* (New York: Oxford University Press, 2001).

22  E.F. Schumacher, *Small Is Beautiful: A Study of Economics As If People Mattered* (London: Blond and Briggs, 1974), p. 20; Wilberforce, *A Practical View of the Prevailing Religious System of Professed Christians*, p. 437; Barbara Wood, *E.F. Schumacher: His Life and Thought* (New York: Harper and Row, 1983), available on-line via the E.F Schumacher Society at http://www.schumachersociety.org/Wood%20bio/index.html, p. 264 (last accessed June 24, 2009).

23  Schumacher, *Small Is Beautiful*, p. 40.

24  Wood, *E.F. Schumacher*, p. 283.

25  *Ibid.*, p. 314.

26  Schumacher, *Small Is Beautiful*, p. 163.

27  Whitaker, *A Bridge of People*, p. 82.

28  Wood, *E.F. Schumacher*, pp. 289–90.

29  *Ibid.*, p. 273.

30  *Ibid.*, pp. 340–41.

31  Whitaker, *A Bridge of People*, p. 36.

32  Greg Philo, *Glasgow Media Group, Volume 2: Industry, Economy, War and Politics* (London: Routledge, 1995), pp. 3–20.

33  Duffield, *Development, Security and Unending War*, pp. 63–64; Whitaker, *A Bridge of People*, pp. 30–32.

34  Deepak Narayan, Robert Chambers, Meera K. Shah, and Patti Petesch (eds.), *Voices of the Poor: Crying Out for Change* (Oxford: Oxford University Press for the World Bank, 2000), p. 21.

35  John Pender, "Empowering the Poorest? The World Bank and 'The Voices of the Poor,'" in David Chandler (ed.), *Rethinking Human Rights: Critical Approaches to International Politics* (Basingstoke, UK: Palgrave Macmillan, 2002).

36  Philip Hammond, *Media, War and Postmodernity* (London: Routledge, 2007).

37  Whitaker, *A Bridge of People*, p. 184.

38  BBC, *Newsnight*, "White Season," March 6, 2008, available on-line at http://news.bbc.co.uk/1/hi/programmes/newsnight/7279997.stm (last accessed June 26, 2009).

39  Josie Appleton, *The Case against Vetting: How the Child Protection Industry Is Poisoning Adult-Child Relations*, available on-line at http://www.manifestoclub.com/files/THE%20CASE%20AGAINST%20VETTING.pdf Recent articles include Stephen Adams, "Philip Pullman Refuses to Undergo 'Insulting' Child Safety Check," *Telegraph*, July 15, 2009, available on-line at http://www.telegraph.co.uk/culture/books/booknews/5834646/Philip-Pullman-refuses-to-undergo-insulting-child-safety-check.html; BBC, "Millions Must Be on Vetting List," June 2, 2008, available on-line at http://news.bbc.co.uk/1/hi/education/7430954.stm; and BBC, "School Safety 'Insult' to Pullman," July 16, 2009, available on-line at http://news.bbc.co.uk/1/hi/uk/8153251.stm (all last accessed September 13, 2009).

40  Seymour Drescher, "The Historical Context of British Abolition," in David Richardson (ed.), *Abolition and Its Aftermath: The Historical Context, 1790–1916* (London: Frank Cass, 1985) pp. 3–24; C.L.R. James, *The Black Jacobins: Toussaint L'Ouverture and the San Domingo Revolution* (New York: Vintage, 1963).

41  Chris McGovern, "The New History Boys," in Robert Whelan (ed.), *The Corruption of the Curriculum* (London: Civitas, 2007), pp. 58–85.

42  Hammond, *Media, War and Postmodernity*.

43  James, *The Black Jacobins*.

44  Aid organizations' involvement in contemporary global governance has been perceptively explored elsewhere, for example, in Duffield, *Development, Security and Unending War*.

45  Tony Vaux, *The Selfish Altruist* (London: Earthscan, 2000), p. 115.

46  Hannah Arendt, "The Crisis in Education," in *Between Past and Present* (London: Penguin, 1993), pp. 173–96.

47  Sarah Moore, *Ribbon Culture: Charity, Compassion and Public Awareness* (Basingstoke, UK: Palgrave, 2008).

48  See http://www.makepovertyhistory.org/whiteband (last accessed June 26, 2009).

49  See http://www.oxfam.org.uk/generationwhy/do_something/campaigns/controlarms/takeaction/millionfaces (last accessed June 26, 2009).

50  See http://www.oxfam.org.uk/generationwhy/index.htm (last accessed June 26, 2009).

51  Jim Butcher, *The Moralisation of Tourism: Sun, Sand…and Saving the World* (London: Routledge, 2007); and *Ecotourism, NGOs and Development: A Critical Analysis* (London: Routledge, 2007).

52  James Rice, "Holidays with a Difference," November 30, 2005, available on-line at Oxfam, "Your Say," http://www.oxfam.org.uk/generationwhy/do_something/ethical/

53  Campaigns aimed at young people strikingly target personal consumption such as Oxfam's Why Generation, which advised "Support campaigns by changing your every day life—from where you shop and what you buy, to what you study and where you work." See http://www.oxfam.org.uk/generationwhy/do_something/ethical (last accessed June 26, 2009).

54  Ian Leggett, Letter to Arthur Ryan, Chairman, Primark, London, February 27, 2007, available on-line at http://peopleandplanet.org/dl/tradejustice/highcost/primarkletter.pdf (last accessed June 26, 2009).

55  James Heartfield, *Green Capitalism: Manufacturing Scarcity in an Age of Abundance* (London: OpenMute, 2008); Joseph Heath and Andrew Potter, *The Rebel Sell: How the Counterculture Became Consumer Culture* (Chichester, UK: Capstone, 2005).

56  Carey, *The Intellectuals and the Masses*; Eliot, *Felix Holt*.

57  Stephen Hopgood, *Keepers of the Flame: Understanding Amnesty International* (Ithaca, NY: Cornell University Press, 2006).

58  Anna Drakes, Web site post, Oxfam Why Generation, September 19, 2006. See http://www.oxfam.org.uk/generationwhy/do_something/ethical/careers/best_ethical_careers (last accessed June 26, 2009).

59  Leggett, Letter to Arthur Ryan.

60  Hoggart, *The Uses of Literacy*.

61  Narayan, Chambers, Shah, and Petesch (eds.), *Voices of the Poor*, pp. 100 and 171.

62  Paul Baer, Tom Athanasiou, Sivan Kartha, and Eric Kemp-Benedict, *The Greenhouse Development Rights Framework: The Right to Development in a Climate Constrained World*, rev. 2nd ed. (2008), p. 33, available on-line at http://www.ecoequity.org/docs/TheGDRsFramework (last accessed June 26, 2009).

63  Heartfield, *Green Capitalism*.

64  Vaux, *The Selfish Altruist*.

PART TWO: SCENES

# From Paradox to Paradigm:
# The Permanent State of Emergency in the Balkans

Mariella Pandolfi

Regardless of their apparent contemporary significance, events encounter one of three fates. They may become fragments of historicity and as such may fall into oblivion, leaving no documentary trace behind, except perhaps for a future archaeologist to uncover in a quest for the foregone potentialities of social struggle.[1] At other times, they may become part of the repertoire of individual or collective memory and thus be woven more or less discernibly into its plot. Finally, phenomena can become paradigmatic: They can help us to cast a critical and problematizing gaze on the processes that characterize a whole epoch or society. Even current events can be quickly forgotten (who still remembers the war in Lebanon of the summer of 2006?), be recuperated by existing discourses, or become harbingers of a whole new order. I evoke these three possibilities in light of my ongoing field experiences and reflections on the war-torn Balkans, a region plagued by ethnic conflicts and locked in a "permanent transition"[2] since the 1990s. Bosnia, Kosovo, and, to a lesser extent, Albania are not simply territories that have been affected by exceptionally dramatic historical events. To my mind, the Balkans, which until recently the Western imaginary constructed as the other,[3] today embody the paradigm of our present predicament, whose fundamental feature is that the state of emergency as such has become a political instrument in its own right.

Giorgio Agamben reminds us that "to give an example is a complex act which supposes that the term functioning as a paradigm is deactivated from its normal use, not in order to be moved into another context but, on the contrary, to present the canon—the rule—of that use, which can not be shown in any other way."[4] In other words, exemplarity paradoxically resides in particularity. What is more, the paradigmatic example stands both inside and outside of historicity. In its particularity, it is neither the contingent product of history nor some underlying principle expressing itself through history. To paraphrase Agamben,[5] it is neither inductive nor deductive, neither *telos* nor *archē*, neither synchronic nor diachronic, but the threshold of such oppositions. The example serves as a key to intelligibility, making sense of a historical epoch even as it finds its particular place within that epoch. The recent history of the Balkans—the breakup of Yugoslavia, the murderous, ethnicized fragmentation of Bosnia, the implosions of Albania, the NATO bombardment of Belgrade, the internationalized protectorate of Kosovo, and the multiple, complex attempts of the "international community" to pick up the pieces—has revived their image as a hopeless backwater of particularism. Locked in this state of exception, the Balkans have become a site for the management of living beings through military intervention and declarations of humanitarian emergencies, a process that places them in the midst of a permanent transition. This political technique simultaneously imposes both a neoliberal market of suffering and its projects for social control, the ambiguous parameters disciplining international aid thus acquiring their paradigmatic exemplariness. The application and development of techniques for managing life in the Balkans in the name of human rights, understood as a globalized form of life, thus are not merely a response to an exceptional historical accident but are paradigmatic features of our times.

Indeed, one could very well interpret the events that followed the breakup of Yugoslavia leading to the re-formation of old/new nation states as an experimental moment of the postbipolar world, where old conflicts and new instabilities interact to generate the perimeter of what Marc Abélès has designated the "global-politique,"[6] in which the value of survival, be it of the self, the nation, or the planet, defines the horizon of political possibilities: security and development, emergency and permanent transition, conditioned sovereignties and mobile sovereignties, peacekeeping missions and militarized safe zones, neoliberalism and…sustainable development, international courts and international opaqueness, soft powers and "empire lite,"[7] old and new wars. Are all of these attempts to conceptualize the global politics of the present oxymora, contradictions, paradoxes, ambiguities? Probably the management of living beings and the management of global chaos have developed, over the last two decades, into a spider-web strategy whose filaments seem randomly woven only from the perspective of obsolete interpretive models while they point to new strategic models for the management of disorder.

## THE AMBIGUITIES OF THE EUROPEAN UNION'S "SOFT POWER" IN THE BALKANS

The Balkans are perhaps the last frontier of the neoliberal utopia of creating a perfectly self-regulating society. There, the West's—and particularly the European Union's—strategies of inclusion and exclusion through the wielding of the carrot and the stick reveal the values underlying Western democracies, namely, the social triage of lives worth living. By manipulating the ghosts of the past through discursive strategies that the international "community" can accept, Western policy designates the "worthy" and the "unworthy," thus perpetuating instability and producing among local communities foolhardy innovations and sudden regressions that further unsettle local societies and makes them even more dependent on Western prescriptions for self-improvement. They are subject to a pedagogy that, whether developed by the West or by the globalized market, nevertheless produces permanent mistrust, especially if the countries at the receiving end are peripheral to or far away from the Western world.

A recent innovation in policy jargon aptly captures this perverse pedagogy. In light of the European Union's ambivalent involvement in the Balkans and debates over enlarging or deepening it, the geographical definition of the region has gradually slipped into a neologistic distinction between "Southeastern Europe" and the "Western Balkans." This change in terminology points to the clear-cut distinction between countries such as Greece, Bulgaria, and Romania, all EU members and thus now part of "us," and those countries that emerged with the breakup of Yugoslavia, which together with Albania now constitute the "Western Balkans," our irreducible "them." This apparently anodyne bureaucratic gesture generates tensions and antagonisms on the ground between possible EU candidates as they jockey for inclusion within the Southeastern European sphere. Bosnia, Albania, and Kosovo were all initially the theater of ostensibly temporary Western intervention in response to humanitarian crises (respectively, ethnicized civil war, economic and political implosion, and purported genocide). More than a decade later, they have shifted from a temporary state of intervention (humanitarian crisis) to a condition of permanent transition, a state of limbo of inclusive exclusion on the threshold of Europe.

The hypothesis that I wish to develop is that in the context of the new world order exemplified by Europe's exclusive inclusion of the "Western Balkans," the "emergency" and the "long term" are not contradictory apparatuses. The emergency, the need to act now—punishing the bad guys and aiding the victims—produces a state of exception that entails the partial abrogation of strategic, economic, and moral standards. From communism to liberalism, from war to peace, from ethnic-religious conflict to cosmopolitanism, in an endless permutation of violence, where once emergency roamed, now postemergency and permanent transition dwell. Yet the contradiction remains, since the temporality of the state of emergency and of the humanitarian and military emergency is only "legitimate" insofar as it is limited in time, insofar as it can unambiguously demarcate the distinction between wartime and peacetime. Thus, in Bosnia and Kosovo, for example, the acronyms, agencies, and actors of the military and civilian missions have morphed to respond to changes in their mandates while still remaining a form of parallel sovereignty. The continuity of such parallel sovereignty from conflict to postconflict conditions can best be seen in two basic spatiotemporal features that inform the actors involved whose actions contribute to generate microemergencies while legitimizing the state of exception. This chain of microemergencies in turn reinforces the situation of permanent transition, since to every microemergency there corresponds a specific tool kit of operative practices specifically tailored to the particular segment of transition that needs to be addressed. Furthermore, each microemergency segment, be it an armed conflict, a humanitarian operation, or development aid, follows symmetrical procedures carried out by the same international and local actors.

## LONG-TERM WARS

These subtle shifts from punctual emergency intervention to permanent tutelary transition have by and large escaped the attention of observers and the ability of existing intellectual frameworks to capture the essence of the emergent order exemplified by the "Western Balkans." Many authors have recently begun to look at the consequences of the end of the bipolar post–World War II order. The asymmetries engendered by the end of the Cold War have led to the development of a wide range of interpretive strategies focusing on global chaos management, on new forms of emergent sovereignties, on flexible modes of domination,[8] and on new ways of conceiving humanitarian aid and international development. The intertwining of military intervention and humanitarian action legitimated by the emergency formula, on the one side, and the processes seeking to stabilize the rule of law, to export democracy, and to generate development through security by so-called "good governance" measures, on the other, all reveal, albeit usually only implicitly, the blueprint of new emergent forms of control and political techniques of the postbipolar world.

Contemporary scholars of international relations have attempted to understand the post–Cold War order in terms of "new wars" and the renewed intensity of localized violence. The point here, however, is not to look back at the historical origins of contemporary violence, but to shift the analysis toward the new modalities of the management of populations, which, having achieved global currency today, also participate in the ambiguous production of violence. Philippe Zarifian reminds us that "the world has entered into a regime of long-term war."[9] This means that we should not think of the process under way as a linear sequence of wars. Rather, we should understand it as a system of dotlike discontinuities, much like the spots of a leopard's skin—a series of operations that produce both security and destruction and that may include a specific form of armed conflict. According to Zarifian, this new regime of war also generates a whole series of parallel activities that make use of all kinds of different discursive apparatuses, from politics to ideology, from the media to legislation.

Whereas Zarifian underscores the new, discontinuous temporality and spatiality of current conflicts and their management, Frédéric Gros points out the diversity of their social agents, showing that the basic feature of the contemporary state of violence is to accustom us to the simultaneous emergence of a series of figures such as the soldier, the mercenary, the computer engineer, and the head of security or the humanitarian worker.[10] The victims, the executioners, the soldiers who fight and build infrastructures, the humanitarians who cure the sick and injured and deploy the emergency logistics, and the legal experts who redesign the democratic juridical order in the name of security are all part of this global environment. The local specificity of violent outbursts is effaced as they become but one in an endless series. An asymmetry thus emerges between the logic of exception (exceptionalism), emergency intervention, and crisis as a chronic state of existence, on the one hand, and violence as a continuous chain of events, on the other.

Perhaps most symptomatic of the emergent paradigm has been the proliferation of discourses of "good governance," which offer both a diagnosis and a remedy for the new world disorder: Violence, corruption, and chaos result from deficient governance, and the techniques of good governance provide a panacea. The term "governance" has been used as a kind of catch-all "to refer to any strategy, tactic, process, procedure or program for controlling, regulating, shaping, mastering or exercising authority and legitimacy over others."[11] "Governance" used in this way introduces new practices of categorization: Who are the humans that are destined for this aid program, the citizens who are the subjects of rights? They are victims or other emergent "political" subjects, such as refugees,[12] nonpersons, biocitizens, liquid lives, discarded lives, wasted lives, bare lives.[13] In *The Origins of Totalitarianism*, Hannah Arendt observes that the problem with human rights is that they are invoked at the precise moment at which the rights of a citizen are stripped away. This removal of the political artifice that confers human dignity leaves us with "the abstract nakedness of being human and nothing but human."[14] The presumption that intervention in a humanitarian perspective is "neutral" and separate from politics produces a paradoxical inversion. Thus, echoing Arendt, David Rieff writes that humanitarian intervention:

> is founded on the belief that people are not meant to suffer and that, when possible, assistance should be given to the victims of war, oppression, hunger, and other calamities. The modern media has reinforced both the urgency and moral authority

of this message, galvanizing support among the "international community" to act, prompting observers to proclaim a "revolution of moral concern" and to hope that humanitarianism might provide a solution for the ills of the world. But these hopes are misplaced.[15]

In fact, bureaucratic language investigating the legitimacy of genocides and massacres, international courts spinning webs of universal rights, and international aid defining the legitimate perimeters of emergency operations all reinforce such phenomena in their self-evident historicity. Thus, dates and numbers transform events into facts that can be "measured" and therefore managed.

### ENEMIES

Gil Anidjar's reassessment of Schmitt's friend/enemy distinction through the question of the theologico-political gives us a conceptual groundwork from which to interpret the different emotional effects and responses to contemporary interventions,[16] particularly in light of the observation that the new wars occur at the merging of the everyday realities of development and security,[17] whose confusion in the discourse of "human security" is the latest articulation of the ambivalent injunction to "love thy enemy." However, who is the enemy on whom war is waged, and who is to be disarmed through development and good governance?[18] The distinction between friend and enemy, central to Schmitt's political theory, is particularly relevant in light of how contemporary efforts to manage the "transition" in the Balkans have fashioned a discourse of a hostile other that, while registering individual anxieties, communitarian exclusion, and rage, allows the international community to justify its ongoing intervention.

The friend/enemy threshold, however, is as fragile as it is porous. Paradigmatic of politics in the preceding modern age, today it serves as an alibi that actualizes ancient myths while enabling all-too contemporary cynical strategies. Radovan Karadzic, the human rights foe, on the run for more than ten years, finally has been apprehended. As he stands trial before the International Criminal Tribunal, the powerful networks that protected him will be as if they had never existed.[19] In their place, we will have the UN and EU discursive strategies narrating the eternal victory of good over evil. At the same time, the ambiguity, the growing hostility toward the newly independent Kosovo on the part of its Balkan neighbors, seems to anticipate the construction of a potential enemy that, by attracting funds and the attention of donors, may put the process of regional integration in jeopardy. Since February 2008, in Albanian territories outside Kosovo, there has been a growing criticism that points to the sociological ambiguities of the new Kosovo nation-state. There is the anger and the fear that international funding agencies will end up concentrating their resources in Kosovo. This possibility may engender the construction of a lesser enemy.

Arjun Appadurai has examined the contemporary macrodynamics of the production of the "inner enemy."[20] He argues that the waning of national state sovereignty with globalization creates favorable conditions for heightened social anxiety to be displaced and transferred onto minorities and marginalities. Talal Asad's examination of the suicide bomber also draws an arresting portrait of Western international law being manipulated in the interest of Western states and the role played in this endeavor by the figure of the terrorist.[21] While these important works do not explicitly theorize the notion of the enemy, they shed light on the many dimensions of different contemporary violent settings, from ordinary life,[22] to the effects of globalization, to the manipulation of international law, and suggest the ways in which an enemy is drawn out in such social contexts as a discursive trope that obscures the ambiguities of survivalist politics.

Thus, in some Balkan states today, the enemy is a rhetorical figure and an ever-changing political strategy. Under the pressure of the ambiguous presence of the international community, anxiety and uncertainty, expectations and disappointments, are the basic ingredients for the construction of the enemy, who may be the alien from far away or the neighbor. Wherever animosities have exploded with the multiplication of fear-engendering discourses, victimization, dependency, tutelage, and uncertainty have created a climate of individual and community inadequacy and self-loathing that is reflected in the articulation of hate as a communal expression of humiliation and rage. The intensive development of nationhood in Kosovo, Albania's joining NATO and later the EU, and the divisive tensions that have recently emerged in the Bosnian parliament have all triggered a frenzy of political activity that in effect marks yet another phase of the state of emergency and a further mutation of the permanent transition.

Indeed, the experience of the "Western Balkans" over the past decades exposes the logic of an enduring postinterventionist order. This new phase is characterized by: a therapeutic approach to society in an endless oscillation between victimization and salvation, the ideology of better governance, that is, the mixture of the developmental and humanitarian canons as a neoliberal agenda, and the conflation of development and security.

## SALVATION AND VICTIMIZATION

Let us first examine the twinned idioms of salvation and victimization. Their linkage signals a shift from a politics of rescue aimed at saving an agonizing polity from potentially annihilating a part of itself to a politics of healing. My own fieldwork

in the Balkans has followed this trajectory, or rather oscillation, from victimization to salvation. Drawn there initially within the framework of an International
Migration Organization's psychotherapeutic mission for victims of violence, I subsequently turned to an ethnography of the huge humanitarian apparatus, only to
discover that its promise of salvation depended on a constant (re)production of
victims, if not immediately victims of war, then of corruption, underdevelopment,
inadequate self-organization, failed markets, and the like.[23] Following Vanessa
Pupavac, we might describe this victimization-salvation cycle as a new global therapeutic order where the emotional norms of donor states and an emphasis on individual vulnerability articulate in new strategic ways a bureaucratic process of good
governance and new cultural sensibilities.[24] Pupavac has described this process as
the medicalization and pharmaceutical treatment of social suffering ("saving the
sick") that has occurred in parallel with redemptionist myths of political liberation
("saving the nation") and the universal mission of the international aid community
("saving the world"), binding previously disparate forms of pathos in a thickening
hegemony of compassion.[25] Our modernity creates a zone of indeterminacy not so
much between the inside and the outside (of the nation, the town, or the home)
but within every subject, as well as within the realm of the political itself, which is
today plagued by devastating misgivings in the face of an elusive horizon of danger and threats. Marc Abélès has argued that the choices and worries that today
structure our public sphere are shaped by the problem of survival, with discourses
of crashes and rescues supplanting those promising a better life.[26] Humanitarian
practices are a major example of the kind of political action typical of this new
survivalist public sphere.

From a different perspective, the work of Mark Duffield and Pupavac highlights many of the material aspects of these new political techniques that, by rendering humanitarian imperatives isomorphic with economic development, end up
endowing their territorial intervention with a therapeutic approach carried out on
the ground by an all-pervasive international community. These two authors, in
particular, have convincingly shown that military intervention and humanitarianism, the stabilization of a territory under the "human rights" label and the ensuing
economic strategies and investment priorities, are not in contradiction with one
another. How can we make sense of this continuum that from humanitarian or military emergency leads to the emergence of a new developmental canon? How can
the experiences of intervention and postintervention be seamlessly constructed by
Western bureaucracies and local communities?

The postintervention sequence refers to a particular historic period in the
multistaged punctuation of the "politico-therapeutic treatment" that aimed at
managing politically the "trauma" of collective violence. On the one hand, we

thus have a neoliberal version of "healing": humanitarian interventions, plus security and "institutional" pedagogy and, finally, a developmental pedagogy. On the other, such a "healing" process is truly a "therapeutic" relationship in which bodies and development respond to the same imperatives. For example, while Kosovo now seeks to increase its sovereignty as an independent nation-state, Albania is preparing to join NATO. Both territories seek to reconfigure sovereignty in different ways, even though the "graft" of a democratic state has yet to take hold and, in its place, a tissue of international organizations continues to hold sway over key aspects of the economy and society. On this political tabula rasa, the international community has sought to inscribe elements of a democratic civil society. However, the persistence of international mechanisms of governance and their short-circuiting of local forms of politics by the co-opting of local elites into the international apparatus has in effect sterilized the public sphere and neutralized political engagement.

In this void, political negotiation is conducted through the programs of NGOs and international organizations that seek to "build civil society" and repair the wounds of previous conflicts. In these territories, NGOs and political entrepreneurs have tapped into this humanitarian market with growing business acumen. The postintervention sequence could be roughly characterized as a shift from a politics of rescue to a politics of healing. In this phase, the politics of healing imposes a new center of gravity (or reference) on all interventions and provokes a reconfiguration of the political treatment that has been recently applied to Kosovo and Albania. The "post" of postintervention does not mean that the crisis has been dissipated, that the end has been reached, and that nothing else will come after it. In fact, interventions persist under a different figure that purports to repair the impact of insecurity and violence on communities and individuals and to cure the political sources of collective and individual problems.

## BETTER GOVERNANCE
In the war-torn Balkans, Bosnia, and Kosovo have represented a privileged political laboratory of "better governance" in a postbipolar world. Under the "good governance" label, numerous international organizations, driven by a limited number of donor countries, have invested large financial resources not only in the permanent training of judges and police officers, but in the building and modernization of prisons and in drafting constitutions and penal codes. In the process, these agencies have fostered media and economic liberalization. Constant references to the Marshall Plan are supposed to reassure the public that this process is not a new form of global colonialism. On the contrary, they seek to imply that European democracies had benefited from an earlier version of better-governance

assistance. This parallel is untenable. Today, mobile oligarchies, which elsewhere I have identified as mobile sovereignties,[28] are ever-changing apparatuses that bind NGOs operating in the field and multilateral diplomatic agencies in a common constellation. Contemporary better-governance assistance thus enforces a uniform strategy horizontally, even though communication between different multilateral sectors may be inefficient and at times even contradictory (for example, between an occupying military force and political representatives, or between a UN development agency and the UN High Commissioner for Refugees, or between the Organization for Security and Co-operation in Europe and the United Nations Interim Administration Mission in Kosovo).

The ongoing presence in the crisis zone of military forces with flexible mandates contributes to determining a strategic opacity, or rather, as Duffield suggests, to the rehabilitation of an ambiguous form of development.[29] Such has been the widespread acceptance of this asserted complementariness between the military and the humanitarian and between the developmental and the "good-governmental" that it now qualifies as an accepted truth of our time. Reflecting and orchestrating the international policy consensus, numerous speeches and policy documents have argued that globalization, besides bringing great benefits and opportunities, has also brought into existence a shrinking and radically interconnected world in which distant and hence internationally unimportant problems no longer exist.

In the 1990s, the Balkans, as both the protagonists and the product of violence, have been the scene of this emergent tentacular political rationality. In this novel form of control, we have been able to observe the increasingly opaque succession of "quixotic" utopias of the right/duty to intervene, theorizations of the responsibility to protect, varying definitions of complex emergency, and the proposal of ambiguous conditions for joining NATO or the EU. A complex array of discourses, procedures, and operations all blur into one another to produce an intricate web of pervasive control. More specifically, in Bosnia and Kosovo, after the Dayton Accords of 1995 and the unilateral declaration of independence in 2008, long after the respective peace treaties were signed in 1995 and 1999, the international community is still very much present on the ground. Hence, the position of the high representative for Bosnia and Herzegovina and the Office of the High Representative in Bosnia and Herzegovina, were created in 1995, but were transformed in 2007 into the European Union's special representative, and although the position was to expire on June 30, 2008, it is still very much in place.[30]

The example of Kosovo best captures the paradigmatic quality of recent events in the Balkans. Suspended in what can alternately be described as a state of exception, of limbo, of paradox, or of extreme particularity, for almost ten years following NATO's intervention in the spring of 1999, Kosovo unilaterally declared independence in February 2008. The Albanian majority and we ourselves might understand this gesture to be an attempt to reinsert this territory into the course of history, the recognition of a new nation-state fitting perfectly into the master narrative of political modernity and its subplot of post-Communist transition as catch-up modernization. Precisely this attempt at rehistoricization, however, has revealed the change of paradigm, for the key to the intelligibility of present-day Kosovo lies in the generalization of the state of emergency into an enduring political order, one that the ambiguities of authority fail to dissipate, but rather further complicate. With the ever-changing language of allegedly transparent bureaucracy, the appearance of categories and their subsequent disappearance mark the various stages of the enduring presence of the international community on the ground. For instance, the special representative of the secretary-general and the head of the UN Interim Administration Mission in Kosovo (UNMIK),[31] present in the country since 1999, has now changed status from that of an administrator with full authority. Thus, the recently nominated mission head, the Italian diplomat Lamberto Zannier, has, instead of obtaining the special powers that had been granted to his predecessor Bernard Kouchner in the immediate aftermath of the war, been given the obscure status of "facilitator" (a title of remarkably telling ambiguity) of the mission's reconfiguration process. Within this reconfiguration, the European Union's Rule of Law Mission in Kosovo (EULEX),[32] under a plan devised by UN Secretary General Ban Ki-Moon, was initially supposed to operate under the auspices of the UN Interim Administration Mission, yet at the same time, it was to remain under the sole authority of the EU,[33] which has also taken charge of the Office of the International Civil Representative. In another slippage of usage, EULEX proposed to replace the previous promise of "conditional independence," which implied a sort of long-term UN or EU protectorate, with the more ambiguous formulation of "supervised independence." To add to the confusion of the lines of command in the now nominally independent Kosovo, more than eight months after the unilateral declaration of independence, the EULEX mission had not been formally deployed throughout the territory, because Serbia attempted to negotiate favorable conditions in exchange for EULEX's deployment in the north and Russia threatened to use its Security Council veto to prevent any transfer of UN authority.

The half measures, confused authority, and ambiguous titles such as "facilitator" that have proliferated with a vengeance since Kosovo's declaration of independence all reveal the blurring of roles and practices that I have described as a "gray zone,"[34] a space where the different moments of military intervention, humanitarian operations, security concerns, and foreign investments are seamlessly implicated in one another, ironically all in the name of "good governance" and its alleged principles of transparency, responsibility, and technical efficiency.

To see how the discourse of better governance is not only pervasive, but assimilated on the ground, one need merely read the letter of invitation drafted by the ministers of economy and industry announcing the Kosovo Business and Investment Summit of June 25 and 26, 2008: "we will learn firsthand about all the latest developments from Key government officials, donors, international and local organizations." Moreover, in order to earn further legitimacy in the eyes of the international community at large, in the same letter, the two ministers remind the invitees that "our government is committed to rapid reform and accelerated private sector development." While previous forums focused on the peace process, security, and institution building with the involvement of the same "Key" government officials, donors, and international and local organizations, today, the same procedures involving the same international and local actors are activated under the umbrella of development and good governance. Indeed, as another forum organized by the European Commission in Brussels on July 11, 2008, reminds us, "Kosovo is facing considerable financial requirements to respond to its institution-building and pressing socio-economic development needs. The Kosovo authorities have drawn up their own program for socio-economic development that will address key challenges like investing in the infrastructure to connect Kosovo with the rest of the region, developing Kosovo's institutions to consolidate democracy and rule of law in a multi-ethnic society."

In all emergency-operation tool kits (whether for the purpose of humanitarian aid, security, institution building, or development aid) the International Monetary Fund and the World Bank are sure to play an active role, either with an IMF assessment of the macroeconomic framework and policies or with a statement by the World Bank on policy priorities and aid modalities. Humanitarian aid, security aid, and development aid are thus legitimated from the beginning, starting with the March 1999 armed intervention by NATO through the arrival of the UN Interim Administration Mission in Kosovo in June 1999 and the declaration of independence in February 2008, since "Kosovo is a profoundly European matter. Bringing growth and prosperity to the poorest part of Europe will help secure stability in the Western Balkans." Or as Olli Rehn told the European Parliament in an elision of the political, the strategic, and the economic, there is "no sabbatical from the EU's work for peace and prosperity."[35]

Since the ripple effects of poverty, environmental collapse, civil conflict, health crises, and so on respect no international boundaries, they can easily breach and destabilize the West's carefully balanced way of life unless they are properly managed. The combination of the moral imperative and intervention technologies hence cloaks humanitarian operations with a kind of protective screen whereby any specific procedure is justified in the pursuit of the final objective.[36] In other words, the apparently successful engagement by NGOs or international organizations with the "hard facts" of international crises has resulted in a moral conundrum. The effectiveness of their actions, which they thought would legitimize their ethics, is actually undermining them. Consequently, they risk becoming very much part of the problem they originally set out to solve as they run roughshod over local communities and lives in the name of the higher good.

This moral conundrum lies at the heart of Michel Foucault's critical analysis of neoliberalism, understood as a set of techniques for managing social risk.[37] Toward the end of the 1970s, Foucault developed his analyses of neoliberalism and consequently of the emergencies it entails (or calls into being the better to control them) in the courses he held at the Collège de France. In this respect, his 1977 lectures and most notably his 1979 course on the birth of biopolitics are a crucial point of reference in the development of our own theoretical framework. These lectures are also relevant because they allow us to connect Foucault's work on governmentality with Agamben's argument on the state of exception as the defining characteristic of our time.

However one may choose to interpret the notion of biopolitics, the Balkans seem an apt illustration of the hypothesis. Counter to or in addition to classical theories of domination, the Foucaultian concept of governmentality points to the "active" participation of subjects who are capable of agency, albeit in conditions not of their own choosing. What needs to be noted here is the mobile nature of power relations. Life forms interact with coercive processes—which are flows of independent agency—while technologies repeatedly show how, in the social texture, this web of practices generates an "ideal" of human existence that makes the act of governing at a distance possible through the continuous production of soft power that places the individual in the ambiguous predicament of being free while being dominated.

In postconflict laboratories of biopolitics, where military and humanitarian intervention has paved the way to institution building—in other words in the post-Communist Balkans—the analytical utility of Foucault's concept of neoliberal governmentality can be clearly observed in all its fundamental ambiguity. One needs only to note how the new Kosovar politicians, building their country's state institutions in the aftermath of the 2008 declaration of independence, have embraced the neoliberal dicta shared by the EU, UN agencies, and multilateral bodies such as the Organization for Security and Co-operation in Europe. In so doing, they have deployed governmental procedures that reveal how the state is the mobile effect of a regime of multiple governmentalities, a heterogeneous mixture of apparatuses and technologies of political regulation. As Laurent Jeanpierre summarizes it aptly: "The mobile effect of multiple governmentalities can be appreciated in the official statements issued after every meeting declaring that the market is the avenue for all future progress and that financial aid will be available depending on neoliberal 'professionalism,' strict adherence to the human rights doctrine, respect for ethnic minorities, and a ruthless vision of social and economic policies based on 'competition.'"[38]

To conceive of liberalism as a mode of government by economic means implies that human conduct is to be regulated solely through the dominant economic activities. Legislative and juridical powers are superseded by the market. The market thus is the only authority entitled to define governments, bodies, and populations. Yet one cannot avoid realizing that thirty years after its inception, this mode of planetary management has given birth to a situation in which the market and the state of exception go hand in hand. The juridically legitimated apparatus of exception generated by neoliberal forms of emergency intervention produces the web of relationships so aptly described by Duffield in *Development, Security and Unending War*.[39] He views the relationships between state institutions, NGOs, and multilateral agencies as a direct continuation of neoliberal strategies. Despite, or rather because of their appeal to well-intentioned discourses of sustainable development and local "empowerment," these webs of relationships tend to recreate, through policies of exclusion and reinclusion, two worldwide typologies of human beings: the included and the excluded or, in Duffield's language, socially insured populations (the minority, in the Global North and the West) and ostensibly self-sustaining uninsured and uninsurable populations (the majority, in the rest of the "developing" world). According to Duffield, the neoliberal strategy demonstrates, on the one hand, that to separate NGOs from developed nation-states is impossible and, on the other, that underdeveloped and the insecure states will have to develop themselves ("self-reliance"), but not at the same level as that of the West. In other words, Duffield argues, development (seen either as colonialism or as following struggles of national liberation) cannot be conceived as the extension of social protection for the insecure. It has to be understood as a liberal technology of security that manages and contains the destabilizing effects of underdevelopment. This amounts to discarding the excluded—the lives in excess. After decolonization, Western states based their security on establishing a "developmental trusteeship." Today, in seeking to respond to the challenge of globalization, neoliberal internationalism confirms Duffield's claim that development is an infinite and generalized counterinsurgency strategy that maintains the status quo.

## SECURITY AND DEVELOPMENT

While the generalization today of "good governance" techniques as a means for uninsured populations to self-regulate their biopolitical risks suggests the prescience of Foucault's critique of neoliberal governmentality, the insured West has effectively mobilized the discourse of development as an instrument for enhancing its own security. The end of the Cold War ushered in a normative reevaluation of the notion of international "security." Security now takes as its object the physical and psychic well-being of individuals who are grasped through the notion of the "global population." This new political rationality imposes itself under the name of "human security." It is founded upon a strategy of risk management that focuses on the interrelationships between various threats: threats to health and the environment that stem from migratory flows, poverty, crime, terrorism, and armed conflicts. More recently, the claim that humanitarian governance requires postintervention development, and that development requires security, and that security is impossible without development has been repeated to the point of monotony in countless government reports, policy statements, UN documents, NGO briefs, academic works, and so on. As Duffield bluntly puts it, the new wars must be understood in light of the merging of development and security. In such a context, the notion of development clearly shows the extent to which contemporary domination dons a reassuring guise, as if it were the expression of the communities' autonomous decisions—indeed, "institution building" at its best.

The discourse of "human security" provides the political grounds for justifying the intervention of private actors or state coalitions, whether mandated by the UN or not. In the lexicon of government, "human security" is defined as the capacity of individuals to benefit from a life that by definition should be peaceful and fulfilling. While once relegated solely to the domain of domestic affairs, the doctrine of "human security" has transformed the fulfillment of individual life into a domain of concern for the international community.[40] Over time, human security has inserted itself in the universalist discourse of human rights, which, divorced from local history, is capable of being applied to a multitude of enterprises, from institution building to peacekeeping, invoking its relationship to both democracy and international law. Originally, human security was defined according to seven different dimensions of security: economic, food, health, environmental, personal, community, and political security. This totalizing grid increasingly envelops the individual in its successive layers of insecurity until it finally succeeds in reaching the physical body.[41] In this colonization of political space, humanitarianism is a technology that produces a body that must be transformed through the beneficence of aid. For example, humanitarian intervention claims as its objective the food and health security of refugees. This aid process inevitably recasts the refugee as victim, a remolding that is at the heart of security operations. Human security operations therefore exactly follow the lines of inequality that shape the international order. Security operations create a new space that fosters the

implementation of liberal management on an international scale. In this managerial realm, absolutely every dimension of human life is recast as an issue of security, and the discourse of security gains more and more strength as it penetrates
ever deeper into the body, eventually so circumscribing human life that security
becomes purely a technique of survival.

This silent mechanism is carefully regulated by an ensemble of norms and universal standards. Over the last fifteen years, the projects of human security and
of humanitarian "governance" have emerged as an ever-growing research agenda
in academic and/or operative fields. In strategic terms, "human security" attends
to the well-being of those who would otherwise be a threat to "our" security. In
an enterprise that constantly redefines what it means to be human, target populations have become both subjects and objects of security. The effort to achieve
"human security" is therefore also an act of production. It produces "humans" who
need to be secured through a web of techniques and political practices in which
actors may or not be linked through the state. Is there an alternative interpretation
to such a damning perspective on the neoliberal spider's strategy?

## CONCLUSION

In a recent yearly meeting of the Blue Bird Club,[42] a think tank that brings together
writers, journalists, and intellectuals from the Balkans, participants struggled with
an issue that seems aptly to express the anxiety entailed in the perpetration of
a situation of permanent transition: Are the Balkans the first EU colony? The
answer depends, of course, on how one conceives of colonialism. This is not the
place to rehash debates over direct rule, indirect rule, or the colonization of the
mind. Even from my brief descriptions of the shift from humanitarian emergency
to permanent transition in the post-Communist ("Western") Balkans, however,
it is clear that Europe and the West at large have exercised direct power (con-
ditionality), indirect power ("facilitation"), and subjective/subjectivating power
("good governance"/governmentality) over local societies and individual bodies
there. We might understand these emergent practices as a hybrid form of colonialism or, instead, as I have tried to argue, as the harbingers of a fundamentally
new global-political paradigm. Arriving so close to the end of the Cold War and so
near to the West's European heartland, the humanitarian-security crises in Bosnia, Kosovo, and Albania in fact have become the exemplary sites, or the laboratory, for the experimental application and development of discourses, techniques,
and practices as well as the (perverse) effects of a power that expresses itself
in the three moments of therapeutic victimization and salvation: better (self-)
governance, security, and development. Caught within these moments, the

"Western Balkans" stand on the threshold of Europe, subject to its pedagogy and disciplines and waiting for the gatekeeper of the law to grant them admission. Their inclusive exclusion is not a paradox, but rather is paradigmatic for the vast majority of humankind—suspended in a state of permanent emergency.

## NOTES

1   Michel Foucault, *Il faut défendre la société: Cours au Collège de France (1975–1976)* (Paris: Gallimard, 1997). On the relation between Foucault's archaeological method and his genealogy of contemporary power relations see pp. 11–12. Available in English as *Society Must Be Defended: Lectures at the Collège de France, 1975–76*, ed. Mauro Bertani and Alessandro Fontana, trans. David Macey (New York: Picador 2003). See pp. 24–25.

2   This concept, which was initially developed by sociologists and political scientists, reflects an inherently contradictory social situation. The international community has intervened in an effort to create a democratic, secure society in place of authoritarian regimes and to carve a space for peace from a place of war. In fact, these interventions have created new forms of dependence and violence that have led to a reinvention of the notion of "transition." What was once seen as a temporary, finite period of change has become normalized and is now viewed as a "permanent state." For more on the concept of "permanent transition," see Paul Beckett and Crawford Young, "Introduction: Beyond the Impasse of Permanent Transition in Nigeria," in Paul Beckett and Crawford Young (eds.), *Dilemmas of Democracy in Nigeria* (New York: University of Rochester Press, 1997); Emmanuel O. Oritsejafor, "Permanent Transition: A Conceptual Framework for Understanding the Role of Military in Nigeria," *Journal for Sustainable Development in Africa* 1, no. 2 (1999), available on-line at http://www.jsd-africa. com/Jsda/Winter%201999/articlespdf/ARC-perminant%20transition.pdf (last accessed July 1, 2009); Arpad Szakolczai, "In a Permanent State of Transition: Theorising the East-European Condition," *Limen: Journal of Theory and Practice of Liminal Phenomena* 1 (2001), available on-line at http://limen.mi2.hr/limen1-2001/arpad_szakolczai.html (last accessed July 1, 2009); Harald Wydra, *Continuities in Poland's Permanent Transition* (New York: Macmillan, 2000); and Mariella Pandolfi, "La zone grise des guerres humanitaires," in Ellen Judd (ed.), "War and Peace/La guerre et la paix," special issue, *Anthropologica* 48, no. 1 (2006): pp. 43–58.

3   See Maria N. Todorova, *Imagining the Balkans* (Oxford: Oxford University Press, 1997).

4   Giorgio Agamben, *The Signature of All Things: On Method*, trans. Luca D'Isanto with Kevin Attell (New York: Zone Books, 2009), p. 18.

5   *Ibid.*, pp. 30–31.

6   Marc Abélès, *Politique de la survie* (Paris: Flammarion, 2006), and *Anthropologie de la globalisation* (Paris: Payot & Rivages, 2008). The concept of "global-politique" also refers to the new localities in which these global politics of survival are being played out.

7   Michael Ignatieff, *Empire Lite: Nation Building in Bosnia, Kosovo, Afghanistan* (London: Vintage, 2003).

8   Ignatieff, *Empire Lite*.

9   Philippe Zarifian, "Pourquoi ce nouveau régime de guerre?" *Multitudes* 11 (2003): p. 11.

10  Frédéric Gros, *État de violence: Essai sur la fin de la guerre* (Paris: Gallimard, 2005).

11  Roberto Ciccarelli, "Reframing Political Freedom: An Analysis of Governmentality," *European Journal of Legal Studies* 1, no. 3 (2008): p. 1.

12  Liisa Malkki, "Speechless Emissaries: Refugees, Humanitarianism and Dehistoricization," *Cultural Anthropology* 11, no. 3 (1996): pp. 377–404.

13  Alessandro Dal Lago, *Non-persone: L'esclusione dei migranti in una società globale* (Milan: Feltrinelli, 1999).

14  Hannah Arendt, "The Perplexities of the Rights of Man," in *The Portable Hannah Arendt*, ed. Peter R. Baehr (New York: Penguin, 2003), p. 41.

15  David Rieff, *A Bed for the Night: Humanitarianism in Crisis* (New York: Simon and Schuster, 2002).

16  Gil Anidjar, *The Jew, the Arab: A History of the Enemy* (Stanford, CA: Stanford University Press, 2003) and "L'ennemi théologique," in Marie-Louise Mallet (ed.), *La démocratie à venir: Autour de Jacques Derrida* (Paris: Galilée, 2004), pp. 167–87. For Carl Schmitt on the distinction of friend and enemy as the fundamental political principle, see *The Concept of the Political*, trans. George Schwab (1933; Chicago: University of Chicago Press, 1996).

17  Mark Duffield, *Development, Security and Unending War: Governing the World of Peoples* (Cambridge: Polity, 2007); Mark Duffield, "Securing Humans in a Dangerous World," *International Politics* 43, no. 1 (2006): pp. 1–23; Mark Duffield, "Getting Savages to Fight Barbarians: Development, Security and the Colonial Present," *Conflict, Security & Development* 5, no. 2 (2005): pp. 1–19.

18  Slavoj Žižek, "Are We in a War? Do We Have an Enemy?" *London Review of Books*, May 23, 2002, pp. 3–6.

19  Carla Del Ponte and Chuck Sudetic, *La caccia: Io e i criminali di guerra* (Milan: Feltrinelli, 2008). In this controversial book, Del Ponte and Sudetic denounce the West's hypocritical protection and prosecution of war criminals on all sides of the Kosovo conflict.

20  Arjun Appadurai, *Fear of Small Numbers: An Essay on the Geography of Anger* (Durham, NC: Duke University Press, 2006).

21  Talal Asad, *On Suicide Bombing* (New York: Columbia University Press, 2007).

22  Veena Das, *Life and Words: Violence and the Descent into the Ordinary* (Berkeley: University of California Press, 2007). Das's understanding of violence as inscribed in ordinary social life — and therefore not as an interruption of it — is linked to world making and thus to the drawing of boundaries and limits.

23  Mariella Pandolfi, "L'industrie humanitaire: Une souveraineté mouvante et supracoloniale. Réflexion sur l'expérience des Balkans," *Multitudes* 3 (November 2000): pp. 97–105; and "Laboratory of Intervention: The Humanitarian Governance of the Postcommunist Balkan Territories," in Mary-Jo DelVecchio Good, Sandra Teresa Hyde, Sarah Pinto, and Byron J. Good (eds.), *Postcolonial Disorders* (Berkeley: University of California Press, 2008), pp. 157–86.

24  Vanessa Pupavac, "Psychosocial Interventions and the Demoralization of Humanitarianism," *Journal of Biosocial Science* 36, no. 4 (2004): pp. 491–504.

25  Vanessa Pupavac, "Human Security and the Rise of Global Therapeutic Governance," *Conflict, Security & Development* 5, no. 2 (2005): pp. 161–82 and "Therapeutic Governance: Psycho-Social Intervention and Trauma Risk Management," *Disasters* 25, no. 4 (2001): pp. 358–72. Didier Fassin aptly designates the "humanitarian government" as the administration of

populations in the name of a superior moral motive that aims, first and foremost, at preserving life and alleviating suffering. See Didier Fassin, "L'humanitaire contre l'État, tout contre," *Vacarme* 34 (Winter 2006), pp. 15–19.

26  Abélès, *Politique de la survie*.

27  Pandolfi, "L'industrie humanitaire."

28  Duffield, *Development, Security and Unending War*.

29  European Union Force Althea—EUFOR ALTHEA—is the European peacekeeping force overseeing the military implementation of the Dayton Accords. At the moment, EUFOR deploys around twenty-five hundred troops from twenty-seven countries. See the EUFOR Web site for information: http://www.euforbih.org/eufor/index.php?option=com_frontpage&Itemid=27 (last accessed July 1, 2009).

30  Here is how the UN Interim Administration Mission in Kosovo Web site presents the mission and objectives of the "transitional" administration: "In June 1999, following a 78 day-long NATO campaign, the United Nations was asked to govern Kosovo through its Interim Administration Mission in Kosovo (UNMIK), with an unprecedented sweeping mandate to provide Kosovo with a "transitional administration while establishing and overseeing the development of provisional democratic self-governing institutions to ensure conditions for a peaceful and normal life for all inhabitants in Kosovo." For more information, see http://www.unmikonline.org/intro.htm (last accessed July 1, 2009).

31  "The European Union Rule of Law Mission in Kosovo is the largest civilian mission ever launched under the European Security and Defense Policy (ESDP). The central aim is to assist and support the Kosovo authorities in the rule of law area, specifically in the police, judiciary and customs areas. The mission is not in Kosovo to govern or rule. It is a technical mission which will mentor, monitor and advise whilst retaining a number of limited executive powers. EULEX works under the general framework of United Nations Security Resolution 1244 and has a unified chain of command to Brussels." See http://www.eulex-kosovo.eu/?id=2 (last accessed July 1, 2009).

32  Yves de Kermabon, the French retired general, head of the European Union Rule of Law Mission in Kosovo said: "In this environment EULEX is under very clear chain of command, which is a European chain of command, and we will report through this specific organization in Brussels." See "EULEX: Head EU Mission in Kosovo to Report to Brussels Only," *People's Daily Online*, July 8, 2008, available on-line at http://english.peopledaily.com.cn/90001/90777/90853/6443973.html (last accessed July 1, 2009).

33  See Pandolfi, "La zone grise des guerres humanitaires." In *The Drowned and the Saved*, Primo Levi describes "the gray zone" as the situation of those "privileged" prisoners (those able to obtain a little extra food, for example) who had to collaborate with their torturers to do so. See Primo Levi, *The Drowned and the Saved* (London: Vintage, 1989). The use of "gray zone" in my work was inspired by Primo Levi.

34  According to a European Commission press release, "The international community will invest €1.2 billion in Kosovo's socio-economic development, with the European Union contributing €508 million. The announcement came at the closing of the Kosovo Donors' Conference hosted in Brussels by the European Commission. Enlargement Commissioner Olli Rehn said: 'I am proud that by pledging half a billion euros, the EU today clearly demonstrates its commitment to Kosovo and to the stability of the Western Balkans. I am also thankful to our international partners for their contribution and engagement. The €1.2 billion pledged today will help to

bring about a better future for all living in Kosovo.'" Under the headline "'No sabbatical from the EU's work for peace and prosperity,' "Olli Rehn tells the European Parliament," another European Commission press release declares: "Enlargement policy serves the fundamental interest of the European Union and its citizens, noted Enlargement Commissioner Olli Rehn in his speech at the European Parliament pointing out that 'we cannot take any sabbatical from this work for peace and prosperity'. The Commissioner concluded by underlining that enlargement was always going to be a long-term effort, which has to ride out political storms in Ankara, Belgrade, Brussels and other capitals." See http://ec.europa.eu/enlargement/press_corner/whatsnew/events_en.htm?Page=4 and http://ec.europa.eu/enlargement/press_corner/whatsnew/commissioner_en.htm?Page=2 (last accessed July 1, 2009).

35    See Didier Fassin's essay, "Heart of Humaneness: The Moral Economy of Humanitarian Intervention," in this volume.

36    Michel Foucault, *Naissance de la biopolitique: Cours au Collège de France, 1978–1979* (Paris: Hautes Études-Gallimard-Seuil, 2004), available in English as *The Birth of Biopolitics: Lectures at the Collège de France, 1978–79*, ed. Michel Senellart, trans. Graham Burchell (New York: Palgrave Macmillan, 2008).

37    Laurent Jeanpierre, "Par-delà la biopolitique," *Critique* 61, no. 696 (2005): p. 358 (my translation).

38    Duffield, *Development, Security and Unending War*.

39    Mark Duffield, *Global Governance and the New Wars: The Merging of Development and Security* (New York: Zed Books, 2001).

40    Mariella Pandolfi and Chowra Makaremi, "La sécurité humaine," *Parachute*, no. 124 (October 2006): "Violence Unlimited" issue, pp. 143–48.

41    According to the doctrine of human security, the physical body must be secured against hunger and illness, harkening back to the idea of biopolitics identified by Michel Foucault. Biopolitics represents the point at which politics appropriates human life in its biological form. At this moment, both life and politics are radically transformed, and invested—even circumscribed—by the normative and immanent dimension of biological life.

42    The objective of the Blue Bird Club is to provide a discussion forum for scholars from Eastern Europe and for journalists from all over Europe, bridging gaps in communication, thus contributing to the diversification of the intellectual debate in Europe. The club gathers a group of about twenty-five highly qualified intellectuals from Southeastern Europe—some of them brilliant younger scholars, others experienced, internationally renowned scholars who excite attention among the politically engaged public all over Europe—and journalists from Europe at large to discuss questions and topics of mutual interest. The Blue Bird Club will meet once or twice a year for at least one day at different locations to acquaint participants with the region's diversity.

# The Verge of Crisis:
# Doctors Without Borders in Uganda

Peter Redfield

> For you people coming here, you may see war, but we here, we think of this as a
> peaceful time.
> —Ugandan driver in Gulu, 2006

Most writing about humanitarianism—by practitioners, journalists, and academics
alike—focuses on dramatic episodes of extreme emergency and human tragedy.
Disasters such as the Ethiopian famine and the Rwandan genocide inspire ample
commentary, analysis, and recrimination after the fact. Their significance established, they serve as landmarks for humanitarian chronology, orienting subsequent
problems into a lineage of inhuman events. In this manner, they constitute classic
forms of crisis, moments that appear as decisive turning points, while collectively
suggesting the limits of humanity amid extreme conditions. Neither the focus on
catastrophe nor the ethical framing of it is particularly surprising. As numerous
observers have suggested, the moral force of humanitarian ideals derives from
the apparent clarity of extreme conditions and the imperative to act that they can
evoke. However, it may not present the most accurate portrayal of either humanitarianism or even the "humanitarian crisis" itself. A great deal of actual practice
by humanitarian organizations responds to less spectacular forms of suffering and
more ambiguous contexts, ones that might or might not represent states of emergency. Situations balancing on the "verge" of future disaster or possible recovery
from past devastation only infrequently surface into media view.

In the following essay, I will explore this uncertain zone of suffering directly,
tracking the place of Uganda amid the shifting portfolio of projects maintained by
one major humanitarian organization: Médecins Sans Frontières, known in English as Doctors Without Borders and in the aid world as MSF. This organization has
worked off and on in Uganda for well over two decades, pursuing a variety of

projects ranging from basic health care for refugees to efforts to combat sleeping sickness and HIV-AIDS. During much of this time, the country has been a relatively stable neighbor to more dramatic events in Rwanda, Sudan, and the Democratic Republic of Congo. In 2003, flare-ups in the long-standing northern insurgency prompted many aid agencies, including MSF, to respond to the large number of displaced people living in camps. The situation, however, remained ambiguous and its health issues diffuse: a mixture of malnutrition, sporadic epidemics, potential trauma, and enduring symptoms of poverty. The MSF sections on the ground thus faced a continuing problem of defining and redefining their role.

By focusing on this geographic and temporal borderland of crisis, I seek to reexamine the broader orientation of humanitarianism toward present calamity and its less comfortable sense of the future and the past. Humanitarian action, I suggest, actually involves the margins of crisis far more than its dramatic narration would indicate. In this sense, the uncertainties posed by Uganda for MSF constitute a norm, not an exception. The dilemmas of humanitarianism derive not only from clearly dire situations, but also from those that might be dire and that could either be getting better or be getting worse. Here, the temporal frame expands away from the present, and the limits of humanitarian concern grow less sure.

It is precisely this state of uncertainty, I argue, that ultimately proves most revealing. Inasmuch as humanitarian actors define their ethics around action and present that action as a reaction to suffering, they limit the scope of their perceived responsibility and decision making. The formula is clear: Moral outrage demands response. When faced with a less definite field of potential outrages and responses, however, humanitarians must themselves determine what constitutes a legitimate exception. In doing so, they confront the task of evaluating forms of suffering, comparing cases and recognizing constraints—in effect, adjudicating within the very categorical value of life that they hold dear. Moreover, uncertainty underscores ordinary inequalities between lives and life prospects beyond states of exception and the uneasy boundary between humanitarianism and development. Ambiguous cases such as that of Uganda thus not only provide a less romantic portrayal of humanitarian engagement than those common to media imagery, but also expose a key tension within humanitarian ethics and its relation to crisis, as well as what Didier Fassin terms its "politics of life."[1]

## MSF AND THE CLARITY OF CRISIS

To set the stage for this discussion, I will first outline the trajectory of the organization in question and note its particular relevance for the issues at hand. MSF emerged in France at the end of 1971, ostensibly in response to two crises: the protracted demise of the Biafran rebellion in Nigeria amid manipulated famine and the violent emergence of Bangladesh in the wake of natural disaster. Although the early history of the group may not quite conform to later myth, MSF nonetheless came to embody an alternative Red Cross, shaped by the new conditions of decolonization, youth rebellion, and a new media age.[2] Initially a small and poorly organized shoestring operation, it grew into a significant presence by the later 1980s. As it did so, it became less French and more European, expanding into a federation of loosely connected and often squabbling national sections.[3] It also became more effective, famous, and rich, developing a global system of logistics, an increasingly professional profile, and a fundraising strategy that favored independence by relying less on states than on individual donors. In 1999, the Nobel Committee awarded MSF its Peace Prize, favorably citing that independence, the speed of the organization's response, and its public opposition to abuses of power.[4]

Although the group would devote its prize money to support a new initiative advocating greater pharmaceutical equity, rather than to a response to any specific disaster, the Nobel citation reflects MSF's central public image: an emergency-room team, on call worldwide. The details beneath that image are more complex: The group includes nurses, engineers, and administrators alongside doctors amid its volunteers, relies on an army of local employees to perform a considerable part of the actual labor, and now conducts a range of missions beyond emergency response. Nonetheless, the image does capture a core essence of the organization's ethos. Both "crisis" and "emergency" are native terms for MSF. While the first generally describes a critical condition or conjuncture, often including social and political context, the second most commonly refers to a specific set of medical problems requiring rapid response.[5] Within the organization, emergency missions represent a self-consciously "classic" form of action, if no longer a norm. Although not every member may dream of being "eight to a tent in the Congo," as one veteran put it to me in Kampala in 2003, such dramatic conditions remain romantic points of reference for the collective, and a sense of urgency courses through most of the group's rhetoric. To quote another of its former adherents, MSF "couldn't survive without the word 'emergency.'"[6]

MSF's relatively rapid rise to prominence reflects the proliferation of nongovernmental organizations in the last decades of the twentieth century. In national contexts of wealthy countries, social-science analysts often gloss this pattern with references to "neoliberal" governance, under which policies seek to transfer welfare functions of the state to private entities in the name of efficiency. Internationally, the appearance of a "civil society" form of aid can evoke visions of neocolonialism, with latter-day missionaries now cast in a lead role. Such grand narratives, however, should not obscure the historical specificity of contemporary nongovernmental politics, the relative exhaustion of ideologically based party politics, and the emergence of new concerns (such as environmentalism and human rights) that have modified the political field itself.[7] In this particular case, the details are more revealing, since MSF inherited its oppositional ethos from the political moments of the late 1960s and early 1970s in France.[8] A number of its key early leaders arrived at humanitarianism through political activism. The bloody results of decolonization and wars fought in the name of liberation disillusioned them, and the realities of the "Third World" differed from the conceptual version of café solidarity. Thus, Bernard Kouchner, the most outspoken of MSF's founders and a future political figure, found his calling amid the starving masses in Biafra. For Rony Brauman, ex-Maoist and MSF's later president and intellectual light, the Khmer Rouge debacle in Cambodia brought a final break with Communist ideology, replaced by the specificities of a rural hospital in Benin, an urban hospital in Djibouti, and a refugee camp in Thailand. As he noted in a later interview, the period from 1975 to 1980 was an era of expanding Soviet influence in the Third World, and with the eruption of one refugee crisis after another, MSF's actions in effect began to take an anti-Communist turn.[9] Several prominent figures within the original French group (including Brauman), took public stands against the leftist tradition of *tiers-mondisme* ("Third Worldism"), in opposition to MSF's newly formed Belgian branch, not to mention much of France's intelligentsia.[10] Beyond such bitter internecine struggles, two operational episodes profoundly marked the organization during this time: a partly clandestine and romanticized mission in Afghanistan following the Soviet invasion and MSF-France's noisy opposition to the Ethiopian regime amid the famine of Live Aid fame that led to the group's expulsion from the country. Both experiences contributed to MSF's mythic self-conception and greatly enhanced its public profile.[11]

Although the French section of the group briefly flirted with an ideal of liberty during the mid-1980s, what emerged from this period was less any ideological stand than a focus on life itself. The various strands of the organization and its offshoots might struggle fiercely over the terms of their engagement, but they remained in agreement about the value of life and a refusal to justify present suffering in the name of future utopian ideals. Rather than considering a crisis from the long-term perspective of some unfolding history or liberatory struggle, they perceived it in relation to the immediate needs of the affected population. Moreover, they reinforced this fundamental consensus most powerfully in their operations. During the 1970s and 1980s, the variety of suffering found in refugee camps offered MSF's humanitarians moral clarity at the level of practice. Rather than focusing on political abstractions, their actions could focus on particular bodies suffering in particular times and places. In response to violations, they could both speak out and actively intervene at the level of health.

Thus, MSF focused its energies on a direct response to inhuman conditions, wherever they might be found and whatever their origin. By the early 1990s, they had a global logistics system in place and had become more technically proficient, part of a growing trend of nonprofit professionalization.[12] Even if emergency conditions could rarely be resolved, they did lend themselves to clear technical responses alongside moral denunciation. Biomedicine could contain an outbreak of disease or offer short-term alleviation from a disaster. Undertaking such action could also represent a deeper moral rejection of the very situation itself, an "ethic of refusal," as MSF's Nobel acceptance speech would put it.[13] Amid the compressed time of crisis, humanitarians grasped the clarity of action.

As MSF continued to grow, however, it gradually took on new concerns. Unlike the Red Cross, it had no specific mandate or legal status beyond its internal charter and articles of incorporation. Led by an ever-shifting array of personnel and deeply infused with a global imagination and an oppositional ethos, the group's organizational structure fostered never-ending experimentation and critique. Many initiatives would prove short-lived, withering with the departure of key visionaries or eclipsed by events. But over time, MSF came to sponsor missions far beyond classic emergency response to wars or natural disasters. Although emergencies continued to define the group's public profile and sensibility, its definition of what constitutes a crisis expanded to include problems such as HIV-AIDS and mental health, conditions unlikely to resolve cleanly or conclusively.

To provide a sense of MSF's actual practices, I will review the 2003–2004 edition of the group's *Activity Report*. As in previous years, the volume includes not only a quick country-by-country synopsis of all projects, but also a world map, organizational statistics, a number of reflective and critical essays on humanitarian issues, and a carefully selected array of black-and-white images featuring aid workers and afflicted populations. It constitutes, in this regard, one snapshot of what Craig Calhoun terms "the emergency imaginary."[14] As essays in the report indicate, during the time period, MSF recognized a series of significant challenges. These included the rise of military humanitarianism, which the group blamed for the recent loss of five staff members in Afghanistan, an increasing focus on cost recovery in international health, which it suggested favors macroeconomic theory over human life, and the emerging disaster in Darfur, to which it responded with a large operation and publicity blitz, if stopping short of invoking genocide. In addition, the report highlighted regional issues related to HIV-AIDS in Africa, tuberculosis control in Asia, and the plight of recent immigrants in Europe.

Alongside these general concerns, the statistical record suggests both clear patterns of geographic concentration and considerable variety of topical focus. While MSF's world may center on Africa, the projects it conducts extend well beyond. The group maintained a presence in seventy-seven countries that year: thirty-two in Africa, twenty-one in Asia, eleven in the Americas, and thirteen in Europe and the Middle East. The prevalence of Africa was even higher in monetary terms, as the continent accounted for nearly 70 percent of the organization's program expenditure. Four of the five most expensive programs were in that continent, led by the Democratic Republic of Congo and Sudan. Of the twenty-two programs with expenditures over 3 million euros, only six lay elsewhere: Afghanistan, Chechnya, Iraq, Myanmar, Cambodia, and Russia. Not all of the major programs, however, concentrated on immediate emergency relief. In postconflict settings such as Angola, MSF had treated malaria patients while lobbying to change government protocols, while in Liberia and Burundi, it had begun new initiatives aimed at combating sexual violence. In Kenya and Malawi, the focus was on AIDS, including antiretroviral therapy. Although not on the massive scale of operations in the Democratic Republic of Congo or Sudan (each of which involved over two hundred foreign and several thousand local staff), these programs were nonetheless significant and in aggregate constituted a majority. Away from Africa, missions tended to be smaller and the projects even more varied. In Thailand and Cambodia, for example, MSF was treating AIDS and malaria with less than a tenth of the personnel as in Sudan. In Burkina Faso and Guatemala, it sponsored another AIDS program, as well as health care and psychological counseling for street children. In Nicaragua, it targeted Chagas disease (a tropical disease caused by protozoan parasites) and in Uzbekistan multidrug-resistant tuberculosis.

Even a quick survey of MSF's worldwide activity underscores the extent to which the organization's sense of crisis now reaches well beyond the refugee camp. A similar expansion of concern is evident in the American section's annual list of top ten "underreported humanitarian stories." Released every year since 1998, these lists match entries for specific countries with general problems such as cholera, street children, AIDS, drug resistance, access to medicine, neglected diseases, and malnutrition. Such issues reflect MSF's advocacy priorities and its increasing involvement in efforts to alter health policy and even pharmaceutical research and development. Although stopping short of full political engagement—let alone utopian ideals—such efforts extend beyond the immediacy of charity that David Rieff identifies with Bertolt Brecht's apt phrase "a bed for the night."[15]

While MSF's annual reports and lists constitute snapshots of "the emergency imaginary," as I have suggested above, they also reveal contours that stretch into longer-term ambitions and structural problems of inequality. Reading several of them in a row further clouds the clarity of the concept of crisis itself. Missions open and close, problems reappear, dire predictions sometimes do and sometimes do not come to pass. The larger ensemble of MSF, then, offers an empirical map of ethical turmoil related to the concept of humanitarian emergency. To explore one sector in greater detail, I now turn to the organization's adventures in Uganda.

## UGANDA: A PERIPHERAL CENTER OF ACTION

At the turn of the millennium, Uganda lay amid several significant humanitarian concerns, but was at the center of none. Compared with much of the tumultuous Great Lakes region of Africa, Uganda had its most famous crisis moment relatively early, during and after the rule of Idi Amin in the 1970s and early 1980s. By the early 1990s, the regime of Yoweri Museveni had acquired a reputation for stability and prescient policies on HIV-AIDS, rendering it a potential model for future African governments in the eyes of aid donors. At the same time, Uganda's relatively mild physical and social climate, together with the institutional prominence of the English language at a national level, made it an attractive site for NGOs. Its reputation in the AIDS world made it a favored location for research, and although the public-health infrastructure—large elements of which derived from the colonial era—might be strained and creaky, at least some evidence of state concern existed. Uganda not only offered an easy place to work; from a humanitarian perspective it was also well positioned. South of Sudan, east of the Democratic Republic of Congo, and north of Rwanda, the country could also serve as a base for missions in volatile areas nearby. At various points, refugee populations had spilled over the borders, but not on an unmanageable scale. A long-simmering conflict in the north had produced scattered episodes of sensational violence and large population displacements across the region, but did not appear to threaten the regime. With considerable activity but relatively little damaging drama, the country seemed like a good first assignment for new international personnel. In the memorable phrase of a jaded American expatriate at a party in Kampala, it was "Africa Lite."

MSF first arrived in Uganda in 1980, responding to famine in the northeast and northwest corners of the country. It was the initial famine response by the organization, still a minor actor in the aid world, and the brief operation encountered chaotic conditions and was hardly a resounding success. Two years later, MSF was back again, dealing with the effects of population displacement, malnutrition, and a meningitis outbreak. They stayed to provide health care to alleviate an evolving series of refugee issues under UN sponsorship. In 1986, as Museveni solidified power and the situation stabilized, the organization initiated a new project to combat sleeping sickness. This venture would last nearly two decades at an evolving series of sites. During that period, other sections of the expanding organization opened their own missions alongside those of the French. The Dutch also concentrated on refugee assistance, while in the early 1990s, the Swiss began initial forays into AIDS treatment, including an effort to involve traditional healers. At the end of the decade, MSF-France began an AIDS-related program in Arua, while MSF-Switzerland was on the Kenyan border, treating pastoralists afflicted with kala azar, or visceral leishmaniasis (another disease caused by protozoan parasites). In 2000, the group responded to the ebola outbreak in Gulu. The last sleeping-sickness site closed in late 2002, even as the Arua AIDS program began offering antiretroviral therapy.

Thus, at the time of my initial arrival to visit field sites in 2002, MSF had been running one project or another in the country for two decades. This extended presence was not the result of conscious planning or any long-term policy. Rather, it represented a long and fitful string of projects implemented at different moments by an ever-changing set of personnel. Not all of MSF's constituent sections were equally represented or in agreement over what constituted the greatest need. In 2001, the Dutch pulled out, preferring to devote their resources elsewhere. Over time, however, MSF's presence in the country became something of a tradition, particularly for the French. Some members of earlier missions returned years later in a new capacity, while others rose to positions of influence within the wider organization. Some Ugandan personnel ended up working for years with the group in one setting or another. Meanwhile, other international staff arrived from beyond Europe, while still others brought families. While conditions changed, even on a local scale, MSF grew into an institution.

For an organization ideologically committed to mobility and to addressing the greatest need, wherever it might be found, such extended presence in one setting raises the troubling prospect of stasis. The head of the French mission noted this for me in his office in Kampala, briefly outlining the current roster of projects with the aid of a large map. Speaking about one potential new program, he said: "We don't want to put a foot in the hospital, or we will be there ten years later. We only want to maintain two to three programs per country in order to stay flexible. Five or more is a heavy investment, and then you can't move or be flexible. We always want to be ready for emergency."

Subsequent meetings with his counterparts in later years echoed this sentiment. MSF always needed to be alert that it would not grow complacent or be caught off guard. Over time, I came to recognize this as a common theme, particularly among people with some decision-making capacity. On the one hand, it made perfect sense for a humanitarian organization to be in a setting like Uganda. On the other, the need was neither singular nor indisputable, given that there was no current, overwhelming crisis. The horizon in this context thus extended beyond immediate concerns. One justification given for the organization's continued presence in the region was that something dire might happen at any point. Certainly,

Uganda had no shortage of imaginable disasters, and if one should strike, it would pay to be present on the ground.

It is this edge of uncertainty and anticipation that I wish to explore in some ethnographic detail. Unlike moments of dramatic action, uncertainty and anticipation do not lend themselves to repeated narration. Nonetheless, I suggest, uncertainty and anticipation make up a good deal of the fabric of humanitarian experience and complicate the temporal profile of humanitarian practice.

## A SHADOW IN THE NORTH

In 2002, the Ugandan government launched a military offensive named Iron Fist, seeking to eradicate the main northern insurgency. Although relatively insignificant as a fighting force and unlikely to seize power, the Lord's Resistance Army (LRA) had waged an effective campaign of regional destabilization. The successors of earlier insurgent movements and part of a conflict with longer colonial roots, the LRA itself had acquired a lurid reputation.[16] Numbering at most a few thousand and spending considerable time over the Sudanese border, the group conducted sporadic raids that included episodes of brutal mutilation and the abduction of children. Such practices, combined with elements of spirit possession and references to the biblical commandments in place of an elaborated political agenda, propelled the LRA beyond the pale of conventional story lines. They also spread fear among northern rural populations, driving many from their lands and villages and into resettlement camps. Some northerners speculated that elements of the central regime and national army had a stake in keeping the north weak and thus conspired to keep the conflict alive. Nonetheless, Museveni was under pressure to demonstrate periodic action, and Iron Fist was the latest attempt at a military solution. The result was an escalation in violence. Although the army chased the rebels and destroyed bases in Sudan, the LRA pulled off attacks in new areas in 2003 and 2004. The population of displaced people surged, tripling by some estimates to 1.5 million. Uganda had the makings of another crisis on its hands.

Humanitarian groups took notice of the deteriorating situation. MSF monitored all available information and sent exploratory teams north to evaluate whether to open a mission and if so where to locate it. At a party in Kampala during the summer of 2003, the newly arrived local head of MSF-France and her counterpart for MSF-Switzerland discussed the need to open operations in the region. Although hardly a decision-making forum, the brief exchange over wine and banter reflected the mood of the moment. Something, it seemed, was bound to happen.

I left the country shortly afterward. By the time I returned the following year, both MSF sections had new programs in the north. In addition, MSF-Holland had raced back to Uganda, establishing the largest program of all in the northern town of Lira. I went to see their new head of mission at their reopened office in Kampala, now a hive of activity. A dynamic woman originally from Spain, she spoke passionately about the new project, part of a Dutch effort to get back to the basics of emergency response while also incorporating lessons from the group's nonemergency work on AIDS and malaria. The upsurge of violence in Uganda had coincided with this effort and provided a good context for implementing this latest model of intervention. Uganda, after all, had many medical problems beyond the results of human conflict. At the same time, there were people in the Amsterdam headquarters who felt the group never should have left the country. In retrospect, that decision now looked potentially shortsighted. The head of the mission suspected that the aid community in Uganda had grown too complacent, lulled by the relative calm in the south and the existence of a semifunctioning state. Whereas the Congo region suffered from rich resources, this country, she suggested, was "cursed by a good image." In the north, things were different, with the real brutality of force on display. NGOs were all too often overly cautious, she felt, and became the easy targets of cynical manipulation. The time had come to take more risks.

Although the three MSF sections all represented the same larger movement, in typical fashion, their parallel field ventures remained distinct, and their collaboration was tinged with wariness, if not open rivalry. Each would find and define the crisis for itself. The original Dutch plan had been to focus on the area around Gulu, the long-standing epicenter of the conflict. However, the Swiss section of MSF had arrived there first, and the French were exploring areas around Soroti and Kitgum. The Dutch thus settled on Lira, where the violence had unexpectedly shifted. A commercial center usually beyond the conflict zone, the town was quite unprepared for a sudden influx of displaced people, many suffering from malnutrition, and the local hospital soon found itself overwhelmed. In full emergency mode, the Dutch team concentrated on moving quickly, sending as many people as possible and working out the details afterward. They also began efforts at research and advocacy, to establish the scope of the problem better and to publicize it in national and international media.

Due to a series of contingent circumstances, I visited the French and Swiss missions that year, rather than the Dutch. By the time I arrived, the French were already winding down their operation in the town of Soroti and shifting focus to a smaller community called Amuria farther north. Although Soroti had experienced an unexpected influx of rural people fleeing the fighting and suffering from hunger, conditions had stabilized, and the problem was dissipating. The therapeutic feeding center that MSF had established in the local hospital was largely empty, with only a few painfully thin children still receiving treatment. There, the emergency appeared over.

Amuria, however, still had plenty of needs. The French team struggled to expand the water system to cope with the thousands of new arrivals while also running a health clinic and assessing conditions in the neighboring areas. I participated in a couple of these rapid assessments, judging the nutritional state of the surrounding people by measuring the circumference of small children's upper arms. The results remained ambiguous. Things did not look good, but were not obviously dire, and the team awaited evaluation visits from Kampala before determining how to proceed. The crisis could be moving in either direction.

Meanwhile, in Gulu, the Swiss faced both a cholera outbreak in a nearby camp and a sudden influx of children sent by their parents to sleep in the relative safety of the town. Known as "night commuters," they flooded local institutions, including the hospital where MSF was working. The Swiss team helped set up a center for them and established a counseling program to respond to the potential psychological effects of violence and displacement. The cholera response went smoothly, and the disease was quickly contained. The night commuter program, on the other hand, offered less clear possibilities for closure. Numbers had declined since the peak, but now held steady. The phenomenon derived from a complex mix of social causes, and unlike cholera, mental-health problems are hard to treat quickly.[17] The center also attracted considerable media attention, to the exasperation of some of the staff. Although pleased with the overall publicity, they feared its effects on the program, which they suspected might be acquiring an unintended role as a quasi-youth center. Here the sense of crisis was varied, particular, and unresolved.

In November 2004, MSF-Holland released a research survey assessing baseline health among camp residents in two northern districts. Preliminary findings indicated that crude mortality and under-five mortality rates were above emergency thresholds. Morbidity and insecurity measures were also high, and water supplies appeared deficient. Nonetheless, most respondents indicated they would stay in the camps until the situation eased.[18] A second study focused on mental health. It found evidence of trauma and domestic violence, as well as depression and thoughts of suicide, particularly among women. The need for action appeared evident in order to "achieve normalization and improved quality of life."[19] Even as the conflict in Uganda began to attract greater attention from international media, MSF included it in its annual list of "underreported humanitarian stories."[20] And the new International Criminal Court began investigations, responding to a request from President Museveni. From the outside, at least, a state of crisis had clearly arrived.

On the ground, however, things remained less uniform or determinate. At the time of my visit to Gulu, yet another MSF section arrived in Uganda. A small team from MSF-Spain conducted an exploratory mission around the town, evaluating the situation and looking to see where humanitarian conditions might warrant a project. For several days they roared off in one direction or another, traveling from camp to camp following news of misery. In the evenings, they discussed their findings among themselves and also talked with the Swiss group already in place. Both the severity and the trajectory of the situation were uncertain. Conditions were clearly not good, with many people in undesirable circumstances. But to the team's eyes, the level of misery hovered on the borderline between exceptional disaster and endemic poverty. It was also unclear whether things were disintegrating, improving, or merely holding steady. The decision whether or not to open a mission would not be a simple one, the team leader told me. "We want to act, but don't want to force it. What we see is lots of work around, but no one obvious center." Given the presence of other organizations in the area, including other sections of MSF, they leaned toward a negative recommendation.

When I returned to Uganda in 2006, I was therefore surprised to find that MSF-Spain had indeed launched a mission in Gulu. After debate, the central office had decided to override the initial exploratory team and open a project. Part of their rationale for doing so was that establishing a presence would allow the group to monitor the situation. The project, however, had been slow to take off. The staff experienced personnel issues and chafed at restrictions placed on their movement in the name of security. Several wanted to stay in the camps overnight, as originally planned, and all thought the situation calmer than it appeared from Barcelona. Thus far, their work had been limited to providing basic health care and working on health infrastructure, and it was going more slowly than anticipated. "I'm not always sure what we're doing," one nurse told me, expressing frustration over the slow pace of a government clinic with which she was collaborating. "Nothing has changed in a year. You come, do something, and then 'pfft!' there's nothing left. OK, we save some lives, but...." Her voice trailed off. Nearing the end of her posting, she was annoyed at how little progress had been made and at the continuing sense of limbo. The project field coordinator, newly arrived and assessing the state of things, took a longer-term view. "It really irritates me when MSF is worried that they'll get stuck in one place for ten years. Like an old washing machine, get sucked in and that's that. There are lots of places where we know we'll be in ten, twenty years time. Cambodia, after the genocide, for example." Northern Uganda, he implied, might be just such a setting, less dramatic, perhaps, but requiring similar measures of patience. Beyond their evaluations of this particular program, these two divergent views suggest the deeper problem of humanitarian time frames and the assumed place of emergency within them. How long could an emergency last? Or, put in terms more appropriate for this setting, how long should a group like MSF wait for one?

The problem confronting the organization, I must stress, was not an absence of good works to do. Most health indicators in Northern Uganda were (and remain) far from ideal. The question, rather, was whether they were the right good works for MSF to undertake. Would the group find itself contributing to an aid economy, substituting health services that it felt the government should provide? Would it become an effective accomplice of those seeking to prolong the status quo? Would it succumb to the alluring mirage of development and engage in projects beyond its expertise or capacity to deliver? As an entity committed to engage worldwide, MSF feared investing too heavily in one place and thereby missing a worse problem elsewhere. But conversely, pulling away too soon risked missing a sudden deterioration, and leaving altogether would abandon local populations to the continuing misery of camp life.

That same year, a member of MSF-Holland's office staff in Amsterdam gave me a cogent summary of the challenge the situation presented for her organization:

> In a sense, Uganda is at the edge of crisis. The situation isn't as dramatic as many other contexts. But the population is almost completely dependent on foreign assistance. For whatever reason, the government hasn't been able to protect many people from five hundred LRA soldiers. Uganda managed to convince the international community and has been a model of "good development." But everyone has ignored the north up until now. It's a difficult situation to assess. The conflict doesn't translate into high mortality, but has been enough to keep 1.2 to 1.5 million people hostage for twenty years. So it's difficult to pinpoint just what's going on and to get a handle on this crisis. It's not always visible; it's not like there's been bombing of buildings or anything like that. Rather it's small scale, a few killings, or one car attack at a time. Everyone has a story to tell, but it's not comprehensive, only piecemeal. And there are lots of tensions with the UPDF [the government military]. For MSF, it's a destroyed society, and we're struggling to try and deal with that. Ultimately, most of all it's a social and domestic issue. Put a lot of people together with no space to move for several years, and you'll have your own crisis. In such a chronic sort of crisis, though, what is our role?

The different sections of the MSF responded to this question in somewhat different ways. MSF-Holland and MSF-Switzerland opened major projects, supplementing "classic" refugee relief with programs to treat social problems such as night commuting, attempts to provide counseling for potential trauma, including sexual violence, and (in the Dutch case) offering some treatment for nonemergency conditions such as HIV-AIDS. MSF-France, which had a large AIDS program elsewhere in the country, offered basic health care, therapeutic feeding, and water and sanitation programs while continuing to make exploratory forays and shifting its location when it deemed conditions suitably improved. MSF-Belgium, which had no presence in the country, simply stayed away. And MSF-Spain, late on the scene, tried to find a place to fit in.

All these different efforts encountered moments of uncertainty, even the relatively brisk French forays ("Are we fishing for an emergency?" one project coordinator for them wondered in 2004, amid a nutritional screening in one camp that again yielded borderline results). But the Spanish team had the greatest difficulties of all. They had arrived uncertainly, following an inconclusive initial survey, and were subsequently delayed for months by security concerns. Working in the shadow of the nearby Swiss team, they struggled to get their project fully off the ground and come to an agreement with local officials about the extent of their operations. Their new coordinator, a Quebecois engineer who had recently been in the Democratic Republic of Congo, reflectively compared the problems he faced in this setting with those of his last one:

> Up until now, I don't think we had a precise idea here what we're doing in the field. Things are fuzzy. I don't feel our project is here yet. It's unlike in the DRC; there it only took a week to be clear. There they were lost and needed a leader. But there was no crisis or dissension, like this team has had. In DRC, it was a similar project, primary health care. But there we had a setting where there was no service at all. Here we have to establish a partnership with the Ministry of Health. They could always just continue what they are doing, however inefficiently, so we're not in a powerful position. In Congo it was the reverse; they could do nothing without us.

Beyond personality conflicts between team members, he faced the deeper problem of finding a role in a semifunctional state. Health services in Uganda might be poorly funded, erratically staffed and supplied, and generally inefficient, but they did exist. MSF might build a better clinic or latrine, but providing primary health care quickly led to a morass of longer-term questions about the organization's role if they stayed in place. Like other sections, the Spanish anticipated expanding operations to address other aspects of suffering in the camps, including mental health and sexual violence. But as yet, the team had not found the right venue to address them. In the interim, they offered emergency care in uncertain conditions, warily cooperating with a semifunctional (but hardly "failed") state.

## THE VITAL PRESENT AND THE UNCERTAINTIES OF EXCEPTION

By recounting the trajectory of a particular NGO in one country at some level of detail, I seek to illustrate the complexity often involved in determining whether a given situation constitutes a crisis. Uganda provides a particularly apt example for this endeavor, being a land scarred by multiple problems and intermittent after-shocks, rather than suffering a decisive cataclysm. Part of MSF's challenge in such a context is simply determining whether or not it should act, and if so, on what and where. The result, to quote an article in MSF-France's internal newsletter, is "questions, but no answers."[21] Such an expression of uncertainty, while quite familiar in discussions of humanitarian ethics, is far less common in discussions of humanitarian action. It is also less common in theoretical analyses of the temporal-ity of crisis and "states of exception," to which I now turn.

Concepts of crisis and related terms such as "emergency" carry with them an implied temporality focused on the present and closely tied to action. As noted earlier, the etymology of "crisis" suggests a decisive turning point, while the mod-ern sense of "emergency" connotes a need for immediate response. In an urgent situation, the imperative mode of engagement becomes action, rather than reflec-tion or vacillation. Time, as the saying goes, is of the essence; the one who hesi-tates is lost. Such connections between moment and activity are familiar techni-cal tropes, even commonplace in the sense that all material engagement involves an immanent present, and action occurs in the now. The time of crisis, however, foreshortens the temporal horizon surrounding the moment, subordinating past and future within it. Within such limited temporal parameters, action must occur quickly, if it is to occur at all. Thus, whatever the empirical purchase of any par-ticular crisis claim, the very claim itself frames choice as limited good.

The context of contemporary humanitarianism further highlights the ethical valence of decision within crisis, dividing action and inaction along lines of virtue as well as outcome. A failure to respond becomes a moral failure and a potential source of future anguish and recrimination. The reluctance of the Red Cross to speak out during the Holocaust weighed heavily on their humanitarian successors. In this rhetorical framing, at least, the morality of the moment is essentially clear, even if that clarity may fully emerge only retroactively. Thus, once established as a defined narrative, the Holocaust could cast a long shadow on presents future and past, even in vastly different contexts. The perception of moral failures associ-ated with inaction provided a template for later crises and shaped MSF's instinct to break with the Red Cross's traditions of silence and respect for sovereignty.

The form of action that came to define moral virtue was a response to immedi-ate outrage. As a rationale for their collective endeavor, members of MSF often offer variations of a blunt formulation that "people shouldn't die of stupid things." Or as the head of the Dutch mission in Uganda put it, recounting her own ethical trajectory to humanitarianism: "If somebody's drowning, you save them." The crisis moment can thus supersede ordinary considerations as humanitarians find moral clarity in suffering and elemental matters of life and death.[22] In this sense, the present becomes "vital"—an exceptional and essential point of reference for action.

For MSF, the operational category of the emergency constitutes the most specific form of a vital present. Not only is time of the essence when combating an outbreak disease such as cholera, but decisions remain focused on short-term and technical goals. Moreover, the group has an impressive array of standard equipment and guidelines ready to facilitate rapid treatment and to minimize the significance of local conditions. Within the parameters of a sharply defined emergency, humanitarian morality appears relatively simple: Lives are at risk, and lives should be saved.

Problems that exceed these parameters, however, or fail to fit easily within them, cloud the moral clarity found in crisis. They do so by introducing a critical, complicating ethical dimension: the need for evaluation and decision. Rather than one drowning victim, an indistinct crowd struggles in the surf. How deep is the water? Who is in danger? How might they be reached? And why are they there at all? Once such questions come to the fore, it grows harder to maintain an "ethic of refusal." If the existence of a crisis is no longer a given—defined by a clear state of emergency—then its determination becomes an active problem. MSF confronts the quandary of recognizing and naming the exceptional outrage, not simply the problem of responding to it.

Humanitarians, of course, are hardly alone in investing in the overriding significance of the crisis state and the present moment. Appeals to emergency suffuse contemporary political discourse and order state practice. Past disasters authorize indefinite urgency, while potential scenarios enroll the future into a continuing logic of preparedness.[23] Amid the sea of commentary on the political moment and its longer lineage, I focus on one strand associated with sovereignty, war, and states of exception. My goal here is twofold: to recall humanitarianism's long and intimate association with warfare and to contend with a potential point of clarity. The result, I hope, is a study of temptation and a cautionary tale.

In a recent series of works, the Italian philosopher Giorgio Agamben has elaborated an extended meditation on the legal problem of the exception and its relation to sovereign rule. Following various leads of Walter Benjamin, Hannah Arendt, and particularly Carl Schmitt, Agamben identifies the state of exception as a key political form through which to grasp the nature of rule. As he writes, the exception "is this no-man's-land between public law and political fact, and between the juridical order and life," a limit case intimately tied to civil war, insurrection, and resistance.[24] In keeping with Schmitt's dictum, it is precisely the deep alchemy of this limit case that reveals sovereign power, for the one who designates the state of exception stands above the law.[25] The state of exception thus offers a potential window into political power and its relation to law.

Such an approach to sovereignty, particularly when infused with Agamben's other preoccupations about the status of life within politics, provides a tempting orientation for the study of humanitarianism. As Mariella Pandolfi suggests, one way to understand conjunctures such as the NATO intervention in Kosovo is through a recognition of dual modes of sovereignty, one tied to territory and the other to nonterritorialized logics of global governance and deployed in shifting crisis zones worldwide.[26] Certainly, the confluence of military action with humanitarian concern deserves note, and the Kosovo adventure holds landmark status within humanitarian discourse. The political trajectory of a figure such as Bernard Kouchner, stretching from outspoken critic to government minister, attests to the migratory power of humanitarian ideals and the emergence of what Pandolfi terms the "gray zone" in which military and aid objectives converge.[27] Nonetheless, the apparent collusion of state and nonstate actors in a shared rhetoric and modes of governance in such marquee emergencies—certainly crises—may distort even as it illuminates. As Didier Fassin and Paula Vásquez note, concern over the state of exception is itself historically situated.[28] Facts and discourse together constitute a larger ensemble, one that invites investigation as a problem. The goal is not the generation or evaluation of overarching theoretical claims, but rather specific exploration of the varied terrains they cross and reconnect. Renewed philosophical interest in states of exception and the public emergence of a figure such as Agamben identifies one such terrain. The actual practice of humanitarian organizations across a variety of settings is another.

It would be tempting to draw a single lineage for contemporary humanitarianism through states of war and legal exception, particularly that strand stemming from the nineteenth-century emergence of the Red Cross and subsequent efforts to "civilize" the modern battlefield. As the historian John Hutchinson notes, European states were quick to enlist this humanitarian movement as a quasi-auxiliary medical corps.[29] Outside of sponsoring formal agreements, the Red Cross largely stayed silent, accepting the limits on crises imposed by state power. MSF, in its mythic moment of origin, breaks with Red Cross tradition, challenging and denouncing power in the name of humanity. Furthermore, the "sans frontières" claim it embodies suggests not only the rhetorical refusal of borders, and by implication the limiting force of sovereign power, but also a potential higher claim to moral justification.[30] Schmitt's definition joins sovereignty and exception in a moment of legal action; the sovereign "decides" the exception, claiming status in the act of demarcating the limits of law. A struggle over what constitutes a moment of exception would thus imply a struggle over sovereignty, whether framed in legal or medical terms.[31]

However, I want to suggest that this theoretical portrayal of humanitarianism is overly clear. The work of a group such as MSF in Uganda suggests a prospect in which neither sovereignty nor exception are so sharply drawn. Whereas in theoretical discussions both the exception and the sovereign bear with them the certainty of given concepts, MSF's practice in Uganda involves bodies and populations with uncertain symptoms, a conflict that ebbs and flows, and a state that functions sporadically while hovering between guarantor and threat. In Uganda, and indeed in much of the contemporary world, the practice of war, of crisis, of humanitarianism remains less sharply drawn, less clear, and less amenable to tidy analysis. Rather than stark dictatorship and codes of law at the edge of a single polity, we find what Carolyn Nordstrom terms the "shadows": a more fragmentary realm of long, obscure connections, in and out of legal standing.[32] The results are no less brutal in terms of human suffering. However, the shadow world does not lend itself to either geographical or temporal closure. It is a realm of things that happen amid many others that *almost* do. Determining just what constitutes a crisis here grows difficult. Rather than the certain existence of an emergency, there is a continuing sense of danger, of potential collapse or recovery, all played out against a general backdrop of poverty and material lack.

An NGO in Uganda is hardly sovereign, even in a Schmittian sense. Unlike in the Democratic Republic of Congo, where the state "could do nothing" without MSF, here, the group must negotiate its presence around a Ministry of Health in addition to army regulations. But at the same time, it does participate in a struggle over determining the exception on a regular basis, by recognizing war, evaluating security and health risks, and deciding on a course of action. In the case of MSF in Uganda, situations improve and deteriorate and various iterations of the organization come and go. The group identifies shifting problems (displaced people, sleeping sickness, AIDS, displaced people again) and seeks to respond to them. It participates within a large NGO complex actively pursuing governance projects alongside, in place of, and occasionally at odds with those of the state. At points, ominous stars appear to align. MSF flirts with denunciation and with challenging, to some degree, the continuing state of exception. But the looming tragedy yields no catharsis of certainty. Like the many people in displacement camps, MSF remains waiting.

Amid this other gray zone—the verge of crisis—the decisions that MSF makes also address its fundamental humanitarian values. When a situation drags on, it must determine what constitutes an acceptable "normal" state in this setting and the limits of its own operation. It must decide whether to withdraw, even if other, nonemergency health problems remain. Such a decision is rarely easy. (As a lawyer working for MSF-Holland told me, "How do you argue against human suffering? If you really want to keep a project going, you say: 'Are you going to let those people die?'") And yet here, concern for life confronts the organization's practical constraints and global commitment, its mobility and independence. In pragmatic terms, MSF must carry out a form of triage with regard to its own programs, acknowledging the larger frame of inequality that surrounds each crisis and the fact that lives have different values in ordinary times. It thereby engages in the politics of life, "making a selection of which existences it is possible or legitimate to save."[33] Such a selection stands in contrast to MSF's vision of radical moral equality at the level of life, in which one action should never balance against another.[34] But without a clear emergency, in uncertain states of crisis, the choices that the group makes factor into the work of other organizations, the politics of development, and the realities of poverty. "It's a painful issue, having to accept limitations and accept a different level of care between places like Berlin and here," another MSF administrator in Uganda said with resignation in 2006. "But as an aid worker, you have to, or you can't continue."

## CONCLUSION

One central claim of this work is resolutely banal: that things are more complicated than we often like to think. This is no less true, I suggest with crises, and the humanitarian response to them. Humanitarian practice and its representation diverge, because a crisis is not always as certain as the term itself implies. Amid landmark moments such as Biafra, Rwanda, or Kosovo, exhaustively recorded and debated, much of the humanitarian terrain blends into common forms of suffering and the ethical dilemmas of everyday life. Here, the emergency remains emergent, its temporal form an "almost now," rather than a vital present of pure action. Considered from this perspective, the labors of an entity such as MSF appear cyclical, unresolved, and almost Sisyphean. More importantly, they rarely conform to dramatic expectations. Uganda, in this formulation, appears less the exception than the rule.

My second claim is that situations on the "verge" of crisis reveal a critical humanitarian tension between exceptional states and the ordinary, longer-term problems and inequalities that surround them. For humanitarianism—particularly the heroic medical form personified by MSF and focused on the secular value of life—ethics take definition through action. Amid an emergency, action takes the form of reaction, a response to outrage. Moments of dramatic emergency thus provide temporary moral clarity, providing MSF with the grounds for its "ethic of refusal." When operations extend beyond an emergency response, however, or when a crisis is chronic or uncertain, then action involves an expanding, uncomfortable component of decision. In ancient Greek, Reinhardt Koselleck reminds us, the term *crisis* applied to both ends of the decisive edge of politics, covering not only external conditions, but also their subjective analysis—what we now might term "critique."[35] The decisions facing an organization such as MSF are often ethically hard and politically complex. Slow threats appear alongside quick ones, and life acquires a longer and more troubling frame in which verdicts grow harder to come by. The verge of crisis reveals the degree of uncertainty surrounding the very center of humanitarian conviction. It is thus of little surprise that many humanitarian actors, media observers, and even critics have favored certain disaster.

## NOTES

1    Didier Fassin, "Humanitarianism as a Politics of Life," *Public Culture* 19, no. 3 (2007): pp. 499–520.

2    For a more comprehensive account of MSF's early French evolution, see Anne Vallaeys, *Médecins Sans Frontières: La biographie* (Paris: Fayard, 2004); Bertrand Taithe, "Reinventing (French) Universalism: Religion, Humanitarianism and the 'French Doctors,'" *Modern and Contemporary France*, 12, no. 2 (2004): pp. 147–58, offers an analysis of the context. For a portrait in English, including more on the Dutch section see Dan Bortolotti, *Hope in Hell: Inside the World of Doctors Without Borders* (Buffalo, NY: Firefly Books, 2004).

3    MSF currently has nineteen component sections. The largest and most historically influential of these are MSF-France, MSF-Belgium, MSF-Holland, MSF-Switzerland, and MSF-Spain. MSF-USA (which also uses the name Doctors Without Borders) plays an important role in advocacy and fundraising. Although organized under national headings, the actual membership of each section is heterogeneous and fluid. Thus, a French citizen might work for MSF-Belgium or a Japanese citizen for MSF-France. These subgroups share a general ethos and loose affiliation, but act with considerable independence. For the purposes of this essay, I will refer to MSF in the singular, except at moments where sectional differences are significant.

4    Press release "The Nobel Peace Prize 1999," available on-line at http://nobelprize.org/nobel_prizes/peace/laureates/1999/press.html (last accessed July 3, 2009).

5    For much of this essay, I will use these terms interchangeably in descriptions before suggesting an analysis involving MSF's distinction between them. In etymological terms, the *Oxford English Dictionary* traces "crisis" from a turning point in disease, a critical conjuncture of planets, and a point of immanent change to "times of difficulty, insecurity and suspense," the sense closest to MSF's usage. "Emergency" drifts from a rising above water, an issuing out, and an unexpected event to "a state of things unexpectedly arising, and urgently demanding immediate action." Amid the homogenization of the aid world (now dominated by the English language), I have discerned little difference between the French and English cognates in usage. Some analysts, such as Craig Calhoun, prefer "emergency" to "crisis," given the latter's hint of potential resolution. As this essay suggests, however, the very elasticity of "crisis" itself can prove revealing. For more on the history of "crisis" see Randolph Starn, "Historians

and 'Crisis,'" *Past and Present* 52 (August 1971): pp. 3–22; also Reinhart Koselleck, "Crisis," *Journal of the History of Ideas* 67, no. 2 (April 2006): pp. 357–400.

6   Unless otherwise noted, all quotations derive from ethnographic field notes taken between 2000 and 2006 in Uganda, France, Holland, Belgium, Switzerland, and the United States. In keeping with anthropological convention, I will name only those who are public figures, presenting others in terms of their group identity.

7   See Michel Feher, Gaëlle Krikorian, and Yates McKee (eds.), *Nongovernmental Politics* (New York: Zone Books, 2007).

8   This is the era that saw the founding of the independent newspaper *Libération*, as well as general intellectual ferment in leftist circles. For general background and caustic commentary see Kristin Ross, *May 68 and Its Afterlives* (Chicago: University of Chicago Press, 2002).

9   Stany Grelet and Mathieu Potte-Bonneville, "Qu'est-ce qu'on fait là?" Interview with Rony Brauman, *Vacarme* 4–5 (Summer 1997) available on-line at http://www.vacarme.eu.org/article1174.html (last accessed July 3, 2009). For a larger sociological study of French humanitarian actors, see Pascal Dauvin and Johanna Siméant, *Le travail humanitaire: Les acteurs des ONG, du siege au terrain* (Paris: Presses de Sciences Po, 2002). For a more comprehensive historical overview of the evolving political context around MSF, see Odd Arne Westad, *The Global Cold War* (Cambridge: Cambridge University Press, 2007).

10   MSF-France sponsored an abortive think tank known as Liberté Sans Frontières at the time. The struggles between different sections of MSF and its schismatic offshoots (most prominently, Kouchner had formed a rival group known as MDM, Médecins du Monde [Doctors of the World] in 1980 after a power struggle) would continue in subsequent years. They grew less ideologically charged, however, as all the parties grew more established, expanded, and became more professionalized. By the late 1990s, most of my informants agreed, relations had become far more civil. By 2003, Brauman could describe the LSF episode to me as something of a youthful folly stoked by rival ambitions, albeit one with significant bearing on the goal of humanitarianism. See also Bortolotti, *Hope in Hell*, p. 58 and Vallaeys, *Médecins Sans Frontières*, pp. 461–509.

11   In Afghanistan, members of MSF rode mountain trails with the muhajedin, entering the consciousness of the American press of the day as "French doctors." In Ethiopia, MSF-France publicly opposed government policies of forcible resettlement, perceiving in them the political manipulation of the famine and international relief, a stance that created significant uproar in the aid world. See Vallaeys, *Médecins Sans Frontières*, pp. 397–460 and 511–50.

12   See Peter Redfield, "Vital Mobility and the Humanitarian Kit," in Andrew Lakoff and Stephen Collier (eds.), *Biosecurity Interventions: Global Health and Security in Question* (New York: Columbia University Press, 2008).

13   Nobel lecture by James Orbinski, Médecins Sans Frontières, Oslo, December 10, 1999, available on-line at ahttp://nobelprize.org/nobel_prizes/peace/laureates/1999/msf-lecture.html (last accessed July 3, 2009). For more extensive commentary see Peter Redfield, "Doctors, Borders and Life in Crisis" *Cultural Anthropology* 20, no. 3 (2005): pp. 328–61.

14   Craig Calhoun, "A World of Emergencies: Fear, Intervention and the Limits of Cosmopolitan Order," *Canadian Review of Sociology and Anthropology* 41, no. 4 (2004): pp. 373–95.

15   David Rieff, *A Bed for the Night: Humanitarianism in Crisis* (New York: Simon and Schuster, 2002).

16   For more background on the Lord's Resistance Army and related issues, see Tim Allen, *Trial*

*Justice: The International Criminal Court and the Lord's Resistance Army* (London: Zed Books, 2006); Sverjer Finnström, "'For God and My Life': War and Cosmology in Northern Uganda," in Paul Richards (ed.), *No Peace, No War: An Anthropology of Contemporary Armed Conflicts* (Athens: Ohio State University Press, 2005), pp. 98–116; and Heike Behrend, *Alice Lakwena and the Holy Spirits: War in Northern Uganda, 1985–97* (Oxford: James Currey, 1999).

17  Founded on emergency medicine, MSF long emphasized physical forms of suffering. For an illuminating account and analysis of why the organization came to practice humanitarian psychiatry following the Armenian earthquake of 1988, see Didier Fassin and Richard Rechtman, *The Empire of Trauma: An Inquiry in the Condition of Victimhood* (Princeton, NJ: Princeton University Press, 2009), pp. 163–88. Alongside the organization's various ventures into social programs, psychiatric work remains a topic of debate within as well as between MSF's different sections, in part due to difficulties in accessing impact and finding closure. See, for example, the roundtable discussion on mental health published in MSF-France's house newsletter, entitled "Freud in the Field," *Messages* 142 (September 2006), pp. 1–12.

18  MSF-Holland, "Internally Displaced Camps in Lira and Pader, Northern Uganda: Baseline Health Survey Preliminary Report," November 2004, available on-line at http://www.msf.or.jp/news/baseline/Baseline.pdf (last accessed July 3, 2009). Crude morbidity rates in the Pader and Lira districts sample were found to be 2.79 per 10,000, with the < 5 rate at 5.4 per 10,000. A conventional measure of emergency is a crude mortality rate of over 1 death per 10,000 per day. See Médecins Sans Frontières, *Refugee Health: An Approach to Emergency Situations* (London: Macmillan, 1997), p. 38.

19  MSF-Holland, "Pader: A Community in Crisis: A Preliminary Analysis of MSF Holland's Baseline Mental Health Assessment in Pader, Uganda," November, 2004, available on-line at http://www.aerzte-ohne-grenzen.de/_media/pdf/uganda/2004/uganda-mental-health2004.pdf (last accessed July 3, 2009).

20  See http://www.doctorswithoutborders.org/publications/reports/2005/top10.html, (last accessed July 3, 2009).

21  François Delfosse, "In Uganda, MSF and the 'Decongestion' Process: What Is to Be Done?" *Messages* 141 (July 2006), pp. 26–27.

22  The work of Paul Farmer and associates, as well as its reception, offers a striking example. See the discussion of "areas of moral clarity" in Tracy Kidder's biography, *Mountains beyond Mountains, The Quest of Dr. Paul Farmer, a Man Who Would Cure the World* (New York: Random House, 2003), p. 101.

23  Andrew Lakoff, "Preparing for the Next Emergency," *Public Culture* 19, no. 2 (Spring 2007): pp. 247–71.

24  Giorgio Agamben, *State of Exception*, trans. Kevin Attell (Chicago: University of Chicago Press, 2005), p. 1. See also his *Homo Sacer: Sovereign Power and Bare Life*, trans. Daniel Heller-Roazen (Stanford, CA: Stanford University Press, 1998).

25  Carl Schmitt, *Political Theology: Four Chapters on the Concept of Sovereignty* (1922; Cambridge, MA: The MIT Press, 1985).

26  Mariella Pandolfi, "Contract of Mutual Indifference: Governance and the Humanitarian Apparatus in Contemporary Albania and Kosovo," *Indiana Journal of Global Legal Studies* 10, no. 1 (Winter 2003): pp, 369–81. See also Mariella Pandolfi, "Laboratory of Intervention: The Humanitarian Governance of the Postcommunist Balkan Territories," in Mary-Jo DelVecchio Good, Sandra Hyde, Sarah Pinto, and Byron Good (eds.), *Postcolonial Disorders* (Berkeley:

University of California Press, 2008), pp. 157–86.

27   Mariella Pandolfi, "Vivre la guerre des autres: Notes de terrain," *Humanitaire* 4 (Fall/Winter 2007): pp. 62–68; and "La zone grise des guerres humanitaires," in Ellen Judd (ed.), "War and Peace/La guerre et la paix," special issue, *Anthropologica* 48, no. 1 (2006): pp. 43–58.

28   Didier Fassin and Paula Vásquez, "Humanitarian Exception as the Rule: The Political Theology of the 1999 *Tragedia* in Venezuela," *American Ethnologist* 32, no. 3 (August, 2005): pp. 389–405.

29   See John F. Hutchinson, *Champions of Charity: War and the Rise of the Red Cross* (Boulder, CO: Westview Press, 1996).

30   Certainly, Bernard Kouchner's humanitarian vision—however disavowed by his successors in MSF—suggests as much. Long a champion of a "right of interference," Kouchner's dream arguably would involve a supranational order, mobile and motivated by humanitarian principles. It is one dream of Kosovo (where he served as head of the UN interim administration), more nobly executed, perhaps, but of the same genre. See Bernard Kouchner, *Le malheur des autres* (Paris: Editions Odile Jacob, 1991).

31   To announce a state of crisis, to proclaim an emergency, remains the prerogative of political power. The prototypical state of exception, after all, is war, and particularly civil war, as Agamben duly notes. The time of crisis, like that of ritual, stands outside of ordinary time and regular conventions. Ruptures and cleavages sharpen, alliances are made and reinforced, and stakes are revealed. Furthermore, an effort to respond to a state of crisis either conforms to the definition given by sovereign power or effectively challenges its prerogative. In this sense, militarism and humanitarianism share a conceptual and historical root at the edge of politics.

32   Carolyn Nordstrom, *Shadows of War: Violence, Power, and International Profiteering in the Twenty-First Century* (Berkeley: University of California Press, 2004).

33   Fassin, "Humanitarianism as a Politics of Life," p. 501. See also Peter Redfield, "Sacrifice, Triage, and Global Humanitarianism," in Michael Barnett and Thomas G. Weiss (eds.), *Humanitarianism in Question: Politics, Power, Ethics* (Ithaca, NY: Cornell University Press, 2008).

34   For example, the MSF Nobel Prize lecture declares: "One life today cannot be measured by its value tomorrow: and the relief of suffering 'here', cannot legitimize the abandoning of relief 'over there'. The limitation of means naturally must mean the making of choice, but the context and the constraints of action do not alter the fundamentals of this humanitarian vision. It is a vision that by definition must ignore political choices." Nobel lecture by James Orbinski, Médecins Sans Frontières.

35   Koselleck, "Crisis," pp. 358–59.

# Compassionate Militarization:
# The Management of a Natural Disaster in Venezuela

Paula Vásquez Lezama

"On December 15, 1999, savage nature struck a blow against a country that was advancing optimistically on the path of change."[1] This was the description of the situation in Venezuela offered by a social analyst on December 18. On the morning of December 16, 1999, Venezuelans were awaiting the results of the previous day's referendum, called to validate the new constitutional charter drawn up by the Constituent Assembly convened by President Hugo Chávez following his election in December 1998. The charter was intended to mark the start of a more socially just era. During the night of December 15–16, avalanches, mudslides, and landslides had flowed down the slopes of the El Avila range in the state of Vargas and north of Caracas, carrying with them rocks up to two meters in diameter and huge tree trunks, which rolled down the slopes at a speed of around 100 kilometers per hour, ravaging entire communities, rich and poor alike. La Tragedia, as the disaster has come to be known, left about one thousand dead and two hundred thousand homeless. Because the extraordinary ferocity of the mudslides coincided with the vote to approve the new constitution, exceptional circumstances surrounded the management of the disaster.

In today's world, militarization is a common feature of the long-term management of the aftermath of disasters. The case I examine here is one where the militarization of disaster fell in line with a political project of social transformation that promoted a convergence between the army and the people. Thus, the militarization reflected a long-term process that was closely linked to the chronic crisis affecting the country. The analysis below is based on a study of press reports and official documents produced by the Venezuelan government, together with interviews with approximately thirty people who were involved in managing aid operations and implementing a system of assistance for the disaster victims, and a field study conducted in the victims' shelters between 2000 and 2005.[2] The militarization of the management of the social aftermath of *la Tragedia* prompts reflection on the redefinition of power and the role of the military in society on three levels.

First, the actions taken during the emergency and to deal with the violence (looting and disorder) following the disaster were resituated in the gradual legitimization of the role of the military in social interventions. In the case of *la Tragedia*, the temporal coincidence between the two events created specific modes of legitimization of the articulation between military and civil power during the state of exception declared by the government on December 17, 1999. The fact that the civilian authorities were overwhelmed by the emergency meant that they were in effect removed from the management of the crisis and that the intervention of the armed forces could be easily justified. We therefore need to examine how the political legitimization of the role of the armed forces during the "state of humanitarian exception"[3] heralded the introduction of specific social policies targeted at the victims under the banner of humanitarianism.

Second, the militarization of the management of the disaster takes on a specific meaning in the context of the historic moment of the Bolivarian revolution's refounding of the nation. *La Tragedia* was also a focus of powerful emotion, given the suffering, the grief at the death of the victims, and the compassion shown them by society and by the government. Ethnographic studies conducted in the military camps where victims were sheltered reveal the interaction between officers and the disaster victims who were temporarily housed there. The military took responsibility for lodging families, providing food, and managing the plans for the temporary employment of those affected by the disaster. The fact that shelters were set up inside army camps is exceptional because of the context of political change in which it was decided—that of the coming to power of a government that prioritizes compassion for the poor.

Finally, the program of assistance for the victims, which at the time of the disaster was termed the "Plan for Dignification of the Venezuelan Family," was firmly placed in the context of the revolution's promise of social transformation and a more socially just future. "Policies of compassion" were reinvigorated by a "policy of dignification" for the victims.[4] Care for the victims under the Bolivarian revolution manifested a surge of compassion in the sense proposed by Hannah Arendt, that is, as the emotion felt in proximity to the suffering of others.[5] Against a background of deep social crisis, the aid policy redefined the relationship between the military, as the central actors in the emergency, and the disadvantaged victims. "Dignification" thus became the source of social processes originating in a very effective set of images and metaphors lying at the heart of Chávez's political discourse. The idea of dignity emerged in the assistance provided to the victims of the disaster, but also in the demand for rule by the people and in the use of the army as protagonist in the social transformation initiated by the revolutionary government. Nevertheless, analysis shows how, once the disaster was past, compassionate militarization encountered institutional and social limits imposed by normalization, in both senses of the word.

## THE PERIOD OF THE "HUMANITARIAN EXCEPTION"

In theory, an "emergency" is a specific mode of the state of exception characterized notably by the granting of extraordinary powers to the executive and the restriction of the freedom of circulation and movement. On December 17, 1999, noting the "incapacity of the Civil Defense and the Ministry of the Interior," the Venezuelan National Constituent Assembly declared a "state of emergency." The decree of December 1999 reads as follows:

> Considering that an extraordinary weather situation prevails over the whole of the national territory, caused by continual unusually heavy precipitation…the national executive is empowered to take all necessary provisions and measures to prevent further damage, to care for the people affected and to coordinate the joint action of all national, regional, and municipal bodies…. The people are called on to mobilize in solidarity and to collaborate with the aid operations in response to this natural disaster and are therefore urged to obey the instructions of public authorities, to follow their recommendations, and to cooperate with any preventative or palliative action they may take.[6]

The decree of a "state of alert" issued on December 17, 1999, authorized the president to adopt any measures necessary to "prevent further damage" without impinging on the constitutional guarantees enshrined in the 1961 constitutional charter, which was still valid, because the new constitution had not yet come into force. The decree formally "urged" the people to "act in solidarity" and demanded "strict respect" for the instructions of public authorities. But it made no mention of any potential suspension of constitutional guarantees, which an official declaration of a state of emergency would automatically, by law, have entailed. The decree ratified the extension of the executive's power to adopt any measures necessary to avoid further damage without officially restricting the constitutional guarantees.

According to political philosophy, the state of exception presents a legal ambiguity, "a lacuna in public law" inherent in the relationship between law and anomie.[7] In *State of Exception*, Giorgio Agamben evokes the possibility of creating a permanent state of emergency via a provisional measure without any legal requirement to declare the state of exception—in other words, the possibility of suspending the legal order itself. This is the theory of exception as rule that Agamben sees as characteristic of the contemporary era. In his view, "the voluntary creation of a permanent state of emergency (though perhaps not declared in the technical sense) has become one of the essential practices of contemporary states, including so-called democratic ones."[8] But in the case I examine here, the executive refused to shut itself into the circle of exception by suspending the constitutional guarantees. The situation following *la Tragedia* led to an exception of fact, because there was no exception in law.

On Saturday, December 18, 1999, the government stated categorically that there would be no suspension of the constitution by decree, and at the same time, official spokespeople declared the government's intention to repress looting and impose order by force. José Vicente Rangel,[9] who was minister of foreign affairs at the time of the disaster, stated that the government had ruled out suspending the constitution and imposing a curfew because it did not want to take "an extreme measure."[10] However, he added that "the government will not tolerate looting" and that "any threat to public order would be repressed." Isaías Rodríguez, vice president of the Constituent Assembly, declared: "Far from helping, a decree restricting the constitution might lead people to think that the state of alert is much more serious and to understand it differently from the way in which it is intended."[11] Thus, citizens in the disaster zone were in effect deprived of their rights. This unusual situation provoked no immediate political protest, because the people had confidence that armed forces would fulfill their mission. For several weeks, the security forces, both military and civilian, had extensive powers in the disaster zone. The nation saw nothing to question in this. On the contrary, people saw this demonstration of authority as desirable and necessary and thus gave carte blanche to the forces of order to go beyond their usual roles. This was the background to the violent repression imposed by the army: It was an action derived from a consensual political exception—the humanitarian exception—but was itself violent.[12] This exception was of course legitimized on the grounds of humanitarian mobilization, in which the priority is saving lives: The powerful legitimacy it enjoys derives precisely from the fact that it can point to the number of people saved from death due to famine, epidemic, or injury.[13]

On December 18, rescue operations were transferred to the sole command of the army after the civil authorities' control of operations had been assessed as inefficient and incompetent.[14] What was presented in official reports on the management of the crisis as "a harmonious interinstitutional collaboration" was in fact the subject of powerful tensions between the military and civil servants over areas of operation and expertise. Following the disaster, Minister of Defense Raul Salazar appealed to the United States government, and personally to Bill Clinton, to send four Chinook, eight Black Hawk, and two Galaxy helicopters to assist in rescuing the victims. Salazar also proposed requesting more direct involvement by the U.S. Army by asking for the help of the U.S. Army Corps of Engineers in reconstructing roads and bridges that had been destroyed. However, on January 2, 2000, this initiative was abandoned by President Chávez on the grounds of safeguarding national sovereignty and rejecting interference.[15] Rumors suggest that this decision was based on the president's fear that the massed presence of U.S. soldiers on Venezuelan territory would destabilize the Venezuelan armed forces and encourage a coup d'état.

The armed forces' intervention following the disaster occurred in three stages. The first was the provision of aid, in which all three forces, naval, air, and land, participated. The next stage was the "securing" of the disaster zone—in other words, repressive action aimed at reestablishing order after the looting and disturbances during the second night after the disaster. Members of other forces such as the Guardia Nacional and the Dirección de Servicios de Inteligencia Policial (DISIP),[16] the political police, participated in these operations. The final stage was the temporary housing for approximately one hundred and fifty thousand victims, from the middle of December 1999 on, in military camps and bases—sites that had never before accommodated so many civilians. In official documents, the management of the crisis by the armed forces is constructed politically as an exemplary instance of the union between civil society and the military.[17] In this partnership, the military is portrayed as the only force capable of mobilizing exceptional resources and as taking the preeminent role in the management of the crisis. But looking at this action in the longer-term context, in the case of *la Tragedia*, the militarization implied an immediate, unconditional, and prolonged transfer of power within the framework of a project of social transformation in which the military emerged as the central, crucial protagonist.

The violence that occurred in the aftermath of the disaster nevertheless shook the mystique of power underlying the civil-military union of the Bolivarian revolution to its core. Human rights organizations reported at least sixty "forced disappearances": summary executions, abductions, and violence are documented in the uncompromising report,[18] which led a few years later to the conviction of the Venezuelan government in the Inter-American Court of Human Rights in Costa Rica.[19] The bodies of some of the disappeared were in fact found by researchers, who reported the abuses to the media. The discovery revealed that the victims had been killed by weapons belonging to the state's security forces—in other words, that they were victims of "extrajudicial" execution. But the violent repression was not the end of the involvement by the military and the special forces: They also took part in the disorder and looting. Eye witnesses reported examples of them moving through residential districts to exact a sort of war booty. One inhabitant of the disaster zone who took part in the rescue operations described the abuses of the DISIP thus: On December 19, "once we had arrived [at La Guaira], we discovered that DISIP agents had been there and had set up an operation so they could steal the cars parked in buildings and loot apartments. They were the first to loot apartments. They took away the cars with cranes and looted the apartments. I saw them, on Tanaguarena Hill, I saw them looting a house and stealing valuables." The modus operandi reveals the complex interplay between the different bodies providing assistance.[20] A civilian aid worker who had stayed in the disaster zone told me:

> The shooting went on all night: There was gunfire for hours. The DISIP against the *malandros* [delinquents]. And everyone was looting.... I was the first to report the violations of human rights, but I didn't go to give evidence. I was scared the army would find me and kill me, because there were only three of us. I was the only one with a camera, and they knew that. One morning, we heard a noise, hammering on the doors to force them open. It was soldiers, with a major. They were trying to force open a chest. My colleague was armed; he shouted at them to get out, and then I saw a line of rank-and-file soldiers with red berets. I took pictures of them while my friend held his gun on them.

The public condemnation of these abuses and disappearances resulted in a crisis at the heart of the political establishment—not over the methods used to repress looting, but because of disagreements among the senior ranks of the security forces as to who was responsible for the abuses and disappearances. According to the authorities, the reports of these abusive practices were part of an alleged conspiracy. According to Major Jesús Urdaneta Hernandez, the accusations of abuses committed by DISIP officers under his command were part of a political strategy to "sully his reputation."[21] Urdaneta Hernandez was dismissed following this scandal, but the investigation did not lead to any charges. Thus, his explanations served to shore up a system of impunity that is reinforced by intertwined conflicts of interest. The official defense in effect consisted of protecting officers accused of abuses by any means necessary and undermining the reputation of victims and accusers within their local area.

Moreover, analysis of the violent looting and repression during *la Tragedia* brings into focus a long history of urban rioting and of legal ambiguity around the deployment of extreme repressive action going well beyond the powers of the state in law. The nonchalance with which the saying "a good delinquent is a dead delinquent"—"malandro bueno es malandro muerto"—was frequently cited when I interviewed those involved in the crisis gives an indication of the extreme moral tension aroused by this violence in Venezuelan society. The prevalence of this slogan grew out of a frustrated demand for a state of emergency to be imposed and for the violent elimination of looters, the "bad victims" of the disaster, to be normalized. Paradoxically, the background of this exaggerated demand for repression was the hope for a socially more just society. If we examine the narrative ambivalence around the postdisaster violence, three distinct registers emerge.

The first register is that of looting seen as "normal." It is treated as an everyday phenomenon, to be expected and all the easier to understand in the extreme context of struggle for survival. Since December 17, the press had been reporting sporadic looting in Vargas grocery stores. In the media rhetoric, this looting was "justified" by the situation of the survivors, who were homeless and desperately hungry. The spotlight was thus soon placed on the slowness and inefficiency of the aid operations. In such a situation, where the victims saw themselves abandoned, what could be more "normal" than stripping the little grocery stores for provisions to feed their families? This collective justification of looting for survival was contrasted with "bad looting," which was not to be tolerated and which was seen as criminal behavior, committed by "bad victims who are taking advantage of the misfortune of others, of their lack of resources, defenselessness, and isolation."[22]

The second register of the discourse concerning the violence is that of looting viewed as an act of vandalism, that is, as violent and perverse destruction perpetrated by delinquents. And indeed, by December 20, 1999, acts of vandalism in the zone had degenerated into extremely violent situations that persisted until around January 20, 2000.[23] According to this line of thinking, the looting, devastation, and gun battles between the security forces and the gangs in the zone were more "dramatic" than the mudslides. This register extends into dehumanizing the bad victims as socially illegitimate and therefore liable to be eliminated without this being seen as injustice. The press reported a few cases where "bad looters" were lynched. These reports justified the actions as a response to "unhealthy" looting perpetrated by the profiteers of misfortune and thus offered a collective legitimization in this specific case. The lynchers were seen first and foremost as survivors who needed to be able to defend their families or what remained of their property. The moral boundaries between "survival looting" and "looting by vandalism" therefore determined representations of the limits on the "right to loot" and whether the elimination of looters was seen as unjust or not.

The third register in this narrative relates to the perception of abuses committed by soldiers and officials. This register supplements a heavy burden of resentment against the security forces of a collapsed state whose abuses almost always went unpunished. "The Vargas human rights affair," "el asunto de los derechos humanos en Vargas," as it has come to be known in Venezuelan popular parlance, has become a veiled reference to the first major political crisis of the Chávez government, in which the repressive practices of the old regime came into conflict with the hope for a state that would show greater respect for human rights.

## FROM NATURAL EMERGENCY TO SOCIAL EMERGENCY

On December 19, 1999, President Chávez visited the fifteen thousand victims of the mudslides and landslides that had devastated the state of Vargas and the metropolitan zone of Caracas the week before. The families made homeless by the disaster were temporarily housed in the city's largest concert hall, the Poliedro. During his visit, the president, dressed in military uniform, announced his intention to adapt army camps and military garrisons so that they could house the disaster victims and enable them to enjoy "the Christmas dinner they deserve."[24] Chávez's decision to evacuate the Poliedro quickly persuaded the victims to leave the hall and depart for army camps located in other Venezuelan towns and communities. The wave of optimism generated a collective agreement among these residents of poor urban neighborhoods to leave Caracas, either for army camps or for places where the government had accommodations available, often thousands of miles from the capital.

Thus, there was a general social and political consensus around the opening of barracks to the people hit by *la Tragedia*, a consensus that had its roots in the political situation—Chávez's government was already relying on support from the army—but also in history and ideology. In May 2000, a commandant at one of the garrisons in Fort Tiuna, where homeless families were lodged, was organizing monthly parties to celebrate children's birthdays. One of my interviewees had by chance found out the date of the commandant's birthday and had organized a surprise party for him. This situation suggested a normal, everyday order in which people had reorganized their lives and their routines, and the barracks had thus become a social space where a "return to normality" was being played out for many of the victims that also extended to the informal practices of the refugees and of the military. For example, in one shelter I visited in April 2003, at the navy police base of Maiquetía, an admiral was looking after families. He organized special activities, such as putting the refugee children onto a bus every weekend and taking them to the swimming pool at Club Mamo, the army beach club a few kilometers away, which was normally reserved for the families of career soldiers. It requires a particular shift of mind-set to conceptualize this militarization on the basis of reconstruction of data and scenes at the shelter in the Maiquetía naval police base. Part of this shift involves deconstructing the stereotype of the Venezuelan and more generally the Latin American military. In these spaces, the apparently clearly defined categories became somewhat vague and inconsistent: What, in the end, did this "militarization of society" actually imply?

Plan Bolívar 2000 is a social program driven by a humanitarian initiative aimed at pulling Venezuela out of a serious social situation. As early as January 1999, the government had declared that its duty was to respond to the "social emergency generated by the destitution and poverty of the people who suffered under the old national order." Plan Bolívar 2000, under which social intervention by the armed forces was introduced, was designed as an essential emergency humanitarian action, rather than as a public political initiative, although it did define the time-table for this militarization: Soldiers would not return to their barracks as long as people had need of them, for the social emergency extended beyond the disaster.

What the Bolivarian government means by "social emergency" is the chronic social crisis that has affected the country since 1980. In 1974, oil prices reached exorbitant levels, and Venezuela doubled or even tripled its revenue from oil. On January 10, 1976, Carlos Andrés Pérez of the Acción Democrática Party, national-ized the oil and steel industries. Venezuelan oil was at that time in the hands of North American companies that had been extracting it since the discovery of oil deposits in the early twentieth century. When these concessions were withdrawn under Pérez, the country's oil revenues rose from $1,400 million in 1970 (around 10 percent of GDP) to $9,000 million in 1974 (around 40 percent of GDP).[25] The state set up huge national oil consortia based on the way the fields had been organized by the multinationals who had been operating in the country since the 1920s, and the exceptional rise in prices guaranteed the political success of the operation. But in 1978, oil-price stagnation heralded the beginning of the end for this strategy as a politically viable method of development.[26] The collapse of the landowner econ-omy that had been fed by oil revenues had a profound effect on the social situa-tion of Venezuelan families and shattered the foundations of the consensus around the political model based on it. The sudden fall in per-capita government income from oil, the drop in imports, and the rise in inflation had devastating effects on an economy managed by an oligopolistic state. The Venezuelan state began gradu-ally to lose its capacity to resolve social conflicts by allocating resources to the sectors concerned.

In February 1983, the economic crisis led to the collapse of the system, sig-naled by the devaluation of the bolivar, and inevitably undermined the legitimacy of political parties as mediators between government and citizens. The crisis led successive governments to reduce public spending, particularly on physical infra-structure. Furthermore these governments had raised taxes, doubling tax rates since 1984 and privatizing public enterprises. The riots in Caracas in February 1989 and the two failed coup attempts in 1992 (on February 4 and November 27), shat-tered the foundations of the constitutional order, instituting a new political rheto-ric that transformed allegiances, radically altered the patterns of communication between social actors, and broke the political consensus established in 1961 by the Pacto de Punto Fijo—an agreement drawn up between the political parties that were by now hegemonic and under which the armed forces had been banned from political life for almost three decades.[27]

In 1993, the National Assembly removed from office President Carlos Andrés Pérez—who was already detested by his own Acción Democrática Party—signaling an early end to his second term as president. The Supreme Court of Justice agreed to the initiation of court proceedings against Pérez for embezzlement and misappropriation of public funds to his personal bank accounts in New York, thus opening the way for Venezuelans to voice vociferous demands for a new political and social order. Under the government of Rafael Caldera, a policy of "economic opening" recalled the big oil companies, awarding them exploration and production concessions once more. At the same time, 70 percent of the financial system collapsed. The crisis meant that the political parties that had been in power since 1961 could no longer be seen as in any way representative.

Hugo Chávez's discourse during the failed coup d'état of February 1992, after which he was arrested and imprisoned, was not a statement of left-wing principles, but rather a denunciation of the corruption of the Punto Fijo regime. Chávez remained in prison until March 27, 1994, when he was freed by Caldera's presidential decree. The other leaders of the coup were also released at that time. The alliance between Chávez and the left, which was orchestrated by Luis Miquilena, was cemented in 1997 with the establishment first of the MVR Party, the Movimiento V República, or Fifth Republic Movement, and then of the Polo Patriótico, an alliance of left-wing parties around Chávez, who was becoming a powerful figure in politics. The political activity of the Bolivarians between 1994 and 1997 focused on giving a political content to the image of the *Libertador*, Simón Bolívar. The political capitalization on the "Bolívar cult" was part of a strategy of transforming despair into the hope of a feeling of nationhood.

In 1999, Chávez was defining his project as giving the army back to the people, placing it at the service of citizens. This premise formed the basis of the military social program of Plan Bolívar 2000, under which the army used its staff, funds, and resources to implement aid and development programs. Plan Bolívar 2000 was defined as an "emergency program for reconstruction of the infrastructure of poor neighborhoods, schools, clinics, the construction of housing, and the distribution of food in isolated settlements."[28] But it later became consolidated as a permanent public policy.[29] This process is typical of a mode of management in which the temporary eventually becomes permanent. Often described by analysts as the expression of a "probably temporary militarization of public policy,"[30] Plan Bolívar 2000 is the most concrete expression of militarized social emergency policies.[31]

Under such policies, military personnel are used to carry out tasks that are deemed to be beyond the capacity of traditional state institutions, which are judged by the revolution to be too corrupted by political parties. These social policies, detailed in the National Economic and Social Plan, 2001–2007,[32] are directly funded by oil revenues, which have been increasing since 1999 as a result of the world market situation.

While Plan Bolívar 2000, which was the subject of my study, distributed "work grants" to victims housed at Fort Tiuna, the officer responsible for the battalion often told me that the victims—socially disadvantaged families who had no choice but to stay in the army camps—were socially "rehabilitated" (*se rehabilitan*) when they undertook cleaning jobs they were offered under one of the "Rapid Employment Plans." The new social order advocated by the Chávez regime, which underlaid the organization of everyday life in shelters in military zones, was now no longer unusual.

When I arrived at the barracks to which I had been assigned in May 2000, I noted that families were free to enter and leave the camp during the day. The following rules were posted on a notice at the entrance to the building: "Drink only drinking water; no bathing in the fountains; keep the communal areas clean; wear shoes; avoid keeping rubbish [in rooms] and drinking alcohol; you have half an hour to get your food from the refectory; stay in your apartment after 9:00 p.m." The families had been living there for three months, and the rules had become a little more flexible, particularly those concerning mealtimes: in principle, dinner was at 6:00 p.m., the same time as for the troops, since soldiers get up at 5:00 a.m. During our first conversations, officials from the Consolidated Social Fund (the Fondo Unico Social) told me that the curfew was much more restrictive for men than for women. Military police watchmen at the camp gate had already forbidden men from entering after 9:00 p.m. several times. The men were left to sleep in the street. The soldiers I interviewed at Fort Tiuna worked hard to show me that the military was providing appropriately for the needs of the civilians housed in the barracks: "Write in your notebook, Madam, that we organize sports activities for their children every weekend, which they didn't have before," when they lived in the poor neighborhoods."[33] This lieutenant colonel, who was responsible for organizing the battalion's leisure activities, wanted to persuade me of the benefits of military discipline for "straightening out all these problems." In his view, victims of the disaster had an opportunity to improve their future situation during their stay in Fort Tiuna.

This long-term militarization is a form of political action to provide compensation and relief that at the same time makes clear the new relationship between the military and the people enshrined in the new constitution. Under Article 328 of the Bolivarian Constitution (1999), the new role of the armed forces is to send personnel from the three forces "out into the social arena." The way the military is now integrated into the organization of civilian institutions and the articulation between new social policies and the armed forces, particularly the army, are representative of the militarization of the institutions of the Venezuelan state. According to Bolivarian principles, the harmony of national unity is based on the army's identification with the "people," and the need to make the army an institution of social support is justified in these terms.

The politicians argued that it was necessary to militarize management of the disaster and its social consequences beyond the immediate emergency. In 2004, Ana Elisa Osorio, minister for the environment and natural resources, described "the civil-military alliance" as a fundamental element of the Bolivarian revolution. Explaining the direct participation of armed-forces personnel in the planning and execution of social programs, she referred to *la Tragedia*:

> Just at the moment when the new Constitution was being approved, in December 1999, disaster struck in Vargas: over 20,000 dead and the need to take care of tens of thousands of refugees and relocate them in different areas of the country. This was a great tragedy and also involved unforeseen expenditure. But it was also a great opportunity to roll out joint action between the people and the armed forces. President Chávez, as commander in chief of the armed forces, linked them to emergency programs that allow us to speed up payment of the social debt to the people...helping to reinforce the civilian-military relationship. The armed forces were involved in social labor, and this fits in with a new vision of national security, a vision that is not restricted to the military environment or to the protection of borders, but extends to all aspects of the security of the people.[34]

This speech incorporates two new rhetorical elements that seek to legitimize the presence of the armed forces in the management of disaster victims and by extension the management of other disadvantaged groups in Venezuelan society while making a distinction between emergency and postemergency situations. The first of these rhetorical devices is the redefinition of disaster as a "great opportunity to roll out joint action between the people and the armed forces," that is, as an opportunity to legitimize military power in the administration of a public project that will last well beyond the emergency. Given an "overwhelmed and failing" civil administration, the legitimization of the armed forces follows "naturally." Thus, compassion serves to justify prolonging the emergency, understood within the military establishment as the conduct of "special actions." In this way, the "supply effect of emergency" identified by Zaki Laïdi and noted by Mariella Pandolfi in relation to NGO activity in Kosovo is maintained.[35] The indefinite extension of the crisis situation is in fact one of the characteristics of exception as a paradigm of government.[36] Thus, Osorio was using an argument typically deployed to justify the militarization of social programs, supported by the logic of the legitimization of "emergency on the grounds of urgent problems."[37] In this representation of the management of disaster, the minister revealed the moral basis for Bolivarian civil-military governance in relation to the socially disadvantaged victims of the disaster.

The second rhetorical device is redefining the "security" of the people in terms of "payment" of the Venezuelan state's "social debt" to its people. Thus, Osorio asserts that "national security" is no longer a matter of state security, but is broadened to include taking care of the needs of the people. This political justification of the presence of the armed forces in the "fight against exclusion" supports the official position, which automatically links aid for the disaster victims to a long-term social policy, in this case, Plan Bolívar 2000. This argument is a typical example of the way the "military doctrine of national security" is ideologically transformed into a social mandate for the armed forces in relation to the disadvantaged. The military dictatorships in Latin America exerted their authority through a range of legal devices—a state of siege or of war, the suspension of constitutional guarantees, and so on—in order to use the violence of the state for politically repressive purposes.[38] Under these regimes, inspired by the "doctrine of security and defense," repression was one of the tools used to apply the security paradigm, which became a normal technique of government. The Bolivarian social contract, in contrast is based on a "civil-military" union, in other words, "an alliance between the people, organized, and the armed forces to ensure popular and national sovereignty."[39] According to this rhetoric, the Bolivarian army is a bearer of social "goodwill" and desires only to contribute to and participate benevolently in national life—and thus to go beyond the tasks of security and defense imposed on it by the former national order. The idea of popular sovereignty itself, to which official rhetoric always has recourse, in fact underlies this speech without defining precisely the institutional channels through which it is exercised.

## DIGNIFICATION AND SOVEREIGN POWER—THOSE LEFT BEHIND

Following *la Tragedia*, the military embodied the state's compassion for the victims. Compassion for the victims is part of a politically and historically based claim of responsibility in which the government responds to the social vulnerability of the poor. The rapid sociological and political development of active military participation under the "dignification" program clearly demonstrates the place and the polysemic character of the Bolivarian revolution's moral universe.

In his daily radio broadcast *Aló Presidente*,[40] President Chávez demonstrated his lexical creativity, proposing that once they were under the protection of the government organizations responsible for their care, the victims of *la Tragedia* should be known as *dignificados*, a neologism based on the word for dignity. The term aims to restore the "lost dignity" suggested by the Spanish word *damnificado* ("victim"). The word *damnificado* has the same root as "damn" and "condemn," from ecclesiastical Latin *condemnare* and Latin *damnun*, from which derive the Spanish verb *condenar* and noun *condena* ("condemnation"). Thus, the official rhetoric invoked the ugliness of the term *damnificado* to create a neologism emphasizing dignity (*dignificados*), which was to have immediate practical manifestation in the provision, experience, and expectations of the assistance offered. This was in effect a political development. The new description of the victims of *la Tragedia* as *dignificados* rather than *damnificados* is therefore above all the formulation of a political promise—that of a better time to come.

Thus, dignity acquires multiple meanings. On the one hand, there is the sense of the victims being identified as poor, which is embedded in modern Western societies' conception of human integrity, in which autonomy and respect are linked,[41] but at the same time, the concept returns to the telos of the Bolivarian revolution. The promise of restoring to the people their lost dignity is set against a social history of violence and inequality in which the political recognition of the poorer communities previously ignored in the social order finds its full meaning. Accounts of the cholera epidemic in the Orinoco delta in 1992 and of the social treatment of "street children" in Caracas demonstrate to what extent the social representations put forward by state institutions before the current revolution reinforced, through their intrinsic violence toward the disadvantaged, the social problems they were supposed to tackle.[42] But in the dignification process, the shift from "forgotten victims" (those ignored by the political order that dominated in the past) to "victims taken care of" (by the Bolivarian government) that defines the *damnificados-dignificados* opposition is put forward by planners as a national initiative aimed at the "poorest" people, stipulating that this work should be undertaken by the army. Thus, the dignification process set in motion a broad sociological process of the moral contamination of the military,[43] who are required to take care of a population that was previously stigmatized and is now celebrated.

The political reorientation of the army that was intrinsic to military participation in the dignification programs also ties in with the historical discrediting of the military. Chávez often says that in February 1989, the armed forces had become "unworthy" because of the repression of the riots protesting at the neoliberal structural readjustment during the Caracazo, the riots of 1989.[44] The Bolivarian rebels' insurrection on February 4, 1992, is thus seen as an act of remission of the sin of the excessive repression of the riots, which occupy a central place in the collective memory and political imaginary in Venezuela. Taking power and making soldiers leave their barracks returns dignity to the armed forces at the same time as it returns dignity to the poor of whom they now take care. This rhetoric is part of an extreme dramatization of the popular imaginary in which the new rulers impose equitable distribution of oil revenues.[45]

This shift is clearly evident in the military's attitude toward activities with the most disadvantaged people in their work. The shelter at the Maiquetía Naval Police base was constructed in the "Casino," an area found in all Venezuelan military camps and used for recreation by the ranks and noncommissioned officers. It is used for dances and meetings. At Maiquetía, the military had given up this space to the families left homeless by *la Tragedia*. During my visits in 2003, I met Ana and her family there. Between twenty and forty families were housed in this *refugio* (shelter) for over a year. The February 2003 census listed sixteen families, numbering fifty-seven people in all. By June, only ten families remained.

In this shelter, which was about to close for good, Ana talked of the victims' difficulty in getting the authorities to listen to them and explained the conditions imposed by institutional bodies (in this case, the Fondo Unico Social) when they negotiated rehousing "solutions." That day, some families had received notification that they were to be rehoused imminently. The number of people at the shelter was dwindling. But Ana was still there, and the decreasing number of families provoked a very strong feeling of invisibility among those who remained. She told me that the long wait had meant her children lost a year of school: School places were not allocated to those who were due to move during the year, and the Social Affairs Department of the Vargas regional government had stopped providing transport for children in the mornings. In front of the junior officer who was with us that morning, Ana said: "I'm sure our president Chávez doesn't know that we're living in these conditions. Our situation is terrible, and I'm sure my president doesn't know anything about all of this," that is the conditions in the shelter and the delays in allocation of housing. By speaking in this way, she conveyed to the soldier, who was visibly embarrassed by the situation, that her words implied no criticism of the president. She was trying to explain why she was still living in the shelter when she had been offered housing in San Carlos, in the state of Cojedes, which she had eventually left because "it was too far away from everything."

Ana's words are typical of the rhetoric of the victims (*damnificados*) who were taken care of (*dignificados*) and who, three years later, came to criticize the rehousing programs. While blaming officials for inefficiency, they exonerated the president and his project of transforming society of all responsibility. This judgment arose as the emotional experience of political polarization in the shelters converged with the hope inspired by the discourse of "dignification." On that April day in 2003, when Ana spoke to me, the fear of the victims, dissatisfied with the dignification program, was that the government would take their complaints as political criticism. Ana complained about very specific conditions that resulted from the gap between her expectations created by the discourse of the dignification and the reality of the relocations. But saying this in the context of a deep political polarization, she feared being identified as an opponent of the government. This fear prevented any negotiation and began to operate as an instrument of blackmail by civil servants and army officers in the shelters.

## CONCLUSION

On November 29, 2006, a man and a woman nailed their hands to the trunk of a tree at the entrance to the Ministry of Housing and the Environment in Caracas. Shortly before, ten people from the same group had slashed their arms, thus keeping the pledge they had made two weeks earlier, when they began a hunger strike, to mount a "blood strike" if their demands for housing were not met. These people were members of a group of sixty-seven *damnificados* who were staging a round-the-clock vigil at the ministry. The emergency services were called, but the injured man and woman refused to leave without first talking to senior officials at the ministry. They stayed for hours with their hands nailed to the tree without receiving any response. In the afternoon, senior ministry officials called a press conference to explain the dramatic events. The ministry's spokesman explained that the process of rehousing the victims had been somewhat delayed because documents had to be verified. He maintained that the certificates of loss of housing supplied by the victims were often forged and that they needed to be validated by the fire service. The following day, representatives of the victims, who were continuing their vigil, responded that the root of the problem lay in the application of arbitrary and unjust criteria in the allocation of housing and in the corruption of some of the officials managing their cases. But the strongest argument against the ministry came from a victim who said that she would not do herself any harm, but added in a furious tone: "I will do something worse if they don't listen to me: For the first time, I will not vote for Chávez!"[46] Nevertheless, in the election held four days later, on Sunday, December 3, the president was triumphantly reelected with 61 percent of the vote. The dramatic image of the "crucifixion" of disaster victims thus gained little media exposure at this moment, when all attention was focused on the coming election, for, although opinion polls indicated he would win, it was the first time since 2000 that the president had faced an opposition candidate: Manuel Rosales, who won over 37 percent of the vote.

Let us look briefly at some of the more salient elements of the cacophonous exchange between ministry officials and the disaster victims. By taking up residence in the street, the victims were presenting a dramatic enactment of their pain and suffering in a desperate last attempt to show the world how they had been ignored by an institution where they had to queue for an average of a week to hand in an application. In inflicting painful, bloody wounds on themselves and exhibiting them, they were making an appeal for compassion, mobilizing the image of the Crucifixion. They were taking this extreme measure to demonstrate their powerlessness and their anger, their blood and their pain offering proof of their honesty. For its part, the ministry reasserted doubts as to whether victims applying for housing were genuinely homeless. Their numbers had continued to increase since *la Tragedia* because of the extreme vulnerability of these neighborhoods to heavier seasonal rains and because of the national housing crisis. The ministry spokesman's discourse was more technocratic than emotional and thus signaled his refusal to be drawn into this act of manipulation.

Thus, the scene testifies to an appeal for compassion and communicates to those in power a call for a final act of salvation. When the victims are called on to prove their status, they enter into conflict with the rule-based logic created by the institution that is supposed to be sensitive to their situation. But the scene also reveals the limits of a government policy organized around special, emergency actions as a way of providing the protection promised to the poor. The Bolivarian process of dignification came face to face with the limits of its own institutions. As well as being a strategy to attract media attention, the extreme act of victims nailing their hands to a tree highlighted the articulation of different critical dimensions in the relationship that has developed between rulers and the ruled under the Bolivarian revolution. The radical action of crucifixion demonstrates how the poor have reappropriated Bolivarianism's theological-political dimension. These people put their bodies and their lives at risk in order to reignite emotion—this time on the political level—among the military. The latter were by this time increasingly less sympathetic toward the disaster victims, who now occupied the lowest place in the hierarchy of those suffering.[47] By nailing their hands to the tree, they were calling, in the most extreme way, for the unfulfilled promise of rehousing all the victims—in other words, dignifying them—to be kept.

*Translation by Rachel Gomme*

## NOTES

1   Tulio Hernández, "Dolor avisado," *El Nacional*, "Siete días" supplement (December 18, 1999).

2   For an analysis of this disaster from the point of view of political anthropology, see Paula Vásquez, "Les politiques de catastrophe en temps de 'révolution bolivarienne': La gestion des sinistrés de la Tragedia de 1999 au Venezuela," Ph.D. diss., École des Hautes Études en Sciences Sociales, Paris, 2007.

3   Didier Fassin and Paula Vásquez, "Humanitarian Exception as the Rule: The Political Theology of the 1999 Tragedia in Venezuela," *American Ethnologist* 32, no. 3 (August 2005): pp. 389–405.

4   Didier Fassin, "La supplique: Stratégies rhétoriques et constructions identitaires dans les demandes d'aide d'urgence," *Annales: Histoire, Sciences Sociales* 55 (2000): p. 975.

5   Hannah Arendt, *On Revolution* (London: Penguin Books, 1990), p. 135.

6   Cenovia Casas, "Asamblea Constituyente decretó estado de alarma," *El Nacional*, December 17, 1999.

7   Giorgio Agamben, *State of Exception*, trans. Kevin Attell (Chicago: University of Chicago Press, 2005), p. 31.

8   Agamben, *State of Exception*, p. 2.

9   A left-wing politician, Rangel ran for the presidency several times during the 1970s and 1980s. He is an active member of Hugo Chávez's government and has served as chancellor, minister of defense and vice president. However, for reasons that remain unclear, he was not appointed to the government following Chávez's reelection in December 2006.

10  Abraham Rivero Pérez, "Se reprimirán intentos de saqueo en las zonas de desastre," *El Nacional*, December 20, 1999.

11  Alcides Castillo, "El Ejecutivo restringirá circulación de vehículos," *El Nacional*, December 18, 1999.

12  Fassin and Vásquez, "Humanitarian Exception as the Rule," p. 399.

13  Giorgio Agamben, *Homo Sacer: Sovereign Power and Bare Life*, trans. Daniel Heller-Roazen (Stanford, CA: Stanford University Press, 1998).

14  The parliamentary deputies' report indicates: "management of the national emergency was the sole responsibility of the national executive through the high-level committee it set up (Decree No. 577 of December 15,1999). The members of the committee were the minister of the interior and justice, the minister of defense, the minister of science and technology, and the minister of health and social development." See the *Informe de la Comisión especial para el tratamiento de los distintos casos del estado Vargas* (Caracas: Asamblea Nacional, 2000).

15  Fired from his post as minister of defense, General Salazar was subsequently appointed ambassador to Spain. He resigned and finally left the ranks of the Chávez movement in protest against the repression of the opposition demonstrations during the events leading up to the failed coup against Chávez in April 2002.

16  The Dirección de Servicios de Inteligencia Policial is the best-equipped and most feared security corps of the Venezuelan security forces. Organizations defending human rights, such as COFAVIC and PROVEA argue that its very existence is unconstitutional.

17  Hugo Chávez, *Understanding the Venezuelan Revolution: Hugo Chávez Talks with Marta Harnecker* (New York: Monthly Review Press, 2005), p. 81. See also Juan Miguel Díaz Ferrer, "Fuerzas armadas y alternativas al neoliberalismo: el caso de Venezuela," in Oscar Azócar

(ed.), *Fuerzas armadas: Democracia y alternativas al neoliberalismo en América Latina* (Santiago de Chile: Instituto de Ciencias Alejandro Lipschutz, 2005), p. 115.

18   PROVEA, *Caso Vargas: Justiciabilidad del derecho a la vida, a la integridad, al debido proceso y prohibición de la desaparición forzada* (Caracas: Programa Venezolano de Educación-Acción en Derechos Humanos, 1999).

19   Vanesa Gómez Quiroz, "Cofavic rechazó posición del Gobierno por desapariciones en Vargas," *El Nacional*, July 23, 2005.

20   The PROVEA report refers in particular to the disappearance of Marco Antonio Monasterio Pérez and Oscar Blanco, who were arrested at Valle de Pino by army paratroopers and then handed over to the DISIP, and of José Francisco Rivas Fernandez, arrested at Caraballeda on Tuesday, December 21, 1999. A witness testified to having seen the three men executed by the DISIP at Los Corales. It is obviously impossible to determine whether one of those executed was Oscar Blanco. See PROVEA, *Caso Vargas*.

21   Agustín Blanco Muñoz, *Habla Jesús Urdaneta Hernández: El comandante irreductible* (Caracas: Fundación Cátedra Pío Tamayo, 2003), p. 242.

22   Morelia Morillo Ramos, "Los casos de Vargas generan dudas y diferencias en opinión del público," *El Universal*, January 25, 2000.

23   Javier Ignacio Mayorca, "Ejecutivo endurece vigilancia para impedir nuevos saqueos en Vargas," *El Nacional*, December 23, 1999. See also Javier Ignacio Mayorca, "Militarizado el puerto de La Guaira para evitar nuevos saqueos," *El Nacional*, December 22, 1999.

24   "Trasladados más de 12000 afectados a Carabobo," *El Nacional*, December 21, 1999.

25   Macroeconomic data are taken from my analysis of Asdrúbal Baptista, *Bases cuantitativas de la economía venezolana, 1830–2002* (Caracas: Fundación Polar, 2002).

26   Luis Gomez Calcaño, "Venezuela: organisations sociales et luttes pour la citoyenneté," *Problèmes d'Amérique Latine* 29 (April–June 1998): p. 31.

27   Punto Fijo is the residence of Rafael Caldera, the leader of the Christian Socialist Party, where the agreement was signed. The riots on February 27 and March 3, 1989, also known as "the Caracazo," saw the most violent popular demonstrations and the bloodiest repression by the security forces in the context of a program of economic readjustment anywhere in Latin America.

28   Edgardo Lander, "Venezuela: La búsqueda de un modelo contrahegemónico," *Question*, July 2004, available on-line at:http://www.tni.org/detail_page.phtml?act_id=17437&username=guest@tni.org&password=9999&publish=Y (last accessed July 5, 2009).

29   William Fariñas, *Plan Cívico Militar Bolívar 2000* (Caracas, Comisión Interministerial, 1999).

30   Olivier Dabène, "Un pari néo-populiste au Venezuela," *Critique Internationale* 4 (1999): pp. 31–38.

31   Hugo Chávez, *Discurso del presidente de la república bolivariana, Hugo Chavez Frías, con motivo de la conmemoración del 4 de febrero de 1992. Poliedro de Caracas, 4 de febrero de 2003.* Available on line at http://www.presidencia.gob.ve/images/publicaciones/discursos/discursos_2003.pdf. pp. 132–152. (last accessed August 25, 2009).

32   *Líneas generales del Plan de Desarrollo Económico y Social de la Nación, 2001–2007* (Caracas: República Bolivariana de Venezuela, 2001).

33   Interview with the army lieutenant colonel supervising the barracks, May 10, 2000, Briceño Méndez Battalion Barracks, Fort Tiuna, Caracas.

34   Extracts from Ana Elisa Osorio Granados, *El proceso venezolano, una expresión nacional de la*

*lucha global de los pueblos contra el imperialismo* [The Venezuelan process: A national expression of the global struggle of peoples against imperialism, available on-line at http://www.geocities.com/nuestrotiempo/300sorio.html (last accessed July 5, 2009).

35 See Zaki Laïdi, "L'urgence ou la dévalorisation culturelle de l'avenir," in Marc-Henry Soulet (ed.), *Urgence, souffrance, misère: Lutte humanitaire ou politique sociale?* (Fribourg, Switzerland: Editions Universitaires, 1998), pp. 43–59, and Mariella Pandolfi, "Contract of Mutual (In)Difference: Governance and the Humanitarian Apparatus in Contemporary Albania and Kosovo," *Indiana Journal of Global Legal Studies* 10, no. 1 (2003): p. 380, available on-line at http://muse.jhu.edu/journals/indiana_journal_of_global_legal_studies/v010/10.1pandolfi.html#REF24 (last accessed July 5, 2009).

36 Agamben, *State of Exception*.

37 Mariella Pandolfi, "'Moral entrepreneurs,' souverainetés mouvants et barbelés: Le biopolitique dans les Balkans post-communistes," in Mariella Pandolfi and Marc Abélès (eds.), "Politiques: Jeux d'espaces," special issue, *Anthropologie et Sociétés* 26, no. 1 (2002): p. 38.

38 Daniel Zovato G, *Los estados de excepción y los derechos humanos en América latina* (Caracas, Venezuela/San José, Costa Rica: Instituto Interamericano de Derechos Humanos, Editorial Jurídica Venezolana, 1990).

39 Díaz Ferrer, "Fuerzas armadas y alternativas al neoliberalismo: El caso de Venezuela," p. 117.

40 The president's daily broadcast forms part of the government's communication policy. The program is also available on-line at http://www.alopresidente.gob.ve (last accessed July 5, 2009).

41 Charles Taylor, *Sources of the Self: The Making of Modern Identity* (Cambridge: Cambridge University Press, 1989).

42 Charles Briggs and Clara Mantini-Briggs, *Stories in Time of Cholera: Racial Profiling during a Medical Nightmare* (Berkeley: University of California Press, 2003); Patricia C. Márquez, *The Street Is My Home: Youth and Violence in Caracas* (Stanford, CA: Stanford University Press, 1999).

43 Erving Goffman, *Asylums: Essays on the Social Situation of Mental Patients and Other Inmates* (New York, Anchor Books, 1961).

44 "We would never have fired on the people, but the higher echelons of the armed forces were at the service of a corrupt regime." Chávez, *Alocución del presidente de la República, Hugo Rafael Chávez Frías, ante el Parlamento de Canarias*.

45 Yolanda Salas, "La dramatización social y política del imaginario popular: El fenómeno del bolivarismo en Venezuela," in Daniel Mato (ed.) *Estudios Latinoamericanos sobre la cultura y transformaciónes sociales en tiempos de globalización* (Buenos Aires, CLACSO, 2001), pp. 201–21. The Venezuelan state is the permanent recipient/payee of income from oil revenues. The criteria for its redistribution in Venezuelan society have always been political, as is shown by the analysis in Asdrúbal Baptista, "Justicia distributiva y renta del petróleo," in María Ramírez Ribes (ed.) *¿Cabemos todos? Desafíos de la inclusion* (Caracas: Club of Rome, 2004).

46 "Sangre por una vivienda," *El Nacional*, November 29, 2006.

47 Didier Fassin, "La souffrance du monde: Considérations anthropologiques sur les politiques contemporaines de la compassion," *Evolution Psychiatrique* 67, no. 4 (October–December 2002): p. 688.

# From Denial to Emergency:
# Governing Indigenous Communities in Australia

Deirdre Howard-Wagner

In June 2007, within two weeks of the release of *Ampe Akelyernemane Meke Mek-arle, 'Little Children Are Sacred,'*[1] the report of an inquiry into child sexual abuse in Indigenous communities of Australia's Northern Territory,[2] the federal government declared a state of emergency in the region. The report had been commissioned by the Australian Northern Territory government to examine the extent, nature, and contributing factors of sexual abuse of Aboriginal children in the territory. It acknowledged there was "nothing new or extraordinary about the allegation of sexual abuse of Aboriginal children of the Northern Territory." It confirmed that all categories of child abuse, including neglect, existed in Indigenous communities of the Northern Territory, that child abuse and neglect was "serious, widespread and often unreported" and "symptomatic of the breakdown of Aboriginal culture and society." The report stated: "What is required is a determined, coordinated effort to break the cycle and provide the necessary strengths, power and appropriate support to local communities, so they can lead themselves out of the malaise; in a word, empowerment."[3] In announcing shortly after his government's intention to intervene in the affairs of the Northern Territory and in what had been essentially self-governing Indigenous communities since the 1970s, the then prime minister, John Howard, proclaimed that children in remote communities of the territory were "living out a Hobbesian nightmare of violence, abuse and neglect."[4] Using its constitutional and political powers to intervene in the affairs of the territory, combined with its *parens patria* power, the state asserted its "duty of care."[5] This so-called Hobbesian nightmare had provided a strategic moment in which deci-sive intervention could be made, justifying the suspension of the existing statu-tory laws and political regimes. The state's emergency response to violence, abuse, and neglect was "radical, comprehensive and highly interventionist" and involved seizing control of seventy-three Indigenous communities, including town camps, in the Northern Territory, sending in troops, and instigating a major rebuilding of social order in these Indigenous communities. Indigenous communities and the Northern Territory government were denied the right to engage in designing initiatives and strategies to overcome violence, abuse, and neglect.

This strategic moment of intervention relied heavily on rhetorical tactics and linguistic devices to construct a state of emergency in the minds of the Australian populace.[6] Tales of Indigenous-community dysfunction and failure worked to define the crisis and shape its future in particular ways. The "national emergency" was constructed as appearing in "an environment where there is no natural social order of production and distribution," one in which "the combination of free money (in relatively large sums), free time and ready access to drugs and alcohol has created appalling conditions for community members, particularly children."[7] Government discourses attributed violence to situational factors such as welfare dependency and alcohol abuse, rather than to historical and underlying factors. Intervention in the affairs of Indigenous communities of the Northern Territory was premised on the inability of communities to realize their full economic and democratic potential.[8] Indigenous "failure" validated the setting aside of the normal state of affairs. A zone of exception was established.

The discursive construction of Indigenous communities of the Northern Territory as failed social enclaves in which violence and child sexual abuse was rife allowed for new disciplining, prohibitive, and corrective practices. Federal government strategies were aimed at getting "tough on violence and child sexual abuse" through extra police to reestablish law and order, harsh penalties for the purchase, supply, or consumption of alcohol and pornography, the surveillance of people's movements through the use of photographic identification, used to stem the flow of alcohol, drugs, and pornography, as well as the management of welfare payments to limit the amount of cash available for alcohol, drugs, gambling, and pornography.[9] A blueprint for the rebuilding of social order in seventy-three Indigenous communities of the Northern Territory was announced, one in which viable economies and an entrepreneurial culture were to be the new norm. Social order was to be facilitated through the incorporation of these communities into mainstream society through participation in "Australia's prosperous economy."[10] The failed apparatuses of welfarism were to be dismantled, along with the vestiges of self-determination and autonomy with the initiation of new mechanisms of intervention and regulation. The state's declaration of a "national emergency" in Indigenous communities of the Northern Territory allowed for the creation of a new social order within these communities, particularly the introduction of new legal provisions that initiated new types of normalization practices.[11] This essay explores how the declaration of a state of emergency and subsequent changes to the governance of Indigenous communities in the Northern Territory implemented a qualitatively different form of state governmentality.[12] New laws instituted new modes of governance that reflected associated changes in the governmentality of Indigenous affairs.[13] This is a particular historical juncture in state governmentality with regard to Indigenous affairs,[14] which was decontextualized from the historical backdrop of violent practices that had operated through different modes of social ordering. It ignored the history of the placelessness of Indigenous peoples within the state, the indelible state of anomie endemic to that placelessness, and the consequent effects.[15] But first, I will give consideration to historical junctures in the governance of the Indigenous population of the Northern Territory and to family violence in Indigenous communities in the context of this history.

## RACE, STATE INTERVENTION, AND SPATIAL GOVERNANCE

On settlement, the British transported both convicts and the English common law to Australia, arriving on January 26, 1788. Unlike in New Zealand, Canada, and the United States, no treaty was established. Australia was deemed to be uninhabited and to be settled, rather than conquered.[16] Settlement occurred under the legal aegis of the doctrine of *terra nullius* (land belonging to no one), removing any legal recognition of preexisting Indigenous institutions. Practices of dispossession emanated from this principle, resulting in not only the physical removal of Indigenes from their land, but the exclusion, control, and destruction of Indigenes.[17] The Indigenous peoples were given no rights, and these events occurred in a context where Indigenous people had little protection except, ambivalently, the common law. The colonial form of sovereignty and the mode of rapid land appropriation did much to shape conflictual colonial relations between the preexisting Indigenous peoples and the colonizing settlers in Australia. Murders, massacres, dispossession, dispersal, and marginalization of the Indigenous population were the major consequences of colonial conquest.

In the late nineteenth and twentieth centuries, blatant murderous acts were replaced with policies of protection that were intended to assist the dying out of Aborigines. Legislation brought into force to protect Aborigines in the 1840s was "predicated on the philosophy of 'soothing the dying pillow' of a race near extinction"—philosophies premised on Social Darwinism or "scientific" race theory.[18] Protection amounted to separation and incarceration, with Indigenous people removed from their land and placed on government-managed reserves or in church-run missions. Ronald M. Berndt argues: "In effect, the 'white' arrogated to himself the right to decide that the 'black' should be given no new opportunity to change, either in his own environment or in 'white' society."[19] Further, as Colin

Tatz comments, "the intent was...to await the 'natural' death of the 'full-blood' peoples and to socially engineer the disappearance, forever, of all those 'natives of Aboriginal origin.'"[20] Law and policy were oriented toward their "protection" by the state, but excluded them from citizenship and the social rights of the modern state. The science of "race" difference continued to influence the public administration of and policy concerning Aborigines until the late 1940s.[21]

When the modern Australian nation-state was formed in 1901, the Australian Constitution had no place for its Indigenous peoples as citizens. The "race power" under section 51 (xxvi) of the constitution gave the federal parliament "the power to make laws with respect to the people of any race, other than the Aboriginal race in any state, for whom it is deemed necessary to make special laws." Section 127 of the constitution stated that "in reckoning the numbers of people of the Commonwealth or of a state or other part of the Commonwealth, Aboriginal natives shall not be counted." Indigenous people were relegated to a zone of exception in which they became noncitizens denied basic citizen rights, including the right to protection within the new state. Their exclusion "from the census meant their homo sacer status as non-persons was empirically assured."[22] The colonial status of Aborigines remained constant after federation, because the law continued to deny Aborigines social and civil rights in the new nation. The Aborigine was left to the custodianship of the former colonial governments. Aborigines were "wards" of the states and subject to the laws of those states. The attention of the newly formed nation was redirected to debating miscegenation. It was not the existence of Aborigines, but the consequences of miscegenation that seemed to be the central issue for administrators. Academics, such as the leading pathologist, Professor J.B. Cleland, and various state and territory chief protectors of Aborigines, such as Walter Baldwin Spencer, John William Bleakley, and A.O. Neville, saw miscegenation as a solution to the race "problem." For administrators in more remote areas of Australia with large Indigenous populations, however, miscegenation was seen as a threat to the "ideal of White Australia." Cecil Cook, the administrator of the Northern Territory, was more ambivalent about miscegnation, as a natural solution to racial difference, if not opposed to it. In fearing it "to be a matter of only a few decades before the half-castes equal or exceed in number the white population," Cook argued that steps should be taken to "limit the multiplication of the hybrid coloured population."[23]

In 1910, the newly formed nation-state took over control of the Northern Territory, which had been previously annexed to South Australia, providing for the provisional government of this federal territory and establishing an administrator for the affairs of the Northern Territory.[24] The nation-state achieved legal segregation of "Aborigines" by passing the Northern Territories Aborigines Act that same year, administering their lives through Aboriginal protections boards, reserves, and guardianship. Protectors had the power to remove Aboriginal children from their families and/or communities and the power to place Aborigines on reserves and arrest those who left or refused to go. In effect, what occurred here was what Michel Foucault describes as the emergence of a juridical combination of laws and regulations that brought about a binary division in society.[25] In this case, it was a system that ensured miscegenation did not take place. The regulation of Aborigines of the Northern Territory involved literally removing them from their traditional land. Different tribes were placed together and institutionalized in centralized reserves that were in effect penitentiaries, a segregation that achieved the spatial division and separation of Aborigines and whites. A disciplinary system dealt with the problem of exclusion that functioned to modify the biological destiny of the Aborigines, limiting multiplication of a hybrid population. Discipline was also exercised on the bodies of the Aborigine. As Richard Broome writes: "The inmates...were subject to orders, discipline, a loss of privacy and removal if they tried to resist."[26] The traditional ways of life "were attacked with regimented effort," and the identities of individuals "were threatened by giving them European names." Disciplinary regimes eroded the powers and authority of traditional elders and leaders. Traditional ceremonies, traditional marriage, and Indigenous languages were banned.[27] This regulated and controlled environment produced a dependent population whose affairs and every decision were managed.[28]

After World War II, biologists, geneticists, and social scientists recognized that the notion of how "races" are constituted has no biological basis—mainly as a result of a reaction to the atrocities committed against Jews, Romanies, and other minorities in Nazi Germany in the lead-up to and during World War II. This recognition led to a new era of reflection on the way that the colonized peoples of the world had been treated. The United Nations had condemned colonialism and all practices of segregation and discrimination associated with colonialism in the Declaration on the Granting of Independence to Colonial Countries and Peoples on December 14, 1960, General Assembly Resolution 1514, XV. The treatment of "racial" groups within Western nation-states received greater attention, particularly the treatment of racial groups oppressed as a result of Western colonization. Increasingly, in the postcolonial world, pressure was placed on Australia to implement a nondiscriminatory policy in Indigenous affairs. The response to this international criticism was defensive. Although the federal parliament formally deliberated these issues in terms of citizenship rights and, hence, inclusion and equality, Aborigines generally remained excluded from citizenship and the social rights of the modern nation-state.

The Australian state, as "the custodian of the national reputation in the world at large," believed it had a responsibility to "move to a new era in which the social advancement rather than the crude protection of the native should be the objective."[29] This transition in dominant rationalities about Indigenous difference resulted from the adaptation of assimilation in line with Western liberal thought. However, the policy of assimilation continued the belief that Aboriginal culture is incompatible with the "white way of life." Race took on a new cultural signification. What was different was the expectation that Aborigines would assimilate into the wider society and culture, which was unquestionably regarded as superior. For the minister for territories, Paul Hasluck, assimilation did not mean the "suppression of Aboriginal culture but rather that, for generation over generation, cultural adjustments would take place. The native people [would] grow into the society in which, by force of history they are bound to live."[30] The Aborigine was now constructed as a "human personality" to be assimilated into mainstream society.

Welfare rationalities and technologies instituted new mechanisms of social ordering based on the idea that the Aboriginal problem was a "social problem," rather than a "racial problem." A new instrument of Aboriginal governance was introduced in 1953 in the form of the Northern Territory Welfare Ordinance, later amended by the Social Welfare Ordinance 1964.[31] Referring to the management of "wards" of the state, rather than the management of Aborigines, these laws were an attempt by the state to abolish race as a blatantly negative legal category. The "Aboriginal problem" as a "social problem," as Hasluck defined it, could be remedied through "welfare" programs. The concept of welfare did not have "welfare state connotations of 'cradle to the grave' provisions of services by the State." The minister of territories was opposed to "passive welfare" and argued that "the payment of social benefits to natives [had], in fact, led to a decline in their living standards and [had] halted the advancement of their welfare in as much as they [had] accepted social benefit payments as a means of livelihood and [had] been content to live at the standard which such an income provides and give up wage-earning." The Welfare Ordinance was not about welfare payments per se, but detailed the mechanisms for improving the well-being of Indigenous peoples, which was to be achieved through the expansion of assimilation, education, employment, housing, and health services. The process of continuing domination was now facilitated by "the development of relations of dependency between Indigenous minorities and welfare departments."[32] Indigenous people declared these policies and programs to be paternalistic and a form of systemic racism.[33]

The most dramatic shift occurred in the positioning of Indigenous people in Australian society following the 1967 referendum that resulted in amendment of Section 51—the "race power" clause—of the constitution. Australians eligible to vote in federal elections gave constitutional power to the federal government, concurrent with the states and territories, with the federal government's power having precedent in the event of inconsistency, allowing it to make "special" laws relating to Aboriginal people. Previously, the federal government's responsibility was limited to the Northern Territory and the Australian Capital Territory. Section 127 of the constitution was also repealed as a result of the 1967 referendum, which now allowed Indigenous people to be counted as citizens in the Australian census, beginning in 1971.

In the 1970s, the politics of welfarism and self-determination combined to form new models of governance. According to Tatz, the reserves were "euphemistically re-named as 'communities,'" and "bureaucrats eventually gave these prison-like institutions 'freedom', a budget and autonomy of a limited kind."[34] There was no training in autonomy: "Nobody remembered, or wanted to remember, that the inmates-turned-citizens were often people who had been moved or exiled to these places, people who had had to be disciplined or punished, or people who had been rounded up by desert patrols and simply placed there for the 'social engineering' experiment of assimilation in the deserts and monsoon lands." Self-determination and autonomy in this form was a federal-government construct. Thus, the belated postcolonial move to recognize retroactively Indigenous peoples' rights was based on government largesse and willingness. Indigenous people, their historical exclusion from the broader community, and then their incorporation into the broader community, the expression of their culture, and the struggle for their rights, were and continued to be spatially managed by governments and bureaucrats.

What was striking in this contemporary period were the Indigenous claims for integrity, rights, autonomy, self-governance and self-determination, which became an irrepressible element of the postcolonial landscape in Australia beginning in the 1950s. In the late 1960s, the agenda for assimilation and inclusion had been confronted by a different set of demands that emanated from the Indigenous community itself, which sought to address questions of prior occupancy, compensation for their dispossession as a colonized people, as well as recognition of Indigenous rights consistent with international customary and treaty law. Indigenous spokespeople and scholars pushed for change, continually critiquing laws and policies and engaging in public struggles for rights, self-determination, and Indigenous governance. The Gurindji strike and land claim that began in 1967, known as the Wave Hill Walk-Off, in the Northern Territory, was as much an industrial dispute for improved wages and conditions for the Gurindji stockmen and workers as it was a struggle for Aboriginal justice. However, it developed into a major national industrial and political dispute that had far-reaching ramifications in terms of Indigenous people's rights in Australia, resulting in the passing of the Aboriginal Land Rights (Northern Territory) Act 1976 and, subsequently, Aboriginal people of the Northern Territory regaining almost half of the land mass over the period of twenty years that followed.

## VIOLENCE AND CHILD SEXUAL ABUSE IN INDIGENOUS COMMUNITIES

However, placelessness as a consequence of being excluded into zones of exception had had its consequent social and psychological effects.[35] The history of Indigenous "communities" in the context of the history of reserves and the removal of Indigenous peoples from their lands, as well as in the context of the laws, policies, and practices affecting Indigenous peoples, is important for understanding violence and sexual abuse in contemporary Indigenous society. For the past thirty years, scholarship by Indigenous people, has linked violence and abuse in Indigenous communities to the "artificial" nature of contemporary communities,[36] suggesting that Indigenous "communities" were a construct of both historical and more recent government intervention. Reference has also been made to the "traumatised community," that is, to problems within Indigenous communities brought on by the traumas of the past, such as the history of colonization, dispossession, violence, segregation, and intervention.[37] Also, the term "dysfunctional community" has been used to describe the social breakdown within Indigenous communities associated with historical, structural, and situational factors.[38]

Violent colonization, the often-violent enforcement or imposition of discriminatory laws and social policies, and individual experiences of violation and violence as children had resulted in transgenerational trauma. Violence, abuse, and neglect in Indigenous communities is thus identified as a community-based social problem deeply rooted in a social context of colonization, loss of land and traditional culture, racism, marginalization and dispossession, entrenched poverty, and alcohol and drug abuse.[39] Indigenous scholars have emphasized the importance of allowing Indigenous peoples and communities to be "the architects of their own solutions."[40] Over the last thirty years, the system, as it presently stood, was perceived as inhibiting autonomy and self-determination. Indigenous communities called for real autonomy and basic funding for specialized services, such as programs to combat family violence. Boni Robertson, for example, argued that the "time is overdue for politicians and service providers to hear and acknowledge the voices of Indigenous people."[41] The constructive features of Indigenous community approaches to address family violence, such as night patrols ("voluntary community policing") that started in Julalikari in the Northern Territory in the 1980s and that had been implemented in over fifty Indigenous communities of the Northern Territory since, were increasingly turned to as an alternative to law-and-order and Western models of policing.[42] National and international research supported the proposition that, if appropriately funded, community-based strategies for addressing family violence had been most successful.

What can also be determined from this literature on family violence in Indigenous communities is that establishing a precise historical moment in which the situation in Indigenous communities became a national emergency is difficult. Nonetheless, it was more than ten years prior to the federal government's declaration of a state of emergency. Quantitative facts and figures and qualitative accounts detailing the extent and affects of family violence in Indigenous communities had been presented to Australian federal, state, and territory governments since the 1980s. Family violence had been reported as endemic to and an epidemic within Indigenous communities as early as 1990.[43] Reports, major studies, and national summits continued to be produced throughout the first ten years of the Howard government's federal leadership. Even so, "rationalization, trivialization and denial" had served to delay the application of strategies recommended for overcoming family violence in Indigenous communities.[44] In 2001, the *Herald Sun*, an Australian newspaper, featured a story detailing accounts of rape of an eight-month-old baby and a three-year-old toddler in remote communities in the Northern Territory.[45] The report indicated that academic research had found the problem was particularly dire in some remote Northern Territory, Queensland, and Western Australian Indigenous communities, where "a typical cluster of violence types in such a dysfunctional community would be male-on-male and female-on-female fighting, child abuse, alcohol violence, male suicide, pack rape, infant rape, rape of grandmothers, self-mutilation, spouse assault and homicide" and that "such communities need to be viewed as in a state of dire emergency." The article detailed how a report of the findings of research undertaken by Dr. Paul Memmott, who had conducted surveys of the research literature and interviews with 100 Indigenous organizations around Australia, had been presented to the Howard government in August 1999—eighteen months earlier.[46] The National Campaign against Violence and Crime within the federal attorney general's department had commissioned the report.

A few months later, the Secretariat of National Aboriginal and Islander Child Care released a study written and researched by Julian Pocock detailing the neglect and abuse of Indigenous children in the Northern Territory.[47] The study established that the child protection system in the Northern Territory "was seriously failing" and that "the Northern Territory has the highest levels of hidden or ignored child abuse and neglect in Australia." The report, entitled *State of Denial*, drew on and reiterated the findings of previous studies, making thirteen recommendations for addressing child neglect in Indigenous communities of the Northern Territory, which included child removal and national reforms to child welfare policy to pre-vent child abuse and neglect in the Northern Territory. The report claimed that a "state of denial" had existed for nearly twenty-five years. It was not the truth claims that were being denied.[48] The government officials, bureaucrats, media, and academics working in this field knew that alcohol and substance overuse were rife in Indigenous communities. Violence and child sexual abuse were con-sidered endemic, too. That same year, the report of a six-month inquiry into fam-ily violence had revealed a "shocking level of child sexual abuse and violence in Indigenous communities in Western Australia."[49] The inquiry, chaired by Western Australian Children's Court magistrate Sue Gordon, had found that the situation was also endemic and an epidemic within Indigenous communities of Western Australia. The Western Australian premier described the situation as a "national disaster," calling on the prime minister to take action.

The following year, Professor Mick Dodson, director of the Australian National University's National Centre for Indigenous Studies and former Aboriginal and Torres Strait Islander social justice commissioner, presented a speech entitled "Vio-lence Dysfunction Aboriginality" at the National Press Club in Canberra. In the speech, Dodson declared that "extreme situations require extreme responses.... Violence must be tackled as a priority, not part of some other secondary program, but as a central feature in Aboriginal social and economic policy across all of gov-ernment—all of community priorities."[50] Later that year, the then prime minister, John Howard, convened a national summit on Aboriginal family violence, includ-ing child abuse, which brought together twenty Indigenous spokespeople, mostly Indigenous women, who provided graphic details of violence, abuse, and neglect in Indigenous communities. Afterward, in a press interview, Howard stated: "I don't think there's any doubt...it is the most important issue facing the [Indig-enous] community.... Violence is a hugely important issue because it is destroying communities." The situation was declared a "national crisis."[51]

On May 15, 2006, *Lateline*, the leading current affairs television program of the Australian Broadcasting Corporation (ABC), featured a story about sexual abuse and violence toward Aboriginal women and children in Indigenous communities of the Northern Territory. In a lengthy interview, the crown prosecutor for Cen-tral Australia, Dr. Nanette Rogers, voiced concerns about the difficulties associated with prosecuting child sexual abuse in Indigenous communities because of cul-tural issues. Rogers gave graphic details of cases of child sexual abuse purportedly resulting from Indigenous cultural practices, revealing explicit details of one man's repetitive child sexual abuse, which she linked, in part, to the problem of the cul-tural practice of "promising wives," that is, girls promised in marriage at birth to older men according to traditional custom. Rogers also revealed that "the volume of violence" in Indigenous communities of Central Australia "was so huge" and conditions were "so depraved and dysfunctional as to defy belief."

Violence and sexual abuse were thus discursively constructed as a feature of Aboriginal culture in government and media narratives about violence and sexual abuse in Indigenous communities. In an interview on ABC's *Lateline* on May 16, 2006, the then minister for families, community services, and Indigenous affairs, Mal Brough, implied that child sexual abuse in Indigenous communities was related to the cultural and social values of patriarchal Indigenous societies in which women and children have an inferior social status.[52] The media in general claimed that Indigenous male culture and the web of kinship had contributed to a "conspiracy of silence" around violence and child sexual abuse in Indigenous communities. Anecdotal reports of the child "promised wife" being sexually assaulted by old men with the consent of the family dominated the media, causing a "ripple of outrage across the country."[53] In that same interview, Brough declared that "paedophile rings were working behind a veil of customary law" in the Northern Territory and that "everybody who lives in those communities knows who runs the pedophile rings, they know who brings in the [sniffable] petrol, they know who sells the ganja.... They need to be taken out of the community and dealt with, not by tribal law, but by the judicial system that operates throughout Australia." Brough alleged that the police force had turned a blind eye to such practices and that the Northern Territory government had been negligent.[54] He announced that if the Northern Territory government did not do something about the situation, then the federal government would step in.

Soon after, an intergovernmental summit involving federal, state, and territory ministers was convened on the topic of violence and child abuse in Indigenous communities. As Kyllie Cripps notes, within a month, the federal government had committed "$130 million over four years to address social problems in remote communities" that was targeted at police stations and police housing in remote communities ($40 million), drug and alcohol rehabilitation services ($50 million), twenty-six Australian federal intelligence-gathering and "strike teams" ($15 million), and setting up advisory networks of senior women ($4 million).[55] Suggesting again that somehow customary law and Indigenous culture had provided an excuse for family violence in Indigenous communities and had allowed offenders to get away with family violence using customary law as a mitigating factor, the Howard government's commitment of funding to states and territories "was conditional on all references to customary law and Indigenous culture being removed from the Crimes Acts in each State and Territory."[56] The federal government had amended the Commonwealth Crimes Act 1914 by passing the Crimes Amendment (Bails and Sentencing) Act 2006 with the intent of ensuring that "Indigenous [customary] law and cultural belonging" were not used "as a basis for defence or to mitigate the sentence imposed."[57]

In his speech of 2003, Dodson had pointed out that while violence and sexual abuse were endemic to Indigenous communities, they were not and never were part of Aboriginal tradition.[58] Other Indigenous spokespeople and scholars had long referred to the claim that these were cultural customs as what Indigenous peoples refer to as "bullshit law," arguing that it was distortion or falsification of Aboriginal customary law, stigmatizing the claim as "a misuse of culture."[59] They argued that a "state of denial" indeed had existed, but with family violence being normalized within government and media discourses,[60] so it was not true that "no one was listening." Indigenous women had long critiqued the judiciary's biased assumptions that violence is part of Indigenous culture and its inability to make a distinction between actual customary law and "bullshit" law.[61] Hannah McGlade has asserted that, rather than a "veil of secrecy" existing, the systemic problems in the criminal justice system contributed to fears about reporting violence and sexual abuse.[62] With the fracturing of Indigenous law and the breakdown of tradition, Indigenous women had had to turn to Australian law for protection. Yet many argued that the Australian legal system had failed Indigenous women time and again, leaving them with no faith in it, and that this was a contributing factor in their failure to report violence.[63] Many argued, too, that a major part of the problem was that government had failed either to support or to adequately fund Indigenous initiatives.

Twelve months later, the report of that inquiry, written by Rex Wild, Queen's Counsel, and Pat Anderson, entitled *Ampe Akelyernemane Meke Mekarle, 'Little Children Are Sacred,'* was presented to the Northern Territory government, detailing cases of child sexual abuse in at least forty-three Indigenous communities in the Northern Territory. The report gave accounts of serious sexual contact offenses, yet it noted that the exact rate of child sexual abuse remained unclear because no detailed child-maltreatment or abuse-prevalence studies had been conducted. It noted that available information was only an aggregate collection of administrative data based on the reported figures of child-protection services and the findings of sexual-health and primary-care practitioners.[64] The report expanded its focus to include all forms of child abuse (physical, emotional, psychological, and sexual) and neglect,[65] and it also placed child abuse and neglect under the rubric of family violence within Indigenous communities. It argued that explanations for child abuse and neglect are, by and large, also the basis of explanations for family violence. The findings and recommendations considered child abuse and neglect as symptomatic of historical, structural, and situational factors that had resulted in social dysfunction in Indigenous communities. The report recommended that successful Indigenous models, including national and international models, be considered for addressing serious trauma, dysfunction, and law-and-order problems in Indigenous communities. These had been adopted to address family violence, including child abuse and neglect, in Indigenous communities elsewhere, such as the Hollow Water program in Canada. In 1984, Hollow Water, an Indigenous reserve in the central-western plains of Canada, had reached a point of crisis—75 percent of the community were victims of sexual abuse, 35 percent were the perpetrators of sexual abuse, and violence was the norm. Indigenous strategies and dispute-resolution processes had successfully restored law and order and community well-being in Hollow Water.[66] Such a model was considered attractive by many of the Aboriginal communities consulted by the inquiry.

While it is difficult to isolate the exact historical moment that family violence, including child abuse and neglect, became a national crisis, the moment was long before June 2007. Also, a disjunction had occurred between Indigenous representations of family violence, child abuse and neglect, and federal government and media representations, which tended to attribute blame for them to Indigenous culture or to an inherent failure of Indigenous society itself.

## THE "NT INTERVENTION"

It was only within about two weeks of the release of *Ampe Akelyernemane Meke Mekarle, 'Little Children Are Sacred,'* that the federal government announced that it would be taking control of seventy-three Indigenous communities in the Northern Territory (NT). The declaration of a state of emergency in these Indigenous communities involved the suspension of statutory laws and legal norms in the form of the suspension of the recognized rights of Indigenous peoples who live there. A multiplicity of discursive practices and rhetorical strategies were deployed to rationalize the severity of the federal government's intervention. War metaphors, such as the "deploying of troops into the Northern Territory to fight against this community problem" and "troops seizing control of Aboriginal communities" operated as powerful symbolism, performing their role in the fictitious production of the state of emergency by the executive and providing a level of authentication to the extreme measures adopted, including the suspension of the existing regime. Troops and police were sent in to "stabilise the situation" and "to make communities safe," and within the first few weeks, the army and police had conducted "almost 500 health checks of Aboriginal children under 16."[67] The rhetorical framing of the situation in Indigenous communities of the Northern Territory as a crisis in the context of other crises and disasters, such as the political crisis in East Timor and the crisis in New Orleans following Hurricane Katrina, functioned in the same way. In drawing this parallel between Hurricane Katrina and the crisis in the Northern Territory, the failure of the American federal system of government to cope adequately with the human misery and lawlessness occasioned by Hurricane Katrina allowed the Australian federal government to configure its own intervention in what was constructed as a crisis of human misery and lawlessness in Indigenous communities of the Northern Territory.

It was in this climate that the exception quickly became the norm with the rapid passing of five interrelated pieces of "emergency response" legislation, which repealed the existing regime and legislated into effect a new model of governance. Intervention of the most extreme kind occurred: Troops and the police were sent in, the sale and consumption of alcohol was banned, and filters were put into computers to control access to pornography. The intervention extended beyond establishing new law-and-order regimes operating to regulate and intervene in the day-to-day affairs of Indigenous peoples and communities of the Northern Territory. The new laws changed the very land tenure arrangements that had been put in place to ingest and disalienate the placeless.[68] The Families, Community Services and Indigenous Affairs and Other Legislation Amendment (Northern Territory National Emergency Response and Other Measures) Act 2007 (Cth) suspended the existing model of self-governance and Aboriginal communal land ownership, giving the federal government "special jurisdiction" over the land belonging to those same communities. This was a significant shift in the governance of Indigenous communities of the Northern Territory.

The new laws made changes to Aboriginal property rights in the Northern Territory by scrapping the permit system put in place to allow Aboriginal peoples the right to determine who enters their community or township, such as government officials, media, researchers and tourists, acquiring Indigenous townships through five-year leases, and setting up a framework of individual private-property ownership by building houses and introducing market-based rents and normal tenancy agreements.[69] Commodification of the land was therefore central to the amendments to land-tenure arrangements. That is, a restructuring of land use and tenure was aimed at facilitating entrepreneurial initiatives through a move away from a community-based approach to land management and ownership to a model of individual housing/leasehold tenure.[70] (It is a modernization logic that, as Paul Havemann argues, "requires the conversion of place into commodified and controlled space to effect order building and growth."[71]) While neoliberal rationalities view land as an economic commodity to be parceled, packaged, and sold, projecting Indigenous people into the market economy, Indigenous peoples do not regard land as an economic commodity.

Thus, the "NT Intervention"—or "the Intervention," as it has come to be called by Indigenous people in the Northern Territory—and the accompanying array of laws set out new models of governance of which the long-term objective is to encourage self-governance and localized, community "responsibilisation"[72] by empowering entrepreneurial subjects to govern themselves economically, through participation in the broader market economy. In this context, "community responsibilisation" refers to the legitimization of the localization of responsibility for service provision.[73] However, while the end game is a multiplicity of self-governing communities in accordance with neoliberal principles of economic and entrepreneurial governance, the initial intervention, which aims to institute and provide the foundations for this new economic and social order, is highly interventionist, once again attempting to restructure the cultural, communal, and place-based origin of these communities. The end game is inconsistent with Indigenous models of self-governance and self-determination.

These new laws were not simply aimed at projecting Indigenous people into the market economy. They also sought to shape and regulate the Indigenous population upon which they acted.[74] The Aboriginal people affected by these laws slipped further into a biopolitical zone of exception when the state took over determining their day-to-day existence by quarantining welfare payments and stipulating what they could and could not spend their money on.[75] For example, the Social Security and Other Legislation Amendment (Welfare Payment Reform) Act 2007 contained provisions aimed at dealing with "the scourge of passive welfare" and aimed "to reinforce responsible behaviour" through a new Income Management Regime.[76] The then prime minister argued that the new laws were "designed to stem the flow of cash going towards alcohol abuse and to ensure that the funds meant to be used for children's welfare are actually used for that purpose."[77] He noted that "we're going to enforce school attendance by linking income support and family assistance payments to school attendance for all people living on Aboriginal land. We'll be ensuring that meals are provided for children at school with parents paying for the meals."[78] It is a rationality in which Indigenous people are "judged to be incompetent as autonomous individuals" and are therefore deemed incapable and unfit to exercise the freedom of the capable subject.[79] Such rationalities provide for the rationalization of authoritarian rule. Indigenous people are subjected to various techniques of improvement aimed at fostering capable, self-regulating subjects.[80]

Thus, community dysfunction provided a pretext for the regulation of social life in that it provided a means for programming and transforming social fields and a technique for managing the Indigenous population.[81] It provided a pretext for suspending existing governance, the failure of which gave the federal government the coercive license to govern, and allowed for the introduction of new legal provisions that initiated new types of normalization practices, as well as the creation of a new social and economic order within these communities—a zone of governance in which Indigenous society was constructed to exist for the purpose of intervention.[82]

## CONCLUSION

I have explored here historical junctures in the constitution of different forms of state governmentality involving the Indigenous population of Australia's Northern Territory. I have demonstrated how historical state projects have regulated the Indigenous population through, for example, isolation and segregation in state reserves or church missions and the consequent effects. State tactics and strategies have had dire consequences for the Indigenous population of the Northern Territory, and for Australia more generally, in terms of the loss of land and traditional culture, including kinship systems, customary law, and traditional roles. Colonization, racism, marginalization, and dispossession also paved the way for community-based social problems, such as social dysfunction, entrenched poverty, alcohol and drug abuse, and family violence, including child abuse and neglect.

While the invocation of a state of emergency in Indigenous communities involved implementing a qualitatively different state governmentality, once again, it rested upon the operative biopolitical categorization of Indigenous people in a state of exception. The lack of social order within Indigenous communities of the Northern Territory was decontextualized from the historical background of violent practices of state governmentality and attributed to situational factors, such as alcohol abuse and "passive welfare." Community dysfunction provided a pretext for the moral regulation of social life in that it provided a means for programming and transforming social fields and a technique for shaping and managing the Indigenous population of the Northern Territory. The sudden and urgent shift from a state of denial to the declaring of a state of emergency and the passing of laws to manage Indigenous community dysfunction involved intervention of the most extreme kind, denying Indigenous people the right to engage in meaningful community strategies.

The blueprint for the rebuilding of social order in seventy-three Indigenous communities of the Northern Territory was one in which viable economies, individual home ownership, and entrepreneurship were to be the new norm. Social order was to be facilitated by the incorporation of these communities into mainstream society through participation in "Australia's prosperous economy." Yet the NT Intervention does not incorporate the Indigenous population of the Northern Territory into Australian society. Rather, state governmentality once again isolates Indigenous people of the Northern Territory from the Australian population through their subjection to models of governance that again render them the exception. The consequent effects of this new form of state governmentality is the loss of Indigenous communal land-management frameworks, the loss of not only Indigenous peoples' rights to self-determination, but also their equal citizenship rights through their subjection to extreme measures of surveillance and the monitoring and policing of their movements, as well as through highly interventionist and regulatory government strategies managing their daily lives.

## NOTES

The author wishes to thank Professor Duncan Chappel, Dr. Murray Lee, Professor Pat O'Malley, Dr. Rebecca Scott Bray, Professor Julie Stubbs, and Associate Professor Robert van Krieken for their comments on the first draft of this paper. The argument presented here is explored in more detail in the context of neoliberalism and neoconservatism in Deirdre Howard-Wagner, "Northern Territory National Emergency Response: Governing the Indigenous Population through Violence and Child Sexual Abuse in Indigenous Communities," in Craig Browne and Justine McGill (eds.), *Violence and the Postcolonial Welfare State in France and Australia* (Sydney: University of Sydney Press, 2009).

1    Rex Wild and Patricia Anderson, *Ampe Akelyernemane Meke Mekarle, 'Little Children are Sacred,'* Report of the Northern Territory Board of Inquiry into the Protection of Aboriginal Children from Sexual Abuse 2007, June 2007, available on-line at http://www.inquirysaac. nt.gov.au/pdf/bipacsa_final_report.pdf (last accessed July 5, 2009).

2    The terms "Indigenous" and "Aboriginal" peoples tend to be used interchangeably in Australia and, therefore, throughout the paper. Australia's Indigenous population is 2.4 percent of the Australian population and is composed of Aboriginal and Torres Strait Islander peoples and communities located around Australia, including the Torres Strait Islands off the coast of the northeastern tip of Australia. Almost 14 percent of Australia's Indigenous population lives in the Northern Territory. The terms "Aborigine" and "Indigenous" are white constructs. It has been estimated that over two hundred and fifty language groups existed at the time of settlement in 1788. Indigenous people refer to their land as "country" and refer to themselves as "peoples of that country," such as "Larrakia land" and "Larrakia people," and tend to refer to themselves as "Indigenous" only in a broader societal and political context. The various peoples of the Northern Territory include, for example, the Gurindji, Kija, Jaru, Jawoyn, Larrakia, Miriwoong, Warlpiri, Warray, and Yolgnu peoples.

3    Wild and Anderson, *Ampe Akelyernemane Meke Mekarle, 'Little Children are Sacred,'* pp. 5, 12, 13.

4    John Howard, quoted in "PM Likens Crisis to Hurricane Katrina," *ABC News*, Australian Broadcasting Corporation, June 26, 2007, p. 1, available on-line at http://www.abc.net.au/news/stories/2007/06/26/1961802.htm (last accessed July 5, 2009).

5   In 1910, the Northern Territory became a federal territory of the commonwealth, giving the federal government control. Self-government was conferred in 1978, yet the federal government retained its political and constitutional powers to intervene in the affairs of the Northern Territory, including the power to override its laws.

6   Colin Hay, "Narrating Crisis: The Discursive Construction of the Winter of Discontent," *Sociology* 30, no. 2 (1996): p. 254.

7   Senator Nigel Scullion, Social Security and Other Legislation Amendment (Welfare Payment Reform) Bill 2007, Northern Territory National Emergency Response Bill 2007, Families, Community Services And Indigenous Affairs and Other Legislation Amendment (Northern Territory National Emergency Response And Other Measures) Bill 2007, Appropriation (Northern Territory National Emergency Response) Bill (No. 1) 2007–2008, Appropriation (Northern Territory National Emergency Response) Bill (No. 2) 2007–2008, "Second Reading Speech," Australian *Senate Hansard*, Wednesday, August 8, 2007, p. 25.

8   John Howard, "To Stabilise and Protect," Address to the Sydney Institute, June 25, 2007; John Howard Joint Press Conference with the Hon. Mal Brough, Minister for Families, Community Services and Indigenous Affairs, Canberra, June 21, 2007, p. 1, available on-line at http://pandora.nla.gov.au/pan/10052/20080118-1528/pm.gov.au/media/Interview/2007/Interview24380.html (last accessed July 5, 2009); Scullion, "Second Reading Speech," p. 11.

9   Scullion, "Second Reading Speech," pp. 15–16.

10  Howard, Joint Press Conference with the Hon. Mal Brough, p. 11.

11  Giorgio Agamben, *State of Exception*, trans. Kevin Attel (Chicago: The University of Chicago Press, 2005).

12  Dennis Rodgers, "The State as a Gang—Conceptualizing the Governmentality of Violence in Contemporary Nicaragua," *Critique of Anthropology* 26, no. 3 (2006): p. 325.

13  The five new Acts were the Northern Territory National Emergency Response Act 2007 (Cth), the Families, Community Services and Indigenous Affairs and Other Legislation Amendment (Northern Territory National Emergency Response and Other Measures) Act 2007 (Cth), the Social Security and Other Legislation Amendment (Welfare Payment Reform) Act 2007 (Cth), the Appropriation (Northern Territory National Emergency Response Act (No.1) 2007–2008 (Cth), and the Appropriation (Northern Territory National Emergency Response Act (No. 2) 2007–2008 (Cth).

14  State governmentality here differs from a Weberian-inspired thinking in which states are solely defined in terms of their outcomes. See Rodgers, "The State as a Gang," p. 324. The state is given no universal or general essence. Rather, state governmentality is viewed in terms of the tactics of governmentality, the governing of populations and citizenry, and as an instrument and effect of political strategies. See Judith Butler, *Precarious Life: The Powers of Mourning and Violence* (London: Verso, 2004); Bob Jessop, "From Micro-Powers to Governmentality: Foucault's Work on Statehood, State Formation, Statecraft and State Power," *Political Geography* 26, no. 1 (2007): pp. 34–40; and Thomas Lemke, "An Indigestible Meal?: Foucault, Governmentality and State Theory," *Distinktion: Scandinavian Journal of Social Theory*, no. 15 (2007), available on-line at http://www.thomaslemkeweb.de/publikationen/IndigestibleMealfinal5.pdf (last accessed September 13, 2009).

15  Paul Havemann, "Denial, Modernity and Exclusion: Indigenous Placelessness in Australia," *Macquarie Law Journal* 5, (2005): p. 78, available on-line at http://www.austlii.edu.au/au/journals/MqLJ/2005/4.html (last accessed July 23, 2009).

16  Indigenous discourses have historically represented Australia as conquered; not only did boundaries exist demarcating tribal ownership, but also Indigenous peoples had their own political culture and system of law. Hence, to date, the deeming of Australia as "settled" under English law, rather than "conquered," remains a contentious issue.

17  Ghassan Hage, *White Nation: Fantasies of White Supremacy in a Multicultural Society* (Sydney: Pluto Press, 1998), p. 336.

18  Colin Tatz, *Genocide in Australia*, Australian Institute of Aboriginal and Torres Strait Islander Studies Research Discussion Paper no. 8 (Canberra: Aboriginal Studies Press, 1999), pp. 17–18.

19  Ronald M. Berndt, *A Question of Choice: An Australian Aboriginal Dilemma* (Nedlands: University of Western Australia Press, 1971), p. 20.

20  Tatz, *Genocide in Australia*, p. 28.

21  Deirdre Howard-Wagner, "Colonialism and the Science of Race Difference," in Bruce Curtis, Steve Matthewman, and Tracey McIntosh (eds.) *TASA and SAANZ Joint Conference Refereed Conference Proceedings—Public Sociologies: Lessons and Trans-Tasman Comparisons 7* (Auckland, New Zealand: Department of Sociology, University of Auckland, 2007).

22  Havemann, "Denial, Modernity and Exclusion," p. 67.

23  Henry Reynolds, *An Indelible Stain: The Question of Genocide in Australia's History* (Ringwood, Victoria: Viking, 2001), p. 149.

24  The Australian Northern Territory was not settled until the 1860s. Land dispossession there was much slower, however, as Richard Broome notes, "it was likely that a greater proportion of the Aboriginal depopulation on the northern frontier was due to violent death than in the south." Richard Broome, *Aboriginal Australians: Black Responses to White Dominance, 1788–2001*, 3rd ed. (Crows Nest, Australia: Allen and Unwin, 2002), p. 99. Missions were not established until the late 1800s.

25  Michel Foucault, *Security, Territory, Population: Lectures at the Collège De France, 1977–1978*, ed. Michel Senellart, trans. Graham Burchell (New York: Palgrave Macmillan, 2007), pp. 9 and 31.

26  Broome, *Aboriginal Australians*, p. 103.

27  National Crime Prevention Indigenous Report, *Violence in Indigenous Communities* (Canberra: Australian Government Publishing Service, 2001), p. 12.

28  Broome, *Aboriginal Australians*, p. 103.

29  Paul Hasluck, Debates, *Senate and the House of Representatives Hansards* 208 (June 8, 1950), pp. 3976–77. Paul Hasluck, who became the federal minister for territories in 1951, which included responsibility for Aboriginal policy in the Northern Territory, was a main advocate of assimilation.

30  Paul Hasluck, Debates, *Senate and House of Representatives Hansards* 214 (October 18, 1951), pp. 875–76.

31  Russell McGregor, "Avoiding 'Aborigines': Paul Hasluck and the Northern Territory Welfare Ordinance, 1953," *Australian Journal of Politics and History* 51, no. 4 (2005): pp. 513–29.

32  Barry Morris, "The Politics of Identity: From Aborigines to the First Australian," in Jeremy Beckett (ed.), *Past and Present: The Construction of Aboriginality* (Canberra: Aboriginal Studies Press, 1988), p. 65.

33  Morris, "The Politics of Identity," p. 64; Commonwealth of Australia *Aboriginal and Torres Strait Islander Social Justice Commissioner Second Report* (Canberra: Human Rights and Equal Opportunity Commission, Australian Government Printing Service, 1994), pp. 27–28.

34  Tatz, *Genocide in Australia*, p. 30.

35  Havemann, "Denial, Modernity and Exclusion," p. 78.

36  Barbara Miller, "Community Development Approach to Crime Prevention in Aboriginal Communities," in Sandra McKillop (ed.), *Aboriginal Justice Issues: Proceedings of a Conference Held 23–25 June 1992* (Canberra: Australian Institute of Criminology, 1992).

37  Noel Pearson, *Our Right to Take Responsibility* (Cairns: Noel Pearson and Associates, 2000).

38  Mick Dodson, "Violence Dysfunction Aboriginality," speech presented at National Press Club, June 11, 2003, available on-line at http://law.anu.edu.au/anuiia/dodson.pdf (last accessed July 7, 2009).

39  Paul R. Wilson, *Black Death: White Hands* (Sydney: George Allen and Unwin, 1981); Ernest Hunter, "Changing Aboriginal Mortality Patterns in the Kimberley Region of Western Australia, 1957–86: The Impact of Deaths from External Causes," *Aboriginal Health Information Bulletin* 11 (1989); Ernest Hunter, "Images of Violence in Aboriginal Australia," *Aboriginal Law Review* 2, no. 46 (1990): p. 12; Ernest E. Hunter, "Demographic Factors Contributing to Patterns of Violence in Aboriginal Communities," *Australasian Psychiatry* 1, no. 4 (1993): pp. 152–53; Judy Atkinson, "Violence against Aboriginal Women: Reconstitution of Community Law—The Way Forward," *Aboriginal Law Bulletin* 2, no. 46 (1990): p. 6; Judy Atkinson, "Violence in Aboriginal Australia: Colonisation and Its Impacts on Gender," *Refractory Girl*, no. 36, pp. 21–24; Judy Atkinson, "Stinkin Thinkin—Alcohol, Violence and Government Responses," *Aboriginal Law Bulletin* 2, no. 51 (1991): pp. 4–6; Judy Atkinson, "Aboriginal People, Domestic Violence and the Law," in Dimity Lawrence (ed.), *Future Directions: Proceedings of Queensland Domestic Violence Conference* (Rockhampton: Rural Social and Economic Research Centre, Central Queensland University); Audrey Bolger, *Aboriginal Women and Violence: A Report for the Criminal Research Council and the Northern Territory Commissioner for Police* (Casuarina: Northern Territory University, 1990); Harry Blagg, *Crisis Intervention in Aboriginal Family Violence: Summary Report* (Canberra: Partnerships against Domestic Violence, Office of the Status of Women, 2000); Monique Keel, *Family Violence and Sexual Assault in Indigenous Communities*, Australian Centre for the Study of Sexual Assault Briefing no.4 (Canberra: Australian Institute of Family Studies, 2004).

40  Indigenous scholars, in particular, direct attention away from references to the dominant paradigm of Western conceptualizations of, say, domestic violence, preferring instead to use the concept of family violence to include extended families and intergenerational issues, thus allowing for different forms of violence, such as child abuse and neglect, to be situated within this framework of family violence. See Janet Stanley, Adam M. Tomison, and Julian Pocock, "Child Abuse and Neglect in Indigenous Australian Communities," Australian Institute of Family Studies, Child Abuse Prevention Issues, no.19 (Spring 2003), available on-line at http://www.aifs.gov.au/nch/pubs/issues/issues19/issues19.html (last accessed September 13, 2009).

41  Boni Robertson, *The Aboriginal and Torres Strait Islander Women's Task Force on Violence Report*, Queensland Department of Aboriginal and Torres Strait Islander Policy and Development, p. 111, available on-line at http://www.women.qld.gov.au/resources/indigenous/documents/atsi-violence-report.pdf (last accessed July 7, 2009).

42  Alexis Wright, *Grog War* (Stanley: Magabala Books, 1997); Janet Stanley, Katie Kovacs, Adam Tomison, and Kyllie Cripps, *Child Abuse and Family Violence in Aboriginal Communities—Exploring Child Sexual Abuse in Western Australia*, Australian Institute of Family Studies,

May 2002, available on-line at http://www.aifs.gov.au/nch/pubs/reports/wabrief.pdf (last accessed July 7, 2009).

43  National Committee on Violence, *Violence: Directions for Australia* (Canberra: Australian Institute of Criminology, 1990).

44  Havemann, "Denial, Modernity and Exclusion," p. 70.

45  Debra Jopson, "Black Australia: A Picture of Despair, Rage and Violence," *Sydney Morning Herald*, February 16, 2001, p. 2.

46  *Ibid.*, p. 2.

47  Julian Pocock, *State of Denial: The Neglect and Abuse of Indigenous Children in the Northern Territory*, Report for the Secretariat of National Aboriginal and Islander Child Care, SNAICC Incorporated, available on-line at http://www.snaicc.asn.au/_uploads/rsfil/00110.pdf (last accessed July 7, 2009).

48  Stanley Cohen, *States of Denial: Knowing about Atrocities and Suffering* (Cambridge: Polity Press, 2001).

49  Alison Wright, "Call for a National Response to Child Sexual Abuse Report," *The 7.30 Report*, Australian Broadcasting Corporation television program transcript, August 15, 2002, p. 1, available on-line at http://www.abc.net.au/7.30/content/2002/s650033.htm (last accessed July 7, 2009).

50  Dodson, "Violence Dysfunction Aboriginality," pp. 6–7.

51  John Howard, "Summit on the Domestic Violence in Indigenous Communities," *PM* ABC Radio, July 23, 2003, p. 1, available on-line at http://www.abc.net.au/pm/content/2003/s908693.htm (last accessed July 7, 2009); Noel Pearson, "Forget Excuses, We Need a Plan to Reduce Indigenous Violence," *The Australian*, July 24, 2003, p. 13.

52  Mal Brough, Mutitjulu Sexual Abuse Story, *Lateline*, Australian Broadcasting Commission, May 16, 2006.

53  Miranda Devine, "A Culture of Violence that Must Change," *Sydney Morning Herald*, May 18, 2006, p. 1, available on-line at http://www.smh.com.au/news/opinion/a-culture-of-violence-that-must-change/2006/05/17/1147545387118.html?page=fullpage#contentSwap2 (last accessed July 7, 2009).

54  Tony Jones, "Paedophile Rings Operating in Remote Communities: Brough," *Lateline*, May 16, 2006, available on-line at http://www.abc.net.au/lateline/content/2006/s1640148.htm (last accessed July 7, 2009).

55  Kyllie Cripps "Indigenous Family Violence: Towards Committed Long-Term Action," *Australian Indigenous Law Review* 11, no. 2 (2007): p. 6.

56  *Ibid.*

57  Deirdre Howard-Wagner, "Legislating Away Indigenous Rights," in Luke McNamara (ed.) "The Protection of Law," special issue, *Law Text Culture* 12 (December 2008): pp. 45–68.

58  Dodson, "Violence Dysfunction Aboriginality," pp. 2–3.

59  Bolger, *Aboriginal Women and Violence*; Hannah McGlade, "Our Own Backyards," *Indigenous Law Bulletin* 5, no. 23 (2003): p. 6.

60  Pocock, *State of Denial*.

61  Bolger, *Aboriginal Women and Violence*; Atkinson, "Violence against Aboriginal Women: Reconstitution of Community Law," pp. 4–9.

62  McGlade, "Our Own Backyards," p. 6

63  Atkinson, "Violence against Aboriginal Women: Reconstitution of Community Law, pp. 4–9;

Judy Atkinson, "To Do Nothing Is Tantamount to Genocide," *Indigenous Law Bulletin* 6, no. 20 (2006): pp. 20–22; Stanley, Tomison, and Pocock, "Child Abuse and Neglect in Indigenous Australian Communities."

64  Wild and Anderson, *Ampe Akelyernemane Meke Mekarle, 'Little Children are Sacred,'* p. 235.

65  The Australian Institute of Health and Welfare child-protection figures for 2006–2007 indicate that the rate of child abuse and neglect for Indigenous children in the Northern Territory was 16.8 per 1000. Of these cases, 30.1 percent were cases of physical abuse, 30.1 percent were cases of emotional abuse, 29.9 percent were cases of neglect, and, 9.9 percent were cases of sexual abuse. These figures are based on child-protection matters documented by child-protection services within Northern Territory government departments. See Australian Institute of Health and Welfare, *Child Protection Australia, 2006–2007*, available on-line at http://www.aihw.gov.au/publications/index.cfm/title/10566 (last accessed July 8, 2009).

66  Australian Broadcasting Corporation Radio, *The Law Report*, "Canadian Indigenous Community Tackles Sexual Abuse," July 3, 2007, available on-line at http://www.abc.net.au/rn/lawreport/stories/2007/1967700.htm (last accessed July 8, 2009).

67  Scullion, "Second Reading Speech," p. 15.

68  Havemann, "Denial, Modernity and Exclusion," p. 78.

69  The land that this applied to was land "scheduled under the Commonwealth Aboriginal Land Rights (Northern Territory) Act 1976 (Cth); community living areas, which are located on a form of freehold title issued by the Northern Territory Government to Aboriginal corporations; and town camps, in the vicinity of major urban areas, held by Aboriginal associations on special leases from the Northern Territory Government."

70  Scullion, "Second Reading Speech," pp. 10–18.

71  Havemann, "Denial, Modernity and Exclusion," p. 68.

72  "Responsibilisation" is a term coined by Michel Foucault and is used by Nikolas Rose to denote the effort "to reconstruct self-reliance in those who are excluded." See Nikolas Rose, "Government and Control," in David Garland and Richard Sparks (eds.), *Criminology and Social Theory* (Oxford: Oxford University Press, 2000), p. 201.

73  Martin Mowbray, "Localising Responsibility: The Application of the Harvard Project on American Indian Economic Development to Australia," *Australian Journal of Social Issues* 41, no. 1 (Autumn 2006): p. 88.

74  Deirdre Howard-Wagner, "Restoring Social Order through Tackling 'Passive Welfare': The Statutory Intent of the *Northern Territory National Emergency Response Act 2007 (Cth) and Social Security and Other Legislation Amendment (Welfare Payment Reform) Bill 2007 (Cth)*," *Current Issues in Criminal Justice* 19, no. 2 (2007): pp. 1–9.

75  Wendell Kisner, "Agamben, Hegel and the State of Exception," *Cosmos and History: The Journal of Natural and Social Philosophy* 3, nos. 2–3 (2007): p. 223.

76  Scullion, "Second Reading Speech," p. 11.

77  Howard, "To Stabilise and Protect," p. 1.

78  Howard, quoted in "PM Likens Crisis to Hurricane Katrina."

79  Barry Hindess, "The Liberal Government of Unfreedom," *Alternatives: Global, Local, Political* 26, no. 1 (2001): pp. 93–112; Rebecca Lawrence, "Governing Warlpiri Subjects: Indigenous Employment and Training Programs in the Central Australian Mining Industry," *Geographical Research* 43, no. 1 (2005): p. 44.

80  Mitchell Dean, "Liberal Government and Authoritarianism," *Economy and Society* 3, no. 1

(2002): pp. 37–61; Lawrence, "Governing Warlpiri Subjects," p. 44.

81 Peter Miller and Nikolas Rose, "Governing Economic Life," *Economy and Society* 19, no. 1 (1990): p. 24; Toby Miller, *Technologies of Truth: Cultural Citizenship and the Popular Media* (Minneapolis: University of Minnesota Press, 1998), p. 71.

82 Giorgio Agamben, *Homo Sacer: Sovereign Power and Bare Life*, trans. Daniel Heller-Roazen (Stanford, CA: Stanford University Press, 1998), pp. 15–16.

# Complex Engagements: Responding to Violence in Postconflict Aceh

Mary-Jo DelVecchio Good, Byron J. Good, and Jesse Grayman

In February 2006, we led a research team for the International Organization for Migration (IOM) in "a psychosocial needs assessment" (PNA) in post-tsunami, postconflict Aceh, the province on the northern tip of the Indonesian island of Sumatra. The field survey was undertaken not in the tsunami area, but in thirty villages in three districts known to have suffered particularly high levels of violence during the two previous decades of armed conflict between the forces of the government of Indonesia and GAM—Gerakan Aceh Merdeka, the Free Aceh Movement. We and our Indonesian colleagues heard terrible stories as villagers described sustained violence by Indonesian special forces against their communities, with houses and schools razed or burned and villagers beaten, tortured, or killed—often in retaliation for attacks by GAM on the Indonesian military. Men and women told of being forced to watch spouses killed and sons taken to the forest to be executed and of their own beatings and humiliation. They complained of waking up with vivid images of what happened and being unable to return to sleep,[1] the constant fear and sadness that made daily activities difficult, and their anger and inability to forget inflicted traumas.

By mid-March, the survey data were ready for our analysis, following a month of exchange and correcting data with our Indonesian colleagues. With the data set and initial analyses complete, two of us (Mary-Jo and Byron), began to review the statistics on traumatic events with a growing sense of horror. Of the 596 randomly selected adult villagers, 78 percent had experienced combat and firefights, 38 percent had fled burning buildings, 39 percent reported being beaten, 25 percent of the men and 11 percent of the women reported being tortured, 41 percent had family members or friends killed, 8 percent of women had husbands killed and 5 percent of all adults reported children killed in the conflict. We had hoped that stories heard during our February field trip represented particularly egregious events suffered by a limited number of individuals in the most severely affected villages. As we scanned the data, we were stunned at how widespread acts of violence against civilian communities had been.

Just what should we do with these findings? The peace process was still fragile, with the military denying human rights violations. How could we represent these data in ways that would support the ongoing peace process, yet bring help to those who had suffered the most? How could we respond appropriately to villagers who had told us and our colleagues their experiences? Was there a role for medical responses to those who had suffered trauma? Had the very act of conducting the survey put our interviewing teams and the Acehnese doctors and nurses who participated in this project at risk?

This paper is a reflection on work we began in June 2005, following the tsunami that devastated the coast of Aceh. We were initially invited to consult with IOM (pronounced in Indonesian with a lilt as *eeyom*) about mental-health responses to tsunami-affected communities. However, after the signing of the Memorandum of Understanding between the government of Indonesia and GAM on August 15, 2005, we became engaged in a major postconflict mental-health assessment and subsequently in designing a mental-health-services outreach program, which continues with our support into 2009.

Our reflections are situated amid a proliferation of writings about humanitarian work, particularly in conflict and postconflict settings. One strand produced by those actively engaged in humanitarian work includes polemics and advocacy, documents to mobilize resources and political will to respond to particular crises, reflexive narratives and historical accounts, and guides to action and discussions of the effectiveness of specialized interventions. Such writings often convey a sense of urgency and moral imperative, as well as technical expertise. This literature is matched by rapidly evolving critical analyses of intervention and the global humanitarian enterprise that challenge assumptions about the evident good of humanitarian responses to natural disasters and conflict. The work of Mariella Pandolfi and Didier Fassin has been particularly influential in launching this field.[2] Pandolfi, drawing on the work of Giorgio Agamben and her own ethnographic studies in the Balkans, elaborates a critical view of the rise of the international "humanitarian apparatus," interlinking military, humanitarian, and financial organizations that create "gray zones" as "laboratories of intervention," and new forms of "mobile global sovereignty."[3] Fassin's analyses, ranging from Palestine to South Africa and Venezuela, bring a particular focus on the "moral" aspects of humanitarian interventions, the politics of trauma, and the production of new categories of victims.[4] In these and other recent writings in this new field, special attention has been given to the increasing interdependence of security forces and humanitarian organizations,[5] and analyses of states of exception, intervention, mobile sovereignty, the humanitarian-military complex, zones of abandonment, bare life, and necropolitics have joined Foucault's analysis of biopolitics to constitute a dense network of analytical concepts in scholarly work on an emergent global humanitarianism.[6]

Given these critical analyses of the humanitarian enterprise, is there an appropriate role for anthropologists working in postconflict programs in settings such as Aceh? In particular, given critical debates about trauma and psychosocial interventions, should anthropologists with deep understandings of particular societies contribute to programs aimed at responding to "the remainders of violence"?[7] What can be learned about the everyday structures and assumptions of large-scale humanitarian organizations such as IOM by collaborating with them, and how can such situated research add to the emerging critical literature? How do crises such as natural disasters or conflicts and a society's accommodation to humanitarian responses reveal larger social and political forces usually hidden from view? In the Indonesian case, what do the responses to the tsunami by the central government and provincial authorities and the evolution of the peace process in Aceh, both of which developed in interaction with the global humanitarian apparatus, tell us about the reshaping of relations between Indonesia's political center and its peripheries?

In this paper, we only begin to address such basic issues. We briefly describe the crises that placed Aceh on the global humanitarian stage and the international response to those crises. We then describe our own participation in one postconflict mental-health program, analyzing this experience as a basis for responding to several of these questions.


## THE TSUNAMI AND AFTER

The province of Aceh, located at the northwest tip of Sumatra and having a population of over four million, came into popular global awareness on December 26, 2004, when the Indian Ocean earthquake (9.2 on the Richter scale) triggered a massive tsunami, killing between one hundred and thirty thousand and one hundred and sixty-eight thousand in Aceh alone and approximately two hundred and thirty thousand people in eleven affected countries.[8] In Aceh, more than four hundred thousand persons were displaced, their houses, animals, and lands destroyed, and many swallowed by the sea. Indonesia's Metro TV featured round-the-clock coverage of an endless loop of video taken by a wedding videographer as he struggled to escape the rising water twisting houses, vehicles, and people into its blackness. Videos and photos sent by private citizens and string reporters conveyed early forays into this devastated land, while a newly composed song, "Indonesia Menangis," "Indonesia Cries" (or "Indonesia Grieves"?), became the disaster's theme.

The Indonesian government, overwhelmed by the loss of local communications and unable to respond effectively, reluctantly granted permission to foreign military and humanitarian workers to step ashore on the "verandah of violence"— Anthony Reid's characterization of Aceh and its decades of deadly conflict with the national military (the Tentara Nasional Indonesia, TNI) in *Verandah of Violence: The Background to the Aceh Problem*.[9] Into this state of astonishing natural disaster came thousands of emergency responders from over 132 international and local humanitarian organizations. When the tsunami struck, IOM, an intergovernmental organization with over 120 member and 19 observer states, was one of the few international humanitarian organizations based in Aceh. Under contract with the Indonesian Ministry of Law and Human Rights, IOM had been charged with resettling communities displaced by the conflict between GAM and the national military and police. After the tsunami, IOM rapidly mustered a highly visible and largely successful emergency disaster response, providing emergency shelter and relief and contracting to build homes in the demolished areas. Its outreach teams, its vehicles with blue-and-white IOM logos, and its refugee services were soon easily recognized and widely appreciated by victims throughout the tsunami-affected areas.

IOM quickly added temporary health clinics and maternal health-outreach programs to shelter projects, and IOM's health officer sought international donor funding to develop new initiatives in "psychosocial and mental health." As part of her effort to expand IOM's portfolio, she recruited an Acehnese psychiatrist—one of four psychiatrists practicing in Aceh—from the medical faculty at Syiah Kuala University in Banda Aceh to lead these initiatives. In the spring of 2005, she invited us to join her team for these new initiatives, with Byron and Mary-Jo as consultants and Jesse as an IOM intern. Thus began our engagement with IOM's humanitarian interventions in the "psychosocial" domain. Our initial IOM trip to Aceh in June was to gain a sense of mental health problems caused by the tsunami and the vast range of psychosocial and mental-health interventions already underway, to consult with IOM staff, particularly the Acehnese psychiatrist, and to recommend ways in which IOM should contribute to this area. The popular understanding of trauma as a natural response to such a disaster legitimized the need for mental-health responses for donors and humanitarian organizations. It also opened the way for the concept of trauma to enter the postconflict humanitarian interventions.

Many Acehnese speak about the tsunami as sent "by God" to end the long conflict between GAM and the government of Indonesia. Indeed, the Memorandum of Understanding signed in Helsinki on August 15, 2005, by representatives of GAM and the government of Indonesia unleashed a project with nearly revolutionary consequences for the province of Aceh, its people, and its local political world. Aceh has a reputation as a fiercely independent "nation" that resisted Dutch incorporation into its East Indies colonies well into the twentieth century. Aceh was active in the national independence struggle after World War II, but Acehnese relations with the national government deteriorated when promises of provincial autonomy were abrogated by Indonesia's first president, Sukarno. Subsequently, under Suharto's New Order regime (1966–98), Acehnese struggles with the central government for control over local politics and natural resources, particularly a vast natural gas reserve off the coast, intensified. By 1976, a Free Aceh Movement (GAM) was launched, with demands for increased autonomy, then independence from the Indonesian state. Many of its leaders, studying and working in Europe, the United States, and Malaysia, engaged in a concerted effort to internationalize the GAM cause. During the 1990s, the armed conflict between GAM and the Indonesian national military and police forces (TNI and the national police special-forces unit BRIMOB, the Brigade Mobil) intensified as local resistance and popular anger spread in reaction to "the militarization of predatory economics" and the stripping of Aceh's oil and gas wealth, its forests and plantations, even its fish and coffee. Local villagers, loggers, farmers, fishermen, merchants, businessmen, and traders were extorted and terrorized.[10] Zones of military operation (DOM, daerah operasi militer) were zones of heightened insecurity for ordinary citizens. The violence was particularly intense in Aceh's northeastern districts from 1989 to 1998 and again in 2003–2004. It was interrupted by two short and unsuccessful ceasefires under the post-Suharto presidencies until the tsunami. The loss of East Timor increased the nationalist military's resolve, and the odds of noncombatants suffering relentless chronic conflict and aggression increased throughout Aceh after 2001. The Acehnese have a saying: "The mountain goat eats the corn, the village goat takes the beating."[11] Through decades of conflict, while GAM guerilla forces waged their battles against the TNI from remote bases in the hills and forests (the mountain goats), many civilian Acehnese were beaten and tortured in their own communities (the village goats) by forces intent on destroying GAM "at its roots"—at the household, kinship, community, and economic levels.[12]

The tsunami profoundly changed the dynamics of efforts to broker a peace agreement between GAM and the government of Indonesia. All post-Suharto presidents of Indonesia—B.J. Habibie, Abdurrahman Wahid, and Megawati Soekarnoputri—vowed to stop the bloodshed in Aceh, but negotiations failed, ceasefires fell apart, and both President Wahid and President Megawati instituted martial law, unleashing new violence. President Susilo Bambang Yudhoyono, the first president directly elected (in 2004) and many of his supporters, particularly

Vice President Yusuf Kalla, were deeply invested in brokering peace with GAM, but they, too, were unsuccessful prior to the tsunami.[13]

The tsunami brought widespread international attention to Aceh, and the massive humanitarian response made continued violence by the military against the people of Aceh politically and morally unsupportable. The August 15, 2005, peace agreement signed in Helsinki was far more wide-ranging than the previous cease-fires, initiating a serious peace process under the watchful eye of a multinational Aceh Monitoring Mission staffed by European Union and regional observers. The Helsinki Memorandum of Understanding led to a cessation of combat and a nearly total end to incidents of violence, the immediate release of Acehnese political prisoners, the demobilization of the GAM forces, and the gradual withdrawal of non-Acehnese national military forces from the province. Politically, the government of Indonesia granted increased provincial autonomy to Aceh. In exchange, the GAM leadership renounced claims to independence and was granted increased control of Aceh's natural resources,[14] special political autonomy, including the right to hold direct elections for provincial governor and district heads, and the right of Acehnese, including GAM members, to form local political parties and run for office without membership in a national party.[15]

Having developed a working relationship with members of President Susilo's government during the early phases of the peace process, IOM was designated as the intergovernmental organization with primary responsibility to implement DDR (demobilization, demilitarization, and reintegration) activities specified in the Memorandum of Understanding, including reintegration services for newly released political prisoners and former GAM combatants. IOM established ICRS (information, counseling, and referral services) offices in each district center of Aceh and extended services to families of former prisoners and former combatants as well as communities most severely affected by the conflict. The IOM health officer secured donor funds to staff each ICRS office with a medical team and acquired separate funds from the Foreign Ministry of Canada for a "psychosocial needs assessment" in villages in three districts along the northeast coast of Aceh where overt conflict had been the most long lasting and intense of any region of Aceh.

In November 2005, the health officer invited us to design and direct the needs assessment. Byron, as chair of Social Medicine at Harvard Medical School, had earlier begun negotiations with the country director of IOM-Indonesia, agreeing to develop a collaboration in which the Department of Social Medicine would provide technical support and IOM would manage operational activities for future community and mental-health programs in both tsunami-affected and conflict-affected regions of Aceh. We argued that our collaboration was contingent on the potential for long-term capacity building in Aceh, rather than on undertaking crisis-related activities alone. The IOM director agreed. He noted that tsunami money would come and go quite rapidly, but postconflict initiatives would last much longer. Thus, we became involved in postconflict mental-health interventions. On a visit to Aceh in November, Byron recruited Acehnese colleagues from Syiah Kuala University, with whom we had reestablished ties during our June consultancy, to participate in the first psychosocial needs assessment.

## THE ACEH POSTCONFLICT PSYCHOSOCIAL NEEDS ASSESSMENT

The first psychosocial needs assessment (PNA1)[16] was to be completed following a typical intergovernmental organization (IGO) emergency operations schedule, rather than an academic research schedule. To academics, it was daunting: The project methods were to be designed in December, the staff recruited and trained in January, the field research conducted in February, data analysis completed in March, and an executive report written by April. Donor funding required that the fieldwork be concluded by mid-February. Our Harvard group designed a quantitative and qualitative adult survey and a qualitative key informant interview in December 2005.[17] In January 2006, instruments were translated and field tested, villages selected, field teams recruited and trained, and logistics for the survey resolved. During the first two weeks of February, just six months after the signing of the Helsinki Accords and as the Indonesian special military forces were just beginning to be withdrawn, the field teams conducted interviews with 596 adults and 75 key informants in thirty villages. Jesse oversaw the field study and Byron and Mary-Jo joined the field researchers for the second week. The three of us visited numerous villages and arranged a focus group with former GAM members to discuss GAM perspectives on health care and mental-health services for individuals and communities affected by the violence.

The following two scenes, based on field experiences during the February survey, illustrate how we learned firsthand about the violence in Acehnese villages.

SCENE 1, FEBRUARY 2006: FOCUS GROUP DISCUSSION WITH GAM MEMBERS We invited a district GAM commander, whom Byron and Jesse had initially met in November, to bring together a group of GAM members to discuss health-care issues and the psychosocial needs of conflict-affected communities. He agreed and invited twelve GAM political leaders and former combatants—all men—to the discussion. The IOM mental-health nurse (an Acehnese male) opened the discussion in Acehnese, followed by Jesse and Byron speaking Indonesian, noting that the purpose of the gathering was to inform IOM about needs for services. The GAM men spoke openly with us (in Indonesian) and were vociferous. When discussing the suffering of women and children, they directed their comments to Mary-Jo and her female colleague, a lecturer at Syiah Kuala University.

They spoke of the oppression of the Acehnese by national forces and about personal experiences that drove them to join GAM, in some cases leaving government posts and lucrative positions—a district administrator, a high-ranking Indonesian military officer. While acknowledging the difficulties they experienced in combat, they argued that the greatest "trauma" and "stress" (terms now fully integrated, with local meaning, into the Indonesian lexicon) were suffered by their families, their mothers, fathers, children, and spouses. They spoke in detail about their losses—the burning of their houses, the robbery of their possessions—and detailed GAM policies on widows, orphans, and former combatants and the need for jobs and economic justice. They described their concerns about their children's education and their future. They argued for private health insurance; they did not trust the public health-care system. We later learned that mistrust of the public health-care system went beyond the sense shared throughout Indonesia of the inadequacy of public health clinics; in Aceh, during the conflict, military forces would often monitor government clinics and demand that health-care workers give information about GAM members who sought care. They expressed frustration at the NGOs: "If IOM is really serious, they would build houses to replace those lost in the conflict. Victims of conflict are like victims of tsunami. Both need housing." They asked IOM to help with reconstructing the economy and with providing jobs: "Why not hire GAM members to be consultants in these projects?" They concluded, responding to a question by Byron suggesting that as veterans, they might need services for war trauma, as Vietnam veterans in the United States had, that they did not need to be "reintegrated," that they were "home," and that "trauma" was not their primary concern. "Trauma is not our language; human rights is our language."[18]

**SCENE 2, FEBRUARY 2006: VILLAGE TRAUMA CLINIC** Interviewers had alerted the outreach medical team that one village they visited had suffered particularly severe torture, interrogation, house burnings, and destruction of resources. They asked that we and the medical team make a visit. It was rainy season, and the dirt road to the village was deeply rutted and slick; the IOM vehicles, all with four-wheel drive, slithered clumsily up the hill. People passed on motorcycles and on foot. We were expected, preceded by text messages via cell phones.

Upon arrival, we were received not with solemn greetings, but with amusement, playfulness, and coffee in the marketplace. The market street was covered with trash, flies, and garbage. Shop shelves were mostly bare. Citrus and snake fruit brought from town, along with cigarettes and coffee, were for sale. TVs flickered in the back of shops. Cloudy skies cast a dank grayness.

We drank sweetened coffee sitting with village men as they spoke of soccer and *rantau* — trips in their youth, seeking fortunes, adventure, even wives — in Jakarta or throughout the archipelago. Slowly, yet spontaneously, they began to talk of the torture and violence suffered by the community before the Memorandum of Understanding. A man told of his brother, who had witnessed his two sons shot by the military: "He is depressed." He then told his own story: "they" were going to shoot him, but his Javanese wife stood in front of him, arms wide apart, and shouted at the Javanese troops: "I am Javanese, shoot me, not him!" We heard this story a number of times that afternoon, along with many others. Soon women of all ages, most dressed in new, brightly colored and well-pressed sarongs and scarves, emerged from the back of market stalls and village houses, and along with their children and the village men, and with our psychiatrist colleague and the IOM medical team, we merged into a village procession to the *meunasah*, a community center typical in Acehnese villages. The IOM vehicles followed us closely — lurking security.

In front of the *meunasah*, a tall, thin man in his forties awaited the medical team, choking, sobbing, embraced by village men. The psychiatrist raised his eyebrows, asking what had happened. "He was accused of telling GAM to run.... They [the military] took him in the night, in the very early morning, they hung him with a plastic bag over his face, strangled him.... They hung him like a goat, they beat him in the head, beat him senseless.... He has depression and trauma.... He can't breathe, he can't work," his men friends lamented. "He was tortured." The women whispered to Mary-Jo and her SKU colleague, "He cries because he can't work and he can't earn money for his family. He can't be a man." All present looked upon the man with compassion and concern. He had been sobbing uncontrollably for months, since before the tsunami, when the villagers were sent away from their homes "for security reasons," only to return to find their houses shot up, their belongings gone, with "not one plate left!"

The group climbed to the second floor of the community house. A succession of men, women, and children dressed in their best continued to arrive throughout the afternoon. The psychiatrist settled on a straw mat and leaned against a wall, while the young female doctors and male nurses set up medication and examination stations along another wall. Byron sat beside the psychiatrist, Jesse sat with the male nurse and female general practitioner, Mary-Jo and her SKU colleague with the women and children. The psychiatrist examined the inconsolable man, spoke briefly to calm him, held his hand, laid him gently on a straw mat, and injected him with a sedative. The suffering man soon fell into a deep sleep. Trauma clinic had begun.

Five hours later, the psychiatrist drew the clinic to a close. He was rewarded with a traditional body massage by a professional soccer player in the village, who had talked with us at the coffeehouse upon our arrival. The village men looked on appreciatively, expressing sympathy for hard work done graciously and well and satisfaction that one of their own could offer a gift of caring and healing in exchange. As we left the *meunasah*, people asked us into their homes, urged more coffee, wished us a safe journey. "Trauma stories," "trauma healing," and "witnessing" took on special meaning that day as the villagers told their stories to the IOM medical team, the local university researchers, the American anthropologists, and to each other.

Following the field survey, data were recorded in Excel and transferred to Boston in March, where quantitative data were analyzed in the Department of Social Medicine. Qualitative data were analyzed primarily in Aceh. The PNA1 documented remarkably high levels of traumatic violence inflicted on civilian communities and even higher levels than anticipated of psychological symptoms, including classic symptoms of depression, anxiety, and PTSD (post-traumatic stress disorder). Initial findings were reported in an executive summary to IOM in early April and formally to the donor in June 2006. The most significant recommendation—that since formal mental-health services were unavailable to those suffering extraordinary levels of conflict-related mental-health problems, outreach teams should be developed and sent into villages to provide such services directly to these communities—was delivered to IOM in April.

We reported findings of the research in a number of settings in July 2006—to a psychiatry conference held in Jakarta by the Association of Southeast Asian Nations (ASEAN) and to IOM staff; to the field researchers and faculty of Syiah Kuala University; to a workshop in Banda Aceh of activists, NGO workers, and professionals attempting to develop a viable mental-health policy for Aceh; and to a workshop for the Aceh Police Force (Scene 3 below). When we presented the statistical data, audiences fell silent, stunned, as we had been on first seeing the survey findings, at how widespread the violence against communities had been. Most understood that the violence was primarily by Indonesian soldiers against their countrymen. The statistics carried political potency beyond that of narratives of individual suffering. The response of the Aceh Police Force was unexpected.

**SCENE 3, BANDA ACEH, JULY 2006** Today, I (Jesse) presented the results of the PNA to the Aceh Police Force. The IOM police project is holding a three-day "local content" workshop, with members of the police from throughout Aceh contributing material to the community-policing curriculum concerning the need to adapt the curriculum for the Aceh context. A strong religious identity, a long history of conflict against the state, the devastating tsunami, and the implementation of

Syariah Islamic law in Aceh truly sets this province apart from the rest of Indonesia, requiring tailoring of the curriculum for the Aceh context.

I presented the results of the PNA as a way to help the police understand the effects of the conflict on ordinary Acehnese civilians. Everyone knows that the police are implicated in much of the violence perpetrated against civilians during the conflict, but no one is allowed to say it. So it was a sensitive issue to present findings concerning past traumatic events for which some of the people in the room may have been responsible. Fortunately, from the very beginning, we wrote a report that avoids references to perpetrators and a human rights framework, so it was fairly easy to translate our findings into a format that was appropriate for this audience of police. Also, I had presented this material five times, three times in Indonesian, so I was nervous only at the beginning of the talk as I got comfortable with the audience.

Although all previous presentations were fine, I think this one went especially well. Typically, in Indonesia, one has to bear chatter on cell phones and among the participants themselves during proceedings of a seminar or workshop. This did not happen when any of us presented the results of the PNA. For the fifth time before an Indonesian audience, I had the good fortune of having the group's full and rapt attention the entire time. The only distraction was a soft murmur coming from the back of the room, and that was someone quietly translating my presentation for foreigners who were present. The audience was patient with my Indonesian language. Sometimes I could see them hanging on every word I spoke, ready at an instant to help me get a word out of my mouth if I stumbled with my pronunciation or my translation. I found this to be very comforting and supportive. Actually, I think this was the best audience I have had so far, and for a group of nonspecialists in mental health, this is remarkable.

I should remember that this is important, sobering, and gripping data. And even though everyone knows these things happened, the data are still surprising when we find out that the numbers are even higher than we suspected. I should remember that I have become immune to it; even though I have seen this project from start to finish, and have visited nearly every region of Aceh to talk about mental health effects of the conflict in people's lives, these numbers are still a little bit unreal to me.

I reel off the numbers totally deadpan: "8 percent of women had their husbands killed...5 percent of all respondents lost a child during the conflict...47 percent of the sample were forced to evacuate their homes at least once during the conflict...64 percent of young men in Bireuen got bashed in the head or suffered some other form of physical head trauma at least once during the conflict...." I think and recite these data with such a mundane attitude that if the numbers themselves were not so shocking, people would be falling asleep listening to me. My presentation covered all ten items listed in the executive summary of our report, and then suddenly it was over. I spoke just over forty minutes. The audience was so quiet and attentive during my talk that I really did not quite know what to expect, but it turned out to be one of my most gratifying experiences in Aceh.

The first question was posed by an officer from Bireuen. He started quite formally by reciting back to me that we had interviewed 596 adults, and that 30 percent of them were from Bireuen, and I was preparing myself for a critique of the claims I made with our data, a challenge to the representativeness of our findings. Instead, he took the opportunity to ask if there were any police in my sample. I told him that it was a random sample that did not target any specific type of respondent, that we might have had some police in the sample, or more likely, some retired police, but we do not have the information on occupational status yet. So then a second officer from Bireuen continued with a follow-up question to the first that I could not have planted among the participants better myself. After formally introducing himself, he said:

> We police are also members of the community. We have also experienced the effects
> of the conflict, and many of us are victims, or at least we all know of other victims
> in the police. One of our colleagues in Bireuen is certifiably insane after his con-
> flict experience…he talks and laughs to himself, and he cannot put down his gun.
> He suffers because of what happened to him during the conflict. My question is,
> are you going to conduct similar research among the police forces here in Aceh?
> Because we could really use these data to understand the effects of the conflict on
> our own men and women.

I thanked him by his name for his question and explained that to date we have not conducted any comprehensive research among the Indonesian police, but that I strongly agreed with his suggestion. I mentioned that we have evidence from GAM security forces that there were serious mental-health effects among their troops, and so why should we not expect similar findings on the police and military side of the conflict? I said that it might be possible, through collaboration between the IOM police project and the IOM postconflict program, to conduct such research in the future.

Then one of the moderators, Karlina Laksono, a philosophy professor at the Jesuit university in Jakarta, shared her experience working with conflict victims in Aceh, Jakarta, East Timor, and Maluku. Using the word *tutur* (which I have known to be translated as "to narrate"), she described a program that was a mix between storytelling and getting one's experience into words and out of their heads. This *tutur* process, she said, was a great way to redirect victims' suffering outside of themselves, to understand that their experience was not their fault. Is this a possible kind of therapeutic intervention that we might try in the future?

It was another great question and allowed me to share our experience when we conducted a trial clinic wherein the very experience of storytelling for the villagers definitely felt like an act of witnessing in which people felt a kind of catharsis because they were able to tell their story to an outsider for the first time ever. It appears to us to be a very effective kind of group therapy process, as well. But I was struck by the way she used the language of *mengalihkan sengsara* (redirecting suffering), because it reminded me of what I heard the research staff saying in the field when they described the process of listening to respondents tell their stories. They used the term *melampiaskan penderitaan*, which I can only best translate as "to expunge one's suffering out of oneself," and it has a very physical, almost sexual connotation, because the verb *melampiaskan* is also used with respect to getting one's "lust" (*nafsu*) out of one's system and projecting it out, physically, onto something else (usually another person while having sex). But my research teams found this process of expunging one's suffering very difficult because they found themselves to be the receptacles of the suffering that respondents were at last throwing out of their bodies and onto them, the interviewers. One of our team leaders always complained of headaches at the end of our days conducting interviews in the field or after a day of reading interview transcripts during the analysis phase.

Here we have an Indonesian way of talking about intersubjectivity, where suffering is something to be thrown out of someone and into someone else, who then must carry the burden. It is not a new phenomenon, no one is surprised by it, and all therapists are conversant with issues of secondary trauma, or at least burnout. Still, it is the physicality of suffering, or its objectification, that gets highlighted when an act of witnessing is described, and I do not think this is trivial.

The last question was a comment from someone who looked like a human rights activist from Jakarta, who took her opportunity to say, a little bit condescendingly, but correctly, nevertheless, that these data were a "landasan yang kokoh" (a powerful starting point) for the police and that the issue now was how far the police were willing to go to regain the people's trust. She said that there is an embryo of initiative among the Indonesian police to engage in community policing, but just how far are they willing to go in order to win back the hearts and minds of the Acehnese people? And that was a good way to conclude the discussion. Her comment did not require any answer from me, so I left it at that. There was rousing applause, and it was over.

The IOM postconflict program's information officer had come to observe. She said she overheard the women sitting next to her say that they appreciated the delivery, the presentation, in the sense that they noticed the sensitive efforts we made to make these data palatable and acceptable to this audience. They appreciated that I was not casting blame upon anyone or making accusations about past crimes. Sometimes I think it is a little bit disingenuous, not calling a spade a spade, but the fact is that there would be no possibility for progress if I just laid the crimes the police committed right down before them. It would have been a total embarrassment to them, and they would have gotten extremely defensive, then combative during the question-and-answer period. I think we all know who did most of these atrocities. I shudder to think of the truth-and-reconciliation efforts that the peace agreement calls for. What remains unsaid is just as important as what gets said, and just because it was not said does not mean that it was not acknowledged among all of us. I left the event with the assurance in my mind that we really were all on the same page.

Our project recommended that IOM should follow the suggestion of the police and conduct a similar study of experiences of violence among the police force and of the related psychological symptoms, then use these data to work through the past with the police force. Leaders of the force seemed prepared to support this, and it is likely that donor funding could have been found. However, IOM dropped the idea, and our mental-health staff never had further direct contact with the police or with the IOM police project.

The IOM leadership was even more ambivalent about the formal release of the PNA data. First, we decided that as a needs assessment, the report should be framed as "what happened to the villagers of Aceh in high conflict areas and what programs need to be developed for them," rather than "who perpetrated what forms of violence against civilians." This was true to our data. In the survey, we had asked whether people had suffered these events, not who had perpetrated the violence. We also decided not to focus on the worst forms of violence we had learned about. We did not want to force the Indonesian military to deny the veracity of our report, nor did we want to destabilize the peace process or put our researchers at increased risk. In discussions with an official from the Canadian Foreign Ministry and IOM officers, we agreed to "scrub" the report of the most inflammatory stories we had initially included. We used the term "combatant groups," rather than "TNI," "BRIMOB," or "GAM." However, we stood by the power and politics conveyed by the numbers and statistics. These remained untouched, raw, brute, and obvious.

Despite care in framing the document, the IOM leadership remained divided about how to release the data. They insisted on text and tables for a glossy IOM report of the study, invested staff time in preparing English and Indonesian versions of the document, and budgeted money for a formal launch. But they debated to the very end whether to release the study formally and whether IOM, as an intergovernmental organization dependent upon the goodwill of the Indonesian government, should take the risk of releasing the findings.

A note was circulated by the public-relations officer in early August 2006. It was clear, he acknowledged, that the report was designed to develop empirical data to support the development of meaningful and effective mental-health programs in high-conflict areas of Aceh and that it was not structured as a human rights document. At the same time, he noted, the report would be likely to fuel demands by Acehnese civil society groups and/or GAM for a Human Rights Court and a Truth and Reconciliation Commission, both of which were called for in the Memorandum of Understanding, but remained quite sensitive issues for Jakarta. He listed IOM's options: Release the document after circulating it among government agencies, but risk efforts to prevent its release, or give notice of the release in advance, then release it with a day-long symposium on postconflict mental health. He then personally suggested his own preferred third option: Release the document as a "Harvard Report Commissioned by IOM," with only "discrete reference to IOM": "The upside is that Harvard takes the political heat. There is little or no fund-raising downside, as donors are already aware of our role in the study and that IOM is heavily involved in the peace process. However, it does allow to pass a significant opportunity to raise general international awareness through the press of IOM as an institution."

In the end, we were able to secure a letter of support for the report from the Minister of Health, due to the mediation of a courageous and committed national director of mental health. Throughout the process, the bravery of the Acehnese interviewers and medical staff, as well as those Indonesians who supported our work in Jakarta, stands in sharp contrast to the self-interested concerns of those within IOM who resisted the publication of the report. The country director of IOM supported our lobbying for a formal release, suggesting that the concerns of his colleagues were overdrawn, and IOM organized a formal launch within the Department of Psychiatry of the University of Indonesia in Jakarta, with international agencies invited, and a second launch at Syiah Kuala University. No press releases were prepared, and we found only one account of the launch in an Acehnese newspaper. It was not until December 2006, after the election of Irwandi Yusuf, a former GAM member, as governor of Aceh, signaling a dramatic change in the political status of Aceh, that IOM released the report to the press. By this time, the peace process was no longer in such question, and sensitivity about the report was not high. The December release led to wide reporting in the international press.

Even before the formal launch, the PNA report was widely read among international organizations in Indonesia. Findings of the study led the World Bank to support extending the research to eleven more districts of Aceh, allowing a nearly complete mapping of levels of violence throughout the diverse regions of the province. IOM finally concurred with our recommendation that mobile mental-health teams should be developed to go into villages most affected by the conflict, and funds were diverted from a Norwegian government contract, designed to support the medical teams in each ICRS district office, into an intensive pilot project. The program trained doctors (general practitioners) and nurses, then provided medical and mental-health services in twenty-five villages for eight months (January through August 2007), eventually transferring care of 581 patients to the local public health clinics with the support of the district health office.

By the time the second needs assessment in fourteen districts throughout Aceh (PNA2) was complete, IOM fully supported highly public launches. The political situation in Aceh was no longer considered sensitive, though inside Aceh, the peace process never seems fully secure. The launches were well attended, receiving international press coverage. Representatives of the World Bank used the occasion to announce publicly that they would provide a new contract of $1 million to IOM to extend the mental-health outreach program to fifty additional villages. Members of the Ministry of Law and Human Rights and psychiatrists from the Ministry of Health attended the release in public solidarity.

Our work now focuses on supporting the mobile mental-health outreach teams, which are providing care to nearly one thousand patients with diagnosable mental illnesses in fifty villages in Bireuen and Aceh Utara. We are gratified to see individual lives change dramatically when provided appropriate medications and psychological support. We recognize the limitations of the project—mobile teams are ultimately not sustainable—and the project is collaborating with efforts to train primary-care nurses as community mental-health nurses, potentially providing the first real model for community-based mental-health services in low-resource areas of Indonesia. We have also developed a rehabilitation program using IOM 'livelihood' support models for persons with mental illness to determine experimentally whether this improves outcomes.

One last scene, drawn from a mental-health outreach visit, is a reminder that it is ultimately a combination of the peace process and the resilience of local men, women, and children that contributes to recovery for members of these Acehnese communities so deeply affected by years of conflict.

**SCENE 4, APRIL 2007: ON THE ROAD WITH A MOBILE MENTAL-HEALTH OUTREACH TEAM** We joined one of our outreach teams on a lengthy trip deep into the district countryside. The area seemed remote, though homes were strung for electricity, and TV satellite dishes perched on roofs. There was no market center; the team's general medical clinic was held in the village *meunasah*, a large, simple, unpainted wooden structure set in an open field. For almost four months, the team had been screening villagers and offering basic mental-health care to those deemed in need under the supervision of IOM's Acehnese psychiatrist. This village was among those chosen from conflict-affected villages.

Medical visits bring out crowds. On the day of our visit, men, mostly older, and women and children of all ages arrived as soon as the medical team settled. Approximately one hundred persons filled the open-sided community center. The senior IOM psychiatrist spoke to community members as he observed the team physicians and nurses carry out their work. We anthropologists were joined by a psychiatrist from Harvard who had tutored the team in psychiatric diagnosis and counseling on an earlier visit. Toward the end of the treatment session, Mary-Jo asked one of our IOM physicians to ask the women in Acehnese, "Women here seem strong—who owns the houses?" There was much laughter. In chorus, the women surrounding the physician responded loudly, "Women do!" An obviously silly question! We then discussed what women did when the military came to force them from their land. The women responded, again in a chorus, "We defended our land." One commented, "If I am to die, I will die bravely [berani]." Another: "I will die with my children, and I will die defending them and defending my land." Daughters, they said, were sent to town or other safe places during periods of conflict; sons accompanied their fathers into the forest to sleep. The women stayed behind in the houses they owned, with their small children, to guard their land and offspring. They described how soldiers "pulled my hair" or "crushed my feet with their boots."

Their comments rolled forth. Told with fierce toughness, these brief stories seemed to be less personal victim talk than solidarity talk reflecting community defiance. Many of the older men present appeared saddened. I do not know what they spoke about with the psychiatrist. After this visit, in particular, when I had spent much of the clinic afternoon playing with and taking pictures of small children, young girls, and women, I wondered what community and family consequences might have arisen from the years of chronic conflict and family separation. What does the future hold for the children of Aceh who grew up in these zones of insecurity and military conflict? What was the subjective reality of these parents, children, youths? What were their imaginings about the future, and what does the current situation portend for their children?

## ANALYTIC REFLECTIONS

We have described our close collaboration with IOM in assessing and responding to the mental-health problems of villagers in postconflict Aceh. We conclude with several reflections on what we have learned about humanitarian organizations by collaborating in these projects.

**PSYCHOSOCIAL NEEDS ASSESSMENT** We have spoken about our role in producing two "psychosocial needs assessments." The term hides a number of complexities. First, the very genre "needs assessment" is highly contested in settings such as post-tsunami or postconflict Aceh. Humanitarian organizations are often derided for spending far more time and money on assessing what needs to be done than on actually doing it. However, as the first scientifically sound study documenting the distribution and levels of traumatic experience and psychological symptoms across high-conflict subdistricts in Aceh, PNA1 and PNA2 proved highly significant in arguing for the importance of mental-health services for these communities. The study led us to work directly with IOM to develop mobile mental-health teams to respond precisely to the problems identified in the research.

Second, the term "psychosocial," like the terms "trauma" and "trauma treatment," is also contested in postdisaster and postconflict settings.[19] The use of the term "psychosocial" often reflects a strong antipsychiatry bias among humanitarian workers. In our PNA reports, we purposely made use of psychiatric diagnostic categories, including PTSD. While the study was framed as a needs assessment, our larger goal was to support efforts underway to build a new form of community mental-health care linked to the primary care system to respond to the needs of all Acehnese.

At a fundamental level, framing our research as a "psychosocial needs assessment" implied that our studies were not intended to be read primarily as human rights reports. Human rights activities play a critical role in Aceh. We are deeply committed to documenting levels of violence and how violence affected the people of Aceh, as well as supporting the peace process and contributing to systems of transitional justice. In this project, however, our primary goal has been to support efforts to construct mental-health services for a profoundly underserved population.

Finally, we focused the research and reports on quantitative data, rather than on narratives of violence and suffering. Stories have tremendous power— to describe, to move, to provoke. But statistics have their own "aesthetics."[20] It *does* matter that 68 percent of young men between the ages of seventeen and twenty-nine in particular high-conflict areas suffered head trauma, suffocation, or strangulation as part of the systematic efforts to combat GAM. It matters particularly when "assessing needs" or arguing for particular policies. Any sense that statistics imply depoliticization or a representation of those suffering as "bare life" misses the power of numbers. The numbers in our study are critical for telling the story of what happened to the people of Aceh, and although we are anthropologists, we remain committed to using the highest-quality methods in establishing those numbers.

**BEARING WITNESS** Didier Fassin and Richard Rechtman note that many humanitarian organizations see "bearing witness" to atrocities or human rights violations—in the sense of being present for those who have suffered, as well as documenting and publicizing such acts—to be critical to their mission.[21] For mental-health specialists, whose work includes listening to terrible stories of violence, the urge to bear witness in a public way is very strong—and is part of a tradition that goes back at least to Frantz Fanon.[22] But we should note the complexity of the word "witness," both as a noun and a verb. Our reports are certainly intended to bear witness to the violence waged against civilian populations. We did not, however, witness the events as they occurred. Our work was done in an explicitly *postconflict* setting, when one of the most important goals—for anyone interested in mental health—was to support an evolving peace process. Witnessing to past atrocities may be a critical step in long-term efforts to find justice, and many NGOs in Aceh are calling for acknowledgment of what was done. It was our hope that documenting the trauma that people suffered without telling the most vivid stories or making explicit claims about who was responsible for the violence could open a space in which diverse constituencies could acknowledge what happened in a productive manner.

But all of this assumes that the critical "witnesses" to trauma and violence are those of us who are non-Indonesian and non-Acehnese. Bearing witness to atrocities and violence for Acehnese interviewers and mental-health workers had, and continues to have, far more serious implications than it does for those of us who wrote these reports. During the conflict, being witnesses to violence was extraordinarily dangerous. Members of the military would interrogate physicians and community health workers to determine whom they had treated and what they had learned. Simply *knowing* what happened, particularly having information about specific acts of violence, placed the witness at risk of interrogation and possible torture. But this is precisely the work in which our interview teams and our mental health workers, nearly all of whom are Acehnese, have been engaged. They do this work with the full awareness that violence might return someday, that the intelligence services remain active in Aceh, and that should the conflict begin again, this information might be used against them. Those of us who organized this study and released it as a public document have to live with the knowledge that no matter how carefully we maintain confidentiality, it is possible that should the violence return, those who have worked in our projects and even villagers who have told their stories could suffer terrible consequences. Our interviewers and mental-health workers know this, and it is humbling to acknowledge their bravery and commitment.

**WORKING FROM THE INSIDE**  We introduced this paper acknowledging that we are anthropologists conversant with critiques of the humanitarian industry, its distinctive forms of sovereignty, and the displacements associated with interventions. We describe how we were drawn into responding first to the tsunami, then to the postconflict situation, and how we came to work closely with IOM as a means of addressing the practical and moral demands inherent in responding to those affected. We want to reflect briefly on what it has meant to situate our activities in this position.

As we write this, we have been working with IOM for over four years—two of us (Mary-Jo Good and Byron Good) as long-term consultants, one of us (Jesse Grayman) as an IOM employee. Our collaboration with IOM has made it possible to do things that we could not have done as independent scholars in Aceh. In the early phases of the crisis, the only access to work in Aceh was via recognized NGOs or IGOs, and it was through IOM that we were able to work in Aceh. The PNA project grew directly out of the IOM mission—to provide services for populations who have been displaced internally or internationally. Our collaboration with IOM enabled us to conduct the initial PNA project, from funding, to conceptualization and design, to data collection, to analysis, in less than six months. The IOM infrastructure was essential to the conduct of the project, and collaboration with IOM meant that our recommendations led to programs that responded to the needs identified in the survey. At the same time, working with IOM has given us a vivid ethnographic sense of the internal workings of one of the largest international organizations in Aceh. We have had to learn the bureaucratic procedures, politics, and unspoken assumptions that govern its activities. Rather than describe our frustrations with the idiosyncrasies or irrationalities of this organization, which have been legion, it may be useful to note several working assumptions that organize the structure of activities at IOM and that are common to humanitarian organizations.

**PROJECTIZATION**  The basic assumption of organizations such as IOM is that activities will be carried out as "projects." Broad philosophies (the importance of responding to the trauma of residents of postconflict villages to relieve suffering and support the peace process and the commitment to a mental-health approach) and strategies (using doctors and nurses, taking services out to the villages via mobile teams) have real traction only when they are translated into projects. Carrying out activities requires the development of a specific project paid for by a donor, specific objectives and measurable outputs, a management team and funding code, and a team charged with meeting the objectives of the project. Ideas are valuable insofar as they are "projectized." One result is that unlike academics with long-term commitments to work in Indonesia, contracts of IOM staff are linked to specific projects, leading to short-term commitments, constant insecurity, and high turnover, from international management staff to drivers and secretarial support staff.

COMPARTMENTALIZATION Large organizations such as IOM become highly compartmentalized. "Shelter," "postconflict," "livelihood," and "medical" have been critical groupings of IOM projects and management teams in Aceh from the tsunami to the present. "Trafficking," "police," and "human rights training" are other compartments in the IOM portfolio in Indonesia. "Medical" and "psychosocial" are ambiguous and somewhat contested categories for IOM. Providing health and mental-health services for temporary residents displaced by the tsunami or for released political prisoners or former combatants has obvious relevance for the IOM mandate, but many of the specialists who work in areas such as "shelter" (building houses), "livelihood" (providing help to former combatants to start small businesses, microfinancing projects, and so on), or "postconflict" (DDR activities) have little or no understanding of medical or psychosocial/mental-health services and are reluctant to complicate their projects by building in a medical or psychosocial component. Thus, programs that should be deeply interlinked often have virtually no relationship with one another.

PLAYING BY DONOR TIME An organization such as IOM is completely dependent upon donor funding. Developing and maintaining relationships with donors, writing proposals, negotiating budgets and contracts, evaluating work, and providing reports on outcomes constitutes an enormous part of the work of an international organization. All of this work must be done according to "donor time." An RFP (request for proposals) or a rumor that one agency may fund a particular set of activities often leads to project proposals being written in unreasonably short periods of time. IOM may have to wait months for the funding for a project to begin, even when a donor has made a commitment to the project. This was true of our current World Bank–supported mental-health project. Although funding was promised in June 2007 for August/September delivery, funds had not been authorized in September, and our entire medical staff was laid off. It was not until November that funding seemed certain enough to rehire some key staff members, and the program could not hire new doctors and nurses or go into the field until January 2008. The irrationalities of "donor time" are essential to the irrationalities of humanitarian organizations.

**"NATIONAL" AND "INTERNATIONAL" STAFF** One of the fundamental distinctions in international organizations is between national and international staff. "International" staff are often career humanitarian professionals. Many have spent time in numerous crisis or conflict settings and have short-term commitments to any one setting or project. "National" staff are critical to the conduct of any project. Working on humanitarian projects is often crucial to the careers of young national staff members, contributing generally to "capacity building" among young Indonesian professionals. However, they are paid a tiny fraction of the salaries of international staff or consultants. A general practitioner who is an international staff person on a medical project such as ours may be paid six times the salary paid to a local physician, even if the local physician is a specialist. This leads to the tensions between local and national staff members and to the gossip and "everyday forms of resistance" that are a routine part of organizations such as IOM.

**THE QUESTION OF SOVEREIGNTY** Within hours of the earthquake off the coast of Aceh and the resulting tsunami, humanitarian agencies began to arrive. Within days, this influx had swelled to a tidal wave of international workers. Although many eventually registered with the Indonesian government, and there were diverse forms of coordination among the groups and with the local government, no government agency could possibly keep track of the enormously diverse set of interventions undertaken, many with little regard for Indonesian bureaucratic and legal structures.[23] Mariella Pandolfi quite perceptively questions the new forms of "mobile sovereignty" represented by the complex of global humanitarian agencies, particularly when linked with military and "security" forces.[24] One only need review the new Inter-Agency Standing Committee *Guidelines on Mental Health and Psychosocial Support in Emergency Settings* to note the virtual absence of reference to local governments and ministries of health.[25] The guidelines largely employ the passive voice ("activities and programming should be integrated"), and use the abstract terms "agencies" and "communities" to describe the primary actors in emergency settings.

At the same time, our analyses should not take at face value the immodest claims to sovereignty of many humanitarian organizations and actors. Aceh experienced an intense struggle for sovereignty between the central government and GAM and between their respective military forces, and today, largely as a result of the tsunami and the influx of external actors, Aceh is a laboratory for working out new forms of governance, particularly in relations between the Indonesian center and provincial authorities, political parties, and civil society. Humanitarian organizations have extraordinarily limited sovereignty in this setting. They often appear profoundly powerless and largely irrelevant to the dynamics of local struggles, unable to effect the forms of governance to which they are committed. We should take care analytically to avoid elevating their status to that to which they aspire.

## CONCLUSION

What, then, of the "politics of collaboration," in Pandolfi's terms,[26] of anthropologists working in humanitarian settings? "Giving an account of oneself" is no simple matter, as Judith Butler reminds us: "My account of myself is partial, haunted by that for which I can devise no definitive story."[27] There is no easy moral position when participating in the complicated world of humanitarian interventions, even when, as in postconflict Aceh, one's participation is quite divorced from military interventions and security forces. We can say simply that having listened to stories, we felt constrained to respond. Looking into the face of the other demanded something in return. Motives are not pure — a funded program here, a thesis there, the fascination of violence, stories to tell. If human consciousness is the "urgency of a destination leading to the other...a movement toward the other that does not come back to its point of origin," as Levinas writes,[28] then it is no surprise that we are drawn time and again to Aceh and that we never return unscathed to our point of origin.

## NOTES

1   See Jesse Grayman, Mary-Jo DelVecchio Good, and Byron J. Good, "Conflict Nightmares and Trauma in Aceh," *Culture, Medicine and Psychiatry* 33, no. 2 (June 2009): pp. 290–312.

2   Mariella Pandolfi, "Contract of Mutual (In)Difference: Governance and Humanitarian Apparatus in Contemporary Albania and Kosovo," *Indiana Journal of Global Legal Studies* 10, no. 1 (2003): pp. 369–81. The conference Interventions organized by Mariella Pandolfi in October 2003 was a critical moment.

3   Mariella Pandolfi, "Laboratories of Intervention: The Humanitarian Governance of the Postcommunist Balkan Territories," in Mary-Jo DelVecchio Good, Sandra Teresa Hyde, Sarah Pinto, and Byron J. Good (eds.), *Postcolonial Disorders* (Berkeley: University of California Press, 2008), pp. 157–86; Mariella Pandolfi, "The Humanitarian Industry and the Supra-Colonialism in the Balkan Territories," paper presented at the Seminar on Postcoloniality, Subjectivity, and Lived Experience, Friday Morning Seminar on Medical Anthropology and Cultural Psychiatry, Harvard University, Boston, October 2000; Mariella Pandolfi, "L'industrie humanitaire: Une souveraineté mouvante et supracoloniale. Réflexion sur l'expérience des Balkans," *Multitudes* 3 (November 2000): pp. 97–105.

4   Didier Fassin, "Humanitarianism as a Politics of Life," *Public Culture* 19, no. 3 (2007): pp. 499–520; "Humanitarianism: A Nongovernmental Government," in Michel Feher, Gaëlle Krikorian, and Yates McKee (eds.), *Nongovernmental Politics* (New York: Zone Books, 2007), pp. 149–60; Didier Fassin, "Beyond Good and Evil?: Questioning the Anthropological Discomfort with Morals," *Anthropological Theory* 8, no. 4 (2008): pp. 333–44; Didier Fassin and Paula Vásquez, "Humanitarian Exception as the Rule: The Political Theology of the 1999 *Tragedia* in Venezuela," *American Ethnologist* 32, no. 3 (2005): pp. 389–405; Didier Fassin and Richard Rechtman, *L'empire du traumatisme: Enquête sur la condition de victime* (Paris: Flammarion, 2007).

5   For example, Michael Pugh, "Military Intervention and Humanitarian Action: Trends and Issues" *Disasters* 22, no. 4 (1998): pp. 339–51; Susan L. Woodward, "Humanitarian War: A New Consensus?" *Disasters* 25, no. 4 (2001): pp. 331–44; Fabrice Weissman, "Humanitarian Action and Military Intervention: Temptations and Possibilities," trans. Roger Leverdier, *Disasters* 28, no. 2 (2004): pp. 205–15.

6   This literature is set within a large field of ethnographies and social and historical analyses of violence and conflict, states of terror, trauma, and social suffering, as well as truth-and-reconciliation (TRC) processes, disarmament, demobilization, and reintegration (DDR) activities, and therapeutic interventions. Examples include Sharon Abramowitz, "The Poor Have Become Rich, and the Rich Have Become Poor: Collective Trauma in the Guinean Languette," *Social Science and Medicine* 61, no. 10 (2005): pp. 2106–18; Begoña Aretxaga, "Madness and the Politically Real: Reflections on Violence in Postdictatorial Spain," in DelVecchio Good, Hyde, Pinto, and Good (eds.), *Postcolonial Disorders*, pp. 43–61; João Biehl, *Vita: Life in a Zone of Social Abandonment* (Berkeley: University of California Press, 2005); Veena Das, Arthur Kleinman, Mamphela Ramphele, and Pamela Reynolds, (eds.), *Violence and Subjectivity* (Berkeley: University of California Press, 2000); Mark R. Duffield, *Global Governance and the New Wars: The Merging of Development and Security* (London: Zed Books, 2001); Erica C. James, "Haunting Ghosts: Madness, Gender, and Ensekirite in Haiti in the Democratic Era," in DelVecchio Good, Hyde, Pinto, and Good (eds.), *Postcolonial Disorders*, pp. 157–86; Mark Knight, "Expanding the DDR Model: Politics and Organizations," *Journal of Security and Sector Management* 6, no.1 (2008): pp. 1–18; Jennifer Leaning, Susan M. Briggs, and Lincoln C. Chen (eds.), *Humanitarian Crises: The Medical and Public Health Response* (Cambridge, MA: Harvard University Press, 1999); Carolyn Nordstrom, *A Different Kind of War Story* (Philadelphia: University of Pennsylvania Press, 1997); Carolyn Nordstrom, *Shadows of War: Violence, Power, and International Profiteering in the Twenty-First Century* (Berkeley: University of California Press, 2004); Peter Redfield, "Doctors, Borders, and Life in Crisis," *Cultural Anthropology* 20, no. 3 (2005): pp. 328–61; Kimberly Theidon, "Traditional Subjects: The Disarmament, Demobilization and Reintegration of Former Combatants in Columbia," *International Journal of Transitional Justice* 1, no. 1 (2007): pp. 66–90; Neil L. Whitehead, (ed.), *Violence* (Sante Fe, NM: School of American Research Press, 2004).

7   Byron and Mary-Jo Good were organizers of The Peace Process in Aceh: The Remainders of Violence and the Future of NAD, a Harvard University Asia Center conference, held in October 2007.

8   Jose C. Borrero, Costas E. Synolakis, and Hermann Fritz, "Northern Sumatra Field Survey after the December 2004 Sumatra Earthquake and Indian Ocean Tsunami," *Earthquake Spectra* 22, no. S3 (2006): pp. S93–S104.

9   Anthony Reid (ed.), *Verandah of Violence: The Background to the Aceh Problem* (Singapore:

Singapore University Press, 2006). "Verandah of violence" is a play on Aceh's centuries-long role as the "verandah" to Mecca for Muslim pilgrims from East and Southeast Asia and on its people's reputation for fierceness and aggression.

10   Damien Kingsley and Lesley McCulloch, "Military Business in Aceh," in Reid (ed.), *Verandah of Violence*, pp. 199–224.

11   See Aryo Danusiri's documentary film *The Village Goat Takes a Beating* (Kameng Gampoeng Nyang Keunong Geulawa), 1999, produced by ELSAM; Official Selection of Amnesty Film Festival, Amsterdam, 2001.

12   Conflict-affected deaths from the past two decades have been estimated by various sources at between thirty and thirty-five thousand.

13   Edward Aspinall, *The Helsinki Agreement: A More Promising Basis for Peace in Aceh?*, Policy Studies 20 (East-West Center Washington: Washington, D.C., 2005).

14   One widely held view was that there was little left to extract from Aceh. Its oil wealth, in particular, had been stripped.

15   Aspinall, *The Helsinki Agreement*. See Elizabeth F. Drexler, *Aceh, Indonesia: Securing the Insecure State* (Philadelphia: University of Pennsylvania Press, 2008), for a discussion of the DOM period and related human rights documents, and John Martinkus, *Indonesia's Secret War in Aceh* (Sydney: Random House Australia, 2004), for a powerful account of the recent conflict.

16   The PNA1 was funded by a grant from the Canadian government to the International Organization for Migration, Indonesia. Byron and Mary-Jo Good were consultants to IOM and Byron served as project director; Mary-Jo Good directed data analysis. Jesse Grayman, on staff of IOM while conducting his Ph.D. dissertation research, was project coordinator in the field. Faculty from Syiah Kuala University, led by Prof. Bahrein Sugihen, were responsible for recruiting and managing the field survey team. Project statistician at Harvard was Matthew Lakoma. The PNA2, carried out in July–November 2006, surveyed an additional eleven districts and was partially funded by the World Bank. For PNA2, the field team was hired directly by IOM and managed by Jesse Grayman. Data analysis for both projects was funded largely by an IOM–Department of Social Medicine consulting agreement. Study results are published as IOM reports: Byron Good, Mary-Jo DelVecchio Good, Jesse Grayman, and Matthew Lakoma, *Psychosocial Needs Assessment of Communities Affected by the Conflict in the Districts of Pidie, Bireuen, and Aceh Utara* (Jakarta: IOM, 2006 and 2007).

17   The Harvard Trauma Questionnaire was adapted for this purpose. Sharon Abramowitz, our graduate student, who had previously carried out similar studies in Guinea, joined this early design effort, spending two weeks in Aceh assisting Jesse Grayman with overseeing translation of instruments and training.

18   See Didier Fassin, "The Humanitarian Politics of Testimony: Subjectification through Trauma in the Israeli-Palestinian Conflict," *Cultural Anthropology* 23, no. 3 (2008): pp. 531–58 for a comparable perspective on human rights language and trauma in Palestine.

19   We purposely do not take on the difficult issues involved in the terms "trauma" and "PTSD" in this paper.

20   Mary-Jo DelVecchio Good, "The Medical Imaginary and the Biotechnical Embrace," in João Biehl, Byron Good, and Arthur Kleinman (eds.), *Subjectivity: Ethnographic Investigations* (Berkeley: University of California Press, 2008), pp. 362–80.

21   Didier Fassin and Richard Rechtman, *The Empire of Trauma: Inquiry into the Condition of*

*Victimhood* (Princeton, NJ: Princeton University Press, 2009).

22  Frantz Fanon, *The Wretched of the Earth* (New York: Grove Press, 1963); Alice Cherki, *Frantz Fanon: A Portrait* (Ithaca, NY: Cornell University Press, 2000).

23  For example, in some projects, nurses were trained explicitly as "mini psychiatrists" to dispense psychotropic medications without physician oversight, in direct opposition to Indonesian regulations.

24  Pandolfi, "The Humanitarian Industry and the Supra-Colonialism in the Balkan Territories."

25  Inter-Agency Standing Committee (IASC), *IASC Guidelines on Mental Health and Psychosocial Support in Emergency Settings* (Geneva: IASC, 2007).

26  Pandolfi, "Laboratories of Intervention," p. 161.

27  Judith Butler, *Giving an Account of Oneself* (New York: Fordham University Press, 2005), p. 40.

28  Emmanuel Levinas, "Four Talmudic Readings," in *Nine Talmudic Readings*, trans. Annette Aronowicz (Bloomington: Indiana University Press, 1990), p. 48.

PART THREE: LANDSCAPES

# Heart of Humaneness: The Moral Economy of Humanitarian Intervention

Didier Fassin

> By the simple exercise of our will we can exert a power for good practically unbounded.
>
> —Kurtz, in Joseph Conrad, *Heart of Darkness*

Humanitarian government can be defined, in the widest sense, as the introduction of moral sentiments into the political sphere.[1] Government should be understood here as encompassing the ensemble of more or less institutionalized practices by which human beings act on the behavior and destinies of other humans—what Michel Foucault terms the "government of men."[2] These practices are based on apparatuses and technologies that relate particularly to the action of states, supranational bodies, and nongovernmental organizations. And the purview of the humanitarian should not be restricted to extreme and remote situations—war zones, refugee camps, famines, epidemics, and disasters. It also relates to the reality closer to home of the treatment of the poor, immigrants, abused women, children affected by poverty—in short, all those categories constituted in terms of "vulnerability," which is set in opposition to the affirmation of what Hannah Arendt calls the "human condition."[3] There are thus two aspects to humanitarian government—the moral and the sentimental. On the one hand, we have what we might call "humanitarian reason": the principle according to which humans share a condition that inspires solidarity with one another. On the other, we have what we will name "the humanitarian emotion": the affect by virtue of which human beings feel personally concerned by the situation of others. Even though the morality of political action is generally claimed to be built on reason, behind the humanitarian gesture, there is always an emotion toward the suffering of others, without which this gesture would not come into being. It is essential that both elements are combined.

This humanitarian government, derived from rights and compassion, is of course deployed in a context where political and economic interests, the logics of states and agencies, and imperial and nationalist ideologies are at work: Thus in Iraq, as in Somalia, in Kosovo, as in Darfur, it is just one of the multifarious manifestations of power, if we consider power as what makes it possible to act on the course of events. Depending on the context, oil fields and arms factories, the demonstration of might and the desire for vengeance, geostrategic considerations and financial stakes are also at the heart of wars officially waged in the name of values and principles. However, the efficacy of humanitarian rhetoric is evidenced by the fact that it has recently been adopted and even appropriated by a number of social actors to describe a whole range of operations that were hitherto legitimized in other ways, most notably military interventions, which are more and more often justified in humanitarian terms.

Clearly, we must ensure we are not deceived by an inflationary reference to humanitarianism that would merely be a smokescreen for the conduct of what is no more than brutal realpolitik and classical liberalism as usual. But it is not sufficient to offer a distant analysis that simply, almost cynically, observes the misuse of humanitarianism as if nothing had really changed.[4] My argument here is different: I attempt to penetrate what, to use Josiah Heyman's formula,[5] we may call the "moral heart" of humanitarian action, taking seriously what actors in the humanitarian world do and say, what leads them to debate and act. This approach, which returns quite simply to the "emic" principle of any ethnographic study, in other words, the natives' perspective (the natives being here humanitarian workers), will throw light on some of the contradictions and conflicts facing humanitarian actors. I therefore begin with a brief portrait of humanitarianism, then attempt to outline its worldview, and conclude by examining some of the problems of its effective implementation in the conflict situations.

However, before embarking on this analysis, I should point out two important social characteristics of the actors in the French humanitarian organizations that are my field of study. On the one hand, these individuals generally have a lofty idea of their mission—saving lives and relieving suffering, but also denouncing injustice and restoring rights—that places them in some way beyond moral criticism. On the other, they often produce a reflexive discourse about themselves, but also about their humanitarian colleagues, that to some extent limits the scope of questions that can legitimately be raised. This double constraint obviously makes it difficult to take any analytical position, even that of "observant participation."[6] How is the researcher to position himself or herself in relation to agents whose ethical commitment appears to place them above criticism and who, moreover, decide for themselves what form any criticism of their movement may take? Instead of denouncing this constraint, I propose to consider it as a productive requirement for actors whose moral commitments and reflexive abilities need to be recognized without nevertheless exempting them from critical analysis.

## A PORTRAIT OF HUMANITARIANISM

But let us return to the sources of humanitarianism. The idea of "moral sentiments," as developed by Adam Smith and the eighteenth-century Scottish school of moral philosophy, from Shaftesbury to Hutcheson, sets the two dimensions of principle and affect, logical reason and felt emotion, against one another.[7] Countering the strictly rationalist view of morality, these philosophers affirmed both the "sense of good" and the "contagion of passions." Active sympathy felt for those who suffer is, in their view, the product of a meeting between humanitarian reason and humanitarian emotion.

In his analysis of "humanitarian morality" and its "topics of suffering," Luc Boltanski focuses on the affective dimension.[8] As he sees it, there are three positions that the spectator, who is also an actor, can take in the face of misfortune: expressing anger toward the perpetrator, feeling moved by aid workers, or aestheticizing the tragedy of the victims. But this theory of emotions accounts for only one part of what forms the basis for humanitarian government, leaving out the rationality of the ethics that Charles Taylor sees as an important characteristic of "modern identity." For him, the space of morality presupposes a conception of the public good, the good life, and human dignity.[9] It is certainly significant that these two dimensions of humanitarian morality—the emotional and the rational— emerged during the same historical period.

This tension between the two aspects persisted in the two very different uses of the French term *humanité*, which became established in the early nineteenth century. I refer to these specific word and period, since there is no doubt that the humanitarian idea and passion, as analyzed here, are closely related to the pre-Revolutionary and post-Revolutionary context in France. *Humanité* meant both humanity as an ethical category encompassing all human beings, forming the basis for a shared experience (humankind), and humanity as an affective movement toward others, manifested as sympathy with them (humaneness). The commitment of the philanthropists who inherited the legacy of the Enlightenment encompassed both solidarity and compassion, as Catherine Duprat has shown in tracing the history of activities ranging from benevolent societies caring for the poor at home to campaigns for the abolition of slavery abroad.[10] Moreover, she explains, on the eve of the Revolution in 1789, the term "philanthropist" was already considered the equivalent of "citizen," emphasizing the responsibility each person bears toward humans suffering and unjustly treated, but also indicating that this is a public, rather than a private issue. Thus, modern humanitarianism derives from this dual etymology and dual lineage. It relates to a sort of "intelligence of emotions," to use Martha Nussbaum's oxymoron.[11] According to her, our affects are not simply transports of feeling: They involve value judgments.

This historical and semantic digression reminds us that what makes humanitarianism unique in the political arena is the articulation of reason and emotion in the attitude held toward the other as vulnerable human being. This articulation opens up the possibility for all actors, including victims, to claim the authority of law or to excite sympathy and to play on this tension in order to promote interests and defend causes and even to instrumentalize humanitarian action. Thus, for example, in October 1990, a statement by a tearful nurse — later revealed to be the daughter of the Kuwaiti ambassador to the United States in disguise — that several hundred newborn babies had died when their incubators were allegedly switched off by Iraqi soldiers was arranged by the Kuwaiti government and relayed by the U.S. Army and was used successfully to legitimize the intervention of Western powers in the First Gulf War on the basis of humanitarianism. From this brief foray into etymology and history, I formulate three general propositions that may allow us to view humanitarianism beyond the confines of usual assumptions.

First, to counter an overly presentist vision,[12] it is important to grasp how inextricably humanitarian government is linked with our long period of modernity. While so-called "humanitarian wars" go back only a dozen years, and the movement described as "humanitarian" is little more than a hundred years old, the origins of the humanitarian idea and passion go much further back, to that historical moment when moral sentiments became the driving force for a politics, which was not simply a politics of pity, as Hannah Arendt argues,[13] but also one of solidarity. We could even say that this philanthropic politics is a sort of moral counterpoint to the contemporaneous development of both the police state, understood as the ensemble of apparatuses maintaining security and control of populations, and classical liberal reason, understood as the emergence of economic activity into the field of power, which Foucault sees as the two elements of what he calls "biopolitics."[14] Under this hypothesis, modern governance would rest not on two, but on three pillars: to the police and liberalism, we should thus add humanitarianism. In other words, in order to understand the contemporary politics of life, we need to make space for moral economy alongside political economy, with its dual functions of standardization and regulation.

Second, against the tendency to restrict analysis of humanitarianism to its actors and its self-reported actions, we need to take a broader anthropological view that can account for the many situations in which it comes into play.

While, as Françoise Bouchet-Saulnier points out,[15] international humanitarian law, extending the principles of the founders of the Red Cross, essentially operates within the legal field of the law of armed conflict, while many commentators, such as Olivier Weber,[16] see the romance of the humanitarian adventure as essentially synonymous with the epic self-narrative of nongovernmental organizations, and while recently the adjective "humanitarian" has been used as a new way of justifying military action, criticized by Stanley Hoffmann,[17] in fact, the humanitarian venture involves a much broader area of our political space. Humanitarianism is a language whose genealogy can be traced back through the last three centuries and that today structures the way we think of politics almost without our noticing. I am referring here to language in the strict sense of the vocabulary and grammar we take for granted and by which we communicate. When, in April 1999, the president of Czechoslovakia, Vaclav Havel, spoke of a humanitarian intervention to protect the people of Kosovo (rather than suggesting an armed conflict, which would imply massive bombing campaigns), and when French Prime Minister Lionel Jospin announced in February 2001 that the applications of asylum seekers would be assessed on a humanitarian basis (rather than using the criteria of the 1951 Geneva Convention), both were using terms whose meaning is immediately evident to everybody, but that at the same time alter our view of the situations in question because they force us to acknowledge a humanitarian aspect where we might have focused instead on war or asylum. Thus, this language produces a certain kind of understanding of the world and configures a particular form of collective experience. It forms and informs the moral economy of contemporary societies.

Finally, to oppose a reading that tends to separate humanitarianism from politics, seeing them as two unconnected and competing territories, it is important to comprehend that politics is being redefined through its increasing incorporation of the language of humanitarianism. There is a fairly widespread view that humanitarianism is gaining the ascendant over politics, which is deemed to be in decline. Rony Brauman argues that the development of the humanitarian NGO movement in the 1980s was linked to "the slow decline of communism, which took with it the idea of politics in the service of the general interest." It was thus, he continues, that "as the tide of ideology retreated, humanitarian action gradually came to occupy the space left empty by politics, supplying a concrete content for the ideal of solidarity."[18] In Giorgio Agamben's formulation, the phenomenon marks "the separation between humanitarianism and politics that we are experiencing today," which represents "the extreme phase of the separation of the rights of man from the rights of the citizen." In these conditions, he argues, organizations that base themselves on humanitarian principles "despite themselves, maintain a secret solidarity with the very powers they ought to fight."[19] These interpretations, whether the image used to represent this evolution refers to a physical one of communicating vessels between humanitarianism and politics or rather a geological one of the continents of humanitarianism and politics drifting apart, suggest that there are indeed two languages. This is reasserted by the politically committed analysis of Hugo Slim,[20] who calls for "a proper politicization of humanitarian philosophy," returning to international law in an arena where the emotional card is too often played. But the question needs to be posed in a different way. We should consider humanitarianism as a new repertoire for public action at both the international and local levels—in other words, not as something external to politics, but as something that reformulates what is at stake in politics. To paraphrase Clausewitz, one could say that humanitarianism is nothing but the continuation of politics by other means. In France in the 1980s, the administrative terminology indicated that some illegal immigrants could be awarded legal residence on humanitarian grounds when they were seriously ill. At the same time, it was humanitarian organizations that put pressure on the government to allow illegal immigrants access to free health care.[21] In both cases, compassion and law were indissociable. Politics became humanitarian. Hence, it is indeed this dialectic that we need to understand.

These introductory remarks are by way of a sort of portrait of humanitarianism, exploring its two dimensions (reason and emotion), dual domain (historical and semantic), and subject matter (politics). My counterproposals, derived from these remarks, emphasize the embedding of humanitarianism in the longer historical context, its reality as language through which the world as we represent it is brought into being, and its incorporation into the political sphere that it is gradually reconfiguring. They also invite all readers to explore the moral economy of humanitarianism, to adopt a notion introduced by E. P. Thompson,[22] in a very different context. It is this moral economy that I will focus on in the rest of this essay. I will do so within a specific, fairly restricted frame: the intervention of French nongovernmental organizations in conflict zones during the last decade. This restriction might appear to contradict the threefold approach—historical, semantic, and political—that I have put forward, since I am choosing a short period, focusing on war, and addressing only the French nongovernmental movement. In other words, I am omitting important elements of humanitarian government as I described it above. There are two reasons for restricting my analysis to this arena: One is empirical, since it coincides with the territory I have explored in my research and is thus the only one in which I feel competent to speak. The other is methodological, since I believe that this approach allows me, through a focus on a limited area, to throw light on some more general issues.

All moral economies are defined by shared values used as a basis for judgment and a justification for actions. The fundamental value that forms the basis for humanitarian government is human life. The highest justification of humanitarian government's intervention in this context is saving life. It is in this framework that the military can call its intervention "humanitarian":[23] just like the nongovernmental organizations that send volunteers, states deploying troops will claim that their mission is to protect a population or individuals whose lives are in danger, whatever their intentions in other respects, under the banner of the "right to intervene" (*droit d'ingérence*) promoted by the fathers of humanitarianism, most notably, Bernard Kouchner. As Thomas Weiss notes of international politics in the light of the experience of Kosovo: "Humanity, or the sanctity of life, is the only genuine first-order principle for intervention. The protection of the right to life, broadly interpreted, belongs in the category of obligations whose respect is in the interest of all states. Others—including the sacred trio of neutrality, impartiality, and consent, as well as legalistic interpretations of the desirability about UN approval—are second-order principles." But, in reference to the dual emotional and rational registers of humanitarian government in which he attempts to trace contemporary changes, the international expert adds: "Thoughtful reflection has assumed a growing role relative to the visceral reactions to come to the rescue that had heretofore guided humanitarians. Merely wanting to help, however laudable in moral terms, is an insufficient motivation to be present in war zones."[24] In other words, according to him, the lesson to be drawn from recent developments is less compassion, more sense of responsibility. But it seems unlikely that this aim will be achieved anytime soon, nor is it as clearly definable as suggested. Indeed, in relation to the NATO intervention in Kosovo, Barry Burciul has shown how the emotional register was used by the military to mobilize public opinion despite the fact that arguments based on U.S. interests prevailed in decision-making circles: "The emphasis on humanitarianism obscured other motives which—whether wise or unwise—were less palatable to Western audiences," he writes.[25] According to this analysis, which is obviously open to debate,[26] humanitarianism is nothing more than a virtuous disguise for reasons of state.

But perhaps the issues appear simpler for nongovernmental organizations, which in principle do not concern themselves with political or economic interests. This is at least the idea held by their promoters, such as Jean-Hervé Bradol, who writes:

> The production of order at the international level—just as at national or local levels— demands its quota of victims. "Are all these deaths really necessary?" is the question

we systematically address to political powers. Why? Because we have taken the arbitrary and radical decision to help the people society has decided to sacrifice. Consequently, if humanitarian action is to be consistent, it will inevitably clash with the established order.[27]

Thus, according to the president of Médecins Sans Frontières (Doctors Without Borders), the world falls into two camps: politics, which sacrifices, and humanitarianism, which saves.[28] In order for humanitarian agents to claim they are on the side of life, they have to place political actors on the side of death. In denouncing the dangerous Manichaeism of the U.S. moral war on the Forces of Evil, this humanitarian leader is in his own way reconstructing a world of binary oppositions in which "institutional political authorities who have the power to divide the governed between those who should live and those who are expendable" are contrasted with "the responsibility of humanitarian action—to save as many lives as possible." Apparently inspired by Michel Foucault,[29] Bradol claims the project of protecting human beings destined for destruction against the bloody trend of the traditional sovereign power of death: "humanitarian action can still oppose the elimination of a part of humanity by exemplifying an art of living founded on the pleasure of unconditionally offering people at risk of death the assistance that will allow them to survive." In fact what is at stake here is actually differentiated and competing forms of sovereignty, as Mariella Pandolfi suggests: some defined by the boundaries of national space, others mobile and deterritorialized, with the latter finding temporary spatial manifestation in the form of aid corridors (for the humanitarians) and camps (for the refugees) set apart as nonbelligerent zones within the very heart of the conflict.[30]

But nongovernmental organizations usually refuse to see themselves as participating in the competition between sovereignties in any way. On the contrary, the image they seek to promote is one of the doctor intervening precisely in places where sovereignty is either abusively exerted or temporarily suspended. "Médecins Sans Frontières provides assistance to populations in distress, to victims of natural or man-made disasters and to victims of armed conflict," begins that organization's charter. "The first and foremost mission of Médecins du Monde is to provide care. They commit themselves to assisting all vulnerable populations in situations of humanitarian crises resulting from wars or natural disasters, or in conditions of poverty in the most underprivileged areas of the world," reads the statement of principles of that organization.[31] Thus, it seems that the only power claimed by humanitarians is that of aiding "populations in danger"—in other words, a power of the powerless in the service of victims.[32] As it is well known, this was the founding principle of the Red Cross in the late nineteenth century, when the issue was bringing aid to the wounded on the battlefields and later protecting civilians against abuses by the military.

Although all contemporary nongovernmental organizations still cleave to this principle, not all of them claim it as their sole criterion for action. The domain of intervention is the subject of intense debate, and even of political splits, between Médecins Sans Frontières, which has refocused explicitly on the traditional mission of providing aid in the form of health care, and Médecins du Monde (Doctors of the World), which now engages more broadly in challenging attacks on human rights. At the birth of the second wave of the humanitarian movement, in the early 1970s, the major tensions were between an emergency-aid tendency, represented by Médecins Sans Frontières and later by Médecins du Monde, and a Third-Worldist line committed to long-term development initiatives and contesting the inequality of the international order. Thirty years later, the division is between the "aidist" tendency (in French, *urgentiste*, a term used by the actors involved), represented by Médecins Sans Frontières and the Red Cross, and the "human-right-ist" tendency (*droits-de-l'hommiste*, a description generally considered pejorative) represented by Médecins du Monde, which occasionally collaborates with the International Federation for Human Rights. While the charter of Médecins Sans Frontières focuses on "universal medial ethics and the right to humanitarian aid," the motto used as a brand identifier on the Médecins du Monde donors' magazine reads: "We treat all sickness, including injustice." Here we encounter the distinction drawn by jurists between humanitarian law (essentially defined in relation to a war situation) and human rights (which implicitly relate to times of peace). The fundamental principle of humanitarian law, which descends from Henri Dunant, founder of the Red Cross, and the 1949 Geneva Conventions, is the protection of life. The concept of human rights, which draws its heritage from the French Revolution and the 1948 Universal Declaration of Human Rights, centers on human dignity. The former is a law for victims of conflicts, the latter implies rights for citizens of the world.

Nevertheless, it has to be acknowledged that in the field, the differences are much less marked: All humanitarian actors are engaged in more or less the same work of maintaining the operation of aid missions in which the sick and wounded are cared for, nutrition and vaccination programs are instigated, and at the same time, abuses committed against civilians and attacks on basic rights are documented. Some analysts have been misled by these apparent similarities, for example Renée Fox,[33] who enthusiastically and somewhat candidly classes Médecins Sans Frontières and Médecins du Monde together under a shared "non-ideological ideology": Inspired by their altruistic actions, she describes their vision of the world as "transcendentally universalistic as well as militantly pacific." But at times of great crisis, the lines of division are often apparent in the positions taken on the two principles of aid and human rights. For example, during the weeks before the Second Gulf War, humanitarian organizations were divided over the attitude they ought to take toward the U.S. government's willingness to intervene. While one coalition, which included Médecins du Monde, condemned the principle of military intervention on the basis of its likely humanitarian consequences, competing organizations, including Médecins Sans Frontières, commented ironically on their colleagues' pacifism, taking the view that on the contrary, such opposition was not the role of the humanitarian movement. "Neither pro-war nor anti-war," asserted Rony Brauman and Pierre Salignon,[34] who went on: "We should remember that modern humanitarian action developed out of armed conflicts in the nineteenth century by asking, 'who needs help because of this war?' instead of 'who is right in this war?' These origins are not recalled as a dogma to condemn some heresy, but to stress the continued importance of this position if aid is to be effective." It is thus no surprise that once the bombing of Iraq was over, the two sides took diametrically opposed positions on the reality of the "humanitarian crisis." While Médecins du Monde "mobilized to bring aid to an exhausted population" in a country "in chaos" confronted by "a situation which gives cause for alarm," with "800,000 displaced people," Médecins Sans Frontières was calmly asking: "What is humanitarianism's role here?" and firmly concluding: "There is nothing humanitarian about the forthcoming reconstruction."[35] In fact, the reasons for this divergence in analysis are more complex than at first appears, and the withdrawal of the French team of Médecins Sans Frontières was largely the result of the collective trauma caused by the abduction by Iraqi police of two of its members during the first days of the bombing of Baghdad. Thus, it was in the name of humanitarianism that some denounced the war while others refused to question the justification for it, and it was in the name of humanitarianism that the former offered assistance while the latter left the country.

While, as William Fisher notes,[36] all NGOs claim "to do good" and seem to define themselves in terms of "antipolitics," they thus differ widely in the ways they address moral questions and position themselves in the public arena. From this point of view, the "competitive humanitarianism" that Jock Stirrat[37] describes in relation to the tsunami in December 2004 is embedded in the dual social logic of the market and the field.

On the one hand, there is a market, in the Weberian sense,[38] in humanitarianism, with its resources (including symbolic ones) that various suppliers attempt to appropriate. The debate around donations, which in France reached a total of 300 million euros, revealed this clearly. Once again, Médecins Sans Frontières created the event by announcing that it was halting its appeal for donations for tsunami relief on the grounds that the money received was already more than enough and should be redirected to causes that were less in the media spotlight, but of equal concern. Most other organizations, including Médecins du Monde, assured donors on the contrary that all monies collected would go to the Asian victims of the disaster. Thus, the issue was no longer merely economic, but also moral. Rivalry focused not just on financial, but also on ethical resources.

On the other hand, the context of humanitarianism operates like a field, in Pierre Bourdieu's sense.[39] In other words, its actors are committed to competing definitions of the issues involved in humanitarianism and the best way to meet them. On this level, too, the tsunami provided material for sometimes heated exchanges between international organizations. Focusing purely on emergency aid, Médecins Sans Frontières particularly criticized the World Health Organization for its announcement, erroneous in their view, that there was a danger of epidemics. The French NGO argued that humanitarian organizations no longer had a role in the aftermath of the tsunami after the first few weeks. The French Red Cross, the main beneficiary of private donations, and the Fondation de France, which also received substantial funds, asserted that, on the contrary, it was important to invest the money received in long-term reconstruction projects in the affected areas. The huge flows of money resulting from the wave of compassion thus rekindled the old debate that had caused divisions some twenty years earlier between those who supported emergency relief and those who argued for development, but with a significant difference this time. The ideological divisions over the most appropriate form of aid now arose within the humanitarian sphere.

But the fact that humanitarianism operates as a space of competition should not draw us into a narrowly sociological reading. Beyond the logics of the market and the field, which are after all common, the issues relate to competing moral accounts of the world. The question is not simply how to assert oneself over and above one's competitors, it is also how to impose one's ethical truth—or how to establish oneself as the holder of that truth. Médecins Sans Frontières is probably the organization that has taken this logic of the fight between good and evil furthest. As a pioneer of the second generation of humanitarianism and recipient of the Nobel Peace Prize in 1999, the organization not only considers itself a global moral authority, which it indeed is, but also acts as if it is authorized to judge—that is, to condemn—others.

The situation in Angola offers a typical example. On July 2, 2001, Médecins Sans Frontières published a report and gave a press conference condemning the false normalization of the situation in Angola. Their conclusion was damning:

> The Angolan government claims that the situation in the country is returning to normal, but this is a far cry from the reality witnessed by Médecins Sans Frontières'

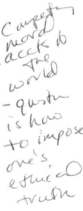

teams working in nine provinces throughout the country. In this new phase of the conflict, the population has been increasingly subjected to the violence of war, abused, displaced, and relocated according to military strategies and political interests, exposed to epidemics and malnutrition. Contrary to the claim made by the Angolan authorities that the situation is simply a consequence of the war, Médecins Sans Frontières finds that it is the result of deliberate choices, on the part of the government, UNITA, the international community, and the United Nations.[40]

All the actors involved were thus criticized with equal severity. Whereas most commentators and aid workers distinguished the legitimate government of President José Eduardo Dos Santos from the UNITA rebels and defended the mediation and aid work of the international community and the United Nations, Médecins Sans Frontières drew no such distinction, casting one side as criminals and the other as complicit. The organization explained that it was issuing this criticism for the sake of saving lives. In a country where over half a million had died and 4 million were displaced, the president of Médecins Sans Frontières pointed to twenty thousand children that his organization had rescued from famine. The UN Humanitarian coordinator responded to this attack by asking "to avoid the cynicism of careless criticism" and asserting that "hundreds of aid workers are aiming for the same objective, saving the lives of people who would otherwise suffer or die." They, too, were saving lives.

Thus, the world according to humanitarianism is laid out in a moral space riven by permanent tensions in which actions and actors are judged by others to be acceptable or rejected. The alleged stark opposition between the humanitarians' politics of life and the states' politics of death draws a first, simple distinction that the former tend to agree on and the latter of course contest.[41] But in a sort of competition of ethics, the protagonists have also established multiple lines of division between NGOs and UN bodies, between supporters and opponents of "humanitarian right to intervene," between prescribers of emergency intervention and proponents of development, between "aidists" and "human-rightists," and even between "humanitarian medicine" and "public health."[42] Thus, it might be more useful to discard the simplistic representation of the world as divided into good and evil in favor of the Dantesque metaphor of the circles of hell, with a gradual progression from dangerous promoters of good (other humanitarians) to evil war criminals (states and their armies), passing through all the forms of what is classified as compromise (intellectual with public health, ideological with Third-Worldism, political with international organizations, military with the principle of intervention). But it is precisely this reassuringly ordered vision of the world that is shaken by concrete intervention.

## HUMANITARIANISM CONFRONTED BY THE REALITY PRINCIPLE

The questions raised and the debates stimulated by humanitarian action are often formulated in terms of "moral dilemmas," a term inherited from moral philosophy.[43] Such a formulation tends to result in a rational and often artificial reading of what is at stake in actual situations. In fact, time rarely stops long enough for a true dilemma to be posed and ultimately resolved. Much more frequently, the moral issues emerge in the course of action, and they are rarely separable from political issues. Thus, I prefer the empirical quality of the term "moral stakes" to the formal qualification of "moral dilemmas"—an essentially reassuring terminology, because it allows problems to be posed in terms of ethical and logical choices outside of historical context and strategic considerations.

In this respect, what we might call the "Kosovo moment"—the period of NATO's intervention in the Serbian province in the spring of 1999—represents a truth test on more than one level. "It was in Kosovo that the battle for independent humanitarianism was probably lost," writes David Rieff: "Humanitarianism had served in Bosnia as pretext for the refusal of the great powers to intervene. In Kosovo humanitarian efforts were deployed for the opposite purpose, as a pretext for what was essentially a political decision by the great powers to put an end militarily once and for all to Slobodan Milosevic's fascist rebellion in the European backlands. By the time the NATO military campaign was over and Serb forces had withdrawn from the rebellious province, Milosevic's days were indeed numbered. But the political instrumentalization of humanitarianism was also nearly complete."[44] This criticism is essentially aimed at the Office of the United Nations High Commissioner for Refugees, which Rieff accuses of working hand-in-hand with NATO and almost all of the NGOs, all too happy, as he sees it, to have a place at the table. Only one organization escapes his opprobrium. For him Médecins Sans Frontières did not become compromised in this merging of categories. But while it is true that this organization continued to condemn the blurring of military and humanitarian intervention, its actions on the ground were not necessarily so clearly separated.

On March 24, 1999, six days after the breakdown of peace talks at Rambouillet, near Paris, NATO began air strikes on Kosovo. As we have noted, the official justification for this intervention was humanitarian. Albanian Kosovars were not only subject to political, economic, and cultural domination, as they had been for several decades, they were also now under direct physical threat from the killings, kidnappings, rape, and even ethnic cleansing that were under way. Thus, although it lacked international legality, the military intervention was justified by Western governments on the grounds of a moral legitimacy, which was easily accepted by public opinion, since it was constructed on what Anne Orford calls "the emotional urgency of intervention narratives."[45] In the month that followed, the NATO bombing and Serbian reprisals resulted in the displacement of hundreds of thousands of Albanian Kosovars, who took refuge in camps on the other side of the border, an exodus described by a NATO spokesperson as a "humanitarian disaster." Médecins Sans Frontières conducted an epidemiological survey on a sample of 1537 refugees, augmented by a collection of short narratives from 639 others: The aim was to build up an account of the crimes committed by the Serbs, in this case, the "deportation" of a people. The report was published on April 30, 1999.[46] On the front pages of the French press, Philippe Biberson, the organization's president at the time, declared: "This is a planned annihilation of a people. Albanian Kosovars are not only being deported, but also systematically robbed of their identification documents, their civil status, and their property deeds." This publication had a major impact. It was used conspicuously by NATO to show that impartial humanitarians were retrospectively providing justification for the intervention. In the intense debates that subsequently took place on Médecins Sans Frontières' Board of Administrators, it was acknowledged that publishing the report at that point in time was a mistake that had contributed to the blurring of military action and humanitarianism in a conflict where the NATO forces had made systematic efforts to act as coordinator of humanitarian operations. Despite Médecins Sans Frontières' much-trumpeted financial independence from the international agencies and Western states, many in the organization took the view that ultimately it had emerged as an objective ally of NATO.

The difficulty of maintaining genuine neutrality in the conflict was made even clearer by the expulsion of Médecins Sans Frontières's Greek section. Neutrality, as is well known, is one of the pillars of humanitarian action, and it is enshrined in the organization's charter. The only side it allows itself to take is that of the victims.[47] In the case of Kosovo, it seemed obvious to many that the victims were the Albanian Kosovars. For months, European and North American journalists, intellectuals, and political representatives had been bearing witness to the abuses that the Serbs were inflicting on them. The need to bring aid to refugees in camps in Albania, Macedonia, and Montenegro was taken as a given, just as was public condemnation of the crimes perpetrated against the Kosovars.

But in the Balkans, some saw things differently. Many Greeks, in particular, were critical of Western countries' positions and reluctant to support the NATO bombings.[48] Their position was clearly inscribed in historical links and geopolitical alliances between Serbia and Greece.[49] The Greek section of Médecins Sans Frontières itself, while officially condemning the Milosevic regime, denounced the NATO air strikes, and when a "humanitarian corridor" was opened by the military on the two sides, members of the Greek section asked permission to use it to bring aid to the people who had been bombed in Kosovo and Serbia. Despite opposition from their French, Belgian, and Dutch colleagues who were present in the war zone, the Greek section sent a team of four persons to bring aid to hospitals in Pristina and Belgrade. The move was immediately denounced by the other sections, and for the first time in Médecins Sans Frontières's history, a section was expelled. For several years, the disagreement and the sanction implemented were experienced within the movement as a deep wound, and merely the mention of it would provoke heated debate.

The breach revealed that in fact there were no universal criteria for the identification of victims and that doing so could be subject to challenge. Humanitarian organizations were for the victims, all the victims, yes; there were no good or bad victims, it went without saying; but on condition that all agreed on who were the victims. But this questioning of whether the moral economy of humanitarian action was so self-evident was barely heard: The official version remained that the Greek section had "excluded itself," as the meeting of the Médecins Sans Frontières International Council on June 6, 1999, put it, since its unilateral decision had demonstrated a lack of independence from statist ideologies and had destabilized operations on the ground. It was considered as an internal problem of not respecting the collective rules, rather than a political issue questioning the absolute truth of victimhood. Moreover, when, with the war barely over, Albanian Kosovars, particularly the UCK (the Ushtria Çlirimtare e Kosovës, the Kosovo Liberation Army, also known as the KLA), indulged in punitive raids, personal vengeance, extrajudicial executions, and bloody settling of scores against the Serbs, but also against the Gypsies, Médecins Sans Frontières made the decision to remain silent about these abuses and the ethnic cleansing that was under way.[50] The organization concentrated on its reconstruction program, which principally consisted of distributing tin roofs to families whose homes had been damaged.

Fiercely proclaiming their independence on both the financial level (by refusing funding from the intervening powers) and the logistical level (staying away from refugee camps controlled by NATO and the UN), but politically supporting the military action by virtue of the belligerent stance taken by their honorary president Rony Brauman and the publication of a widely publicized report on an exodus described as "deportation"; asserting their neutrality in their effort to relieve the victims' suffering, but rejecting any action to support the bombed populations of Belgrade; denouncing the crimes against Albanian Kosovars, but later remaining silent about the abuses against Serbians—the ambiguities of Médecins Sans Frontières' intervention in Kosovo reveal real difficulty in reconciling rationalities, emotions, and political strategies with the ethical principles enshrined in humanitarian organizations' charters. My point is not to add a further moral evaluation to the moral work of humanitarian actors, but to reveal the profound aporia—not simply contradictions—in the stances and positions they take.

The blurring of the boundaries between military and humanitarian action that is so often criticized by nongovernmental organizations who always see it as a form of duplicity on the part of states and their armies, buying legality or legitimacy for their military intervention by adding some humanitarian heart to their operations, is the result of interactions that are much more complex than their protagonists would have us believe. The most extreme form corresponds to the situations where NGOs act as intelligence services for the intervening powers, often justifying this activity by moral arguments such as helping to increase the efficiency of the armies that are supposed to be restoring order. Much more commonly, NGOs collaborate with occupying troops within the context of aid missions to populations, receive financial support from development agencies associated with them, and ultimately merge with the intervening powers in their day-to-day activities to the extent of entering the territory alongside the military. In these cases, they still claim moral justification, but on the grounds of making their own actions more effective. Even those who refuse to collude with or depend on the military cannot completely escape the military-humanitarian nexus in which they are caught. Whether they encourage or deplore it, military forces and humanitarian workers are bound together in the intervention, for better or worse.[51]

Not only do humanitarians need the military to protect them to the extent of setting up aid corridors, not only do they benefit from the essential military logistics and organization, but on a deeper and more subtle level, the two share many more realities and values than they believe or admit to themselves. Their temporalities are linked in the period of emergency, and humanitarian organizations usually leave shortly after the military. They share a habitus, even in their way of isolating themselves from the surrounding population in their separate, guarded living quarters. The organization of their work is often similar in their management of human groups, particularly in the administration of refugee camps. Even their vision of the world, and particularly the way they think of local societies as undifferentiated, treat the sovereignty of national states, and consider their own role above the common law there, are not without unexpected similarities. There have even been cases where humanitarians have committed violence, abuses, and crimes against the populations they were supposed to be protecting, apparently falling into practices that might be more readily seen as crimes of the military.[52] Ultimately, the relations between the two worlds are not just circumstantial and related to the conflict, but essentially structural—the product of intervention itself and the sign of its ambiguities.

However, whereas humanitarian actors rarely have the lucidity to recognize

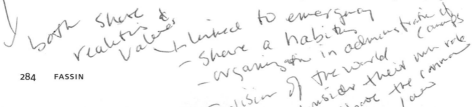

this reality,[53] it does not escape local protagonists. Not only do they not draw any practical distinction between the military and humanitarians, who appear to them to belong to the same entity of an intervention that is both massive and remote, but they see no moral difference between the logic of the military and the intentions of humanitarians.[54] Contrary to the image humanitarians have of themselves, and by contrast, of the military, which they often believe local populations share, those on whose behalf they intervene do not always see them as saviors—or at least not necessarily any more than they see the soldiers in this way—and may even consider them occupiers, just like the armies present in their territory. The targeted killing of aid workers, notably in Afghanistan (a female employee of the UN High Commissioner for Refugees in 2003, five members of Médecins Sans Frontières in 2004, and one person working for the World Food Programme in 2007) offer a tragic demonstration of this fact. Moreover, the consequences of this conflation of organizations seen as Western before they are recognized as humanitarian are usually much more serious for the local employees of these organizations than for the expatriate workers.

Of the fragility of humanitarians' moral representation of the world I had the moving revelation shortly after the release of Kenny Gluck, head of Médecins Sans Frontières' team in Chechnya, who had disappeared for several months in early 2001 when his car was ambushed by unknown militants. There had been great concern. The hypothetical explanation for his abduction, generally agreed upon among the management team in Paris, pointed to the Russian secret services or armed forces, who were known to be unfavorable to the presence of humanitarian agents in the province where they were conducting their repressive operations. The Russian government's denial of responsibility had cut no ice. Suspicion remained targeted at them. But when Gluck was freed, it was learned that he had been held, in comfortable conditions, not by the Russians, but by Chechens, or more precisely by a rebel Chechen group with which Médecins Sans Frontières thought it had built a relationship of trust. Although the Chechen cause was the one to which the organization had shown itself most publicly committed for several years, to the extent of representatives wearing a T-shirt bearing the name of the capital Grozny when receiving the Nobel Prize in 1999, and although there had been regular contact with representatives of rebel groups, both in the Caucasus and in Paris, it was those on whose behalf the organization was working who had put their members, and hence their project, in danger. I had rarely seen such distress on the faces of Médecins Sans Frontières' administrators and directors as when they learned the conditions of their colleague's abduction. With this betrayal, as they saw it, a certain moral order of the world collapsed. Victims could turn on their benefactors, and the space of good and evil was no longer what they had thought.

## CONCLUSION

The supreme value of contemporary societies—at least in the West, but more and more in other regions, too—is life in the sense that Walter Benjamin expressed it: "the simple fact of living." But this does not mean that life does not compete with other values, such as dignity or justice, and other meanings of life, particularly as the good life or the political life. Humanitarian reason, with its law that constitutes its formal expression and its action that represents its translation in practice, essentially consists in drawing attention to this value and implementing it concretely by saving lives. But this does not imply that actors who claim it as their principle do not take on other roles. Considering these principles, it is easy to understand the moral superiority of humanitarian intervention, or rather, of the invocation of the humanitarian argument in order to intervene, whether it is claimed by states at war or by aid organizations. And we can also understand the difficulty of reflecting critically on it, as I am doing here, since such reflection cannot fail to come up against the moral superiority of the action of saving lives.

In fact, rather than contesting this moral economy, on the basis of which those who intervene distinguish the good side from the bad, I have attempted here to analyze it from the inside in order to reveal its ambivalence, contradictions, and its frequent aporia—in other words, to penetrate into the "heart of humaneness," the place where morality can no longer be discussed. It is from this point of view that I have examined how situations are qualified and competitors disqualified, how causes are chosen and victims acknowledged, how social worlds are morally interpreted and their realities confronted.

There is always a political price to be paid for the moral—and often emotional—simplification of what is at stake in conflicts. This has been demonstrated by a number of studies on military interventions justified on humanitarian grounds. And this was what I wished to demonstrate in relation to strictly humanitarian interventions that accompany these military operations. Clearly, there is a risk of misunderstanding here, for it is always easier to criticize those whom one can cast on the side of the politics of death (the military) than those who present themselves as promoters of politics of life (the humanitarians). Certainly, we need to recognize that humanitarian workers are generally motivated by a sense of responsibility toward the world, its violence, and its injustice. But this sense of responsibility is all the more reason to hold them to account for what they say and what they do, before the societies whose values they proclaim and, even more, before those to whom they offer assistance.

*Translated by Rachel Gomme*

I am indebted to those who have agreed to be interviewed for my work and to those who have tolerated my presence, among them the staff of the humanitarian organizations with which and in which I have worked as a researcher and as a companion. If critique means something—and it surely does to me—it is this effort to enter where certainties no longer exist.

1   Didier Fassin, " Humanitarianism: A Nongovernmental Government," in Michel Feher, Gaëlle Krikorian, and Yates McKee (eds.), *Nongovernmental Politics* (New York: Zone Books, 2007), pp. 149–60; and "Le gouvernement humanitaire," in Didier Fassin, *La raison humanitaire: Une histoire morale du temps présent* (Paris: Hautes Études-Gallimard-Seuil, forthcoming). This broad understanding of the term, drawn from the work of Michel Foucault and Hannah Arendt, differs from the definitions of other writers, who limit humanitarian government to the actions of international bodies such as the Office of the UN High Commissioner for Refugees. See, for example, Michel Agier, "Le camp des vulnérables: Les réfugiés face à leur citoyenneté niée," *Les Temps Modernes* 59, no. 627 (May–June 2004), pp. 120–37.

2   Michel Foucault, *Résumé des cours 1970–1982* (Paris: Julliard, 1989). The title of the 1979–80 course at the Collège de France was "Le gouvernement des vivants."

3   Hannah Arendt, *The Human Condition* (Chicago: University of Chicago Press, 1958). Plurality and identity—the fact that we are different and yet the same—form the basis of this human condition.

4   Peter Redfield, "Doctors, Borders and Life in Crisis," *Cultural Anthropology* 20, no. 3 (2005): pp. 328–61. Distancing himself from a critical position that, he argues, "structurally evades the less comfortable possibilities of implication within the process in question and the problem of approaching what is already represented or already familiar," Redfield undertakes "to move away from treating humanitarianism as an absolute value by approaching it as an array of particular embodied, situated practices emanating from the humanitarian desire to alleviate the suffering of others."

5   Josiah Heyman, *Finding a Moral Heart for U.S. Immigration Policy*, American Ethnological Society Monograph Series No. 7 (Arlington, VA: American Anthropological Association, 1998). In contrast to Heyman, my focus is on putting forward not the anthropologist's moral viewpoint, but an anthropology critical of a set of morals, as I also propose in my paper "Beyond Good and Evil?: Questioning the Anthropological Discomfort with Morals," *Anthropological Theory* 8, no. 4 (2008): pp. 333–44.

6   Didier Fassin, "The End of Ethnography as Collateral Damage of Ethical Regulation?" *American Ethnologist* 33, no. 4 (2006): pp. 522–24. One may propose the expression "observant participation" to designate research where the primary function of the researcher is participation in a social activity and the secondary function is the observation of that activity. In this case, my analysis of humanitarian government is based on regular exchanges and occasional collaboration with a number of French nongovernmental organizations over two decades, in particular Médecins Sans Frontières and Médecins du Monde, and more particularly on a deeper involvement as an administrator and then vice president of Médecins Sans Frontières from 1999 to 2003. I have also conducted a more traditional series of interviews with humanitarian workers.

7   Adam Smith, *The Theory of Moral Sentiments* (1759; Oxford: Oxford University Press, 1976). The question of sympathy, often reduced to the purely mechanical dimension of the

communication of emotions between individuals, is at the heart of this essay, which attempts to respond to two questions: What constitutes virtue? And what power or faculty of the mind recommends it to us?

8    Luc Boltanski, *Distant Suffering: Morality, Media and Politics* (Cambridge: Cambridge University Press, 1999). This book focuses mainly on the position of the spectator, although Boltanski makes reference to the humanitarian agent in some of the later developments of his argument.

9    Charles Taylor, *The Sources of the Self* (Cambridge, MA: Harvard University Press, 1989). Taylor connects moral sentiments with what he calls "the affirmation of ordinary life." Extending this observation, we could consider humanitarianism as proceeding from the extension of ordinary life into politics.

10   Catherine Duprat, *"Pour l'amour de l'humanité": Le temps des philanthropes* (Paris: Éditions du Comité des Travaux Historiques et Scientifiques, 1993). Duprat cites François-Vincent Toussaint's 1748 treatise *Les moeurs*, which offers the first "modern" definition of humanity, based on this double meaning: "By humanity, I mean the interest men bear toward their fellows in general, simply because they are men like them. This sentiment, etched in the heart, is the source of the other social virtues."

11   Martha Nussbaum, *Upheavals of Thought: The Intelligence of Emotions* (Cambridge: Cambridge University Press, 2001). Nussbaum focuses particularly on showing how "a society pursuing justice might legitimately rely on and cultivate compassion" (p. 299).

12   François Hartog, *Régimes d'historicité: Présentisme et expériences du temps* (Paris, Seuil, 2003). In particular: "Today, enlightenment is produced by the present and by the present alone. In this sense (only) past, future, and historical time no longer exist" (p. 218).

13   Hannah Arendt, *On Revolution* (New York: Viking, 1963). Arendt contrasts pity as a remote sentiment toward an abstract population (the impoverished masses) with compassion as an affect of proximity relating to a specific individual (the beggar).

14   Michel Foucault, *Security, Territory, Population: Lectures at the Collège de France 1977–1978* (London: Palgrave Macmillan, 2007) and *The Birth of Biopolitics: Lectures at the Collège de France 1978–1979* (New York: Palgrave Macmillan, 2008).

15   Françoise Bouchet-Saulnier, *Dictionnaire pratique du droit humanitaire* (Paris: La Découverte, 2000). In fact, this dictionary covers a field broader than international humanitarian law in the strict sense.

16   Olivier Weber, *French doctors: L'épopée des hommes et des femmes qui ont inventé la médecine humanitaire* (Paris: Robert Laffont, 1995). Besides this book, one can find many autobiographical accounts of a number of these doctors, from Bernard Kouchner to Xavier Emmanuelli, and a series of writings that recount the history of the humanitarian movement in a similarly narrative fashion.

17   Stanley Hoffmann, *The Ethics and Politics of Humanitarian Intervention* (Notre Dame, IN: University of Notre Dame Press, 1996). The emergence of this association between the military and humanitarianism has led to the development of a specific field of research within political science.

18   Rony Brauman, *L'action humanitaire* (Paris: Flammarion, 2000). The end of the Cold War is a historical phenomenon often—no doubt correctly—identified as marking the beginning of the rise of humanitarianism in international politics. But the process probably results from a deeper anthropological reconfiguration of our societies, as evidenced by the rise of the humanitarian paradigm in many areas of social life, and not only in zones of conflict.

19   Giorgio Agamben, *Homo Sacer: Sovereign Power and Bare Life*, trans Daniel Heller-Roazen (Stanford, CA: Stanford University Press, 1998), p. 133. Agamben's critique of humanitarian organizations is based on the fact that their object is bare life, as they reveal it, for example, through images of the imploring gaze of skeletal children.

20   Hugo Slim, "Not Philanthropy but Rights: The Proper Politicisation of Humanitarian Philosophy," *International Journal of Human Rights* 6, no. 2 (2002): pp. 1–22. Slim criticizes the "philanthropic" tendency in humanitarian action (which is based on an "ethics of charity") and calls instead for a "political" approach (couched in the terms of "human rights").

21   Didier Fassin, "Compassion and Repression: The Moral Economy of Immigration Policies in France," *Cultural Anthropology* 20, no. 3 (2005): pp. 362–87. This humanitarianization of policy applies in all areas, not just to repressive policy.

22   Edward Palmer Thompson, "The Moral Economy of the English Crowd in the Eighteenth Century," *Past and Present* 50 (1971): pp. 76–136. In this famous text, Thompson restricts the analysis of moral economies to dominated subjects involved in collective phenomena such as riots. Here I use it in a broader sense, applying it to the sharing and appreciation of values of good and evil on which a social group or an entire society agree.

23   Nicholas Wheeler, *Saving Strangers: Humanitarian Intervention in International Society* (Oxford: Oxford University Press, 2000). Wheeler notes that while the humanitarian argument was never used to justify military intervention in the 1970s, by the 1990s, it had become a legitimate justification.

24   Thomas Weiss, "Instrumental Humanitarianism and the Kosovo Report," *Journal of Human Rights* 1, no. 1 (2002): pp. 121–27. Weiss's reflections in this text relate only to what we might term "state humanitarianism," which is in fact the principal area of research in international-relations studies.

25   Barry Burciul, *Kosovo: The Politics of Humanitarianism*, report for MSF, University of Toronto, p. 34. In order to win public support in the United States for his intervention project, Secretary of Defense William Cohen spoke of one hundred thousand Albanian Kosovars "disappeared," probably murdered: the final tally was less than twenty-five hundred. At the same time, U.S. Balkan envoy Richard Holbrooke explained that the reasons for the intervention were, in this order: maintaining political stability in the region, the survival of the North Atlantic alliance, security in Europe, demonstrating U.S. military power, and, finally, humanitarian concerns.

26   Didier Fassin, "La souffrance du monde: Considérations anthropologiques sur les politiques contemporaines de compassion." *Evolution psychiatrique* 67, no. 4 (2002): pp. 676–89. In this article, I evoke how the emotional reaction to the death of a Palestinian youth at the beginning of the second intifada, given worldwide media publicity, influenced the negotiations between Yasser Arafat and Ehud Barak and especially influenced French President Jacques Chirac, who was mediating the talks. More generally, I defend the idea that there is no doubt that the affective, but also inextricably moral dimensions should not be underestimated in the political analysis of conflicts and their resolution.

27   Jean-Hervé Bradol, "The Sacrificial International Order and Humanitarian Action," in Fabrice Weissman (ed.), *In the Shadow of "Just Wars": Violence, Politics, and Humanitarian Action* (Ithaca, NY: Cornell University Press, 2003), pp. 1–22. This collection of articles represents an updated version of a project initiated ten years earlier by François Jean, giving an inventory of "populations in danger" throughout the world.

28 Didier Fassin, "Humanitarianism as a Politics of Life," *Public Culture* 19, no. 3 (2007): pp. 499–520. Taking the example of Médecins Sans Frontières in Iraq, in this article, I attempted to highlight the ontological inequalities concealed in the humanitarian politics of life.

29 Michel Foucault, *The History of Sexuality, Volume 1: An Introduction*, trans. Robert Hurley (New York: Random House). In the last chapter of this book, Foucault puts forward his idea of the historical succession of the sovereign power to kill and biopower, which determines whether individuals are to live or die.

30 Mariella Pandolfi, "'Moral entrepreneurs,' souverainetés mouvantes et barbelés Le biopolitique dans les Balkans post-communistes," in Mariella Pandolfi and Marc Abélès (eds.), "Politiques: Jeux d'espaces," special issue, *Anthropologie et Sociétés* 26, no. 1 (2002): pp. 29–51.

31 For the charter of MSF, see http://www.msf.org.uk/about_charter.aspx; for the statement of principles of MDM, see http://www.medecinsdumonde.org/fr/qui_sommes_nous/notre_identite (both last accessed July 11, 2009).

32 Jean-Christophe Rufin, "Pour l'humanitaire: Dépasser le sentiment d'échec," *Le Débat* 105 (1999): pp. 4–21. This article ironically presents the ultimate justification for humanitarian action: "If victims were to disappear, everything else would be meaningless," writes the former chair of Action Contre la Faim [Action against Hunger]. But, he continues, almost reassuringly: "not only are they not disappearing, they, too, are proliferating."

33 Renée Fox, "Medical Humanitarianism and Human Rights: Reflections on Doctors Without Borders and Doctors of the World," *Social Science & Medicine* 41, no. 12 (1995): pp. 1607–16. Remarkably, Fox makes no distinction between the two NGOs with respect to the most importatnt difference between them: the "duty to intervene" promoted by Bernard Kouchner and taken up by Médecins du Monde, but condemned by Rony Brauman and Médecins Sans Frontières as the principal cause of confusion between the humanitarian and military roles in international conflict situations.

34 Rony Brauman and Pierre Salignon, "Iraq: In Search of a 'Humanitarian Crisis'," in Weissman (ed.), *In the Shadow of "Just Wars"*, pp. 269–85. Brauman and Salignon add that Médecins Sans Frontières was not immune to this dilemma, with "pacifists" within the organization pointing to the Nobel Peace Prize awarded in 1999.

35 Médecins du Monde, "Après guerre en Irak: Un avenir incertain," *Journal des donateurs* 72, September 2003. Médecins Sans Frontières, "Irak: Quelle place pour l'humanitaire?" *Infos* 100, May 2003; *Rapport annuel d'activités 2002–2003*, May 2003, and DazibAG, "Autour du rapport moral," August 2003. It is worth noting that Bernard Kouchner, founder of both organizations, took neither of these positions. Justifying his stance on the basis of his desire to see an end to the bloody dictatorship of Saddam Hussein, he supported military intervention in Iraq.

36 William Fisher, "Doing Good? The Politics and Antipolitics of NGOs' Practices," *Annual Review of Anthropology* 26 (1997): pp. 439–64.

37 Jock Stirrat, "Competitive Humanitarianism: Relief and the Tsunami in Sri Lanka," *Anthropology Today* 22, no. 5 (2006): pp. 11–26.

38 Max Weber, *Economy and Society*, ed. Guenther Roth and Claus Winch (1921; Berkeley: University of California Press, 1978). Thomas Hofnung assesses NGOs' use of donations for tsunami relief in "Tsunami: Les dons ont-ils fait recette?" *Libération*, December 26, 2005, available on-line at http://www.liberation.fr/evenement/0101552150-tsunami-les-dons-ont-ils-fait-recette (last accessed July 13, 2009).

39  Pierre Bourdieu, *Réponses: Pour une anthropologie reflexive*, ed. Loïc Wacquant (Paris, Le Seuil, 1992). See especially the chapter headed "La logique des champs," pp. 71–90. Two reports, one from the Cour des Comptes [Revenue Court] and one from a French Senate committee, have analyzed how the money had been used and made recommendations.

40  Médecins Sans Frontières, "Angola: Behind the Façade of 'Normalization'—Manipulation, Violence, and Abandoned Populations," available on-line at http://doctorswithoutborders. org/publications/reports/2000/angola_11-2000.pdf (last accessed July 13, 2009). See also Sarah Ramsey, "Agency Condemns 'Near-total Neglect' of Angolans," *The Lancet* 358, no. 9275 (July 7, 2001): p. 41; editorial, "Beyond Trading Insults in International Humanitarian Aid," *The Lancet* 359, no. 9324 (June 22, 2002): p. 2125; and the response of UN Humanitarian coordinator Erick de Mul: "Co-ordination of Humanitarian Aid—A UN Perspective," *The Lancet* 360, no. 9329 (July 27, 2002): pp. 335–36.

41  Christopher Bellamy, *Knights in White Armour: The New Art of War and Peace* (London: Pimlico, 1997). Bellamy is a professor of military science and doctrine; see also his article "Combining Combat Readiness and Compassion," *NATO Review* 49, no. 2 (2001): pp. 9–11, available on-line at http://www.nato.int/docu/review/2001/0102-02.htm (last accessed July 13, 2009). Sherene Razack proposes a much darker vision of military peacekeeping operations, in this case under Canadian command, in *Dark Threats and White Knights: The Somalia Affair, Peacekeeping and the New Imperialism* (Toronto: University of Toronto Press, 2004).

42  Rony Brauman (ed.), *Utopies sanitaires* (Paris: Le Pommier, 2000): "Medicine is first and foremost medicine. It treats people, not statistics," writes Brauman, who challenges public-health policy, arguing that its dual epidemiological and economic rationale leads it to forget basic principles, that is, saving the life of sick people. In another article, "Mission civilisatrice, ingérence humanitaire," *Le Monde diplomatique*, September 2005: p. 2, available on-line at http://www.monde-diplomatique.fr/2005/09/BRAUMAN/12578 (last accessed July 13, 2009), Brauman, former chair of Médecins Sans Frontières, compares public health and military action: "There is obviously a big difference between intruding into people's homes in the name of health and armed intervention in the name of the higher values of humanity, but the same principle is at work: Both take a stance of advanced agents working to free other peoples who are prisoners of archaic traditions or political systems."

43  Jonathan Moore (ed.), *Hard Choices: Moral Dilemmas in Humanitarian Intervention* (Lanham, MD: Roman and Littlefield, 1998); J.L. Holzgrefe and Robert Keohane (eds.), *Humanitarian Intervention: Ethical, Legal and Political Dilemmas* (Cambridge: Cambridge University Press, 2003).

44  David Rieff, *A Bed for the Night: Humanitarianism in Crisis* (New York: Simon and Schuster, 2002), p. 197.

45  Anne Orford, "Muscular Humanitarianism: Reading the Narratives of the New Interventionism," *European Journal of International Law* 10, no. 4 (1999): pp. 679–711, available on-line at http://www.ejil.org/pdfs/10/4/606.pdf (last accessed July 13, 2009). Orford analyzes the way in which interventions are justified not only by logical reasoning, but also by versions of history that bring together violence and emergency, the sense of the intolerable and the need to act. As we have seen, in the case of Kosovo, this narrative strategy included the large-scale exaggeration of the number of victims.

46  Médecins Sans Frontières, *Kosovo: Histoires d'une déportation*, typescript report, 41 pp. The publication of the document was headlined on the front page of French daily *Libération*: "Kosovo: The Humanitarian Survey," April 30, 1999. Three weeks earlier, on April 7, Rony

Brauman, as "honorary president of Médecins Sans Frontières," had written a column in the newspaper entitled "Europe Must Recognize Kosovo as an Independent State: In Support of Military Action."

47 Didier Fassin, "La cause des victims," *Les Temps Modernes* 59, no. 627 (2004): pp. 72–91. "The victims, and all the victims," runs the watchword at Médecins Sans Frontières. "There are no good or bad victims," echoes Médecins du Monde. But this apparent impartiality ignores the reality of choices that are made, including the "tragic choices" they faced in the early AIDS treatment programs: What was never stated publicly and what was a particularly difficult issue within the organizations themselves was the fact that they could not treat everybody. They had to decide which patients would be treated—make what sociologists call "tragic choices." The selection criteria, which were never explicitly stated in full, were presented as purely pragmatic (patients who would comply with the treatment regime), but still implied moral judgments (about who were the "good patients" to be trusted).

48 Keith Brown and Dimitrios Theodossopoulos, "The Performance of Anxiety. Greek Narratives of War in Kosovo," *Anthropology Today* 16, no. 1 (2000): pp. 3–8. See also the same authors' "Rearranging Solidarity: Conspiracy and World Order in Greek and Macedonian Commentaries on Kosovo," *Journal of Southern Europe and the Balkans* 5, no. 3 (2003): pp. 315–35. The only dissenting voice in France was the testimony of Régis Debray: "Lettre d'un voyageur au Président de la République," *Le Monde*, May 13, 1999. This letter provoked a heated debate in which Debray found himself virtually alone against everyone else.

49 Takis Michas, *Unholy Alliance: Greece and Milosevic's Serbia in the Nineties* (College Station: Texas A&M University Press, 2002). The author is very critical of what he sees as ethnonationalism.

50 Médecins Sans Frontières, *Procès-verbal du Conseil d'Administration*, August 27, 1999: "It is clear today that the Albanian Kosovars have adopted the very attitudes toward Serbs and Gypsies of which they were victims for years. Will Médecins Sans Frontières, which played a major role in publicizing and producing evidence of the crime of deportation committed against the Albanian Kosovars, take the same approach and denounce acts of ethnic cleansing against the Serbian Kosovars? The answer is delicate. In a number of cases, we are clearly talking about crimes of the same nature: violence, intimidation, looting, destruction, and murder with the aim of expelling the Serbs on the basis of their nationality. But we believe it would be a mistake if, in a desire to bear witness impartially, we put forward an equivalent depiction of these facts to that of the attacks on the Albanian Kosovars." The motion concluded with a very formal call to "remain extremely vigilant."

51 Neil MacFarlane, "Humanitarian Action and Conflict," *International Journal* 54, no. 4 (1999): pp. 537–61. See also Sarah Kenyon Lischer, *Dangerous Sanctuaries: Refugee Camps, Civil War, and the Dilemma of Humanitarian Aid* (Ithaca, NY: Cornell University Press, 2005).

52 Michel Agier and Françoise Bouchet-Saulnier, "Humanitarian Spaces, Spaces of Exception," in Weissman (ed.), *In the Shadow of "Just Wars,"* pp. 297–313. Making reference to the sexual abuses perpetrated by humanitarian actors in refugee camps in Liberia, Guinea, and Sierra Leone and reported in early 2002, Agier and Bouchet-Saulnier write: "Designed to bring help and protection to people in danger, in some cases humanitarian action has contributed to enclosing people in spaces of exception, spaces of irresponsibility. Far from protecting the international public order, the continued existence of these spaces has reintroduced inhumanity at the heart of all societies" (p. 313).

53  Fiona Terry, *Condemned to Repeat?: The Paradox of Humanitarian Action* (Ithaca, NY: Cornell University Press, 2002). After presenting a series of tragic case studies in which humanitarian action played a role that can be described at the very least as ambivalent, Terry, a director of research at MSF, who is one of the few to take a genuinely analytical approach from the inside, offers two explanations for NGOs' inability to question their work: "the culture of justification that stems from individual defensiveness in the face of criticism" and "a logic of institutional self-preservation that determines much of the interagency dynamic that occurs within the aid system" (p. 229).

54  Isabelle Delpla, "Une chute dans l'échelle de l'humanité, ou les topiques de l'aide humanitaire pour ses récipiendaires," *Mots: Les discours de la guerre* 73 (November 2003), pp. 97–116. On the basis of a study conducted in Bosnia-Herzegovina, Delpla reveals the dissatisfaction, frustration, and anger aroused by the presence of the military and humanitarian organizations, which are barely distinguished from one another: "The discourse about humanitarians is indissociable from that about the war."

# An Emancipatory Imperium?: Power and Principle in the Humanitarian International

Alex de Waal

This essay explores the evolution of humanitarian interventionism, focusing on two episodes of clamor for military action by politicians and activists on both the political left and right in America. Operation Restore Hope was mounted in Somalia in 1992 in the hopeful dawn of humanitarian internationalism. America's Save Darfur campaign reprised many interventionist themes in 2005–2008 during the twilight of America's uncontested hegemony. The actors involved in Save Darfur are different from those in the humanitarian NGOs who pushed for the Somali intervention, as are their moral narratives and the outcomes of their efforts.

The comparison shows how the international humanitarian agencies and human rights organizations have changed over fifteen years and illuminates the conflicts of principles that arise. Central is the tension between sustaining a liberal internationalist constituency in the United States and responding effectively to complicated humanitarian crises. The context of recent international civic activism helps us to characterize America's aspiration to an emancipatory imperium.

## SOMALIA: THE VANGUARD OF THE HUMANITARIAN INTERNATIONAL

In the bright morning of America's fifteen-year moment of undisputed global hegemony, in the wake of its triumphs over the Soviet Union and Iraq, President George H. W. Bush dispatched thirty-five thousand marines on the unlikeliest of missions—"creating a secure environment for the delivery of humanitarian relief" in Somalia. Bush senior and the chairman of the Joint Chiefs of Staff, Colin Powell, had reputations as realpolitik conservatives who would not risk American lives in a venture that did not involve the hard interests of the United States. Although Somalia had been a strategic asset in the Cold War and an important recipient of U.S. assistance, Washington had abandoned any political interest in the country as it slid into civil war and famine. Suddenly, the U.S. administration reversed its course and used its military to try to end the famine. The Somali intervention has been widely regarded as an aberration—a one-off adventure initiated by an outgoing president with nothing to lose—that illustrated only the bizarre turns of political life at such points of triumphal disorientation. It was these things, but it also reveals much about the relationship between divergent humanitarian principles and political power as American global hegemony reached its zenith.

Operation Restore Hope defied a string of preconceptions. As the marines stormed ashore in Mogadishu in December 1992, met by the cameras of the international media covering the event, a Republican administration earned praise from the political left for pioneering a new era of ethical policies. Liberal American NGOs, including CARE and the International Rescue Committee, called for sending in the troops, and many more welcomed it. Bernard Kouchner carried a sack of food up Mogadishu's beach for the cameras. Most of the small band of critics of the operation hailed from the right—conservative realists who did not think Somalia was worth the effort. Alongside them was a very small number of liberal skeptics who feared that *any* exercise of American military force was ipso facto a disempowerment of Somalis.

To the incredulity of most of our American activist colleagues, my colleague Rakiya Omaar and I opposed it. We argued that the rationale for Operation Restore Hope was based on false claims about the situation in Somalia, that opportunities for nonmilitary methods of solving the problem had not been properly tried, that it would not resolve the political crisis, that Somalis had not been consulted about it, and that the intervention itself lacked guarantees that it would be respectful of human rights.[1] In my resignation letter to Human Rights Watch, I asked whether the U.S. Marine Corps represented the vanguard of the humanitarian international or the shock troops of a new philanthropic imperialism.

Ten months later, the world's sole superpower was humbled by the local militia of General Mohamed Farah Aideed and forced to withdraw in disgrace. The hastily written obituary on the mission was that its early, "humanitarian" phase succeeded under U.S. leadership, but its later, "political" phase under the UN failed. This account does not bear scrutiny—the key political decisions were made in the "humanitarian" phase, and the Americans remained very much in charge during the later, "political" phase. But arguments over the allocation of blame obscure the deeper issue—how a foreign military adventure was inspired, shaped, and terminated by a particular moral narrative.

A set of moral precepts—both deeply familiar and, in these circumstances, unexpected—led a conservative American president to send troops on a mission without any discernible political payoff. When serving as director of the CIA fifteen years earlier, the elder Bush would never have proposed such an operation to his political masters. But the same sense of moral entitlement—that America's exceptional place in the world, as a nation above others—that drove the CIA's sorry history of interventions in the political affairs of other countries made Operation Restore Hope thinkable. Powell compared the dispatch of the marines to the U.S. cavalry riding to the rescue, going on to say that in a few months the American saviors would be gone, handing over to the "marshals"—the UN.[2]

For many of the humanitarian advocates of the intervention, success was axiomatic—they simply assumed that the U.S. Marine Corps, with its vastly superior weaponry and training, would impose its will on Somalia and save hundreds of thousands of lives of people at risk of starvation. Humanitarian advocacy is all about deriving an "ought" from an "is"—the very label "emergency" is both a descriptor and a prescription for (urgent) action. By the same token whereby human suffering *demands* an international response, such a response *must* work. The question of efficacy simply did not arise. In all the discussions of humanitarian intervention that have since followed, one criterion borrowed from just war theory—the necessity of success—is routinely mentioned, but then passed over as not requiring further attention. In fact, the success requirement is the most onerous of all the tests for an intervention of any kind.

Bush senior and Powell were old Cold Warriors who were not taking chances. The marines were entering the middle of an ongoing civil war, and they dispatched a hard-bitten old-style diplomat, Robert Oakley, as special envoy to Mogadishu to cut the necessary deals to allow the marines to land unopposed and leave with nearly zero casualties within a few months. Oakley delivered and in doing so deferred the tough political issues. For example, he ordered U.S. and Belgian troops not to intervene in an interfactional battle that saw the city of Kismayo change hands.[3] "Success" in stage one in Somalia was carefully choreographed— the humanitarians could declare victory and add "military intervention" to their arsenal of relief technologies.

Sooner than the skeptics had anticipated, the contradictions within Operation Restore Hope surfaced. For the U.S. leaders, saving Somali lives was not a charter for risking American ones. Indeed, the rationale for the intervention was as much to protect (foreign) aid workers' lives as it was to save Somali children. Both of the foreign relief-worker fatalities in the previous year had led to soul-searching among international NGOs about whether it was worth operating in Somalia—with the significant, if erroneous implication that if the international staff left, the operations would close. Foreign aid workers were medevaced when injured or seriously ill, and outposts were closed down when they were attacked. Somali aid workers were extended these privileges only in a minor way—a double standard that caused considerable resentment—and ordinary Somali civilians did not receive them at all.

The first murder of a foreign humanitarian after the intervention—the UNICEF employee Sean Devereux, shot dead in January 1993—came as a shock to the Western public. Was not the intervention supposed to stop such killings? In fact, as the International Committee of the Red Cross had discreetly warned, the intervention actually increased the risks to aid workers.[4] Aid workers cannot do their jobs properly from inside sandbagged garrisons and armored cars—their protection is the respect they hold among the local community. While the question of whether NGOs should stay or leave had regularly been raised over the year previous to the intervention, this debate fell curiously silent after American soldiers arrived in Somalia. The *actual risks* to aid workers may not have decreased, but the *moral logic* of danger had changed. Before December 1992, when aid workers served without the protection of American troops, they were labeled as brave and compassionate volunteers and, so governments and publics assumed, ran risks in a spirit of individual self-sacrifice. Despite the fact that the marines are all volunteers, as well, and, one assumes, had accepted a level of risk when joining the corps, both the U.S. president and the public assumed that they would surmount the risks entailed in the Somali operation through their technology and prowess and return home without sacrificing their lives. In the case of the military, the responsibility for fatalities lay not with the individual volunteer, but with the commander in chief. The soldiers' bravery was supposed to be risk free, and when fatalities occurred, they were treated as accidents, such as sometimes occur during training or everyday noncombat activities. In this context, a murder of a relief worker was to be seen as just that—an individual crime—and not a challenge to the rationale of the humanitarian mission itself. For an American relief agency to withdraw would have been seen as an act of ingratitude, even disloyalty.

An intervention in an unresolved war requires readiness to use force. The American approach to this was a massive military presence that served as a deterrent to any would-be assailants. This worked for four months. For the United Nations Department of Peacekeeping Operations, the use of force is a different matter. The UN Operation in Somalia (UNOSOM), which took over from the American-led task force in April 1993, had a Chapter VII mandate and was thus authorized to use force as necessary. Its preparedness to use force was much less, primarily because the troop-contributing countries were sending soldiers trained for peacekeeping, and their publics and political leaders were not prepared for casualties. They relied on remaining U.S. contingents for heavy firepower. However, the political ambitions of UNOSOM, especially when it came to disarming the factions, were not compatible with a traditional peacekeeping approach, and UNOSOM blundered into a war. This began with a mismanaged disarmament exercise in June 1993, which quickly escalated into three months of urban warfare. The United States provided the Special Forces units that spearheaded the assault on the militia of General Mohamed Farah Aideed.[5] In a series of battles that culminated in the failed attempt to capture Aideed in October, the U.S. troops used massive force, killing thousands of Somalis, both combatants and noncombatants, in encounters that would have been described as massacres were it not for the extraordinary bravery of their opponents, who despite the imbalance of casualties, still managed to prevail. The American limit seemed to be a dozen dead in one battle, and when this was reached, the U.S. forces quit.

The book and feature film *Black Hawk Down* recount the final battle of America's Mogadishu war from the viewpoint of the U.S. soldiers.[6] The other side of the story is the largely undocumented slaughter of thousands of Somalis.[7] Such asymmetry of human cost was inevitable once the U.S. military began to apply its twin doctrines of overwhelming force and nearly zero own-side casualties. A more than symbolic manifestation of this was the American military attorney's insistence that the Geneva Conventions did not apply in this war.[8] Prisoners of war were held without access to the International Committee of the Red Cross, hospitals were attacked, and civilians indiscriminately fired upon. The pretext was that the soldiers were serving under UN command, and the UN had never signed the Geneva Conventions. The thinking was that "the normal rules of engagement don't apply in this situation."[9] The moral logic was that the saviors—be they the humanitarians or the cavalry—are above the fray, an external and unsullied moral force, and as such enjoy immunity from the ordinary rules that govern behavior, including actions during war.

## THE MORALITIES OF A TRAGEDY

The Somali intervention was a tragedy, and not merely in the everyday sense of a litany of human suffering. Rather, it represented a conflict between different moral claims, each of them of value—and in a sense, "right." For the internationals, four competing ethical imperatives were at work, and the deeper tragedy lay in the fact that the unresolved (and never fully acknowledged) clash between them contributed to a failure on most counts.

The first moral imperative was the humanitarian demand of saving lives. In the Somali instance, before December 1992, this entailed making compromises with the factional leaders who controlled Mogadishu and the surrounding regions in order to deliver food. The relief agencies did this all the time, and the most effective ones (such as the International Committee of the Red Cross and Save the Children

UK) were those that employed the most politically skilled Somali staff, who could navigate the intricate dangers of the war. For most operational NGOs, including CARE and the International Rescue Committee, the prospect of making similar compromises with the U.S. Marine Corps appeared preferable, but the end result was little different. There is no doubt that lives were saved by these compromises, both before and during the intervention, though not on the scale that the humanitarian enthusiasts predicted.[10]

The second moral imperative was witnessing to human rights abuses and campaigning for an end to such violations and the punishment of those responsible. However, exposing the level of atrocious violence could have imperiled the working relations that aid agencies had with local political-military leaders, and exposing the amount of aid that was taxed or looted could have undermined the agencies' public-relations efforts in Europe and America. The logic of speaking out is also "right," in that an end to such abuses would without doubt mean an end to the human suffering that necessitates emergency relief.

The third imperative was political: managing the political dynamic in which the Somali military-political factions were undergoing a painful process of political change that, if well guided, could lead to a political agreement that would make the area secure. (In Somaliland, formerly northwestern Somalia, the armed factions succeeded in doing precisely that.) This is the mediator's morality: the need to cut deals among warring parties whose behavior is by definition violent and destructive.

These three sets of ethical demands are hard to square, and the basic principle subsequently adopted by relief agencies in their codes of conduct, drawn up in the late 1990s, is "do no harm."[11]

The fourth ethical impulse was the desire among international agencies to set new universal standards—in this case, declaring that insecurity and the collapse of government should not be considered a reason for failing to respond to human suffering—while also setting the precedent for military intervention as a tool for humanitarian action. This can be seen as an attempt at secular moral progress, raising awareness in the global public about both a moral emergency and its proposed solution, or setting a new global norm.

Much has been written on the tensions between humanitarian relief and human rights advocacy, and between each of them and the search for peace and stability. Less attention has been given to the potential contradiction between the demands of finding effective responses to local situations (variants of the first three frameworks) and the project of building a global humanitarian system (the fourth). The latter requires strong support among both the general public and political leaders in Western nations, which in turn requires that its messages are simple, morally clear, and resonant and that its remedies are attractive to those constituencies whose backing is needed. The portrayal of Somalia needed to be crafted carefully in order for its most important points to be unmistakable, and the moral logic of the intervention needed to be similarly unassailable.[12] Both goals were achieved at the time of the intervention in December 1992 by means of some selective representation of facts, the invention of others, and the careful use of language.

In the month before the intervention, the famine was waning—both death rates and food prices were dropping—and the rate of diversion of humanitarian assistance, although much higher than most aid agencies would consider acceptable, was less than the figures bandied about in the press. Most importantly for the outcome of the intervention, however, the political situation was rather more complex than the label of "anarchy" implied, and the factional leaders, as well as being "warlords," also possessed political constituencies. The advocacy narrative diverged from the realities of Somalia in important respects. While the improving humanitarian situation made it relatively easy for the intervention to declare success, the political mission quickly came unstuck.

Failure is an orphan. Evaluations of the intervention have tended to focus on the mechanics of what was done by the military and the relations between the military and the humanitarians. Neither the overall conceptualization of the mission nor the portrayal of the Somali emergency that prompted the intervention have been scrutinized to the same degree. But the trajectory of Operation Restore Hope cannot be understood outside the context of how the crisis was originally represented, such that a universal principle of international (American) salvation triumphed over other ethical concerns and sociopolitical narratives. The universalism that justified the mission presented the intervening force as something above and apart from Somali society and politics, rather than as an enterprise that would inevitably and rapidly become part of Somali realities. As with other complex civil wars intertwined with organized criminality, the Somali conflict should be analyzed as a system in which those who control the means of violence can pursue their interests, often in collusion with their supposed enemies.[13] The emergency relief effort was already, by the end of 1992, becoming entwined in a war economy in which humanitarian resources were both among the means of conducting the war and part of the prize. This, indeed, was one of the rationalizations for sending in foreign troops. They, however, also became part of the conflict, and not simply as a belligerent force on their own account. The UN operation became an important part of the Mogadishu economy and politics, to the extent that it ended up contributing to a revived civil war.

The repercussions of the failure in Somalia were felt immediately in Bosnia and Rwanda, where the U.S. government either delayed or blocked military action to stop genocidal killings. The U.S. Presidential Decision Directive 25 was issued in March 1994 insisting that the United States would intervene only when its national interests were at stake and there was a clear exit strategy. By terrible coincidence, the genocide in Rwanda was launched barely a week later, and the United States resisted proposals to intervene, even to strengthen the small UN force already deployed. Nonintervention in Rwanda and Bosnia became scandals that ultimately overshadowed the Mogadishu debacle. It was not until NATO's Kosovo intervention in 1999 that the United States succeeded in combining the operational military lessons of Somalia with the political outcome of defeating an adversary responsible for serial aggression and atrocity. NATO's campaign was conducted from a sufficiently high altitude that, for the first time, the U.S. doctrine of zero own-side casualties was a reality, rather than an aspiration.

The international humanitarian enterprise, in its broadest sense, consists of a dialectic between the moral uplift of universalism and the pedestrian demands of actually delivering the technologies that save lives in the "field." In some respects, this resembles the division of tasks between a wartime propagandist and a general, and indeed, between the seasoned political leaders in Washington, D.C., who ordered the Somali intervention, and the envoy they dispatched to Mogadishu to ensure that it passed off safely. During the Somali crisis, humanitarian organizations attempted to undertake both universalist advocacy and practical relief work and found themselves divided among themselves or oscillating between the different roles. In Rwanda and the subsequent refugee crisis, a similar set of dilemmas and contradictions was exposed even more starkly. The soul-searching among humanitarian agencies that followed Rwanda led to the adoption of principles and codes of conduct. It also led informally to better mutual understanding—and in many cases, an informal division of labor—between operational agencies and advocacy organizations. These arrangements helped manage the tragic dilemmas of what were increasingly called "complex emergencies," but did not resolve them.

## THE HEGEMONY OF ETHICS

The Somali intervention was mounted in a moment of hubris following the fall of the Berlin Wall and the American-led war to liberate Kuwait. At that moment, America was shifting from its Cold War self-conceptualization as a defender of imperiled liberty against a Communist power of parity status to global hegemon. This change coincided with—and helped usher in—a new politics of global ethics, with democracy and human rights advocates in triumphal mode. America's unexpected victory over the Eastern Bloc came about in significant part because of the persistent moral activism of human rights defenders in Communist countries, whose victory gave an immeasurable boost to those who believed that ethics should guide Western nations' foreign policies. In 1993, many of those who had stood in solidarity with human rights activists in Eastern Europe (and also Latin America) through the long years of Republican government in Washington took office in a new administration. What was new in the 1990s was neither the fact of global ethical sensibility nor the activities of activists without borders, but rather new relations between ethical practice and the projection of power. One of the most powerful sentiments was that the triumph of liberal democracy meant—in a famous phrase—"the end of history" and therefore that there was no need to analyze the complicated realities of the old authoritarian order, because it was already history.[14]

The post–World War II architecture of formal state sovereignty was preserved in the shadow of competing superpowers. With the thawing of the Cold War, sovereignty was unfrozen, too. Humanitarian action was released from its tight constraints, and its leading practitioners relished the opportunity to fulfill a mission untrammeled by the restrictions of borders and control by the same governments that had all too often created humanitarian disasters in the first place. Humanitarianism unbound sought to co-opt the instruments of political control—military forces and government budgets—to pursue its ambitions. Western human rights organizations projected their formula of civil and political liberties as the answer to complex challenges of governance. In turn, the World Bank and European and American governments adopted similar formulas.

Equally significant was the democratization of the policy-making process in Western capitals. Coincident with the end of Communism, the institutions, technologies, and social movements of industrial democracies gained greater access to the executives of foreign ministries and aid departments. Alongside this, government money poured into expanding and professionalizing NGOs, and individuals rotated between the voluntary sector and the civil service. Human rights organizations increased their insider advocacy activities. A small, but influential industry of promoting good governance thrived as a specialized variant of human rights work. It appeared that the humanitarian international and its human rights counterpart were moving from being the cutting edge of voluntarism to becoming the agents of a new project of managing the global peripheries through relief aid and governance tutelage. This Wilsonian mission was—for a while at least—displacing the sensibility of a mass popular movement against injustice.

An instance of a new form of civic mobilization in this era was the campaign to ban landmines. Often described as a broad-based social movement, it was in fact closer to a network of existing NGOs with established mandates and interests that adopted an issue, made alliances with medium-sized states and some policymakers in big states, and created a new moral reality.[15] From very modest beginnings in 1990, within three years, the campaign had won influential friends in Western legislatures and across the NGO sector, and by the end of 1997 had achieved an international treaty to ban antipersonnel landmines at a conference in Ottawa and won the Nobel Prize for Peace for its efforts. It was heralded as an example of the "democratization" of foreign policy and of the role that a medium power (Canada) could play in corralling international actors to create a global norm in defiance of U.S. intransigence.[16] While some of the campaign's leaders considered both the international ban adopted in Ottawa and the Nobel Peace Prize to be premature or inappropriate—given that some of the main objectives of the campaign remained unmet, among them U.S. support, and that a declaration of "victory" was likely to demobilize the campaign's supporters,[17] there is no doubt that a new global norm was established.

An example of how an ethical framework could drive global public policy, empowering certain groups of local activists, is provided by the global AIDS treatment campaign. In this case, the early lead was taken within the UN system, where Jonathan Mann pioneered a human rights approach to health within the World Health Organization, and UNAIDS subsequently became a vanguard for innovative ways of approaching policy advocacy, programming, and the involvement of civil society in multilateral governance. Critics have argued that "AIDS exceptionalism" has meant that well-proven public-health instruments—which may involve some abrogation of privacy or other personal liberties—have been cast aside in favor of an approach that emphasizes a fallible epidemiological individualism.[18] However, there is no doubt that this approach has given confidence and influence to some groups and individuals who would otherwise have been among the most marginalized in global public policy. African AIDS activists have gained access to international policy-making circles in ways that would have been unthinkable a decade earlier.[19] This is a form of emancipation through access to the global metropolis.

America was a relative latecomer to global AIDS policy and funding and—remarkably—this occurred under the George W. Bush presidency. While many aspects of U.S. AIDS policy have been deeply controversial (notably the strong preference for promoting abstinence over condoms), American support for treatment programs has surpassed all others. Funding for global AIDS treatment was an unusual area of bipartisan consensus in a sharply divided American political landscape.

With the expansion and popularization of governmental humanitarianism came the moralization of development assistance in general. In Europe, this proceeded cautiously—European discourse emphasizes shared values and common projects and is self-consciously hesitant about imposing its moral values on others. In this respect, Tony Blair struck Europeans as being an outlier, almost a zealot in his belief that Britain and its G8 partners should lead the world in a crusade to conquer poverty and end dictatorship and civil war. The U.S. language has been much more strident and self-assured, and, especially under George W. Bush, explicitly Christian. At a time in which U.S. politics has been exceptionally polarized and acrimonious, there was a bipartisan consensus on Africa policy, notably including HIV-AIDS, Darfur, and increased assistance levels. These African issues became the neutral ground of American politics, an imaginary space in which partisan interests could dissolve in favor of purely moral motives. The existence of this untheorized consensus that humanitarian action in Africa is an unqualified good demands that we scrutinize it ever more closely.

## DARFUR: ASPIRATION FOR A HUMAN RIGHTS IMPERIUM

The Western narrative for Somalia in 1992 revolved around the terms "anarchy" and "humanitarian emergency." In retrospect, these look like anachronistic and even quaint labels from an era in which the collapse of order on the global peripheries was seen as a strategic threat.[20] The descriptors could equally well have been "genocide" or "chaos by design," both of which could serve as apt depictions of the wars that former President Mohamed Siad Barre unleashed after 1988.[21] Twelve years later, as a comparably brutal war was fought in Darfur, Sudan, the parallel chosen by activists and columnists was Rwanda in 1994,[22] although the similarities with the final years of Siad Barre's rule are at least as compelling to scholars of African politics. The marines' mission in Somalia was to protect the humanitarians who were feeding the hungry. The mission called for in Darfur was to stop the atrocities—President Bush "wanted to go in and kill the Janjaweed"—while others focused on the "responsibility to protect."[23] The humanitarian agencies that had been so prominent in calling for intervention in Somalia were conspicuously quiet amid an extraordinary clamor for a similar operation in Darfur, led by American advocacy groups.

In 2003, the name "Darfur" was little known, even among Africanists. When the conflict in Darfur—and more specifically, the massacre and mass displacement of civilians—seized the attention of journalists and activists in 2004, there was not a single English-language book in print dealing exclusively with Darfur's politics, history, or geography.[24] In 2006, subway stations in New York and other major U.S. cities were adorned with advertisements paid for by the Save Darfur Coalition demanding public action to stop genocide. No urban American could plead ignorance that Darfur existed and that people were dying there. Yet the "Darfur" of the Save Darfur advertisements, and the statements of Democratic presidential hopefuls and some of their political advisors was a construction of a particular narrative that became increasingly disconnected from what was happening in the region itself. Mahmood Mamdani provocatively has argued that Darfur was not considered a place with politics and history, but rather had become a "moral high ground."[25]

As the war raged in 2003–2004, the U.S. public discourse on Darfur was conducted in an informational near vacuum. In her study of eighty-three editorials and opinion articles on Darfur published in leading U.S. newspapers during 2004, Deborah Murphy found that while a third referred to Rwanda, just seven compared Darfur with Sudan's North-South civil war.[26] Murphy concluded that "in many ways most of the articles reviewed were not really about Darfur itself. They could have been written about any instance of mass violence that prompts a debate over humanitarian intervention."[27] The early and decisive identification of Darfur as an instance of genocide placed the crisis within a Manichean framework that was defined by the Holocaust and Rwanda. This removed it from the more proximate frameworks of Sudan and Chad—histories that would logically have more explanatory power than the paradigmatic cases of genocide. Reference to genocide and the "responsibility to protect" also prioritized the human rights dimension of the Darfur emergency over its humanitarian and conflict dimensions.

The American movement for Darfur took off in mid-2004 when the U.S. Holocaust Memorial Museum and the American Jewish World Service founded the Save Darfur Coalition, building on the efforts of Christian groups focusing on southern Sudan, human rights organizations, and the concern of members of Congress. Campus activist groups, including the Genocide Intervention Fund (later GI-Net) and Students Taking Action Now—Darfur! (STAND) turned an elite advocacy campaign into a genuine grassroots activist movement that could mobilize hundreds of thousands of people for rallies and letter-writing campaigns.[28] Central to this new activist vanguard was the description of what was going on in Darfur as "genocide" and a strong argument, at least in the early days, for military intervention.

Most mainstream human rights organizations, including Amnesty International and Human Rights Watch, have preferred not to describe the atrocities as genocide. The humanitarian agencies present on the ground were notable for not speaking out in favor of armed intervention, and the InterAction network of U.S. agencies publicly distanced itself from the Save Darfur viewpoint in early 2007, causing a crisis in the leadership of the latter. The years that had passed since the Somali debacle had caused leading humanitarian agencies to adopt sets of practices for operating in war zones and to become more experienced about working alongside peace support operations and hence more skeptical about the value of international protection forces for humanitarian work. Indeed, one of the lessons of Somalia—that foreign troops can actually increase the dangers to relief workers—meant that some agencies working in Darfur preferred not to make use of African Union military escorts that were available to them. At the other end of this spectrum of views and strategies were some activist groups.

Despite its controversial views, Save Darfur came to dominate the stage. One of the reasons for this dominance was the silence of the operational agencies, whose leaders feared that their field programs were vulnerable to punitive action by the Sudan government if they spoke out against atrocities and harassment and who feared the scorn of the most vocal activists if they criticized the punitive measures favored by Save Darfur. In these circumstances of hazard and uncertainty, the safest action was to remain quiet.

The operational humanitarians' silence also reflected their awareness of the moral complexities of Darfur. The advocacy campaign brought them tangible benefits, especially funds for their programs. But it was also a long-awaited test of the claim that the best way of resolving Sudan's recurrent man-made famines is a political challenge to the government that has been responsible for them. Many aid workers in the field, as well as the numerous critics of wartime humanitarianism in southern Sudan, had repeatedly argued this point.[29] There was a diversity of shades of opinion among the relief community, with some emphasizing peace negotiations, others stressing political pressure to end abuses, and others prioritizing providing assistance within the existing constraints—and all recognizing that there were no simple solutions or self-evidently right answers.

## THE WISH FOR INTERVENTION

America's Darfur movement has gained greater popular support and political profile for an African issue than any cause since the antiapartheid movement.[30] The campaign holds out the promise, in the words of Mark Hanis, the founder of the Genocide Intervention Network, of establishing a "permanent anti-genocide constituency."[31] The campaign describes itself as "the project to end genocide and crimes against humanity." Save Darfur is a tremendous outpouring of moral outrage, idealism, and energy. Its leaders are understandably awed at the sentiments they have helped unleash and commensurately anxious that this movement should not be demobilized or disillusioned. They are also giddy with their ability to influence the public pronouncements of political leaders from George W. Bush to Barack Obama, at least during the latter's presidential campaign. Having entered the domestic political arena, "Darfur" became the reference point for presidential aspirants to prove that they were at once humanitarian and tough—there were no prizes for going soft on Sudan. The tough rhetoric included calls for no-fly zones, for military attacks on the Sudanese Air Force, for blockading Port Sudan, and for sanctions. Other proposals were more modest—such as appointing a special American envoy for Sudan or paying more attention to the peace process—but these were things that would probably have occurred anyway.[32] The toughest of these calls—NATO ground intervention—could be made safely because of the improbability of Washington or any other Western capital actually following through on its threats. But for the leaders of the Darfur campaign, who also wanted to retain credibility among humanitarians in the field, professional peacekeepers, others with experience in trying to resolve complicated wars—not to mention the inquiring students and scholars in their own ranks—nuance was necessary. The campaign generated a huge number of Web sites and reports and some interesting debates. Some of the prominent activists attempted a balancing act, rallying the popular base and flattering their political patrons and friends while also keeping a line open to the specialists. But the bottom line of the campaign was that empirical complications and competing ethical considerations should not deflect the world's conscience from a simple fact and its moral consequences: Genocide was being committed, and it had to be stopped.

In Bush's America, where African policy occupied a unique political space of bipartisan consensus, Darfur represented the epicenter of this politics-free zone. At a time when Congress was divided on just about every issue, it was united on Darfur, which was the occasion for political adversaries to make common cause. Even in criticizing the administration, the Darfur advocates on Capitol Hill and in the Save Darfur movement acknowledged that George Bush had said most of the right things and had done many of them, too—just too slowly and halfheartedly. This consensus was upheld by an insistence that describing the crisis as anything other than genocide was itself morally reprehensible and hence that only the toughest and most resolute action was sufficient to stop it.

Insofar as this narrative brushed aside the concerns of the humanitarians in the field and the diplomats in the negotiating chamber, it can be characterized as a form of human rights fundamentalism. Among the most prolific champions of the Darfur cause, any political dealings with Khartoum other than direct threats was considered an unacceptable compromise with evil. The African Union–mediated peace talks were never supported, and indeed the fragile peace deal was attacked even while its possible success lay in the balance. The prospect of Sudan's national elections, scheduled for 2010, heralding change was also given no consideration—as with peace talks, trusting Khartoum to hold elections was a compromise going too far. Mahmood Mamdani has analyzed the Save Darfur movement as a strategic displacement of moral concern away from the U.S. involvement in and responsibility for the Iraq war.[33]

The Darfur campaign's leaders tended not to criticize voluntary agencies working in the field, but the relationship between the two was one of unstated tension. The interventionist position was the polar opposite of the deliberately apolitical stand of relief agencies during war famines in the 1980s. Insofar as it was advocating robust actions aimed at dramatically changing a government's policy—and perhaps (though most Save Darfur leaders disavowed it) changing that government itself—it was overtly political. But in terms of Sudanese realities, the Darfur campaign was curiously nonpolitical. It did not want to engage in any of the complexities and compromises whereby political change occurs, incrementally, in a country such as Sudan. It wanted to remove the Sudanese state and its baleful influence from Darfur. Saving Darfur was a utopian project.

The Darfur campaign got its wish for intervention only in a minimal form, namely, the UN-African Union Mission in Darfur (UNAMID). Although it has a Chapter VII mandate—authorizing it to use force—the circumstances in which UNAMID can do so are so restricted that it is in reality a classic peacekeeping mission dispatched to a place where such a mission is not appropriate. UNAMID is not what the activists wanted—it is a stepchild that they are likely to disavow as soon as it disappoints.

Darfur's war was always complex and not reducible to simple categorizations. It became more so as it dragged on and especially as the rebels fragmented and the Arab militias began to lose confidence in the government, so that some of them switched sides. After the firestorm years of 2003–2004, in which about two hundred thousand civilians died, fatalities from violence amounted to approximately nine thousand (civilians and combatants) over the four and a half years from 2005 to mid-2009, while mortality rates among the general population were reduced to approximately pre-war levels. Darfur was in fact a complex emergency with many of the familiar facets of such a crisis, including a criminalized war economy and collusion among supposed adversaries. None of these facts specifically preclude the possibility of Darfur in 2005–2009 being an instance of genocide, but where there is a level of violent deaths of about thirty per hundred thousand per year in a multisided war with "Arabs" and "Africans" on both sides, the burden of proving "genocide" becomes rather more onerous. These are not mere details—they were the basic facts in Darfur in 2009.

Despite these statistics, any mention of "improvement" was taboo—commentators insisted with almost total unanimity that "things are getting worse" and condemned those who dared suggest otherwise.[34] The chief indicator that supported this statement was a steady increase in attacks on humanitarian agencies. The dangers faced by the agents of philanthropy were the yardstick for the severity of the crisis.

The problem facing the Darfur activists is that, having described Darfur in both Manichean and apocalyptic terms and also having called for extreme action—military intervention, or at least a UN peacekeeping force capable of providing "coercive protection"—their campaign was sure to falter once the complicated contours of Darfur's reality became more widely understood or should the international troops fail to deliver. This dilemma has the makings of a tragedy in which the moral demands for sustaining a liberal internationalist constituency in America come into conflict with the requirements of finding solutions in Darfur.

The American movement for Darfur articulates its program as a defense of human rights, and it is focused on an instance of the extreme violation of human rights, both as an objective description and as a call to action. Among Democrats, it is political liberals who have mobilized the larger constituencies and who have forced the pace of the political debate. Many of those who supported military action in Darfur opposed the invasion of Iraq, and indeed, one of the arguments they proffered was that the Iraq occupation was an error precisely because it prevented U.S. forces from going to Darfur. On the Republican side, some neoconservatives supported military action in Darfur not only because it would strike a blow at an authoritarian Arab regime, but also because it would vindicate the larger project of using American military power to transformative effect.

## ELEMENTS FOR A COMPARISON

There are logical isomorphisms between the argument for intervention in Darfur and the case for military action in Iraq and the "global war on terror." One clear similarity is Manichean moral argument and the identification of evil as a real thing that possesses specific people. Osama bin Laden and Saddam Hussein are the archetypes of evil for the "war on terror," while Omar al-Bashir and the Janjaweed perform the same function for the campaign against genocide. Columnists and academics who would hesitate to use the word "evil" to apply to anything other than the Holocaust use it liberally with regard to the Khartoum government and its actions in Darfur.[35] There is an appealing logic to both interventions: Bad things happen because bad men do them, so if we eliminate the bad men, the problem is solved. Just as the war on terror demands a body count, so the war on genocide demands the physical removal of the *genocidaires*. A generation ago, leftist political activists in solidarity with the overseas oppressed would have taken sides and backed the victims. A previous generation of idealists supported the African National Congress, the Eritrean People's Liberation Front, and the Sandinistas. Contemporary genocide activism stresses intervention and the ability and duty of the activists' *own* society to solve the problem.

A second parallel is the axiom that good intentions are transparent and self-justifying. Thus, the Pentagon refused to engage in postinvasion planning for Iraq because its leaders assumed that the overthrow of Saddam would be so welcomed that it would ipso facto create a new and positive reality. Many who have called for a no-fly zone or ground intervention in Darfur make very similar assumptions—including the unspoken one that it is simple to distinguish "good" from "evil" on the ground in Darfur. The debate over military humanitarian intervention is conducted in purely ethical terms, with little regard to the hard-learned lessons of war fighting and peacekeeping.[36] The empirical historical study of how wars and atrocities actually end and what actually happens during military interventions and peacekeeping operations was considered a detail rendered irrelevant by the moral urgency of the case and the assumption of American military might. In her study of the U.S. press, Murphy notes that "there was no debate over whether the U.S. *could* stop the violence if it were willing to use (or threaten to use) force. Instead the debate was over whether the U.S. *should* take such strong measures."[37]

These elements add up to a contemporary variant of American exceptionalism, which takes the form of a moral imperative for the United States to do what is right and an unquestioned assumption that America has the power and the right—indeed, the duty—to use it. The historical points of reference are the defeat of Nazi Germany and NATO's 1999 Kosovo campaign. The logic of military intervention to defeat genocide is a rerun of the Allied armies' arrival at the Nazi death camps, except that in the repeat performance, the cavalry arrives in time to stop the slaughter, redeeming its fatal tardiness in 1945 and the later repeat nonperformances in Sarajevo and Kigali.[38] The Kosovo campaign was atonement for Bosnia, and so Darfur should be for Rwanda. In a landmark opinion piece published in the *Washington Post* on October 2, 2006, Anthony Lake (former national security advisor to President Bill Clinton), Susan Rice (former assistant secretary of state for Africa) and Democratic Congressman Donald Payne asked "We saved Europeans. Why not Africans?" Making the parallel with Kosovo, the article advocated air strikes against the Sudanese Air Force and a blockade of Port Sudan. The response in the Save Darfur community was jubilation, with e-mails circulating and blog entries posted to the tune of, "At last someone is getting serious!" For the international troops in Somalia, combat was a deviation from their mission. Should there be such a mission to "save" Darfur, humanitarian action and combat will be one and the same.

A final comparison between Save Darfur and Operation Restore Hope is relevant—the role of Iraq. Colin Powell is reported to have argued in favor of a Somali mission and against a Bosnian one with the words "We do deserts, we don't do mountains."[39] The Somali intervention was mounted in the wake of Operation

Desert Storm, a triumph of American arms.[40] Save Darfur was mounted in the shadow of an Iraqi war that was a humiliation for American foreign policy and a challenge to the capacity and credibility of the U.S. Army. This not only shackled America and raised the political costs of any military action that bypassed the UN Security Council, but it also emboldened America's adversaries in the Arab world. Responding to a remark that America was now a "wounded superpower," Nafie Ali Nafie, assistant president of Sudan and one of the main architects of a hard-line policy of resisting international troops in Darfur, asked rhetorically with a smile, "And who wounded the superpower?"[41] The prospects of a military intervention at scale in Darfur, from the moment at which Colin Powell declared the situation to be "genocide" on September 9, 2004, and then went on to say that this determination would have no impact on U.S. policy, were zero. Realistically, the maximum outcome was a classical, albeit large peacekeeping mission backed by a great deal of rhetoric. Hence, the dominant feature of Save Darfur has been the *campaign* for a deployment that its leaders know is a fantasy.

Internationally, the Darfur crisis has largely been a war of words. There has been a slew of Security Council resolutions, several of them demanding the impossible (for example, in July 2004, the disarmament of the Janjaweed within thirty days) and others setting up investigations and panels of inquiry that have drawn up lists of individuals to be sanctioned. The International Criminal Court was put on the case in April 2005, setting in motion a process subject to no political control that resulted in an arrest warrant against President Omar al-Bashir in March 2009. The U.S. government has imposed targeted sanctions—but the measures in place fall well short of the level of ostracism that Khartoum faced in the mid-1990s, when not only America, but Sudan's neighbors, too, were aligned against it, and several of the latter were militarily involved in supporting the opposition. The escalation of rhetoric and largely toothless resolutions on Darfur held little meaning unless the United States was prepared to use the kinds of measures advocated by Lake, Rice, and Payne—measures that were a geopolitical impossibility.

## CONCLUSION

How to analyze the exuberantly harsh, but practically vapid rhetoric that swirls around "Darfur" in America? In part, it reflects the anguished hangover from America's brief period of unchallenged global hegemony. The outrage of the Save Darfur movement is aimed as much at the dilatory actions of the administration in Washington, the lack of moral clarity and courage in Europe, and—most vigorously—the presumed complicity of China,[42] as it is at the powers that be in Khartoum. Precisely because the United States could no longer impose its will unilaterally, as it presumed to do in the 1990s, the calls for moral leadership are all the stronger. While the Somali intervention was mounted amid a triumphal giddiness that led to a belief that American troops and goodwill could conquer all, the Darfur intervention has been called amid the vertigo of America looking over the edge into a world in which its supremacy is passing into history.

Save Darfur's analysis has had difficulty with competing moral claims. In 2007, a quiet challenge from the operational relief agencies, which did not want to be associated with its demands, caused a major crisis in the campaign—but the established humanitarian NGOs chose not to press home the critique, leaving an uneasy truce between the institutions and their respective ethical frameworks. Those who insisted on the label and analysis of "genocide" also stepped back from challenging the established human rights organizations that chose not to define what was happening in Darfur as genocide, though they had no such qualms when criticizing the UN on the same grounds. The peacemakers were an easier target for Save Darfur's ethical critique, especially because the Darfur Peace Agreement of May 2006 failed. At its peak in 2006, Save Darfur encompassed an amalgam of moral concerns, and its response to the challenge of sifting or prioritizing among them was to insist that *all* should be pursued. This, of course, was no answer. It was a movement primarily concerned with what *Americans* could do to "save" Darfur, but the tools at the disposal of America were few and blunt, and success was measured by the extent to which the most dramatic of these tools, notably the use of military force, was threatened or actually used.

The liberal American imperium has rapidly moved from aspirational to endangered status. In its challenged condition, it needs its enemies in precisely the same way that the neocons need bin Laden, and their efforts to defeat them are similarly limited—they are determined to defeat them only in the way of their own choosing. Washington neocons have taken to calling the war on terror "the long war." Using its chosen tools, the war on genocide will also be long. This may be Darfur's tragedy: The hugely commendable aim of securing a liberal, internationalist, and morally fired constituency in America may mean that other ways of looking at the world and responding to some of the most egregious instances of human suffering are lost. In his critique of the humanitarian enterprise, David Kennedy has written:

> Imagine an international humanitarianism which took a break from preoccupation with the justifications for "intervention." Which no longer imagined the world from high above, on the "international plane," in the "international community." Which saw itself in a location, among others, as an interest among others.... Such a heuristic might...prevent us from overestimating the possibilities for a costless, neutral engagement in far away places, or underestimating our ongoing political role in governance.[43]

The tragedy of Save Darfur parallels that of Operation Restore Hope and is also distinctive. It is not that its advocates are wrong, but their rightness is one-dimensional, and their sense of moral certainty prevents them from standing outside themselves to see their activities in a critical light. In Somalia, the humanitarian international had the opportunity to try to implement its ambitions and did not succeed, but it was not until the aftermath of Rwanda that the dilemmas of conflicting ethical demands were addressed. Meanwhile, in important ways, the elements of the international humanitarian enterprise became more diverse, accessible to African actors, and intertwined with governments. That permeability and multidimensionality did not, however, fundamentally change power relations, which remained dominated by Europe and North America. In the case of Darfur, a new configuration of humanitarian and human rights actors emerged in America, enthusiastic with a vast moral energy and espousing a huge ambition, that was at once part of the mainstream U.S. political system and set up as a utopian critique of that system. Its characteristic has been reaching for a "solution" that its advocates well know is impossible internationally and unworkable in Sudan, but that makes perfect sense within liberal America's aspirations for global leadership. What may provide the campaign's redeeming feature is its capacity for autocritique: College students and liberals are ready to learn. But amid the transformations of the last fifteen years, one constant is clear between Somalia and Darfur: The campaigns for vigorous action on both have at least as much to do with America's position in the world as they do with the objects of their concern.

## NOTES

1  African Rights, *Operation Restore Hope: A Preliminary Assessment*, London, March 1993.

2  John Lancaster, "Powell Says Mission Duration is Flexible," *Washington Post*, December 5, 1992, p. A17.

3  This episode is skipped over in his account of his role in Somalia. See Robert Oakley and John Hirsch, *Somalia and Operation Restore Hope: Reflections on Peacekeeping and Peacemaking* (Washington, D.C.: US Institute of Peace, 1995).

4  African Rights, *Operation Restore Hope*. Two expatriates were killed in the two years prior to the intervention, and two were killed in the first two months of the intervention. Six Somali relief workers were killed in December 1992 and January 1993.

5  James L. Woods, "U.S. Decision Making During Humanitarian Operations in Somalia," in Walter S. Clarke and Jeffrey Ira Herbst (eds.), *Learning from Somalia: The Lessons of Armed Intervention* (Boulder, CO: Westview Press, 1997).

6  Mark Bowden, *Black Hawk Down: A Story of Modern War* (New York: Penguin, 2000).

7    Alex de Waal, "US War Crimes in Somalia," *New Left Review* 1, no. 230, (July–August 1998).

8    Major Frank Fountain, interviewed by the author, Mogadishu, July 1993.

9    Liz Sly, "UN Raises the Ante in Somalia Attacks," *Chicago Tribune*, June 20, 1993.

10   Refugee Policy Group, "Hope Restored?: Humanitarian Aid in Somalia 1990–1994" (Washington, D.C.: Refugee Policy Group, Center for Policy Analysis and Research on Refugee Issues, 1994), available on-line at http://repository.forcedmigration.org/show_metadata.jsp?pid=fmo:3778 (last accessed July 13, 2009).

11   Mary Anderson, *Do No Harm: How Aid Can Support Peace—Or War* (Boulder, CO: Lynn Reiner, 1999).

12   Alex de Waal, *Famine Crimes: Politics and the Disaster Relief Industry in Africa* (London: James Currey, 1997).

13   See David Keen, *Conflict and Collusion in Sierra Leone* (Oxford: James Currey, 2005).

14   Francis Fukuyama, *The End of History and the Last Man* (New York: Free Press, 1992).

15   Leon V. Sigal, *Negotiating Minefields: The Landmines Ban in American Politics* (New York: Routledge, 2006).

16   Maxwell A. Cameron, "Democratization of Foreign Policy: The Ottawa Process as a Model," in Maxwell A. Cameron, Robert J. Lawson, and Brian W. Tomlin (eds.), *To Walk Without Fear: The Global Movement to Ban Landmines* (Toronto: Oxford University Press, 1998).

17   See Jerry White, cited in Sigal 2006, p. 228.

18   Kevin M. De Cock, and Anne M. Johnson, "From Exceptionalism to Normalisation: A Reappraisal of Attitudes and Practice around HIV Testing," *British Medical Journal* 316, no. 7127 (January 24, 1998): pp. 290–93.

19   Alex de Waal, *AIDS and Power: Why There Is No Political Crisis—Yet* (London: Zed Books, 2006).

20   Robert Kaplan, "The Coming Anarchy: How Scarcity, Crime, Overpopulation, Tribalism and Disease Are Rapidly Destroying the Social Fabric of Our Planet," *Atlantic Monthly*, February 1994; Mark R. Duffield, "Getting Savages to Fight Barbarians: Development, Security and the Colonial Present," *Conflict, Security and Development* 5, no. 2 (August 2005).

21   The destruction of the city of Hargaisa, the ethnic cleansing of the Jubba Valley, and the group-targeted violence in the Bay and Shebelle regions and in Mogadishu itself all qualify as no less genocidal than the Sudan government's campaigns in Darfur, while Siad Barre's boast that he would take Somalia to Hell with him, should he be overthrown, was made real by his arming of clan militias and practice of "divide and rule." Diagnosis of "chaos by design" may ascribe some form of political responsibility or even identify a conspiracy, but does not help us progress in finding solutions. See Human Rights Watch, "Darfur 2007: Chaos by Design: Peacekeeping Challenges for AMIS and UNAMID," *Human Rights Watch* 19, no. 15(A) (September 20, 2007).

22   Samantha Power, "Remember Rwanda, But Take Action in Sudan," *New York Times*, April 6, 2004.

23   Michael Abramowitz, "U.S. Promises on Darfur Don't Match Actions," *Washington Post*, October 29, 2007; International Crisis Group, *To Save Darfur*, Report 105, March 17, 2006.

24   About ten books were published, but are out of print.

25   Mahmood Mamdani, "The Politics of Naming: Genocide, Civil War, Insurgency," *London Review of Books* 29, no. 8 (March 2007).

26   Deborah Murphy, "Narrating Darfur: Darfur in the U.S. Press, March–September 2004," in

Alex de Waal (ed.), *War in Darfur and the Search for Peace* (Cambridge, MA: Harvard University Press, 2007).

27   *Ibid.*, p. 235.

28   Rebecca Hamilton and Chad Hazlett, "'Not on Our Watch': The Emergence of the American Movement for Darfur," in de Waal (ed.), *War in Darfur and the Search for Peace*.

29   African Rights, *Food and Power in Sudan: A Critique of Humanitarianism* (London: African Rights, 1997).

30   Hamilton and Hazlett, "Not on Our Watch."

31   Quoted in *ibid.*

32   The appointment of Jerry Fowler as head of the Save Darfur Coalition in 2008 heralded a more moderate and thoughtful approach. But the wilder wing of the Darfur activist constituency, including columnists and some political aspirants, continued to advocate truly draconian measures.

33   Mamdani, 'The Politics of Naming."

34   A tabulation of 134 statements, undertaken for this author by Sam Rosmarin, undertaken for this author, from a number of the most prominent activists and advocacy groups between April 2005 and August 2007, finds that variants of this refrain—assertions or predictions of deterioration—accounted for all but 7 statements.

35   Mamdani, "The Politics of Naming."

36   See Victoria Holt and Tobias Berkman, *The Impossible Mandate?: Military Preparedness, the Responsibility to Protect and Modern Peace Operations* (Washington, D.C.: The Henry L. Stimson Center, 2006).

37   Murphy, "Narrating Darfur: Darfur in the U.S. Press, March–September 2004," p. 336.

38   Samantha Power, *A Problem from Hell: America and the Age of Genocide* (New York: Basic Books, 2002); Alex de Waal and Bridget Conley-Zilkic, "Reflections on How Genocidal Killings Are Brought to an End," Social Science Research Council Webforum, How Genocides End, December 2006, available on-line at http://howgenocidesend.ssrc.org/de_Waal (last accessed July 13, 2009).

39   "Reluctant Warrior," *The Observer*, September 30, 2001.

40   The Marine Corps was chagrined by its minor role in the 1991 Iraq war and felt the need to grasp a share in military glory. Interservice rivalry is often an important factor determining what wars are fought, when, and how.

41   Interviewed in Khartoum, November 2007.

42   Stephen Morrison, "Will Darfur Steal the Olympic Spotlight?" *Washington Quarterly*, Summer 2008.

43   David Kennedy, *The Dark Sides of Virtue: Reassessing International Humanitarianism* (Princeton, NJ: Princeton University Press, 2004), p. 351.

# Benevolent Dictatorship: The Formal Logic
of Humanitarian Government

Laurence McFalls

I recently asked a bright and ambitious seventeen-year-old what she planned on doing after completing secondary school. Without hesitation, she responded, "Work for a humanitarian organization abroad." I did not dare call her aspiration into question. Indeed, how could I? Her youthful enthusiasm, good intentions, and selfless idealism were beyond reproach. At her age, I, too, had hoped to save the world, but I had wanted to go into law or politics to defend the poor and the downtrodden, the victims of the iniquities of the capitalist system. A generation later, such an overtly political ambition would appear to be opportunistic or anachronistic, that is, symptomatic of a prepostmodern faith in social progress and reform, if not revolution. Although my youthful interlocutor would not have articulated it as such, her (a)political engagement reflected the contemporary postpostmodern ethical sensibility whereby the good can reside only in the immediate relief of suffering. Unlike postmodernism's relativism, if not cynicism, the contemporary humanitarian ethic raises the alleviation of physical suffering into a moral absolute, a transcendent norm of universal *agape*. Humanitarianism, it is by now banal to observe, has become, with its rights and duties to protect, the secular religion of the new millennium.

Just as I did not question my seventeen-year-old Good Samaritan's ethical position, it is not my intention here to engage in a normative or ideological critique of humanitarianism. Although some humanitarian theorists argue that the immediate concern for the prevention of suffering occupies a minimal moral space beyond the realm of particularistic political contention,[1] any ethical stance implies more or less explicit value choices always subject to political or ideological debate. In this essay, I am concerned not with the substantive rationality, but with the formal rationality of politics in the age of humanitarian intervention. Although I will focus on international humanitarian interventions, my argument seeks to uncover the particular form of "legitimate" domination obtained whenever and wherever social agents base their claim to authority over others on the benevolence of their actions to the governed.

I begin the essay by drawing an analogy to medical authority in order to understand a perverse, but intrinsic concrete effect of humanitarian intervention, namely, what I label "iatrogenic violence"—violence as the inadvertent product of care. In order to identify the formal logic of this form of violence, I then turn to Max Weber's tripartite typology of legitimate domination, arguing that a fourth ideal-typical form of domination, which I label "therapeutic," a form grounded on the claim of scientific expertise, is implicit in Weber's typology. I contend that the logic of humanitarianism's therapeutic domination corresponds to the "structure of exception" that Giorgio Agamben, drawing on Carl Schmitt, has identified at the center of the Western metaphysical and political tradition. After briefly exploring a few cases in which the ideal type of therapeutic domination manifests itself, I conclude that the benevolent dictatorship of humanitarian government based on scientific expertise and relying on the institutional form of the nongovernmental organization has become the uncontested and uncontestable radical biopower of our age.

## IATROGENIC VIOLENCE

The language of international intervention into political, social, and demographic crisis zones draws heavily on medical metaphors. While proponents may, for example, celebrate the scientific precision of "surgical strikes," critics may attack "Band-Aid solutions" to profound problems, and all may debate the appropriate doses of "shock therapy," the discourse of intervention commonly constructs the eruptions of violence or the failure of state institutions that elicit outside attention and intervention in terms of pathology, drawing on the organicist logic of structural-functionalist social theory. The pathologizing analogy gathers strength empirically, if not logically, from the apparent symptoms of a "sick" society: death, injury, impoverishment, famine, and actual medical epidemics.

As descriptively fitting as it may be, the medical metaphor is of course politically hardly innocent. Medicine responds to illness through intervention, an authoritative form of social action enjoying the double legitimacy of scientific rationality and of traditional shamanistic awe. The apparent political neutrality of the Hippocratic commitment to human life and well-being, moreover, exempts (medical) intervention from ethical critique. Thus providing the ideological cover of humanitarianism, the medical metaphor helps to conceal the political stakes of intervention (not only internationally, but domestically, with attempts to pass off social policies as technical solutions to social pathologies)—but only as long as the metaphor remains superficially and superstitiously reverential.

Truly conservative critics of intervention can turn the medical metaphor into an argument against virtually any kind of international or domestic political action by simply noting that the placebo and the waiting list constitute the two most successful medical treatments of all time, followed by hand washing and a good night's rest. Those on the left can also point to public-health studies showing that socioeconomic equality and spending on public goods such as drinking water, schools, and parks improve health statistics more than does spending on drugs, doctors, and hospitals. Applied metaphorically to the sphere of international military-humanitarian interventions, whose number have risen dramatically since the end of the Cold War, these critiques of medicine raise serious questions about the legitimacy and the efficacy of outside intervention into crisis zones such as those of the Balkans in the 1990s.

While the principles and premises of intervention do require debate, I do not propose here to explore alternatives to the practice of military-humanitarian intervention as it has developed over the past fifteen years.[2] Instead, I wish to examine another critical avenue arising from a further medical analogy, namely, that of iatrogenic violence.

Iatrogenic (literally: physician-induced) morbidity refers to disease or injury that medical intervention itself produces. With the term "iatrogenic violence," I designate social disruption and political violence that results from outside intervention (military and/or "humanitarian") intended to stop or to prevent such violence. The most blatant example of iatrogenic violence is of course the aftermath of the American invasion and ongoing occupation of Iraq. Carried out by the United States and its "coalition" partners with dubious to nonexistent international legal sanction, the intervention in Iraq allegedly aimed, among other vague and shifting goals, to shut down Iraq as a breeding ground for international terrorism and other forms of internal and external belligerence. As a consequence of the invasion, Iraq has indeed become such a breeding ground. The treatment is the cause of the illness it purported to be curing.

One might object that the example of Iraq actually calls into question the precise meaning of iatrogenics. If we were to give the Bush administration a huge benefit of the doubt, then we might say that the present violence emanating from and in Iraq is more the result of a misdiagnosis than an inappropriate treatment, though more cynically, we might simply dismiss U.S. policy in Iraq as willful malpractice.

Still, bona fide cases of iatrogenic illness and epidemics do exist, with patients falling ill from the best-intended state-of-the-art medical interventions. For example, recent fatal outbreaks of infection from *Clostridium difficile*, a cause of antibiotic-associated diarrhea, can be traced to doctors' perhaps overzealous prescription of antibiotics, which weakens immune systems and generates resistant strains of bacteria. Although we might also blame drug-company profit incentives and patients' magical belief in the power of the prescription pad, the use of antibiotics is nonetheless the medically indicated treatment for bacterial infection, even if it ultimately favors more severe infection.

Similarly, it is at least ideal-typically imaginable that cases of iatrogenic violence exist in a pure form, that is, cases where outside intervention occurs exclusively in the best interest of the afflicted society and according to the most appropriate and efficient technical means, yet nonetheless generates social disruption and violence. For example, the massive intervention in Kosovo since 1999, largely inspired and informed by the relative failures of intervention in Bosnia and other previous ex-Yugoslav crises, might be seen as a best-case, albeit far from perfect, scenario in which an effective use of armed force followed by a centrally coordinated, coherent multilateral and multilevel effort at political, economic, social, and ethnic reconstruction which nonetheless failed to prevent or even prompted large-scale fatal interethnic violence and rioting in March 2004.

To be sure, any complex social action such as multilateral intervention will suffer from shortcomings, inconsistencies, and paradoxical consequences, as Annie Lafontaine has shown for the unexpected conflicts arising from the repatriation of refugees in Kosovo.[3] I do not intend here, however, to catalogue the practical pitfalls of even the most welcome and well-planned interventions. Instead, the *theoretical* argument that I wish to develop claims that iatrogenic violence is inherent in the *formal* structure of international intervention, regardless of the substantive means, motives, or context of intervention. Drawing for the last time on the anthropomorphic medical metaphor, I mean to argue that this form of iatrogenic illness does not arise from the qualifications and intentions of the treating physician, or from the treatment and its potential side effects, or from the particular morphology and possible pathology of the patient, but from the structure of the doctor-patient relationship itself.

## THERAPEUTIC LEGITIMATE DOMINATION

Every instance of international intervention is of course sui generis, yet whatever the particular causes, contents, and contexts of intervention, we can identify common features of contemporary international interventionism that distinguish it, at least ideal-typically, from "good old-fashioned" conquest and colonialism.[4] These features, each of which could be critically elaborated in depth, include: the request for or consent to outside intervention from some significant population group (typically, an ethnic minority or other category of "victim") or its apparent representatives in order to help resolve a social or natural problem surpassing the capacity or will of local authorities (epidemic, armed insurrection, ethnic conflict, and so on); the quest for normative or legal approbation for the requested or proposed intervention by a supranational body recognized as competent by international law or treaty (the United Nations, the Organization for Security and Cooperation in Europe, or other regional organizations to which the territory of intervention is at least nominally a party); and of historical novelty and perhaps of greatest significance, the involvement in the intervention, alongside of traditionally state-based actors such as armed forces, of a corps of experts organized within the parallel and cross-cutting hierarchies of multilateral international agencies and formally autonomous nongovernmental organizations, NGOs.

Taken together, these features have contributed to the emergence of what Mariella Pandolfi has dubbed "mobile sovereignty."[5] This paradoxical formulation captures well the political complexity of the formal structure of contemporary international intervention. Understood traditionally as an attribute of the modern territorial state, sovereignty refers to the highest possible instance of social authority responsible for the maintenance of internal order and its protection from the interference of competing external orders through the exercise of a monopoly of legitimate violence within a delimited territory, according to Max Weber's classic definition of the state.[6] Sovereignty is thus spatially bounded, yet, at least in theory, absolute. The ideal-typical sovereign state is consequently subject to international legal norms only insofar as it authorizes those norms itself (though only the United States today approaches this ideal-typical status). The expression "mobile sovereignty," however, not only contradicts the bounded territorial character of the sovereign state, but relativizes authority, as well: Sometimes it is there, sometimes it is not. Pandolfi uses the term to describe the authority exercised by the corps of expert interveners who migrate from crisis zone to crisis zone, but its mobility is not only empirically geographical. That is, "mobile sovereignty" also theoretically describes the authoritative relationship between interveners and local populations in any particular site of intervention, regardless of the cosmopolitan or for that matter parochial character of the corps of interveners.

In an ideal-typical site of intervention, we encounter a local population "in need" and a corps of interveners. Although the latter may be a complex amalgam of soldiers, administrators, doctors, and other technical experts subject to the more or less coherent competing logics and command structures of states, multilateral agencies, and NGOs, the relationship between "locals" and "internationals" always has the same slippery or "mobile" authority structure, a peculiar form of "legitimate domination," which, as we will see, escapes Max Weber's well-known tripartite typology.[7] The "internationals" obviously occupy the position of dominance, ultimately by virtue of their superior firepower, if nothing else. The existence of social domination is not a problem, but a universal. The locals, in their subordinate position, necessarily engage in some form of resistance, again a universal within the sociology of domination and therefore not the source per se of iatrogenic violence. Substantively, the sociological categories of domination, subordination, and resistance vary almost endlessly in their contents according to the innumerable social inequalities that enter into the play of social interaction, but formally, as Weber's sociology of domination posits, relations of domination vacillate between the types of claims to *legitimate* domination.

According to Weber's *Herrschaftssoziologie*, any given social order relies, at the microsocial level, on dominant actors' particular normative claims to legitimate authority. Weber identifies three "pure," or ideal-typical forms that such claims can take: the traditional, the charismatic, and the legal-rational. These three modes of legitimation do not describe the normative contents of the claims that rulers make to justify obedience to their commands, but derive from the formal structure of the relationship between rulers and subordinates. Thus, traditional authority refers to a relationship in which the norm for obedience is inherent in the ruler's person, embodying values in a "timeless" regime of continuity, whereas charismatic authority emanates from the person of the ruler in an extraordinary, revolutionary regime of rupture. By contrast, legal-rational authority is literally disembodied, in that the ruler appeals to an entirely impersonal norm or procedure necessarily in a regime of continuity, the validity of the norm depending on its personal and temporal decontextualization.

This formal typology logically suggests a fourth mode of legitimation, one in which a dominant actor makes an impersonal claim to authority in a context of rupture with existing norms.[8] I have elsewhere associated this fourth form with scientific authority, under which the impersonal procedure of scientific method challenges existing orders of knowledge in a revolutionary process of scientific advancement,[9] but by metonymic analogy to medical knowledge, we can also call this fourth pure form of authority "therapeutic domination." Under this form, as in the doctor-patient relationship of command, the ruler claims obedience by virtue of the application of a scientifically valid, impersonal procedure—a treatment protocol—in the extraordinary context of crisis. As Vanessa Pupavac has argued, humanitarian interventions have in empirical practice taken on the quite literally medicalized form of what she calls "therapeutic governance," that is, the application of social and clinical psychological treatments to traumatized or otherwise stressed target populations.[10] While it encompasses substantive practices of therapeutic governance in Pupavac's sense, the concept of therapeutic domination abstractly describes any relationship of command justified by an appeal to an impersonal rule or procedure in rupture with a previous enduring order. Nonetheless, the formal structure of figuratively therapeutic domination logically suggests that the substantive contents of its normative claims will be literally therapeutic. As with legal-rational claims to authority, therapeutic domination's appeal to impersonal procedure applies to nobody (and no body) in particular and hence to everybody (and every body) in general.

Paradoxically, and in contrast to legal-rational authority, the apparently disembodied norms of therapeutic authority focus precisely on the human body itself because of this mode of domination's extraordinary temporal quality. Intervening in rupture with established practices, therapeutic domination not only depersonalizes, but decontextualizes social relationships. Without any reference to culture or to history, therapeutic domination reduces social agents to human bodies. Thus, unlike charismatic, traditional, or even legal-rational authority, no particular conception of the good life, but only the minimal, but absolute value of life itself can inform therapeutic domination.

Before further exploring the logical and substantive, biopolitical consequences of an impersonal, extraordinary mode of domination, we might ask why Weber did not name, let alone elaborate upon, such a form of legitimate authority implicit in his classic typology. Self-avowedly antitheoretical in personal character, if not in practice, Weber claimed to have fit his theoretical apparatus to the empirical objectives of his *Wirklichkeitswissenschaft* (science of reality), and he may therefore not have elaborated a type that no historical example with which he was familiar began to approach. Alternatively, he may have found it empirically implausible that anyone might in the future accept an extraordinary norm that did not have an exemplary personal embodiment. In other words, Weber did not anticipate the possibility, in the absence of clear charismatic leadership, of revolutionary upheavals such as those that occurred in Eastern Europe in the name of the formal procedures of privatization, liberal democratization, and European integration. Finally, on a more philosophical plane, Weber may have wished to avoid the contradictions of the Western metaphysical tradition, which he knew all too well that Nietzsche had exposed.

These philosophical contradictions inherent in an impersonal, but extraordinary mode of legitimation become evident if we associate with each kind of relation of legitimate (that is, rationalized) domination Weber's four ideal-typical modes of rationality: habit, affectivity, value rationality (*Wertrationalität*), and instrumental rationality (*Zweckrationalität*). We can map these types of rational motives for social action along the two dimensions of their relative motivational strength and of their degree of conscious (intellectual) articulation, with habit (for example, custom) being a relatively weak and unconscious "reason" for action; affect (for example, eros) being a potentially powerful, but not necessarily self-conscious motive; the rationality of ultimate value ends (for example, salvation) being also very powerful and usually subject to conscious articulation; and finally instrumental rationality (for example, utility maximization) being absolutely self-conscious in its calculations, but relatively weak in its motivational strength precisely because of the fungibility of its ends. In purely abstract terms, then, the quotidian and personalized claims of traditional authority appeal to habit and affect, whereas charisma, by virtue of its personal and extraordinary quality, appeals to affect and value rationality and legalist proceduralism in its impersonal routine to instrumental rationality and habit. Logically, a simultaneously extraordinary and impersonal claim to authority would have to appeal to both value rationality and instrumental rationality at the same time, that is, to the substantive rationality of ends and the formal rationality of means, two conscious, but contradictory motives for action.

The centrality of an unnamed impersonal, but extraordinary mode of legitimation both to intervention and to Western politics as a whole is the thesis — translated into Weberian terms — that the contemporary Italian philosopher Giorgio Agamben advances in *Homo Sacer: Sovereign Power and Bare Life*.[11] Starting from Carl Schmitt's premise that the power to declare a state of exception defines the sovereign,[12] Agamben tracks the "structure of exception" as the formal paradox at the core of and permeating the Western political and metaphysical tradition at least since Aristotle excluded "mere (or naked) life" (*zoē*) from the ends of the polis in its self-legislating pursuit of the "good life" (*bios*). Whether it exists between the "good life" and "bare life," civil society and the state of nature, constitutional order and the state of emergency, law and force, or language and being, the structure of exception entails a relationship of "inclusive exclusion" where the existence of the first term both depends on and negates the second. The state of exception *proves* the rule (of law) — in both senses of the verb: to confirm and to contest.

The most vivid contemporary illustration of the state of exception's political fecundity is no doubt the American detention center in Guantánamo Bay, the so-called "Camp Justice": extraterritorial, extraconstitutional, outside of international law, and yet heralded by the Bush administration as a vital instrument in the "war on terror." The example is not an aberration, or an exception itself (or inasmuch as it is, it is a revelation of the fundamental structure of American politics), for as Agamben argues (and he did so well before September 11, 2001), the concentration camp is the "biopolitical paradigm of modernity," a delocalized space where totalitarian state power reduces politics to control and to the extermination of bare life. Less brutal, but at least equally biopolitical, modern democratic politics have, more even than Michel Foucault anticipated,[13] concentrated on the control of bodies and populations, from the birthright of citizenship to sexuality, stem cells, security, and euthanasia.

Totalitarian and democratic biopolitics converged in the exceptional political context of former Yugoslavia in the 1990s. As Agamben writes, the Yugoslav civil wars, with their systematic rape and gratuitous slaughter, surpassed totalitarian genocide as well as the traditionally modern redrawing of ethnic and state boundaries. The subsequent "democratic" intervention, understood and justified as temporary and as a restoration of political and social order, has become an indefinite state of exception, a "permanent transition."[14] Under these circumstances, Agamben writes (even before the scale and permanency of intervention became evident):

> what is happening in ex-Yugoslavia and, more generally, what is happening in the process of dissolution of traditional State organisms in Eastern Europe should be viewed not as a reemergence of the natural state of struggle of all against all—which functions as a prelude to new social contracts and new national and State localizations—but rather as the coming to light of the state of exception as the permanent structure of juridico-political de-localization and dis-location. Political organization is not regressing toward outdated forms; rather, premonitory events are, like bloody masses, announcing the new *nomos* of the earth, which (if its grounding principle is not called into question) will soon extend itself over the entire planet.[15]

Regardless of whether Agamben's dystopian biopolitical premonitions come to pass, his analysis of the structure of exception can help us to explicate the more immediate problem of iatrogenic violence within sites of intervention. Following Weber, we saw that the abstract form of legitimate domination on a site of intervention is not legal-rational, or charismatic, or a hybrid of them (as in party democracy, when a leader alternately claims authority by virtue of personal merit or formal electoral approbation), but rather an unnamed, extraordinary, yet impersonal form simultaneously appealing to the apparently contradictory rationalities of efficient means versus ultimate ends. The relation between these two rationalities, however, corresponds to Agamben's structure of exception, where one term depends on and negates the other. Specifically, instrumental reason, which is impersonal in that its validity is internal and autonomous of any particular subject engaged in ratiocination, depends on value rationality, since its "objective" validity exists only relative to a given end. But it must also negate value rationality, which is extraordinary, or unpredictable, and varies from person to person. In other words (which may appear banal), ordinary, impersonal bureaucracy reposes on extraordinary, personal charisma, just as the rule of law obscures the arbitrary force from which it derives.

Such a "dialectical unity of opposites" derives from the formal logic of their definition, but this binary structure of Western thought is not without political consequences, especially since it goes through its own historical moments. Thus, different periods have experienced the ideal-typical predominance of one or another form of legitimate domination with its incumbent rationality. Modernity was the age of the instrumental legal rationality of bureaucracy, indispensable to the emergence of industrial capitalism and the democratic state. It would be ideal-ist nonsense, however, to pretend that the march of (instrumental) reason alone gave rise to these (or other) historical structures. As Weber's historical sociology establishes, the translation of different forms of (ir)rationality into social struc-tures depends on social carriers with material and ideal interests, as well as on the technical means at their disposal. It also gives rise to distinctive institutions and modes of violence. To caricature: Modern bureaucratic society was carried on largely by an intellectual proletariat/petty bourgeoisie of technicians and man-agers organized in distinctive organizations such as political parties, public-sector unions, and public or private national economic enterprises. Whereas traditional societies practiced externalized, ritual forms of violence, modern societies, as Nor-bert Elias and Michel Foucault have respectively shown, depended on the inter-nalized violence of self-discipline.[16] By contrast, the more ephemeral charismatic social orders and movements have typically flourished with exuberant, external-ized violence (looting, pillage, warfare, purges, genocide) and have relied on loose institutional structures such as warrior commensality and communism.

## THE SOCIAL CARRIERS AND INSTITUTIONAL FORMS OF THERAPEUTIC DOMINATION

If, as Agamben suggests, the indefinite extension of states of exception and the exacerbation of biopower characterize the emergent postmodern sociopoliti-cal order, then we must ask not only who the social carriers of its arbitrary, but efficient rationality and legitimation are, but what kinds of institutions, technical means, and social violence they animate. Concretely, the sites of intervention in the Balkans and in other instances of permanent transition around the planet offer an answer. The participation of a migratory corps of experts represents a novel, defining feature of the new international interventionism. Indeed, in the absence of a growing cosmopolitan body of professionals with expert training and experi-ence as well as material and ideal interests in the perpetuation and proliferation of intervention sites, the phenomenon would not be technically feasible. The social origins and resources of these interveners require closer empirical scrutiny, but clearly, most belong to highly educated, mobile, privileged social strata and all derive social prestige, if not always their material livelihood, from an activity distinct from government and business. Thus, the innovative social institution within which they typically function is fittingly the nonprofit nongovernmental organization devoted to a particular normative cause.

The NGO's negative form of self-definition clearly signals the shift in rationality away from the legal-rational instrumentalism of the modern state. Just as the explosive economic growth of modern capitalism depended on a shift from a rationality of ends (that is, wealth) to a rationality of means (productivity), the unprecedented development of the bureaucratic, sovereign state resulted from the Western European political dynamic of the pursuit of power as an end in itself, that is, from the subjection of politics to a purely instrumental rationality. As Agamben shows, the internal, circular logic of the preservation and aggrandizement of state capacities obscured the inclusive exclusion of political value rationality, which manifested itself in the growing biopoliticization of modern state power. The emergence, since the 1970s, of the NGO has simply completed the backdoor return of political value rationality. Performing social functions previously associated with the state and doing so largely with funding of state origin, NGOs short-circuit the self-sustaining circular logic of the bureaucratic state's formal, impersonal rationality. More than a neoliberal privatization of an allegedly bloated, inefficient, and self-serving (but procedurally legitimate) state bureaucracy, NGOs confer the means of legitimate violence on particular, personal, and passing substantive value rationalities. Feigning a nonpolitical, humanitarian vocation, NGOs, whose missions and methods can change with the prevailing wind, in fact embody a politics of arbitrary life force imposing its values and visions.

Again, the normative violence of NGOs as central actors of the new interventionism does not simply signal an incursion of charismatic authority into contemporary politics, for the particular mode of violence they exercise in sites of intervention differs significantly. Charismatic violence seeks a revolutionary transformation of the social order in the image of the values emanating from the leader. By contrast, the extraordinary, but impersonal legitimacy of intervention shapes its characteristic mode of violence, which forces conformity not with a substantive value, but with a formal method. In an inversion of the structure of exception, intervention occurs in the name of an overarching normative principle (health, security, "freedom") that denies the formal instrumental rationality of state sovereignty only the better to apply its own technical rationality.

We can thus characterize its typical mode of violence as "therapeutic," because ostensibly, it pursues a value emanating from the object of intervention (a population "in need"), but its actual end is the proficient application of a treatment protocol captured by the quip "the surgery was successful, but the patient died." The therapeutic structure of domination also determines the mode of resistance principally as "patient noncompliance": usually passive-aggressive, often self-destructive, and occasionally prone to apparently irrational outbursts directed at "care givers" as the patient futilely attempts to reappropriate control over his or her body. Thus, paraphrasing Agamben, we might say that the suicide bomber has become a "biopolitical paradigm of our contemporaneity."

As an ideal type in the Weberian sense, therapeutic domination is, of course, a utopia. It exists nowhere in pure form. Logically and historically, legitimate domination always takes on hybrid forms, with bureaucratic legal rationalism, for example, drawing on charismatic renewal, or with revolutionary regimes routinizing into neotraditional patrimonialism. Thus, therapeutic NGOs today have not supplanted the bureaucratic state, but exist in close symbiosis with states and intergovernmental agencies. Although NGOs enjoyed a relative autonomy from the state during the Cold War, in the heyday of military-humanitarian interventionism in the 1990s, they became financially and organizationally more linked to the state before becoming more subordinated to the new state-centered security agenda after 2001.[17] We can only begin to hint at the hybrid complexity of authority relations between NGOs and state actors as expert personnel migrate back and forth between the public, the private, and the nonprofit sectors, as states subcontract services to NGOs while the latter articulate public policies, or as charismatic celebrities found and fund NGOs and hobnob with democratically elected leaders and top civil servants at international forums. A few brief examples from current field research, however, can illustrate the analytical fecundity of the concept of therapeutic domination.

As I have already indicated, the Balkan crises, and the case of Kosovo in particular, initially prompted my articulation of the concepts of iatrogenic violence and of therapeutic domination. Indeed, my colleague and collaborator Mariella Pandolfi's ethnographic research in Kosovo and into the earlier, less well-known case of military humanitarian intervention in Albania has shown how ostensibly temporary interventions have morphed into an enduring order of permanent transition.[18] Initially a response to the breakdown of state authority resulting from economic chaos in the aftermath of pyramid schemes in Albania and resulting from ethnic warfare in Kosovo, international intervention obviously took on a therapeutic character as a host of military and humanitarian organizations of state and nonstate origin applied their standard operating procedures and honed their technical proficiency in establishing safe havens, "green zones," and refugee processing facilities. If these therapeutic responses to social disorder had quickly restored order, as they pretended, or if they had established a legal-rational legitimate order, be it an autonomous state or a neocolonial administration, then the extraordinary, but normalized means of intervention could be understood as an exception that ultimately proves the rule of bureaucratic, legal-rational modern social order.

However, it is precisely the political limbo from which Kosovo and Albania have not yet escaped that demonstrates the peculiar form of social order that therapeutic domination can sustain. Almost a decade after NATO's bombing campaign, Kosovo remains in a state of exception, with tens of thousands of foreign experts not only maintaining local society, but finding their raison d'être in unending economic, ethnic, and political crisis. Even when Kosovo unilaterally declared its independence in early 2008, it simply passed from one state of uncertainty to another as an initial wave of recognition failed to clarify the (former) Serbian province's political status. Tellingly, Serbian violence in Kosovo in response to the Albanophone majority's declaration of independence did not target the new allegedly dominant ethnic group, but rather the international agencies and actors who in fact hold (therapeutic) legitimate authority. In other words, the Serbs' iatrogenic violence in response to the international community's therapeutic domination not only debunked the notion that the eventual new Kosovo state has an ethnic national basis, but also reinforced the claim of the military-humanitarian intervention corps to be necessary to the pacification of a still-conflict-ridden society.

In the case of Albania, the perpetuation of a therapeutic order of domination is much more insidious, since all but a handful of the foreign military personnel and other experts have left the country since surging into it in 1997. Pandolfi's ethnographic research, however, has shown how local elites have internalized the logic of therapeutic domination in a process of self-pathologization that has paralyzed the country's politics. The legacy of therapeutic intervention is particularly evident in the protodemocratic public sphere, where different media outlets and forms reflect elite rivalries sown by the international community in the 1990s.[19] Because the common diagnosis of the causes of democratic deficiencies in post-Communist transition societies pointed to the corruption of established elites and to the underdevelopment of civil society, international agencies and NGOs prescribed the massive funding and training of local NGOs to constitute the tissue of organized civil society and to recruit ersatz elites. In Albania, as elsewhere in the Balkans, the Soros Foundation played a key role in cultivating a new cosmopolitan and media-savvy elite, which still draws its material resources and symbolic legitimacy from its insertion into international networks and from its reproduction of international norms of "good governance," transparency, responsibility, and so on. In other words, with the retreat of international interveners, this new cosmopolitan elite has donned the cloak of therapeutic domination. In the process, it has encouraged a form of symbolic iatrogenic violence within the Albanian media landscape, where traditional and other, more locally based new elites have, in response, adopted populist, nationalist, ethnicizing, and sensationalist discourses, which in turn have comforted the cosmopolitan elite's claim to be defenders of civilization against barbarism.

A similar dynamic of local elite appropriation of external therapeutic legitimacy is at work in Liberia, a case that well illustrates the complex hybridization of different modes of domination. Sub-Saharan Africa's first independent state, with a long tradition of neopatrimonial rule, Liberia, since 1989, has been the site of two civil wars and of two UN-mandated peacekeeping missions backed up by a host of humanitarian agencies notably devoted to demobilizing, disarming, reintegrating, and reconciling the child soldiers of brutal warlord armies.[20] Ongoing field research among demobilized soldiers subject to therapeutic intervention suggests not only that competing warlord regimes drew their legitimacy at least in part from their integration into international networks, including humanitarian NGOs, as well as into foreign resource-extraction companies, but that remarkable continuities in personnel and organizational actors span the transition from civil war to internationally supervised pacification.[21] Perhaps most telling about the integration of therapeutic legitimacy into Liberian politics is the career trajectory of Liberia's current president, Ellen Johnson-Sirleaf. A Harvard-educated member of the Americo-Liberian elite, she participated in the last traditionally neopatrimonial Tolbert government until Samuel Doe's bloody coup in 1980. Subsequently an ally and then an opponent of notorious warlord Charles Taylor, Johnson-Sirleaf spent the war years abroad, working for Citibank, the World Bank, and the UN Development Programme, and returned to Liberia in 2004 to head the Commission on Good Governance, thus making clear that her bid for the presidency in 2005 rested on her appeal to the therapeutic legitimacy of her technical expertise and integration into the international aid community and its norms.

A further and final illustration of the empirical relevance of the concept of therapeutic domination is evident in neighboring Ivory Coast. There, in the context of civil war, medical anthropologist Vinh-Kim Nguyen has observed the emergence of what he labels a "military-therapeutic complex" within the framework of the U.S.-government-sponsored HIV-AIDS relief program known as PEPFAR.[22] Combining resources of the U.S. military, private security and logistics firms, medical NGOs, and pharmaceutical companies, this program has established parallel or substitute authority in large regions of the country where central government control has receded. Beyond the application of established medical, humanitarian, and military logistical "treatment" protocols, this multilevel intervention has become a laboratory not only for trials of new drugs, but for developing mechanisms for controlling the population, whose resistance seems to take the iatrogenic forms of refusal of treatment and even willful promiscuity by HIV-positive subjects. This self-destructive and irresponsible resistance feeds back into the moral absolutism of therapeutic domination through its development of moralizing and individualizing practices of subjectivating "confessional technologies." Therapeutic domination thus produces what Nguyen calls "therapeutic citizenship," a governmentality whereby individuals take charge of their own moral and physical health by adopting best practices, beginning, of course, with safe sex.

## CONCLUSION

In sum, from NATO bombing in Kosovo to AIDS relief in Ivory Coast, the therapeutic social relation of domination and its concomitant iatrogenic violence has attained its highest form in the military-humanitarian interventions of the past fifteen years. Although they still rely on the typically modern legal-rational authority and bureaucratic capacities of sovereign states and international law and institutions, these operations have introduced a new, extraordinary, impersonal form of legitimate domination that escapes the bureaucratic rationality of the modern state. This apparently paradoxical form of authority has more or less latently permeated the Western political and metaphysical tradition, expressing itself today in rampant biopoliticization. Convinced perhaps of the inescapability of the iron cages of the instrumentally rational modern state and capitalism, Weber skirted the naming and theoretical elaboration of this extraordinary, impersonal form logically implied by his typology of legitimate dominations. His typology thus reproduced the structure of exception underlying Western political and metaphysical thought, suggesting the hidden pervasiveness of a kind of authority that characterizes the purely logical structure of both politics and science.[23] Both of these are Promethean efforts to lend meaning to a godless, meaningless world, where the creative genius must deny and negate his or her arbitrary power.[24] Intervention reproduces this godless, godlike structure of authority, whence its banal claim to be a matter of life and death. Thus reduced to the efficient and effective protection of bare life, politics has become the science of survival.[25] With the proliferation of threats to the survival of the species, from ethnic conflict to global warming, a permanent state of emergency has transformed humanitarian government into a dictatorship above and beyond the discussion, debates, and contestations of ordinary politics. To be sure, it is a benevolent dictatorship, but it is one that suspends or makes obsolete political action in pursuit of a just, equitable, or otherwise good social order. This is what I blasphemously wanted to tell my young humanitarian volunteer, but did not dare.

## NOTES

1   See Michael Walzer, *Interpretation and Social Criticism* (Cambridge, MA: Harvard University Press, 1987); and Thomas Pogge (ed.), *Freedom from Poverty as a Human Right: Who Owes What to the Very Poor?* (Oxford: Oxford University Press, 2007).

2   For a critique of military and humanitarian intervention, see Mark Duffield, *Global Governance and the New Wars: The Merging of Development and Security* (London: Zed Books, 2001), as well as *Development, Security and Unending War: Governing the World of Peoples* (Cambridge: Polity, 2007).

3   Annie Lafontaine, "Le rapatriement des réfugiés albanais au Kosovo (1999–2001): Discours, pratiques et effets sociaux," Ph.D. thesis, Université de Montréal, 2003.

4   Duffield, *Development, Security and Unending War*, pp. 39–46.

5   Mariella Pandolfi, "L'industrie humanitaire: Une souveraineté mouvante et supracoloniale. Réflexion sur l'expérience des Balkans," *Multitudes* 3 (November 2000): pp. 97–105; "'Moral entrepreneurs,' souverainetés mouvantes et barbelé: Le bio-politique dans les Balkans post-communistes," in Mariella Pandolfi and Marc Abélès (eds.), "Politiques: Jeux d'espaces," special issue, *Anthropologie et Sociétés* 26, no. 1 (2002): pp. 1–24.

6   Max Weber, "Politik als Beruf," in Max Weber, *Gesammelte politische Schriften* (Tübingen: Mohr, 1988).

7   Max Weber, *Economy and Society* (Berkeley: University of California Press, 1978).

8   I owe the (im)personal/(extra)ordinary typological scheme to Augustin Simard, *La loi désarmée* (Québec: Presses de l'Université Laval, 2009). Also, a nearly identical theoretical presentation of my concept of therapeutic domination appeared in Laurence McFalls and Mariella Pandolfi, "Intervention as Therapeutic Order," *AM: Rivista della società italiana di antropologia*, no. 27-28 (December 2009).

9   Laurence McFalls, "The Objectivist Ethic and the 'Spirit' of Science," in Laurence McFalls (ed.), *Max Weber's 'Objectivity' Reconsidered* (Toronto: University of Toronto Press, 2007).

10   See Vanessa Pupavac, "Therapeutic Governance: Psycho-Social Intervention and Trauma Risk Management," *Disasters* 25, no. 4 (2001): pp. 358–72; and "Human Security and the Rise of Global Therapeutic Governance," *Conflict, Development and Security* 5, no. 2 (2005): pp. 161–82.

11   Giorgio Agamben, *Homo Sacer: Sovereign Power and Bare Life*, trans. Daniel Heller-Roazen (Stanford, CA: Stanford University Press, 1998).

12   Carl Schmitt, *Politische Theologie* (Berlin: Duncker & Humblot, 1922), available in English as *Political Theology: Four Chapters on the Concept of Sovereignty*, trans. George Schwab (Chicago: University of Chicago Press, 2005).

13   For the elaboration of his concept of biopolitics, see Michel Foucault, *"Il faut défendre la société": Cours au Collège de France (1975–1976)* (Paris: Gallimard, 1997); *Sécurité, territoire,*

population: Cours au Collège de France, 1977–1978 (Paris: Gallimard, 2004); and *Naissance de la biopolitique: Cours au Collège de France (1978–1979)* (Paris: Gallimard, 2004). Available in English as *Society Must Be Defended: Lectures at the Collège de France, 1975–76*, ed. Mauro Bertani and Alessandro Fontana, trans. David Macey (New York: Picador, 2003); *Security, Territory, Population: Lectures at the Collège de France, 1977–78*, ed. Michel Senellart, trans. Graham Burchell (New York: Palgrave Macmillan, 2007); and *The Birth of Biopolitics: Lectures at the Collège de France, 1978-79*, ed. Michel Senellart, trans. Graham Burchell (New York: Palgrave Macmillan, 2008).

14   For a note surveying the provenance of the concept of "permanent transition," see Mariella Pandolfi's essay "From Paradox to Paradigm: The Permanent State of Emergency in the Balkans" in this volume.

15   Agamben, *Homo Sacer*, p. 38.

16   Norbert Elias, *The Civilizing Process*, trans. Edmund Jephcott (Cambridge, MA: Blackwell, 1994) and Michel Foucault, *Discipline and Punish: The Birth of the Prison*, trans. Alan Sheridan (New York: Vintage, 1979).

17   Duffield, *Development, Security and Unending War*, pp. 32–65.

18   Mariella Pandolfi, "La zone grise des guerres humanitaires," *Anthropologica* 48, no. 1 (2006): pp. 43–58; "Industrie humanitaire"; and "'Moral Entrepreneurs.'" Mariella Pandolfi, Annie Lafontaine, Marie-Joëlle Zahar, and Laurence McFalls, "Paradoxes et démocratie de l'information en Albanie contemporaine," *Transitions* 44, no. 2 (2005): pp. 11–30. Laurence McFalls and Mariella Pandolfi, "Souveraineté mobile et cosmopolice humanitaire," in Dietmar Köveker (ed.), *Lieux et emprises de la souveraineté* (Québec: Presses de l'Université Laval, forthcoming).

19   Pandolfi et al., "Paradoxes et démocratie de l'information en Albanie contemporaine."

20   On the origins of the Liberian civil wars, see Stephen Ellis, *The Mask of Anarchy: The Destruction of Liberia and the Religious Dimension of an African Civil War* (New York: NYU Press, 2001).

21   Mayra Moro Coco, "The Legitimacy of War Lords and their Successors in Liberia," Ph.D. thesis prospectus, Université de Montréal, 2007.

22   Vinh-Kim Nguyen, "Antiretroviral Globalism, Biopolitics and Therapeutic Citizenship," in Aihwa Ong and Stephen J. Collier (eds.), *Global Assemblages: Technology, Politics and Ethics* (London: Blackwell, 2005); and "Uses and Pleasures: Sexual Modernity, HIV/AIDS, and Confessional Technologies in a West African Metropolis," in Vincanne Adams and Stacey Leigh Pigg (eds.), *The Moral Object of Sex: Science, Development and Sexuality in Global Perspective* (Durham, NC: Duke University Press, 2005). PEPFAR stands for the (U.S.) President's Emergency Plan for AIDS Relief.

23   See McFalls, "The Objectivist Ethic."

24   On Max Weber's heroic self-abnegation as founder of modern social science, see Sheldon Wolin, "Max Weber: Legitimation, Method, and the Politics of Theory," *Political Theory* 9, no. 3 (1981): pp. 401–24.

25   Marc Abélès, *Politique de la survie* (Paris: Flammarion, 2006).

# The Passions of Protection:
# Sovereign Authority and Humanitarian War

Anne Orford

Late in 2007, I attended a workshop that brought together senior legal military advisers—from NATO, the United Kingdom, the United States, Ireland, the Netherlands, Fiji, Sri Lanka, and Sweden—with NGO representatives and academics in order to discuss the relevance of gender to international humanitarian law. International humanitarian law is the body of international law that governs the conduct of parties to armed conflict. I felt a little anxious when the first proposal for institutionalizing gender neutrality to emerge from the workshop involved ensuring that female as well as male figures should pop up as targets during shooting practice. At the end of our two days together, one of the formerly skeptical senior military lawyers told the group that he was a convert to gender analysis. "Gender issues aren't just personnel issues," he announced enthusiastically. "They are intelligence issues! Gender is a force multiplier—if you understand how gender works in a particular society, you can control that society much more effectively!" Perhaps, in what Rey Chow has called "the age of the world target," this should not have surprised me.[1] Chow argues that since at least the dropping of the atomic bombs on Nagasaki and Hiroshima, to become an object of knowledge is to become a potential target. So to introduce gender, or bodies, or human suffering into the system for producing knowledge about war automatically means that knowledge about gender, or bodies, or human suffering becomes part of the targeting machine.

In this essay, I would like to explore the relationship between the vulnerability of human bodies and the logics of state power and militarism. Do suffering bodies accuse or resist power by their very presence? Or might the recollection of human vulnerability and the representation of suffering in fact reinforce or justify power? After all, vulnerable bodies—bodies in pain—are everywhere in representations of war today. Activist Web sites focused on the situation in Darfur, such as the Passion of the Present site or that of the Save Darfur campaign, combine the language of salvation with images of suffering to mobilize military action in the name of our common humanity.[2] The photographs and descriptions of the infliction of pain upon detainees in the camps at Abu Ghraib and Guantánamo Bay have caused outrage around the world. The many recent books about those whom Philippe Sands has named the "torture team" describe in excruciating detail the violence inflicted upon the bodies of those interrogated in the detention centers and prisons controlled by the United States and its allies.[3]

Yet somehow, the two sets of images or scenes of suffering remain separate. The centrality of the U.S. military to much humanitarian strategizing has not been seriously challenged. While much of the human rights movement has been properly appalled by the abuses carried out by U.S. military and security forces in the "war on terror," advocates of humanitarian intervention still do not question whether increased intervention by the U.S. military under its current rules of engagement offers the best strategy for the protection of individuals in Darfur or elsewhere. Indeed, in many critical appraisals of the conduct of the war on terror, politicians and their advisers are indicted, while the U.S. military and the existing laws of war are redeemed. For example, according to legal scholars such as Philippe Sands and Scott Horton, the torture of detainees represents an abandonment of the long-standing disavowal of cruelty in warfare by the professional U.S. military.[4] According to Sands, the interrogation practices involved in the war on terror are a departure from U.S. military tradition, a tradition in which "the US military did not 'do' cruelty or torture."[5] He traces this tradition back to the general orders promulgated by President Lincoln in 1863 stating "Military necessity does not admit of cruelty."

At the same time, the push for greater military intervention in the name of protecting suffering peoples in Africa, Asia, and the Middle East has received an enormous boost through the adoption of the notion of the responsibility to protect in international relations. The language of the responsibility to protect has gradually colonized the legal and political debate internationally since its development by the International Commission on Intervention and State Sovereignty, or ICISS, in 2001.[6] The ICISS was an initiative sponsored by the Canadian government that was designed to respond to the perceived tension between state sovereignty and humanitarian intervention in the aftermath of the NATO action in Kosovo. When the concept of a responsibility to protect was introduced into the mainstream institutional debate by the ICISS report, it was presented as a new way of talking about humanitarian intervention, as well as a new way of talking about sovereignty. Both were organized around protection. The new way of talking about sovereignty was to argue that "its essence should now be seen not as control but as responsibility."[7] If a state is unwilling or unable to meet this responsibility to protect its population, it then falls upon the international community to do so. The new way of talking about humanitarian intervention involved recharacterizing the debate "not as an argument about any right at all but rather about a responsibility— one to protect people at grave risk." The people at grave risk were those "millions of human beings" who, in the words of the ICISS report, "remain at the mercy of civil wars, insurgencies, state repression and state collapse."[8]

Institutionally, the responsibility to protect concept has been successful in a way that humanitarian intervention never was. Actors ranging from U.S. counter-insurgency specialists through UN officials to human rights activists and Christian aid workers have enthusiastically begun to redescribe and reconceptualize their missions in terms of protection. These actors have also begun to integrate activities across a remarkable range of areas within a protection framework. UN agencies from the Office of the UN High Commissioner for Refugees to the World Health Organization now work in protection clusters when they are in the field. At the UN, two senior positions have been created to implement the responsibility to protect—Francis Deng was appointed to the newly styled position of "Special Adviser for the Prevention of Genocide" in 2007, and Edward Luck was appointed to the new position of "Special Adviser to the Secretary-General with a focus on the Responsibility to Protect" in 2008. UN member states have also embraced the concept, apparently with much greater willingness than was the case with humanitarian intervention. Member states voted unanimously in the General Assembly at the 2005 World Summit to adopt the responsibility to protect as an obligation both of individual member states and of the international community,[9] and since then, representatives of states including the United Kingdom, the United States, France, Sweden, and Australia have specifically invoked the responsibility to protect to explain actions taken or proposed by their governments.

In this essay I am interested in making sense of the relation between these two features of contemporary international humanitarianism—the claim that the modern military state, and in particular the United States, has abandoned cruelty as an official instrument of warfare, and the claim that it is through increased international policing and military intervention that the state can be perfected and protection of those at risk achieved. I begin to explore this relation by looking at the way in which international humanitarian law incorporates the killing or wounding of civilians within the calculations of military statecraft. I then turn back to the early history of the modern state to try to make sense of the ways in which international humanitarian law and military practice sanctify certain kinds of killing or wounding in the name of preserving the security of the commonwealth. I conclude by asking what this relationship between law, violence, and the modern state means for understanding and responding to the logics of humanitarian warfare.

Both international humanitarian law and the broader legal prohibition against torture during war or peace can be understood as part of a modern project to eliminate what international law describes as "cruel, inhuman, or degrading treatment or punishment."[10] Humanitarian intervention can be understood as an extension of that project—as an attempt not just to prohibit, but to eliminate certain forms of suffering in this world. Central to this task is the distinction between torture and cruel, inhuman, or degrading treatment, on the one hand, and justifiable suffering, on the other. The infliction of pain is accepted in many modern states as part of "warfare, sport, scientific experimentation, and the death penalty" and more controversially as part of sexual and artistic practice.[11] Military historians have written "of the new practices of 'deliberate cruelty'" employed in war during the twentieth century, from the use of mines filled with jagged metal fragments designed to tear and fracture bodies, to napalm, with its ingredient that "increases the adherence of the burning petrol of human skin surfaces," to possession of chemical, biological, and nuclear weapons of mass destruction that advertise "governmental readiness to inflict cruel death."[12] Yet while war "is the most obvious analogue to torture,"[13] it remains the case that the normal and lawful conduct of war is not understood to involve "cruel, inhuman, or degrading treatment or punishment." Torture and cruelty thus refer to suffering that is essentially gratuitous from the perspective of the state. International law, like modern statecraft, envisages that certain kinds of suffering are authorized. Some forms of suffering are understood as necessary or inevitable—in particular, the suffering that is authorized in terms of the reason of state or proportional to military necessity. International law thus prohibits suffering that is excessive, suffering that is beyond what is calculated as necessary to protect state security or to enable human flourishing. It is on the basis of this logic that the use of military force against peoples and territories in Africa, Asia, and the Middle East can be understood as humanitarian or that aerial bombardment can be understood as humane.

We can see this logic in action if we look at the ways in which international humanitarian law deals with the killing and wounding of civilians. The norms of international humanitarian law prohibit the targeting of civilians in armed conflict, requiring attackers to direct their actions against broadly defined "military objectives," rather than "civilian objects."[14] Civilians can be killed "incidentally," but the risk of endangering civilians as "collateral damage" must not be disproportionate to the military advantage to be gained by the attack.[15] The utilitarian language of this balancing test reveals that the lives of civilians can be sacrificed if the value of their existence is weighed against the importance of "military objectives" and found wanting. Similarly, while it is illegal to target purely civilian infrastructure, "dual use" infrastructure can be targeted. "Dual use" relates to infrastructure that serves both a civilian and a military function. For instance, roads, electricity distribution systems, and communications networks might all have this dual function, depending on the extent to which they form part of the "command and control" aspect of a state's military activities. Of course, attacks on such "targets" can also have severe effects on the lives of civilians. The "harm to the civilian population" caused by attacks on dual-use targets must therefore be weighed against the military objectives that such attacks are calculated to achieve.[16]

As this brief description reveals, international humanitarian law immerses its addressees in a world of military calculations. As General Michael Rose sums this up, "the aim of the law of war is to save life and limb by encouraging humane treatment and by preventing unnecessary suffering and destruction."[17] International humanitarian law addresses us as if we were all military strategists, for to determine when suffering and destruction is "necessary" requires adopting a strategic perspective. In this sense, international humanitarian law reinforces the aesthetic effect of modern televised forms of warfare, in which the audience is invited to occupy the position of the soldier or strategist. "Sighting the target" involves converting "the object into information as a condition of the violence directed towards it." The viewer of such images participates both "in the sighting and eliminating of the enemy target" and does so in a situation in which there is not even "the mediated sense of presence and context experienced by the soldiers viewing the same image in their cockpits and tanks."[18]

The extent to which civilian deaths are seen as legitimate in conflict situations is dependent also upon the determination of the facts of each case. In a subtle way, this also involves taking the perspective of the state in many situations of modern warfare. In international law, as in domestic law, the application of law depends upon the determination of "facts." In the case of international humanitarian law and its capacity to protect civilians, these "facts" include decisions about whether the targeting of a particular object to further a military objective may pose a risk to civilians and whether particular infrastructure is "dual use." Determination of these facts itself depends upon the information provided by intelligence services. This becomes increasingly complicated in times of "networkcentric" warfare such as that conducted in Iraq in 2003, where coalition forces relied on U.S. intelligence and surveillance systems on the battlefield.

The implications of this for the utility of international humanitarian law are illustrated by institutional responses to the criticism of the conduct of the NATO bombing campaign, Operation Allied Force, carried out against the Federal Republic of Yugoslavia from March 24 to June 10, 1999. During that seventy-eight-day campaign, NATO dropped more than twenty-five thousand bombs, killing an estimated five hundred Yugoslav civilians. These deaths resulted partly from the use of cluster bombs, attacks on targets in densely populated urban areas, attacks on mobile targets, use of depleted uranium projectiles, and the practice of dropping bombs from extremely high altitudes to avoid pilot deaths.[19] Attempts to bring the issue of whether this conduct violated international humanitarian law before international judicial forums were remarkably unsuccessful.[20] The Office of the Prosecutor at the International Criminal Tribunal for the Former Yugoslavia received "numerous requests that she investigate allegations that senior political and military figures from NATO countries committed serious violations of international humanitarian law" during the bombing campaign.[21] However, in June 2000, the chief prosecutor announced to the Security Council her decision not to initiate an investigation of the claims that NATO had engaged in serious violations of international humanitarian law in the former Yugoslavia, based upon the report of a committee she had established to review the matter.[22] Of particular interest here are the ways in which that review committee had treated the information and intelligence gathered by NATO in its evaluation of the legality of target selection. In explaining its recommendations, the committee stated:

> One of the principles underlying international humanitarian law is the principle of distinction, which obligates commanders to distinguish between military objectives and civilian persons or objects. The practical application of this principle is effectively encapsulated in Article 57 of Additional Protocol I [to the Geneva Conventions] which, in part, obligates those who plan or decide upon an attack to "do everything feasible to verify that the objectives to be attacked are neither civilians nor civilian objects." The obligation to do everything feasible is high but not absolute. A military commander must set up an effective intelligence gathering system to collect and evaluate information concerning potential targets. The commander must also direct his forces to use available technical means to properly identify targets during operations. Both the commander and the aircrew actually engaged in operations must have some range of discretion to determine which available resources shall be used and how they shall be used.[23]

The "information" produced through intelligence systems is characterized by the committee as a fact that will allow states to distinguish between "potential targets." According to the committee, having set up such an intelligence system, the military has "some range of discretion" in evaluating the "information" it gathers. The implications of this can be seen from the weight given to NATO's perception of the legitimacy of its targets and the information NATO had gathered to form that perception in the committee's determination of the legality of NATO action. The committee found that while NATO's targets included "some loosely defined categories such as military-industrial infrastructure and government ministries and some potential problem categories such as media and refineries," this targeting practice was not illegal as "NATO was attempting to attack objects it perceived to be legitimate military objectives." The committee found that NATO forces did attack, inter alia, a civilian passenger train (killing at least 10 civilians), a convoy of refugees (killing approximately 70 to 75 civilians), the Serbian Television and Radio Station (killing between 10 and 17 civilians), the Chinese Embassy (killing 3 civilians) and Korisa village (killing as many as 87 civilians, mainly refugees). Overall, 495 civilians were killed and 820 civilians wounded in documented instances. However, based upon NATO's military analysis, explanations provided by NATO officials, and the impression they gained by viewing cockpit videos from NATO planes, the committee members concluded that civilians were not deliberately targeted in these incidents and that legitimate mistakes were made by NATO in the conduct of its campaign. In addition, the committee concluded that while there was evidence that NATO forces had dropped depleted uranium and cluster bombs during their campaign, these weapons—though they make it very difficult to distinguish between civilians and combatants—were not absolutely prohibited in all situations, and their use in this case should not be further investigated.[24]

The questions prior to "Who applies the law?" must always be "Who determines the facts?" and "Who determines which facts are relevant?" Facts cannot simply be found. In domestic legal systems, the removal of ambiguity through the writing of facts and the determination of their relevance is part of the practice of judgment.[25] In the world of international humanitarian law, as the reasoning of the review committee illustrates, a great deal of deference is paid to the intelligence, and therefore the sovereign authority, of powerful states. Thus, while some protection is offered to civilians by international humanitarian law, this protection is offered within a framework in which strategic calculations about military necessity and state survival are privileged and in which facts are often determined by the intelligence of the attacking state. Having adopted this perspective, it becomes difficult to argue with the targeting expert who asserts that striking a particular target is proportional and necessary. The deaths of civilians, the ruination of cities, the destruction of livelihoods, and the pollution of the environment can ultimately be justified if these means are deemed proportional to the ends of military necessity.

Indeed, this was the conclusion that the International Court of Justice (ICJ) reached in a remarkable opinion in which the question of the legality of the killing of civilians and the primacy of state security was directly addressed—the 1996 Advisory Opinion on the *Legality of the Threat or Use of Nuclear Weapons*.[26] On

December 15, 1994, the General Assembly adopted a resolution requesting the ICJ urgently to render an advisory opinion on the question "Is the threat or use of nuclear weapons permitted under international law?"[27] In its advisory opinion, the court confirmed that international humanitarian law applies to nuclear weapons. This conclusion flowed from the "intrinsically humanitarian character of the legal principles in question…which permeates the entire law of armed conflict and applies to all forms of warfare and to all kinds of weapons, those of the past, those of the present and those of the future."[28] The court noted that the first cardinal principle contained in the texts of international humanitarian law is "aimed at the protection of the civilian population and civilian objects and establishes the distinction between combatants and non-combatants; States must never make civilians the object of attack and must consequently never use weapons that are incapable of distinguishing between civilian and military targets."[29] The court recognized the unique characteristics of nuclear weapons, including the inability to distinguish between civilian objects and military objectives in the use of those weapons, the largely uncontrollable and necessarily indiscriminate effects of their use, and the enormous number of casualties that would result from the use of such weapons.[30]

Yet while the court held that due to these characteristics, "the use of such weapons in fact seems scarcely reconcilable" with the principles of international humanitarian law, it could not "lose sight of the fundamental right of every State to survival, and thus its right to resort to self-defence…when its survival is at stake."[31] The court thus held, by seven votes to seven, with the president providing the deciding vote, that:

> while the threat or use of nuclear weapons would generally be contrary to the rules of international law applicable in armed conflict…in view of the current state of international law, and of the elements of fact at its disposal, the Court cannot conclude definitively whether the threat or use of nuclear weapons would be lawful or unlawful in an extreme circumstance of self-defence, in which the very survival of a State would be at stake.[32]

This, then, is the logical if troubling conclusion of a form of law that treats the state as its principal referent. While international lawyers may at times see themselves as the representatives of a civilized conscience or shared sensibility that transcends the state, they still rely upon the state as the vehicle through which this universal law is to find expression. The international order brought into being through international law depends upon state power. States are the authors of international law, whether as negotiators of treaties or as generators of customary practice. States are the agents of coercion, whether through collective security mechanisms or the use of force in self-defense or as countermeasures. States are the creators of courts and the implementers of international obligations domestically. Thus, international law can have nothing to say in the face of the demand made by the modern state that, in some circumstances, the state must remain free to kill and maim those who threaten its existence.

Underpinning the legal recognition of the modern state as the de facto authority in the international system is the question of why this fact has a normative value. That question is no longer addressed in most accounts of the validity of international law. It is as if positive international law, like other forms of modern law, can no longer give an account of its own authority or even "articulate the terms of its own existence."[33] It is to that question of the grounds of the authority of the modern state and modern law that I want now to turn.

## PROTECTION, SHOCK, AND AWE

So far, this essay has explored the implications of the representation of military statecraft as a rational process involving the weighing and balancing of individual life and state survival. I would like now to argue that the history of the modern state suggests grounds for questioning even this claim that reasoned calculation governs the practice of statecraft. And while the rational explanation for state violence would seem to make human beings disposable, the irrational or perhaps passionate explanation for state authority renders us even more vulnerable.

The state is often represented as the ultimate achievement or expression of rationality. Modern state theorists certainly promoted the idea that obedience to the state is a rational choice on the part of its subjects. Thomas Hobbes, for example, famously urged moderns to understand that the commonwealth represents the individual's best chance for self-preservation in a time of civil war. In his classic treatise *Leviathan*, Hobbes sought to develop a theory that would explain why it is rational to submit to an absolute political authority capable of containing the warring religious factions threatening the continued existence of the commonwealth.[34] He did so at a time in which the legitimacy of public authority had become a serious question. The wars of religion that had been waged throughout Europe had undermined appeals to a universal and shared set of values that might ground political and legal authority.[35] Appeals to the truth of competing religious beliefs and the postskeptical spirit of the new sciences were everywhere shaking the foundations of established political orders. In *Leviathan*, Hobbes therefore did not seek to ground authority upon inheritance, or conformity with custom or precedent, or a shared set of moral values, or some authentic relationship with the people. For Hobbes, the authority of the state or the commonwealth is based upon its capacity to guarantee protection. Hobbes argued that an earthly power was needed to bring into being a condition in which the laws of nature could be realized on earth. In particular, the existence of a common power or common wealth would make possible the realization of the first of these natural or divine laws—that men "seek peace and follow it"—so that the right of each man to self-preservation could be guaranteed.[36] Men covenant with each other as equals to bring into being such a commonwealth. Through that act of covenanting, the commonwealth is entrusted with sovereign power for a particular end, "the procuration of the safety of the people."[37] Individuals, according to Hobbes, should therefore harness their passion for self-preservation to the reason of the state.[38]

Something similar is being staged with the turn to protection as the basis of international authority today. The responsibility to protect concept is presented as a rational solution to the problem of creating political order in situations where such order is nonexistent or under threat. It is premised on the notion that authority, to be legitimate, must be effective. To quote former UN Secretary-General Kofi Annan, "the primary raison d'être and duty of every state is to protect its population."[39] If a state proves unable to protect its citizens, the responsibility to do so shifts to the international community. The advocates of the responsibility to protect seek to make an argument for the lawfulness of both state and international authority without reference to self-determination, popular sovereignty, or to other romantic or nationalist bases for determining who should have the power to govern in a particular territory. Rather, the legitimacy of authority is determinable by reference to the *fact* of protection.

This grounding of authority on the capacity to preserve life and protect populations rejects the more familiar claims to authority grounded on right, whether that right be understood in historical, universal, or democratic terms. By focusing upon de facto authority, the responsibility to protect concept implicitly asserts not only that an international community exists, but that its authority to govern is, at least in situations of civil war and repression, superior to that of the state. Yet for the advocates of the responsibility to protect concept, as for Hobbes, this championing of a new form of authority is not understood to be a denial of freedom. Rather, freedom is believed to be realizable only under the protection of an authority with the capacity to safeguard the well-being of the population. What matters for those advocating the responsibility to protect is the effectiveness of the techniques available to achieve protection and the maintenance of a functioning security machine. War or police action may be necessary—and thus individual lives may have to be sacrificed—in order to protect a population at risk. The population here functions as a "transcendental form of life" in the name of which mere "biological life" can reasonably be sacrificed.[40]

Yet in the seventeenth century, and again today, reason cannot fully explain the violence unleashed by the state—or the international community—in the name of protection. Again, I think Hobbes helps to show why. Hobbes argued that for the commonwealth as the protective authority to last, more is needed than an appeal to reason. For Hobbes, "there be somewhat else required (besides covenant)."[41] In order for sovereignty to be "constant and lasting," the common power must also act to keep the people in "awe" (or perhaps in "shock and awe").[42] A "visible power to keep them in awe" is necessary to ensure the performance of the covenants that found the commonwealth. Covenants might be binding, but "covenants, without the sword, are but words."[43] Fear and violence therefore have a complicated position in the theory of Hobbes. On the one hand, fear is the rational basis for submission to the Leviathan. Fear is a response to what Hobbes portrays as objective threats, such as the need to defend against attacks by other subjects or the violence of an invading power. On the other hand, fear is potentially as "artificial" as the sovereign, in that the sovereign must perform as the visible power that keeps the people in awe if their agreement (and thus the commonwealth that it generates) is to last. Thus, while Hobbes sought to persuade his readers that sovereign power is not the result of "sacral authority," but rather comes about "as a consequence of the rational acts of will of the people," he nonetheless suggested that "the sovereign should not be demystified altogether."[44]

It is in this sense that the modern state is the inheritor of the religious foundations of European law and authority.[45] In early modern Europe, no state could have commanded the unquestioned obedience that states take for granted today.[46] That kind of obedience, to the extent that it was owed, was owed to God. By the eighteenth century, Europe had witnessed the shift of authority from God and his worldly representatives to the state. Thus, Kant could argue in 1797 that we should act as if certain things were true if to do so would help to move us toward the civil state and that one of the things we should treat as if true is that "all authority comes from God."[47] Kant was very clear that the citizen owes total obedience to authority in the form of the state. The supreme power is constituted in order to secure "the rightful state, especially against external enemies of the people." "The aim is not, as it were, to make the people happy against its will, but only to ensure its continued existence as a commonwealth."[48] It follows from this counter-revolutionary reasoning that "all resistance against the supreme legislative power, all incitement of the subjects to violent expressions of discontent, all defiance which breaks out into rebellion, is the greatest and most punishable crime in a commonwealth, for it destroys its very foundations."[49] There can "be no rightful resistance on the part of the people," because "a state of right becomes possible only through submission" to the "universal general will."[50] Not long afterward, Hegel would assert that "man must…venerate the state as a secular deity."[51]

As the state became identified with the task of preserving the common wealth and thus realizing the laws of nature in this world, the violence of the state was in turn sanctified. According to Hobbes, "The office of the sovereign (be it a monarch or an assembly) consisteth in the end, for which he was trusted with the sovereign power, namely the procuration of the safety of the people, to which he is obliged by the law of nature."[52]

It was that sense of protection as "procuration of the safety of the people" that would translate into the broader jurisprudence of security and policing in the late seventeenth and eighteenth centuries in Europe and into the representation of war as a political instrument for realizing the will of the people in the nineteenth century.[53] War and policing would come to be understood as means for realizing the safety of the people. While this was perhaps already of concern in the Europe of Kant and Hegel, by the twentieth century, the violence of the modern state—with its concentration camps, its firebombs, its napalm, and its Hiroshimas—would come to exceed not only rational justification, but also rational comprehension.

Something similar is happening with the tendency to sanctify the violence inflicted by the representatives of the international community during humanitarian war. Much of the prohumanitarian intervention literature has tended to treat the international community as the benevolent representative of humanitarian universalism and has argued that its authority to protect those at risk in exceptional situations should not be limited by law. This tendency is perhaps best illustrated by the decision of the European Court of Human Rights in the cases of *Behrami and Behrami v. France* and *Saramati v. France, Germany and Norway*.[54] The Grand Chamber of the court there declared inadmissible two cases in which applicants sought to hold European states accountable for the acts of their military personnel participating in the "international security force" or the international "civil administration" created under the auspices of the UN in Kosovo.

The applicants in the *Behrami and Behrami* case were Agim Behrami (applying on behalf of both himself and his deceased son Gadaf) and his son Bekir Behrami, both of whom lived in the municipality of Mitrovica, Kosovo. In March 2000, Mitrovica was in the sector of Kosovo for which a brigade led by France as part of the international security force (KFOR) in Kosovo was responsible. On March 11, 2000, a group of boys, including Gadaf and Bekir Behrami, came across a number of undetonated cluster bombs while playing in the hills. The bombs had been dropped as part of the NATO bombardment of the area in 1999, and KFOR knew of their presence on the site. The children began playing with the bombs, one of which detonated, killing Gadaf and seriously injuring Bekir. The applicants alleged that the death of Gadaf and injury of Bekir violated Article 2 (the right to life) of the European Convention on Human Rights, because they were caused by the failure of the French KFOR troops to mark or defuse the undetonated bombs. The applicant in the *Saramati* case was Ruzhdi Saramati, who complained that his detention by and under the orders of KFOR between July 13, 2001, and January 26, 2002, violated his right to liberty and security (Article 5) and his right to an effective remedy (Article 13), that his lack of access to a court violated his right to a fair trial (Article 6), and more broadly, that France, Germany, and Norway had failed to guarantee the convention rights of individuals living in Kosovo, in violation of their obligation under Article 1 to secure to everyone within their jurisdiction the rights and freedoms defined in the convention.

In dismissing these cases against states involved in the Kosovo intervention, the court found that it was not competent to review the acts of respondent states carried out on behalf of the UN.[55] It held that operations established by Security Council resolutions, such as that conducted in Kosovo, are "fundamental to the mission of the UN to secure international peace and security."[56] To subject the actions carried out under UN authority to "the scrutiny of the Court" would "interfere with the fulfillment of the UN's key mission in this field including, as argued by certain parties, with the effective conduct of its operations."[57] The actions undertaken by the member states were "directly attributable to the UN, an organization of universal jurisdiction fulfilling its imperative collective security objective."[58]

The court thus identified the UN, and the states and personnel acting under its authority, with the universal. The representatives of universalism should not be asked to take responsibility for the effects of their actions, whether that be the failure to remove unexploded cluster bombs dropped by NATO, resulting in the death and disfigurement of a number of children (the *Behrami* case) or the detention of an individual for eighteen months without trial (the *Saramati* case). Those acting under the authority of the UN represent human rights and the rule of law merely by their presence. In the words of the Danish submission to the court: "States put personnel at the disposal of the UN in Kosovo to pursue the purposes and principles of the UN Charter. A finding of 'no jurisdiction' would not leave the applicants in a human rights' vacuum...given the steps being taken by those international presences to promote human rights' protection."[59]

In this vision, state officials controlled territory and detained individuals not as invaders or occupiers, but as agents of a broader universalism that transcends any particular political order. This focus on that which transcends the imperfections of the present order is illustrated well by the response of Jürgen Habermas to the Kosovo intervention. Habermas endorsed NATO's action on the basis that it was understood by Continental European states "as an 'anticipation' of an effective law of world citizenship—as a step along the path from classical international law to what Kant envisioned as the 'status of world citizen' which would afford legal protection to citizens against their own criminal regimes."[60] The proper measurement of humanitarian action was seen in terms of the extent to which it represented a further step along that path to the coming cosmopolitan order. It becomes difficult to envisage the proper limits to the use of force in the name of goals such as saving humanity, eradicating evil, or bringing into being a cosmopolitan order that would protect citizens against "their own criminal regimes." What sacrifice could be disproportionate to such ends?

## LIFE AND CRITIQUE

What, then, should a critical engagement with military statecraft entail? Do we moderns need to seek a more perfect calibration, a more precise balancing of the costs and benefits involved in warfare? International humanitarian law is in part a call to do just that—to calculate, to evaluate risk, and to measure the suffering that is justified to defend the state. Should we try to respond to this call by entering more fully into the world of "impossible calculations," of "secret debts," of "the charges on the suffering of others"?[61] Should we take part in the ongoing task of differentiating lives to be saved, lives to be risked, and lives to be sacrificed? Should we consider it "moral progress that such a calculation is even possible"—that individual lives count enough that counting deaths seems necessary?[62] If so, the refusal of the ICJ to engage in the political task of weighing the costs and balances of warfare is to be condemned as an abdication of the office of the judge as representative of sovereign authority.

Or should we instead refuse the call to make the suffering inflicted by modern wars, including humanitarian wars, comprehensible? This was the position taken by Martti Koskenniemi in response to the advisory opinion of the ICJ in the nuclear weapons case. According to Koskenniemi, the "silence" of the court was "a wholly appropriate response to the issues at stake." The court's silence was to be welcomed as enabling the voice of justice to be heard: "The Court felt both the law and its own authority to be insufficient for determining the status of the massive killing of the innocent."[63] In one sense, the court simply declared its *inability* to make this calculation, declaring that it could not "conclude definitively whether the threat or use of nuclear weapons would be lawful or unlawful in an extreme circumstance of self-defence, in which the very survival of a State would be at stake." The law, and indeed language itself, can seem inadequate to grasp the reality of nuclear weapons and the destruction that they represent. An American brigadier general who witnessed the first atomic bomb test from a bunker at

Alamogordo commented: "Words are inadequate tools.... It had to be witnessed to be realized."[64] The figure of the civilian who is touched by war, killed or injured during armed conflict or nuclear attack, thus stands at the limits both of language and of modern law. As the international lawyer Hersch Lauterpacht once wrote: "If international law is, in some ways, at the vanishing point of law, the law of war is, perhaps even more conspicuously, at the vanishing point of international law."[65]

But we might take the court to be making a stronger point — that we *should* not look to law or defer to authority to determine the meaning of such violence. To illustrate this last point, I'd like to turn to an incident that accompanied the appearance by U.S. Secretary of State Colin Powell before the Security Council on February 5, 2003.[66] Powell's appearance before the Security Council was designed to explain why the United States could not "risk" leaving Saddam Hussein "in possession of weapons of mass destruction."[67] As Maureen Dowd reported in the *New York Times*, in anticipation of the post-presentation press conference, the UN threw a blue cover over the tapestry reproduction of Picasso's *Guernica* on display at the entrance to the Security Council and then placed the flags of the Security Council in front of that cover.[68] This double veiling served to hide Picasso's famous antiwar image from the television cameras and thus from the global audience that would also judge the adequacy of Powell's information.[69] Why did it become untenable at that moment for the representative of the United States to stand before that backdrop and explain the reasons for bombing the territory and people of Iraq? Perhaps this was simply because, as Dowd commented, "Mr. Powell can't very well seduce the world into bombing Iraq surrounded on camera by shrieking and mutilated women, men, children, bulls and horses."[70] But perhaps it was also because the reproduction of *Guernica* would have served as a reminder that the horror of war lies in its return to the scene that was there veiled.

*Guernica* makes visible the excessive nature of the violence that founds authority. At the moment of constitution of a legal order, that founding violence is neither legal nor illegal. The legitimacy of the law and of authority is established only once that violence has succeeded in creating a new order, and even then only provisionally. Thus, while the legitimacy of the law is in a sense guaranteed by the state, this is always subject to being unsettled. This is perhaps evidenced most clearly in cases of revolution. If a rebellion against an existing government succeeds, the violence of the rebels takes on the legitimacy of the state it founded — if the rebellion fails in founding a new form of the state, the use of force will not receive official legitimation. It is precisely such a potential "founding or revolutionary moment," a moment "before the law,"[71] that *Guernica* portrays. The ambivalence about the meaning of such revolutionary violence for Spain was central to the reception of *Guernica* at its first public display at the Spanish Pavilion of the Paris World's Fair of 1937. The "terror bombing" earlier that year of the town of Guernica, from which the painting took its name, was itself part of the ongoing Spanish Civil War.[72] The bombing of Guernica was an event the meaning of which was still open at the time of the World's Fair. It could only be given a settled meaning as legal or illegal once the revolutionary violence had ended. *Guernica* is thus troubling in part because it freezes time at the moment when the violence that may yet found a new law is not yet "buried, dissimulated, repressed."[73] While *Guernica* circulates as a symbol of democracy and a critique of fascist violence, and while Picasso came down firmly on the side of the Republican government in the Civil War, the painting also retains a sense of the ambiguity inherent in the use of force. As John Berger comments, "there are no enemies to accuse" in the painting.[74] For him, the protest "is in what has happened to the bodies." Thus, *Guernica* stands as a reminder of this "silence walled up in the violent structure of the founding act."[75]

In addition, *Guernica* memorializes an event in the history of warfare that may mark the limit of modern law's capacity to authorize force and to bury the dead. The bombing of the Basque town of Guernica by German planes and pilots flying for General Francisco Franco was the first time that aerial bombardment had been carried out against civilians in Europe. A sense of the horrors of the new form of warfare is clear in the news reports of the event.[76] *Guernica* gives form to the idea of the apocalypse unleashed by such violence through the haunting series of its suffering victims.[77] In so doing, it makes visible the possibility that the capacity of law or the state to secrete this violence in its foundation may be exceeded by the new capacity to cause unprecedented levels of destruction.

Finally, *Guernica* points to that which exceeds the law and which even the law guaranteed by the sovereign cannot contain. For many contemporary viewers of the painting, it was a reminder of mortality. The surrealist poet Michel Leiris saw in the painting a death notice and a farewell: "In the black-and-white rectangle of ancient tragedy, Picasso sends us our death notice: everything we love is going to die, and that is why right now it is important that everything we love be summed up into something unforgettably beautiful, like the shedding of so many tears of farewell."[78] *Guernica* is a reminder that at the foundation of modern state law is the memory of a violence that cannot in the end be authorized—as the poet José Bergamín wrote of his response to the painting in Picasso's studio: "This shockingly naked thing haunts us with the disturbing question of its anxiety."[79]

Each of these themes resonates with contemporary warfare and made it impossible for the reproduction of *Guernica* to be displayed on February 5, 2003. The United States, through its secretary of state, was attempting to perform as a legitimate sovereign before both the Security Council and the mass audience of the subsequent televised news conference. This performance was designed to represent the United States as sovereign, not only over the territory called "the United States of America," but also over the world as a whole. The United States was staged as the sovereign that guaranteed the international law that it sought to bring into being at that performance. This was a version of the law in its own image, an international law that could authorize the violence the United States was soon to bring to bear upon the territory and people of Iraq.

Perhaps, then, as the veiling of *Guernica* suggests, we might better maintain a protest about "what has happened to the bodies" by refusing to give the devastation of war a pattern that is comprehensible or a meaning that is familiar. This was the argument that Koskenniemi was making when he endorsed the silence of the ICJ in the *Nuclear Weapons* case. Koskenniemi argued that we should not look to "technical rules" or defer to "professional authority" to determine "the meaning of the massive killing of the innocent." Rather, he argued, "we need to be able to say that we know that the killing of the innocent is wrong not because of what chains of reasoning we can produce to support it, but because of who we are."[80] On this reading, it is better to *refuse* the invitation made by state militaries and international law—to refuse, in other words, to become part of a system that weighs things that are presented as substitutable one for the other—these human lives, those wounded bodies, that sovereign state. Perhaps, after all, we should welcome the inability of humanitarian law ever successfully to bury the dead.

## CONCLUSION

In contemporary discussions of war and terrorism, passion and reason are often presented as opposites. "Passion" is the term used to describe the investment of religious militants in the beliefs that drive their resort to violence in defense of a faith and a form of life. "Reason," in contrast, is the term used to describe the calculations of statesmen and professional military leaders in defense of national security or in pursuit of military objectives. In this essay, I have suggested that the reason of military statecraft is itself the expression of a passionate attachment to a form of life. As Hobbes showed so clearly, the passion for self-preservation can be translated into the reason of state through the constitution of a common power. Sovereign authority in this tradition is responsible both for preserving life and for protecting the population, both for defending the people against its enemies and for keeping the people in awe. We might understand these disparate tasks of authority in the terms suggested by Michel Foucault—as the power to take life and to make live.[81] Yet the desire to protect the commonwealth or community thus constituted can itself prove a threat, both to the survival of the community and to the life of its members. How, then, might the limits and the ends of protection best be conceived?

Questions about the proper limits and ends of protective authority are raised today by the conduct of the war on terror, the embrace of the responsibility to protect at the UN, the integration of development and security in the work of international and nongovernmental institutions, and the practices of state building and international administration. The projects of international humanitarianism are motivated by the desire to preserve life and overcome suffering, even at the cost of taking life and inflicting suffering. The doctrines of responsibility and of protection that accompany these projects explain that those exercising power, whether as representatives of states or of the international community, are in fact guaranteeing the freedom of those they control, manage, kill, and wound. In light of those developments and at a time when the conflict in Darfur can be described as "the passion of the present," it seems useful to reconsider the theological foundations of the state-making project.[82] The jurisprudence of protection that emerged out of the seventeenth-century wars of religion may still have something to offer for thinking about the proper limits of worldly authority. As that jurisprudence suggests, the representation of power in terms of an office or responsibility to protect involves not only legitimizing new forms of authority, but also marking out the proper limits to the interests of such authorities in the lives (and deaths) of their subjects. It is those questions of the limits and ends of protective authority that international humanitarianism has yet to address.

## NOTES

1   Rey Chow, *The Age of the World Target: Self-Referentiality in War, Theory, and Comparative Work* (Durham, NC: Duke University Press, 2006).

2   See http://passionofthepresent.org and http://www.savedarfur.org (both last accessed July 27, 2009).

3   Philippe Sands, *Torture Team: Deception, Cruelty and the Compromise of Law* (London: Allen Lane, 2008).

4   *Ibid.*; Scott Horton, "'Military Necessity, Torture, and the Criminality of Lawyers," in Wolfgang Kaleck, Michael Ratner, Tobias Singelnstein, and Peter Weiss (eds.), *International Prosecution of Human Rights Crimes* (Berlin: Springer, 2007), p. 183.

5   Sands, *Torture Team*, p. 62.

6   International Commission on Intervention and Sovereignty, *The Responsibility to Protect* (Ottawa: International Development Research Centre, 2001), available on-line at http://www.iciss.ca/pdf/Commission-Report.pdf (last accessed July 14, 2009).

7   Gareth Evans, "From Humanitarian Intervention to the Responsibility to Protect" *Wisconsin International Law Journal* 24, no. 3 (2006): p. 120.

8   International Commission on Intervention and Sovereignty, *The Responsibility to Protect*, p. 11.

9   UN 2005 World Summit, September 14–16, 2005, *2005 World Summit Outcome*, paras. 138–39, UN doc. no. A/60/L.1 (September 15, 2005), available on-line at http://www.unep.org/greenroom/documents/outcome.pdf (last accessed July 14, 2009).

10  Talal Asad, *Formations of the Secular: Christianity, Islam, Modernity* (Stanford, CA: Stanford University Press, 2003), pp. 100–103.

11  *Ibid.*, p. 113.

12  *Ibid.*, pp. 116–17.

13  Elaine Scarry, *The Body in Pain: The Making and Unmaking of the World* (Oxford: Oxford University Press, 1985), p. 61.

14  See A.P.V. Rogers, *Law on the Battlefield*, 2nd ed. (Manchester: Manchester University Press, 2004).

15  See W.J. Fenrick, "Targeting and Proportionality during the NATO Bombing Campaign against Yugoslavia," *European Journal of International Law* 12 (2001): pp. 489–502.

16  Human Rights Watch, *International Humanitarian Law Issues in a Potential War in Iraq*, Human Rights Watch Briefing Paper, February 20, 2003, available on-line at http://www.hrw.org/backgrounder/arms/iraq0202003.htm#5 (last accessed July 14, 2009).

17  General Sir Michael Rose, "Foreword to the First Edition," in A.P.V. Rogers, *Law on the Battlefield*, p. xiv.

18  Michael P. Clark, "The Work of War after the Age of Mechanical Reproduction," in Michael Bibby (ed.), *The Vietnam War and Postmodernity* (Amherst: University of Massachusetts Press, 2000), p. 28.

19  Human Rights Watch, *Civilian Deaths in the NATO Air Campaign* (2000), available on-line at http://www.hrw.org/sites/default/files/reports/natbm002.pdf (last accessed July 14, 2009).

20  See Anne Orford, *Reading Humanitarian Intervention: Human Rights and the Use of Force in International Law* (Cambridge: Cambridge University Press, 2003), pp. 192–94.

21  *Final Report to the Prosecutor by the Committee Established to Review the NATO Bombing Campaign against the Federal Republic of Yugoslavia*, para. 1, available on-line at http://www.icty.org/x/file/About/OTP/otp_report_nato_bombing_en.pdf (last accessed October 14, 2009).

22  *Ibid.*, para. 91, recommendation by the committee "that no investigation be commenced by the OTP [Office of the Prosecutor] in relation to the NATO bombing campaign or incidents occurring during the campaign."

23  *Ibid.*, para. 29.

24  *Ibid.*, paras. 26 and 27.

25  Nina Philadelphoff-Puren and Peter Rush, "Fatal (F)laws: Law, Literature and Writing," *Law and Critique* 14 (2003): p. 201.

26  *Legality of the Threat and Use of Nuclear Weapons*, Advisory Opinion, ICJ Reports, 1996, p. 26, available on-line at http://www.icj-cij.org/docket/files/95/7495.pdf?PHPSESSID=bc7ab6f43c06f38be1bc72bf10e43489 (last accessed July 14, 2009).

27  *Ibid.*, para. 1.

28  *Ibid.*, paras. 85 and 86.

29  *Ibid.*, para. 78.

30  *Ibid.*, para. 92.

31 *Ibid.*, paras. 95–96.

32 *Ibid.*, para. 105.

33 Shaunnagh Dorsett and Shaun McVeigh, "Questions of Jurisdiction," in Shaun McVeigh (ed.), *Jurisprudence of Jurisdiction* (New York: Routledge-Cavendish, 2007), p. 3.

34 Thomas Hobbes, *Leviathan*, ed. J.C.A. Gaskin (Oxford: Oxford University Press, 1996).

35 Richard Tuck, "The 'Modern' Theory of Natural Law," in Anthony Pagden (ed.), *The Languages of Political Theory in Early-Modern Europe* (Cambridge: Cambridge University Press, 1987), p. 118.

36 Hobbes, *Leviathan*, p. 87.

37 *Ibid.*, p. 222.

38 Daniela Coli, "Hobbes's Revolution," in Victoria Kahn, Neil Saccamano, and Daniela Coli (eds.), *Politics and the Passions, 1500–1850* (Princeton, NJ: Princeton University Press, 2006), p. 75.

39 UN Secretary-General Kofi Annan, *In Larger Freedom: Towards Development, Security and Human Rights for All*, para. 135, UN doc no. A/59/2005 (March 21, 2005), available on-line at http://www.un.org/largerfreedom/report-largerfreedom.pdf (last accessed July 14, 2009).

40 On this conception of the relation between a transcendental form of life and biological life, see Timothy Campbell, "*Bios*, Immunity, Life: The Thought of Roberto Esposito," in Roberto Esposito, *Bios: Biopolitics and Philosophy*, trans. Timothy Campbell (Minneapolis: University of Minnesota Press, 2008), pp. vii and xv.

41 Hobbes, *Leviathan*, p. 113.

42 *Ibid.*, pp. 113–14. The U.S. military doctrine of "shock and awe" or "rapid dominance" was developed by Harlan Ullman and James Wade in 1996, and officials in the U.S. armed forces used the language of "shock and awe" to describe their strategy in invading Iraq. See further Harlan K. Ullman and James P. Wade, *Shock and Awe: Achieving Rapid Dominance* (Washington, D.C.: Center for Advanced Concepts and Technology, 1996), pp. xxiv: "The aim of Rapid Dominance is to affect the will, perception, and understanding of the adversary to fit or respond to our strategic policy ends through imposing a regime of Shock and Awe."

43 Hobbes, *Leviathan*, p. 111.

44 Noel Malcolm, *Aspects of Hobbes* (Oxford: Clarendon Press, 2002), p. 228.

45 See Anne Orford, "International Law and the Making of the Modern State: Reflections on a Protestant Project," *In-Spire: Journal of Law, Politics and Societies* 3, no. 1 (2008): pp. 5–11, available on-line at http://www.in-spire.org/archive/vol3-no1/a021072008_international_law.pdf (last accessed July 14, 2009).

46 See Gaines Post, *Studies in Medieval Legal Thought: Public Law and the State, 1100–1322* (Princeton, NJ: Princeton University Press, 1964), p. 569, where he comments that nowhere could the medieval state or royal government "exact that obedience of subjects which is generally obtained by the State in the twentieth century."

47 Immanuel Kant, "The Metaphysics of Morals," in H.S. Reiss (ed.), *Kant: Political Writings*, (Cambridge: Cambridge University Press, 1991) p. 143.

48 Immanuel Kant, "On the Common Saying: 'This May Be True in Theory, But It Does Not Apply in Practice,'" in Reiss (ed), *Kant*, p. 80.

49 *Ibid.*, p. 81.

50 Kant, "The Metaphysics of Morals," p. 144.

51 G.F.W. Hegel, *Hegel's Philosophy of Right*, trans. T.M. Knox (Oxford: Oxford University Press, 1952), p. 285.

52 Hobbes, *Leviathan*, p. 222.

53 See Adam Smith and Edwin Cannan, *Lectures on Justice, Police, Revenue and Arms* (Oxford: Clarendon Press, 1896); Michel Foucault, *Security, Territory, Population: Lectures at the Collège de France 1977–1978*, ed. Michel Senellart, trans. Graham Burchell (New York: Palgrave Mac-Millan, 2007); Carl von Clausewitz, *On War*, trans. Michael Howard and Peter Paret (Princeton, NJ: Princeton University Press, 1976).

54 *Behrami and Behrami v. France*, App. No. 71412/01, *Saramati v. France, Germany, and Norway*, App. No. 78166/01, European Court of Human Rights Grand Chamber, Decision on Admissibility (May 31, 2007).

55 *Ibid.*, para. 146.

56 *Ibid.*, para. 149.

57 *Ibid.*, para. 43.

58 *Ibid.*, para. 151.

59 *Ibid.*, para. 100.

60 Jürgen Habermas, *America and the World*, interview with Eduardo Mendieta, trans. Jeffrey Craig Miller, *LOGOS* 3.3 (Summer 2004), available on-line at http://www.logosjournal.com/issue_3.3/habermas_interview.htm (last accessed July 15, 2009).

61 Jacques Derrida, *The Post Card: From Socrates to Freud and Beyond*, trans. Alan Bass (Chicago: The University of Chicago Press, 1987), p. 56.

62 Didier Fassin, "Humanitarianism as a Politics of Life," *Public Culture* 19, no. 3 (2007): p. 513.

63 Martti Koskenniemi, "'The Silence of Law/The Voice of Justice," in Laurence Boisson de Chazournes and Philippe Sands (eds.), *International Law, the International Court of Justice and Nuclear Weapons* (Cambridge: Cambridge University Press, 1999), p. 488 at pp. 508–509.

64 Brigadier General Thomas F. Farrell, quoted in John Whittier Treat, *Writing Ground Zero: Japanese Literature and the Atomic Bomb* (Chicago: University of Chicago Press, 1995), p. x.

65 Hersch Lauterpacht, "The Problem of the Revision of the Law of War," *British Year Book of International Law* (1952), p. 382.

66 For a more detailed discussion of this incident, see Anne Orford, "The Destiny of International Law," *Leiden Journal of International Law* 17, no. 3 (2004): p. 476.

67 Secretary Colin L. Powell, "Remarks to the United Nations Security Council, February 5, 2003," available on-line at http://www.informationclearinghouse.info/article3710.htm.

68 Maureen Dowd, "Powell without Picasso," *New York Times*, February 5, 2003, p. A27.

69 On the "double veils of cloth and flags," see Miriam Hansen, "Why Media Aesthetics?" *Critical Inquiry* 30, no. 2 (2004): p. 392.

70 Dowd, "Powell without Picasso."

71 Jacques Derrida, "Force of Law: The 'Mystical Foundation of Authority,'" *Cardozo Law Review* 11, nos. 5–6 (July–August 1990): p. 921 at pp. 991–93.

72 The phrase "terror bombing" is taken from Herschel B Chipp, *Picasso's Guernica: History, Transformations, Meanings* (Berkeley: University of California Press, 1988), p. 156.

73 Derrida, "Force of Law," p. 963.

74 John Berger, "'Success and Failure of Picasso," in Ellen C. Oppler (ed.), *Picasso's Guernica* (New York: W. W. Norton, 1988), pp. 267 and 271.

75 Derrida, "Force of Law," p. 943.

76 See, particularly, George L. Steer, "The Tragedy of Guernica: Town Destroyed in Air Attack," *The Times*, April 28, 1937, reprinted in Oppler (ed.), *Picasso's Guernica*, pp. 160 and 161: "In the

form of its execution and the scale of the destruction wrought, no less than in the selection of its objective, the raid on Guernica is unparalleled in military history."

77  On the figure of the fallen warrior as a reference to the eleventh-century manuscript the *Apocalypse of Saint-Sever*, see Ellen C. Oppler, "'Introductory Essay," in Oppler (ed.), *Picasso's Guernica*, pp. 45 and 92.

78  Michel Leiris, "Faire-part," in Oppler (ed.), *Picasso's Guernica*, p. 210.

79  José Bergamín, "Naked Poetic Truth," in Oppler (ed.), *Picasso's Guernica*, pp. 201 and 202.

80  Koskenniemi, "'The Silence of Law/The Voice of Justice," pp. 508 and 510.

81  Michel Foucault, *Society Must Be Defended: Lectures at the Collège de France, 1975–76*, ed. Mauro Bertani and Alessandro Fontana, trans David Macey (New York: Picador, 2003), pp. 246–47.

82  On the relationship of the theological concepts of sin, salvation, and redemption to the internationalist projects of development and state making, see Jennifer Beard, *The Political Economy of Desire: International Law, Development and the Nation State* (New York: Routledge-Cavendish, 2007).

# Experts, Reporters, Witnesses: The Making of Anthropologists in States of Emergency

George E. Marcus

As a longtime supervisor of graduate projects of ethnographic research during a period that spans a seismic shift, since the 1980s, in the character of the conditions, topics, and commitments of anthropology's signature method,[1] I have become increasingly interested in how anthropologists are "made" nowadays as they are sent off to do their first fieldwork, often in troubled lands that are in "states of emergency." Regardless of how careers are developed later, ethnographers in the making are still obliged to produce "basic research" answerable to the academy and its disciplines that credential and confer the status of expertise. This requirement entails some performance of disinterest, objectivity, and distance in the scholarly pursuit of distinctively anthropological knowledge.

Yet ethnography of this character in a strictly disciplinary context is increasingly difficult to conduct and to justify, since the traditional frameworks of anthropological analysis (ending perhaps with Claude Lévi-Strauss in France, Clifford Geertz in the United States, Edmund Leach, and Raymond Firth in Britain) have been largely shelved, and the relative stabilizing conditions of colonial, postcolonial, and Cold War political orders are long gone. Many of the regions of the globe where anthropologists have traditionally worked are now places overtaken by extreme forms of social and political disorder—epidemics, ethnic violence, the dissolution of state apparatuses—necessitating the intervention of supranational forms of aid and authority. Anthropologists, of course, were never oblivious to the social disorder within the order of colonial regimes, but even those who attended to critique (Georges Balandier in France, Max Gluckman in Britain) did so from the canonical concepts and topics of the discipline. This grounding in disciplinary topics is no longer possible, and there arose a general sense of this among U.S. anthropologists, among others, at least by the early 1990s, registered in the first years of the journal *Cultural Anthropology*, as I discuss in a later section.

This essay explores the predicament of the producer of anthropological knowledge "as usual" in contemporary regimes of multilateral intervention, especially with the anthropologist in the making and first fieldwork in mind. A journeyman anthropologist is relatively free to reinvent herself, as researcher, regarding the pace, engagements, and self-fashioning of scholarship, even as activism. The apprentice anthropologist in pursuit of the qualifying dissertation is more constricted and must satisfy disciplinary traditions and the demands of academic authority even as she explores new topics with a mentality of activism and engagement.

What social (rather than required academic) identity does such an anthropologist create for herself? What is the self-claimed rhetoric of authority for research undertaken in situations where the places and scenes of fieldwork are defined by regimes of intervention? In what follows, I survey three alternatives—the consulting expert, the reporter, and the witness—and focus upon the third, since it has increasingly become an expressed self-identity or ideology of anthropological research within such scenes of intervention.[2] I argue that witnessing offers a return to a surrogate position for classic scholarly distance following the binds of postcolonial critiques, which make the presence of independent anthropologists ideologically possible, but conceptually problematic amid projects of interventionist aid, rescue, and military action.

I prepared this essay for the conference evoked in the introduction. This was an extraordinary event, going beyond the academic functions of most conferences in that, in my view, it performed or enacted in its very structure and process key tensions in the terrains of life to which the conference was devoted. The most interesting personal observation that I took away from this event concerned the mutual respect, but almost complete lack of engagement, existing between those participants who were concerned, critically and not, with the management of international regimes of "mobile sovereignty" (to use Mariella Pandolfi's phrase)[3] as they respond to states of emergency (lawyers, diplomats, those with experience in international organizations, political scientists) and those who spoke first-hand of situations on the ground (anthropologists, NGO workers, refugees), primarily relating stories of people caught in traumatic conditions of life. As one partial to the latters' contributions, I was intrigued by the mediating role that anthropology might have been able to play—but did not—between these two levels of discourse by interacting with aid workers, refugees, and so on in the role and ethos of fieldwork while also participating within the culture and discourse of international managerialism—the perhaps passionate, yet rather detached policy concerns of experts. In such a dual, mediating role, a precise identity and authority for the anthropologist would have been crucial. The fact that the anthropologist was a more ambiguous figure, tending to be placed more among the people, locals, and deliverers of aid, rather than among the policy elite, in this conference context, at least, made me reflect even more keenly on the predicament of the uncertain identities of anthropologists during their own research in regimes of intervention, which is the focus of this essay.

For reasons that I discuss, for the anthropologist to be recognized either as an expert (in the service of one of the intervening agencies) or as a mere reporter (having no public for one's reporting, like the actual media does) is unsatisfactory. Yet, the identity of the anthropologist as one in pursuit of independent and self-interested knowledge on the scene of traumatic events is out of place and well nigh unacceptable. How, then, to create the identity of independent, concerned scholarship in its own name and disciplinary tradition in these settings, one that might nonetheless enable the production of a form of knowledge or expression with standing and that might play in between the discourses of the removed bureaucratic managers of mobile sovereignties and those on the scene of intervention, concerned above all with what happens to the people(s) in turmoil? My concern in this essay is with this problem for the anthropologist and with the emergence of the identity of the witness to events — a development that I find both fascinating and worrying.

## SCENES OF INTERVENTION AS SCENES OF FIELDWORK

Intervention, broadly conceived (for example, as encompassing the eras of European colonialism), has been the norm in most regions of fieldwork since the inception of anthropology and has even made anthropology possible in the areas where it has thrived. This evokes the well-rehearsed critique of anthropology in relation to the conditions of European colonialism, also extended into the era of the Cold War: for example, that a Pax Britannica or a Pax Americana over a variety of lands facilitated the most mundane anthropology.[4] But here I am interested specifically in the post–Cold War era that has emerged, which began to take shape in the 1990s and of which anthropologists began to be aware at the time insofar as it affected their work. The setting I have in mind is the failed or weakened state, the breakdown of civil society, and the entrance of international multilateral authorities with various actors on the scene — the UN, NATO, the United States as peacekeepers, humanitarian and other aid organizations, various kinds of NGOs, local political parties, social movements, armed factions, and so on. This is the unmasked regime of intervention "as usual" that has caused the most profound rethinking of the post–Cold War world and the role of the big powers, especially the United States, in it. It has led most recently to macronarrative commentaries and *longue durée* assessments in academia, the media, and policy circles about the concept of empire.

One problem that this poses for anthropology and other disciplines of critical social inquiry that wish to locate themselves in the present, or at least the contemporary, is the utter unreliability or instability of these current macronarrative discussions to serve as framing contexts for the microfocused work of ethnography and fieldwork research. To be effetive, critical anthropology, with its eye on conditions of local social change has always situated itself in the frame of one or another well-developed metanarrative not of its own making in order to give a context of relevance or significance to what was happening in the scene of fieldwork. For example, varieties of Marxist theory, or theories of markets and economic development, were available (Immanuel Wallerstein's world-system theory was the summation of these varieties, I believe), relatively stable in their intellectual production and authoritative so as to yield a perspective for anthropology written in and on the contemporary. They gave the illusion that there might be outside vantage points—intellectual, scholastic platforms—from which to render critical assessments. While such macronarratives are still being created— to wit, the current discussions that are trying to come up with an understanding of empire now,[5] they certainly do not provide the contextualizing terra firma by which anthropologists can establish perspective and context for their ethnography. Without such an intellectual rampart from which to view the events of the world critically, the sense is having to operate, at all levels of articulation of one's scholarship, within the regime of intervention itself, to be complicit with it, to participate within it, even in order to develop a critique of it. The problem is that there are no current models or norms for developing radically immanent critiques, a task that anthropology is facing. For anthropologists, and I suppose for other sorts of scholars, this reflexive distress of how they might situate themselves in relation to objects of study becomes a key problem in rethinking their identities as working scholars involved in the landscapes of the regimes of intervention.

I think the predicament of anthropology is particularly interesting in this search for a mode of delivering critiques without an outside, so to speak. In this time of unusual uncertainty and endlessly speculative representations about the "big picture" and what the emergence of regimes of intervention means for metanarratives of order, it is particularly interesting to look at the identity of a discipline such as anthropology, which has been invested in places all along—or at least for a long time—that are now scenes of intervention, and to ask how it conceives of itself as being able to continue to work in such places now.

While it has been unfashionable for quite some time to characterize the production of anthropological knowledge as disinterested, especially in the context of what is left of its old-style positivist and professional aspirations as a social science, I want to argue that in the predicament of an identity for anthropology that arises when the scene of fieldwork becomes dominated by a contemporary regime of intervention, it is precisely some form or concept of disinterestedness for anthropological presence and its research process that needs to be reintroduced—or at least rethought. But what kind or sense of disinterestedness, if not the old positivist pose and claim to authority, and to what advantage or rationale, and at what cost or implication for the standing (ethical and otherwise) of anthropology in the current world "order" of intervention as usual?[6]

In their institutional face, when anthropologists report to the academy these days, they often appear in venues such as the multidisciplinary conference that occasioned this essay. And in such venues, the critique or defense of the management of big projects dominates—strategies of economic development, for example, in the 1960s and 1970s, post–Cold War nation building in the 1980s and 1990s, and now the management of states of emergency. Evidencing the integral complicity of social science and scholarship in visions of governance, the anthropologist offers something marginal, subordinate, and mediating. Except on rare occasions, such conferences are dominated by political theorists, policy analysts, planners, legal scholars, and economists; the debates are very much pitched with reference to those who move the levers of policy.

The anthropologist's contribution is most often singular and derived from the experiences of fieldwork. The fact that anthropological research is still distinctively organized in terms of lone operatives producing unique narratives from projects of individual fieldwork only determines even more this shape to the discipline's institutional role in the production of knowledge about contemporary events. However, in such conferences, a variety of actors increasingly join the anthropologist in representing the situation on the ground, so to speak—refugees, exiles, aid workers, NGO officials, and journalists. Not yet able or inclined to discuss the management of empire at the highest institutional levels and cleaving to narrating the local scene of change from the experience of fieldwork, yet in a wholly individualistic modality of the lone voice, anthropologists are in a truly "liminal" position,[7] both on the local scenes of intervention as well as in the removed, academic contexts that are always complicit with the formulation of projects of intervention. In either setting, the field or the conference, the identity of anthropology is never clear, or rather, its critical independence or potential lies in sustaining this liminal ambiguity. What is the pose that achieves this independence today?

## THREE POSES OF THE KNOWLEDGE WORKER

There are three identity poses relevant to operating as a knowledge worker within regimes of intervention and as frames in which to consider anthropology's positioning: expertise, reportage, and witnessing, or the expert, the reporter, and the witness. Each encompasses a different kind of norm of disinterestedness and a different kind of struggle of varying intensity to retain an independent space or perspective for claims to knowledge production. All are complicit in their distinctive ways with the various actors defined by regimes of intervention, actors who produce representations, analyses, and commentaries that compete and overlap with any knowledge form that is as deeply attached to a norm of disinterested or independent articulation, as I believe anthropology still very much is, despite its favoring of and commitment to rhetorics of activism. I have argued repeatedly that what distinguishes anthropology now from the discipline in the past is that it enters the field through zones of overlapping representations and power/knowledges that it can no longer ignore or bracket in establishing its own authority or clear vision.[8] The primary complication of anthropology is that in order to establish its own distinctive point of view and space of knowledge creation anywhere, it must work through counterpart or overlapping zones of representation already in and part of the scene. This condition and necessity is what most directly leads to what I have discussed as a multisited design to ethnographic research in which a relation between elites/experts and subalterns becomes part of the terrain of any fieldwork and, indeed, its primary object of understanding. The ethnographer must make expert discourse and practices (previously understood collaterally or collegially) part of the field of ethnography itself,[9] and so fieldwork projects begin with expert subjects with whom the anthropologist does not so much collaborate as exist in a relation of complicity—this founding reflexive complicity with representations already there and the complex ethical and methodological challenges that it poses are what define anthropological research almost anywhere today, but most strikingly in scenes dominated and defined by regimes of intervention. Witnessing, I argue, is the only figure of identity of the three that I indicate that raises the issues of these contemporary challenges of fieldwork and by which the anthropologist retains a modicum of independence, engagement, and self-respect, all at the same time. It is the mold in which the traditional positioning of the anthropologist reinvents itself amid aid workers, peacekeepers, NGO personnel, warlords, social movements, and, indeed, experts and reporters, as well.

I feel that it is worthwhile just to have someone on the scene of intervention to take stock of the situation purely in the name of social inquiry or social theory—trying to take a detached view, if not a relatively disinterested one—rather than in the name of the urgency or present importance of the event that is what attracts journalistic reportage. This, in other words, is the value of the pure and simple "being there" that has given ethnography authority as a form of knowing in the academy. But the old style of positivist disinterestedness won't do, and few are willing to assert it anyhow. For one thing, by the nature of area expertise training, formed as part of the expertise "in reserve" about various parts of the world that the United States supported in universities during its Cold War competition with the Soviets, the anthropologist is already not just "there." Her "being there" is in the name of a specific disciplinary agenda that has been overtaken by events.[10]

What, then, can account for the independence or the use of anthropology in the scene of regimes of intervention? Each of the three identities I suggest deserves extensive discussion. I am going to give the first two short shrift here in order to elaborate upon the more interesting, complicated (exotic?), and least obviously defined identity pose of the witness or witnessing. I became sensitive to the emergence of this positioning for anthropology progressively throughout the 1990s, and I want to register briefly five moments in my own awareness of this identity for anthropology, which I believe is now becoming much more salient and explicit.

But first, a few thoughts about the identities of expertise and reportage within contemporary regimes of intervention. Expert consultancy, formally recruited by one of the actors or organizations on the scene, is perhaps the most likely identity available to anthropologists or other social scientists in regimes of intervention and sometimes the only available or reasonably secure positioning that will allow an anthropologist even to be present in certain places. Anthropologists most often consult on program implementation and assessment in activities ranging from refugee assistance, to the delivery of medical assistance, to military operations. More rarely, they are asked to assess high-level policy processes themselves. Consulting expertise is also, like it or not, the identity that most enhances disciplinary prestige and taps into the deep underlying historical connection of social science itself to the rationale and support for it as expertise "in reserve" for the modern functions of governing and commerce. The classic pose of expertise is disinterestedness—objective commitment to truth finding and the use of methodologies that minimize or at least make rigorously explicit value considerations without necessarily enabling independence.

This pose has been subject to a long history of searching and persuasive critiques and self-critiques among social scientists themselves and especially among anthropologists. This does not mean that expert judgment and knowledge is not honorable or useful, but especially for anthropology, it is difficult to conceive of its base identity resting so substantially on expertise, given its investment in self-critique in recent years. Even insulated disciplinary expertise—the sort that anthropologists judge guildlike, only among themselves—is not in a present state that inspires the sort of confidence that would define a clear-cut disinterested agenda for anthropological research in regimes of intervention. Anthropologists have much to offer in a practical and critical way concerning the follies of policy and politics of others in regimes of intervention, but while they must do so sometimes in the guise or under cover of participating as experts, the heart of the discipline has been too critical of the pose of expert knowledge for anthropologists to believe in it deeply themselves.

As for reportage, (potentially closer to the identity of witnessing than expertise in its self-professed functions), this would be an attractive and available identity for anthropologists if it were not already so well occupied, in many instances, by professional journalists, themselves putative experts in a diverse and complex arena of practice that overlaps and blurs in interesting ways with the classic documentary/descriptive function of anthropological ethnography when it focuses on social change in locales and cultures long studied.[11] There is also an ethic or norm of disinterestedness—in the sense of independence, balance, and fairness—that guides journalistic practice, which, while different from the social-science norm of disinterestedness in which anthropological authority participates, is still very relevant in a de facto way to what ethnographers do in relation to the study of ongoing social change. Short of junking disinterestedness for advocacy, which some anthropologists have chosen to do, the norms of the journalist are perhaps more realistic for them than either the classic norm embedded in social science or the norm of disinterestedness of experts and their knowledge products that has been completely undermined by critique over the past two decades.

Anthropologists are like specialized journalists in some respects, and the overlap can be sensitive, at least to anthropologists who claim a deeper sort of knowledge of other places, but also the ability to interpret events as they happen. The best specialized journalists are better trained and better supported to do in-depth reporting of events and in fact are drawn to places by events where expertise, or its pose, must be rapidly acquired. Anthropologists are already there by dint of disciplinary projects and area-studies traditions and find themselves circumstantially in a situation of reportage. They operate within different temporalities and tempos in producing work than journalists do, even of the most in-depth and specialized sort. They also appeal to different constituencies of readers, even though they might envy the breadth of the publics to which journalists appeal. Still, while the anthropologist may participate in reportage as an overlapping identity, such reportage really does not capture the self-image of the anthropologist or what is distinctive about anthropology caught up in regimes of intervention.

So this leaves me with the third identity, that of the witness, a much more ambiguous, less defined identity than the other two, but one that in a de facto way has emerged in anthropology throughout the 1990s in the ways that anthropologists think about what they do as still disinterested, independent parties in scenes that strongly push them toward either flimsier pleas of detachment or disinterestedness based on professional norms or encouragement to abandon these in favor of explicit activist or advocate roles. Where does the identity of anthropologist as witness leave anthropology in scenes of intervention? How has it emerged?

In evoking the anthropologist as witness, I avoid a full-scale semantic analysis of the range of associations that the concept encompasses, but it is worth alluding to the two major frames, the legal and the sacred, both of which are entwined in the history of the idea of the witness and both of which are implicated in the particular style of anthropological research. Again, it is the distinctive professional modality of the anthropological scholar as lone operative immersed in the particularities of the closely observed circumstances of everyday life, but with the aim of tying those particularities to some transcendent discourse or argument, that creates the cogency of the witnessing pose for anthropologists working in places of political upheaval and the intervention of outside authorities. Yet of the three identities I outlined above, witnessing is the one that anthropologists back into circumstantially, rather than embrace in any explicit and reflected-upon way. It preserves their independence and lends their presence and work a certain authority and purpose when the business of fieldwork as usual is not sustainable. As such, the pose of witness is embraced with both an ethical and a moral purpose in the face of events surrounding fieldwork, but it is perhaps the identity option of the three least reflected upon.

Those whose fieldwork has been a form of witnessing adopt an identity and rhetoric for their work that is as ambiguous as it is powerful and visceral in terms of what it recounts between the covers of an ethnography. Here I have in mind recent influential writing on violence,[12] social suffering,[13] and fieldwork in the midst of political trauma.[14] Certainly originating in religious or sacred authority (with its remnant in the swearing in of witnesses on a Bible in court), the witness in Western law is a truthful observer based on what she or he can describe as having seen, rather than heard.[15] This is the eyewitness, the epitome of whom is the informed or expert witness, whose authority rests on science and disinterestedness. The testimony of such a witness appeals to an ultimate secular or legal authority—the courts and the state, which empowers them—to determine just outcomes.

There is indeed a strong component of this evolved secular role of the witness within the authority of the law in the emergence of the anthropologist as witness, especially in the combined descriptive and analytical skills on which much of the craft of ethnography has traditionally been judged. But this is the part of the identity of the witness that places the anthropologist back into the identity of the expert in the service of other regimes of knowledge—an identity that critical anthropologists routinely call into question. So, in its present incarnation, the identity of the witness as anthropologist appeals much more strongly to the sacred/religious origins of the concept and, in parallel, to the above-noted urge or intention embedded in the articulation of anthropological knowledge to say something transcendent about the closely observed and experienced in fieldwork.

And this discourse of the transcendent comes through allied with the varieties of critical humanism that have so influenced fields such as anthropology in recent years through the various interdisciplinary debates in culture theory. Witnessing itself, as a deeply reflected-upon modality of inquiry in literary and historical scholarship on major political and human traumas, has been subject to penetrating analysis in its critical humanist mode.[16] Always on the side of ordinary human subjects in very complex configurations of macroinstitutional change and social disorder, anthropologists construct arguments or merely sentiments that transcend the specificity of the fieldwork experience by mixed strategies in the use of theory, description, cases, voice, and narration in ethnographic writing. Occupying the surrogate space of the sacred, anthropologists in the midst of regimes of intervention, from which they try to stand apart in the name of commitment to and sympathy with subjects as victims of history writ small and large, are increasingly constructing themselves as witnesses to momentous, large, global processes of change. The anthropologist as witness is thus suspended within the two major sacred and secular senses of the term, but for the sake of a distinctive and independent voice amid the complex array of agents and actors in regimes of intervention, she has gravitated more toward the sacred and its contemporary surrogates that academic humanistic thinking on culture has provided.

## FIVE MOMENTS IN THE EMERGENCE OF THE ANTHROPOLOGIST AS WITNESS

What follows is a selection of examples from my own work and reading through the 1990s and early 2000s that reflect on how the trope of the witness emerged often implicitly as the rationale of research projects caught up in the kinds of local transformations that commonly define or elicit regimes of intervention today.

### REREADING *CULTURAL ANTHROPOLOGY*

At the end of my inaugural editorship of the journal *Cultural Anthropology* (1986–91), I was invited to produce *Rereading Cultural Anthropology*, a reader of selected articles during the first years of the journal.[17] Among several tropes that I used to characterize genres of articles, I chose the category "witnessing." This concept seemed to cover out-of-genre accounts by anthropologists that arose from reflections on long-term fieldwork experience in places that had become markedly destabilized by events of prolonged and traumatic political change and violence. At the time, I associated witnessing with a specialized kind of reportage with which anthropologists were experimenting. They were writings produced somewhere between their firsthand knowledge of locales that were being traumatically transformed and a certain savvy and self-awareness about the forms of rhetoric and representation that the era had so strongly injected into the consciousness of anthropologists, among others, through the so-called *Writing Culture* initiative.[18] My feeling is that these two poles of resources for writing provide the same intellectual inputs for constituting the identity of anthropologist as witnessing now does in regimes of intervention as usual.

At the time, two articles about the Shining Path guerrilla war in Peru were the examples to which I applied the category of witnessing. One article, by Orin Starn,[19] applied a Said/Orientalist–style argument in a charge about the elision of war in anthropological writing on the Andes in the interests of accommodating a disciplinary model of "Andeanism." (This same charge had been laid against a relatively synchronic, politically naïve anthropology several times before, for example, in relation to Vietnam.) Starn's charge was contested in a long and complex piece by Enrique Mayer,[20] who argued that, in fact, there were many examples in which anthropologists had incorporated the presence of political conflict and violence in their writing. Beyond this, he also questioned why the account of Mario Vargas Llosa about the then shocking massacre of a group of journalists, which Mayer criticized severely for its appropriation of pseudoanthropological discourse and flawed assumptions, was so much more powerful and influential than the accounts of anthropologists. In essence, he was raising the stakes of witnessing as a higher form of reportage for which anthropologists were prepared, but only if they were actively engaged in debates and critiques about the nature of representation itself.

Witnessing (my term) thus defined a unique and independent (disinterested?), but engaged identity for anthropology that began with a certain assessment of the politics of representation, not narrowly construed as disciplinary, but worked through available media and prominent examples such as that of Vargas Llosa. In so doing, Mayer provides another suggestion or clue of how anthropology as witnessing might critically situate itself, establish its own contextual frame, as it addresses scenes of political trauma or, now, intervention: Accounts of the politics of representation seem to provide this frame fully within the scene and without aid of a metanarrative.

## AMITAV GHOSH AND THE GLOBAL RESERVATION

Just before Amitav Ghosh established quite the reputation he has now as a novelist, especially within and about realms of the postcolonial (in works such as *In an*

*Antique Land, The Calcutta Chromosome,* and *Glass Palace*), he offered a remark-able small gem of a piece at the 1993 annual meeting of the Society for Cultural Anthropology on the developing modalities of intervention that are now very common and frequently written about in critical and ironic ways.[21] (See, for example, Linda Polman's *We Did Nothing*,[22] about the UN peacekeeping missions in Haiti, Rwanda, Bosnia, and Somalia.) Ghosh writes of being a brief traveler to Cambodia in early 1993. With the keen sensibility of a professional anthropologist, he moved amid officials and volunteers of the UN peacekeeping mission there. His mode is that of an observer witnessing the emergence of new forms of govern-mentality in failed or failing states. As he says, "I would like to think of the notes that follow as an impressionistic contribution to a yet uninvented discipline—the ethnography of international peacekeeping. Or, in other words, an anthropology of the future."[23]

Ghosh claims he is witnessing (my word again) the coming into being of a new technology of containment through nation-state models in the unruly areas of the early post–Cold War world. He does not do so only by the simple cogency of his observations and insights, but through rather shocking conversations with certain Western cultural experts of the UN (trained in area-studies programs) who oper-ate as members of its highly secretive Strategic Investigation Teams charged with ferreting out ethnic Vietnamese passing for Khmer. These are the counterparts of anthropologists deployed as experts charged with defining a country's ethnic boundaries, if only tangentially. By locating and working through the counter-part (doppelganger?) of anthropological expertise in the "cultural work" of UN peacekeeping, Ghosh becomes the ethnographer of a certain kind of deployment of ethnography and thus a witness, in a very micro-observed way, to a new form of containment in the global ordering of unruly areas.

There is, then, in this brief article, the makings of a modality for the world of anthropologist as witness in scenes of intervention. In this case, Ghosh is not the ethnographer of Cambodia caught up in the regime of intervention, but an observant traveler with the sensibility of an anthropologist. He begins to show the moves of the anthropologist as witness caught up in the sometimes analogous operations of authorities who define the parameters of intervention—the *United Nations Transitional Authority in Cambodia* (UNTAC), in this case.

### CATHERINE BESTEMAN AND I. M. LEWIS ON THE ANTHROPOLOGY OF VIOLENCE IN SOMALIA

An exchange that occurred in 1998 between two anthropologists, each having pro-duced scholarship and careers on long-term fieldwork in Somalia, but representing very different generations in the standard practice and style of anthropological research, as well as confronting different situations in Somalia itself, provides the next example. I.M. Lewis worked in Somalia under colonial conditions in the 1950s and 1960s. He practiced with great skill and insight a kind of anthropology that allowed him to perceive ordering principles in the conflict among Somali clans that he observed. He thinks that disorder in Somalia can be understood through an essential structural principle of clanship—and a contribution of reliable anthropological knowledge. He thus presents himself as a scholar and expert who has explanations from the anthropological disciplinary mode of knowledge production for Somali violence, even in its 1990s forms that drew the intervention of international agencies.[24]

Catherine Besteman, formed in a time when the paradigms of anthropology were coming apart and remaking themselves under the sign of critique, contests strongly Lewis's style and claims.[25] Her fieldwork and originating concern with Somalia were caught up within the postcolonial conditions of conflict and the regime of international intervention to which it led. She offers a coherent and deeply informed account of the complexity of the recent history and present conditions of Somali conflict on the ground. For my purpose here, these exchanges are very illuminating of two distinctive styles and eras of anthropological self-fashioning. Lewis's scholarship leads comfortably to an identity of expertise, and if called upon, advising or informing "the external powers that be" about what explains or patterns conflict in Somalia.

Besteman represents the practice of a style of postcolonial anthropology, which, caught within regimes of intervention, moves between a function of reportage and something more. It is this "something more" that interests me here. Her account is too engaged and not clinical enough to be mere reportage. Neither is she addressing an established topic of anthropological specialization or discussion for which there is an established constituency in the discipline to guarantee her the authority of expertise. Nor does she present herself as an activist taking sides. It is in and through gaps such as these that another identity for anthropological work is emerging these days in many places like Somalia, sites of failed states and interventionist emergencies—an identity that takes on the character of witnessing.

**RIGOBERTA MENCHU, DAVID STOLL, *TESTIMONIO*, AND ANTHROPOLOGICAL TRUTH**
In 1999, anthropologist David Stoll published a major exposé of the first-person account of the Nobel Laureate and activist Rigoberta Menchu concerning her experience of the genocidal war conducted by the state in Mayan areas of Guatemala.[26] Through his own fieldwork, Stoll called into question the accuracy and truthfulness of this account, which had circulated worldwide with great emotional

impact. The controversy that Stoll's book generated is interesting here for what it demonstrates about the identity of anthropological representation and presumption in the contemporary world of multiple, widely circulating and overlapping discourses with those of anthropology, and again, especially in those many cases today where anthropologists are working in areas of endemic violence and emergency and that draw international attention, if not direct intervention.[27] Stoll certainly does not portray himself as witness—this investigation involves Rigoberta Menchu's identity, about which he is deeply suspicious. Neither does he portray himself in the identity of anthropological scholar as expert or master ethnographer—even though this was his identity in the field. Rather, he takes on more the guise of investigative reporter observing standards of accuracy and attempting to put truth into a story that has been falsified in another's telling of it.

What the critical and searching commentaries in the wake of his exposé offers is a valuable discussion of the ecology and limits of conventional anthropological representation (and its self-presentations) in highly charged places such as Guatemala. Transcending Stoll's own expression of intent and purpose, the controversy itself demonstrates that witnessing as an option of anthropological purpose and identity (preferable to that of the expert or the reporter, which come in for considerable criticism for their naiveté in this controversy) is always a second-order function, operating through or in dialogue with certain already operating "native points of view" that also share this identity of witnessing, but under different cultural premises and circumstances of positioning.

The lesson for anthropology in this case is in Stoll's failure to anticipate, or else to attend to, the politics to which his own project would give rise and his failure to deliver his own critique by working through the genre of witnessing (*testimonio*) through which Menchu's writing was produced and received. Witnessing in anthropology is not the same as journalistic witnessing as a function of reporting. It is always derivative in that it arises from the anthropological job of translation and figuring out relationships that one constitutes through fieldwork. The same applies especially to the many scenes of fieldwork today, transformed by regimes of intervention. An anthropological account as witnessing, even though directed primarily to a Western or at-home reception, is always produced through local relations and other discourses in which understandings of traumatic events unfolding or in the recent past are likely to be in the form of witnessing genres such as *testimonio* in Guatemala and other places in Latin America. For anthropological accounts that take up such an identity on their own and claim authority for it in their home environments of academia, media, and government, the key ethnographic task—both reflexive and ethical in nature—remains to demonstrate their relation to and derivation from particular politics and situations of fieldwork in which the anthropologist seeks to be both amid and apart from the complexities of international reaction and intervention in places where social order is disintegrating.

## AN ANTHROPOLOGY JOB APPLICANT'S SELF-CHARACTERIZATION

Finally, I conclude these "moments" with an expression of research orientation (from a letter submitted as a "statement of interests") by a young anthropologist with years of fieldwork experience in southern Africa in a place that has been overtaken with HIV-AIDS on the scale of a plague. At the intersection of kinship studies, the anthropology of religion, and medical anthropology—all very traditional areas—he defines his research and his commitments in relation to an anthropology of "social suffering," an emerging field that, while operating with the forms of anthropological inquiry and analysis, moves much more explicitly toward an identity of witnessing for anthropological research amid populations experiencing collective traumas:

> My driving concerns center on how it is possible for people to love one another on global as well as intimate scales. I aim for a comparative perspective on ways in which participation in the suffering and well-being of others creates forms of moral community and makes possible particular kinds of political action. For example, when the World Trade Center collapsed, my sympathy for the victims caused me to feel bereaved for weeks, yet when I read that two million people have died in Congo during the recent war, I acknowledged the tragedy but felt relatively little sympathy. The processes through which people come to participate in the welfare of others, or become indifferent to it, crucially shape patterns of inequality and violence, as well as of care, over a range of social scales. One of my key preoccupations involves how people participate in one another's well-being by communicating sensations and sentiments through a variety of linguistic and embodied forms. A central purpose of my analytical project is to examine the forms—including ethnographic description—through which people narrate suffering and caring to one another. In this respect, I draw on recent work on "social suffering" on the range of languages used to speak and write about pain. Notably, Veena Das has argued that a key task of the analyst is to put pain into words so as to make clear how suffering may be perpetuated through bureaucratic, medical, and nationalist languages which tend to make pain into an abstraction. Yet I regard this approach as too narrow, since putting pain into words is merely one set of means through which people take part in one another's well-being. For example, it may be socially necessary to put love into words, and analytically necessary as well.

I present this expression merely as a document here that serves to register, as an ending frame for a set of examples that might be read as evolving, the most elaborated commitment to the identity of witnessing in research. While cast in the conventional language of anthropological purpose (of ethnography, analysis, and so on) and of anthropological interest, this work, both representative of and creative within an emerging area of fieldwork endeavor, constitutes a close academic parallel to *testimonio*, in my hearing. For whatever "good works" this research accomplishes, as anthropology, it witnesses.

But this paper would not be complete without a brief comparison with the other explicit and much-discussed expression of witnessing as ideology of expert presence in regimes of intervention or states of emergency. This is the "témoignage" self-justification of the organization MSF, Médecins Sans Frontières (Doctors Without Borders).[28] In anthropology, bearing witness emerges from the individual and circumstantial character of anthropological research in the social-science tradition, inserted into situations where the norms of such research practice are insupportable. Witnessing, however sincerely motivated, is a compromise.[29] While in MSF, there are similarities with the problem of rationalizing objective science in zones of political trauma, chaos, violence, and so-called "humanitarian sovereignty," MSF is activist at its core. The ideology of witnessing is another layer upon the justifications of activism that has to do, I believe, with the insufficiencies of both scientific and activist discipline in the face of barely controllable or uncontrollable disaster and human suffering. So anthropology is concerned with the "truth" of complex facts, for which it must offer "disinterest" or objectivity before it offers "engagement." Witnessing serves this latter function in this order—anthropologists come to it naively, so to speak. Complex facts, witnessed with some distance, speak for themselves. In its already embraced activist/advocacy interests, MSF is not concerned with establishing the truth of complex facts, but rather with establishing the testimony of the suffering through their own work. MSF can afford to get to ethics much more quickly and directly than anthropology, which still preserves something of the "modest witness" about it, even amid states of emergency.

## CONCLUSION

There are two current forms of witnessing at play in anthropological identity. On the one hand, there is something akin to testimony (but with a commitment to rigorous truth telling, according to Euro-American norms, unlike the Latin American literary form of *testimonio*), in which accountings and narratives of suffering, victimage, and injustices take center place. This is anthropology as witnessing in the name of harm done to victims and the relatively powerless and is just this side of activism without being activism. It invests in and stays close to the classic documentary function of ethnography. On the other hand, there is a kind of witnessing that is a more intellectualized and conceptually abstracted account or narrative of the emergence of new orders, techniques, structures, and social/cultural forms. This requires a commitment to an interpretation or a "take" on the present—it invests in the stakes of grasping a history of the present moving into an emergent future. Both forms carry a heavy ethical/moral weighting in rhetoric, but both are nonetheless suspect as to their motivations or commitments. In both forms, the anthropologist as scholar remains a classic bystander who in one or another genre witnesses in detachment, despite the moral power of his or her rhetoric.

What witnessing resolves, however imperfectly, is an identity for anthropology that no longer can theorize or envision a point of critique that is somehow outside the situation upon which it focuses. It at least creates a role for critique within the regime of intervention as a form of articulation complicit with and participating within its complex zones of representation. It seems to me, then, that either of these senses of witnessing serve the purpose of providing anthropology with an identity of independence and practical disinterestedness (although not necessarily rhetorical or theoretical disinterestedness) in regimes of intervention where the pressures to align, to be useful, to be active are nearly overwhelming. Witnessing provides purpose to independent inquiry, where having a purpose beyond the conventional academic, scholarly one of curiosity is absolutely necessary to remain present and functioning in a field totally politicized by a history of violence and intervention. The identity of the witness preserves as much as possible the kind of detachment to which I believe even the most committed anthropology is still deeply bound. But it seems to me that such a pose in return for whatever advantages it offers also brings with it a number of difficult problems and implications. On several counts it must remain suspect and itself subject to critique. To wit:

Witnessing as an identity for the anthropologist may fall to the same criticism as would any rhetorical claims to detachment. Witnessing, like the anthropologist's nostalgia for cultures that colonialism is transforming in the very scene of fieldwork,[30] allows the anthropologist to assert detachment from the sorts of processes in which she or he is demonstrably involved or complicit, if only by being on the scene, by continuing to claim the classic authority of "being there." This is one of those stimulating, provocative, but absolutist arguments of critique that there are no self-fashioning or rhetorical fixes for complicity, that there is absolutely no participation outside if you are there on the scene where history is unfolding.

In addition, there is the presumptuousness of taking on the mantle of witnessing, in a challenge of the sort, "Who appointed you?" That is, witnessing has a long-standing association with religious or sacred authority in claiming this identity. If anthropologists or other scholars who witness are not prepared to claim sacred authority, then in whose authority does one witness? Perhaps in the name of a general humanism, but the virtue of humanist authority itself is not innocent either.

Finally, witnessing and the current general fashion for ethics and ethical judgment are the prime modality and function through which humanist disciplines and qualitative social science participate in major governing institutions. I believe that the increasing attractiveness of witnessing as an identity of purpose for anthropological research is not just a solution to the kind of predicament that I have outlined in this paper, but more positively participates in a major trend in the remaking of the place of the humanities and social sciences (at least in the United States) in relation to major institutions and the exercise of power of different sorts. Ethical judgment is a function desired of (or perhaps required of) those who work in the human sciences, and powerful patrons have made a legitimate space for this kind of intellectual activity in hospitals, corporations, governments, and also in regimes of intervention. In short, the credit of ethical judgment as the work of professional scholarship is inflated these days. Anthropologists often arrive on scenes of potential fieldwork in which ethicists already occupy a space similar to the one that the anthropologists themselves would like to occupy as fieldworkers, and they must come to terms with this ideology of practice already in play in order to define their own research agendas. This has given rise to an interesting politics of research(es) and expertise in these constituted domains of ethics in many arenas. There is also an interesting intellectual history to be written on this fashion—its emergence, rationales, and politics. In any case, it seems to me that witnessing is a variation on this contemporary intellectual formation and fashion and ultimately should be understood by investigating its precise relations to it.

For one schooled in the powerful and often liberating critiques of representation and rhetoric in recent years, the above sorts of exceptions to witnessing might be familiar—but of course, no less valid. Yet as a tactic of resistance (in the sense developed by Michel de Certeau),[31] witnessing seems to me still to be an effective way to deal with the pressures in scenes of intervention to become preemptively activist in whoever's name. Witnessing is indeed a form of activism, but ultimately in the interest of detachment and the independent voice. As such, it is a value, at least in support of the conditions that promote distinctively anthropological insight, to be strengthened against the challenges to purpose and identity that regimes of intervention pose generally to any actors (diplomats, humanitarian aid workers, technical advisers, medical personnel, soldiers, and so on) on local scenes of catastrophe from elsewhere.

## NOTES

A different version of this essay was published in *Cultural Politics* 1, no. 1 (2005): pp. 31–49.

1   James Faubion and George E. Marcus (eds.), *Fieldwork Is Not What It Used to Be: Learning Anthropology's Method in Transition* (Ithaca, NY: Cornell University Press, 2009); Paul Rabinow, George E. Marcus, James Faubion, and Tobias Rees, *Designs for an Anthropology of the Contemporary* (Durham, NC: Duke University Press, 2008).

2   The appeal to witnessing as a rationale of ethnography is really quite pervasive in anthropological writing today. I come upon it frequently in my reading. For example, here is a typical quote that I came across in preparing a review article. It is from  Stuart Kirsch, *Reverse Anthropology: Indigenous Analysis of Social and Environmental Relations in New Guinea* (Stanford, CA: Stanford University Press, 2006): "These encounters with the refugees suggest the political and ethnographic responsibilities of anthropologists to bear witness to political violence when it affects the people with whom they work. By documenting political violence and representing its human costs, anthropologists can amplify indigenous forms of political expression, bringing the resources of the discipline and the moral weight of the academy to bear on injustice" (p. 187).

3   Mariella Pandolfi, "L'industrie humanitaire: Une souveraineté mouvante et supracoloniale. Réflexion sur l'expérience des Balkans," *Multitudes* 3 (November 2000): pp. 97–105; "'Moral Entrepreneurs,' souverainetés mouvantes et barbelé: Le bio-politique dans les Balkans post-communistes," in Mariella Pandolfi and Marc Abélès (eds.), "Politiques: Jeux d'espaces," special issue, *Anthropologie et Sociétés* 26, no. 1 (2002): pp. 1–24.

4   During the Cold War development era, primarily the 1950s and 1960s, there was no such thing as a failed state. Many of us as anthropologists would move/work through symbolic states — all presumed to be developing — to find our way to out-of-time ethnographic subjects, where certain histories would be noted, but the contemporary was a temporality in which distinctive systems of kinship, ritual, and so on could be studied as such. Intervention was a fixture of this era, but as a technique of control. Now it is a type of regime that occupies and transforms places where development is not even the issue, in the face of an extreme failure of order.

5   For example, when I began thinking about this paper in 2003, the discussions in the media and the academy about the United States as a contemporary empire and how regimes of intervention might fit into this interest to retheorize empire were very rich and somewhat confident in posing as the frame in which to understand current events. I might easily have invested my remark about anthropology in those discussions as a broader context of reference. Well, this realm of discussion turned out to be very rapidly moving ground, indeed, especially after the conquest of Iraq and the difficulties in the aftermath. The earlier discussions are relevant but have an entirely different cast. This all has the feel of history in the making, and not the creation of stable social theory or perspectives on which fields such as anthropology have depended. In the absence of such conventional means of contextualization and the concomitant sense that critique has a vantage point in the authoritative intellectual work of a macronarrative, how, then, does anthropology situate itself within and in relation to regimes of intervention as the scene of contemporary fieldwork?

6   Perhaps a useful analogy with what I have in mind here is Michael Ignatieff's fascinating discussion in *The Warrior's Honor: Ethnic War and the Modern Conscience* (New York:

Metropolitan Books, 1998) about the conflicting norms of human rights organizations and of the Red Cross, both operating in scenes of intervention. In order to be effective in terms of what it conceives as its mission, the Red Cross remains strictly neutral (radically disinterested?) in the face of human rights violations—so that it can operate across lines of battle, so to speak—while human rights operatives find this neutrality nearly intolerable. Anthropology in the scene of intervention is not quite neutral like the Red Cross, but it should have an analogous alternative to blatant partisanship or advocacy—a sort of positioning that sustains anthropology's distinctiveness despite great pressures to take sides and to help fulfill one or another actor's purposes. It seems to me that an identity of witnessing, as I will argue, with all of its attendant problems, preserves this essential independence of anthropology in the scenes of intervention in a way that no other identity alternative does.

7    Victor Turner, *The Ritual Process: Structure and Anti-Structure* (Chicago: Aldine, 1969).

8    See, for instance, George E. Marcus, *Ethnography Through Thick and Thin* (Princeton, NJ: Princeton University Press, 1998).

9    An excellent example would be James Ferguson, *Anti-Politics Machine: "Development" and Bureaucratic Power in Lesotho* (Cambridge: Cambridge University Press, 1990).

10   This, of course, poses the question of the neophyte ethnographer today, after the vitality of "area studies" has passed, who might enter such regimes for disciplinary purposes without this "innocence" or circumstantiality of the longtime fieldworker overtaken by events.

11   See, for example, the fascinating study by Ulf Hannerz, *Foreign News: Exploring the World of Foreign Correspondents* (Chicago: University of Chicago Press, 2004), in which he systematically frames and compares their writing with that of contemporary anthropological ethnography. As exemplary of contemporary anthropologists who operate in the mode of investigative journalists, I think of Nancy Scheper-Hughes.

12   E. Valentine Daniel, *Charred Lullabies: Chapters in an Anthropology of Violence* (Princeton, NJ: Princeton University Press, 1996); Michael Taussig, *Law in a Lawless Land: Diary of a Limpieza in Colombia* (New York: The New Press, 2003).

13   Arthur Kleinman, Veena Das, and Margaret Lock (eds.), *Social Suffering* (Berkeley: University of California Press, 1997).

14   Antonius Robben and Marcelo Suarez-Orozco (eds.), *Cultures under Siege: Collective Violence and Trauma* (Cambridge: Cambridge University Press, 2000); Carol Greenhouse, Elizabeth Mertz, and Kay B. Warren (eds.), *Ethnography in Unstable Places: Everyday Lives in Contexts of Dramatic Political Change* (Durham, NC: Duke University Press, 2002).

15   See, for example, Talal Asad, "Pain and Truth in Medieval Christian Ritual," in *Genealogies of Religion: Discipline and Reasons of Power in Christianity and Islam* (Baltimore: Johns Hopkins University Press, 1993), pp. 83–124.

16   Shoshana Felman and Dori Laub, *Testimony: Crises of Witnessing in Literature, Psychoanalysis, and History* (New York: Routledge, 1992).

17   George E. Marcus (ed.), *Rereading Cultural Anthropology* (Durham, NC: Duke University Press, 1992).

18   James Clifford and George E. Marcus (eds.), *Writing Culture: The Poetics and Politics of Ethnography* (Berkeley: University of California Press, 1986).

19   Orin Starn, "Missing the Revolution: Anthropologists and the War in Peru," in *Rereading Cultural Anthropology*, pp. 152–80.

20   Enrique Mayer, "Peru in Deep Trouble: Mario Vargas Llosa's 'Inquest in the Andes' Reexam-

ined," in *Rereading Cultural Anthropology*, pp. 181–219.

21  Amitav Ghosh, "The Global Reservation: Notes Toward an Ethnography of International Peacekeeping," *Cultural Anthropology* 9, no. 3 (1994): pp. 412–22.

22  Linda Polman, *We Did Nothing: Why the Truth Doesn't Always Come Out When the UN Goes In* (London: Viking, 2003).

23  Ghosh, "The Global Reservation."

24  I.M. Lewis and Catherine Besteman, "Violence in Somalia: An Exchange," *Cultural Anthropology* 13, no. 1 (1998): pp. 100–114.

25  Catherine Besteman, "Violent Politics and the Politics of Violence: The Dissolution of the Somali Nation State," *American Ethnologist* 23, no. 3 (1996): pp. 579-96; Lewis and Besteman, "Violence in Somalia: An Exchange."

26  David Stoll, *Rigoberta Menchu and the Story of All Poor Guatemalans* (Boulder, CO: Westview Press, 1999).

27  Arturo Arias (ed.), *The Rigoberta Menchu Controversy* (Minneapolis: University of Minnesota Press, 2001).

28  Insightfully analyzed in Peter Redfield, "A Less Modest Witness: Collective Advocacy and Motivated Truth in a Medical Humanitarian Movement," *American Ethnologist* 33, no. 1 (2006): pp. 3–26.

29  Perhaps Donna Haraway's evocation of the "modest witness" lodged on the seams between science and society in her *Modest_Witness@Second _Millennium.FemaleMan©_Meets_Onco-Mouse™* (New York: Routledge, 1997) is a construction of witnessing that comes closer to the predicament of anthropology and thus a resource with which to think through its own tendency to claim the position of witness in the scenes of fieldwork.

30  Renato Rosaldo, "Imperialist Nostalgia," in Renato Rosaldo, *Culture and Truth: the Remaking of Social Analysis* (Boston: Beacon Press, 1989).

31  Michel de Certeau, *The Practice of Everyday Life* (Berkeley: University of California Press, 1985).

# Contributors

CRAIG CALHOUN is president of the Social Science Research Council. He is also University Professor of the Social Sciences at New York University, where he directs the new Institute for Public Knowledge. He received his doctorate from Oxford and has published widely in comparative and historical sociology and social and political theory. His most recent books include *Nations Matter: Culture, History, and the Cosmopolitan Dream* (2007) and *Cosmopolitanism and Belonging: From European Integration to Global Hopes and Fears* (2007). He has also edited four recent collections: *Lessons of Empire: Historical Contexts for Understanding America's Global Power*, with Frederick Cooper and Kevin Moore (2006), *Sociology in America* (2007), *Practicing Culture*, with Richard Sennett (2007), and *The Public Mission of the University*, with Diana Rhoten (forthcoming). Among his best-known earlier books are *Critical Social Theory: Culture, History and the Problem of Specificity* (1995) and *Neither Gods Nor Emperors: Students and the Struggle for Democracy in China* (1994).

MARY-JO DEL VECCHIO GOOD, a comparative sociologist and medical anthropologist, is professor of social medicine in Harvard Medical School's Department of Social Medicine. She also teaches in the Sociology Department at Harvard University, and is a faculty affiliate of the Asia Center, the Center for Middle Eastern Studies, and the Weatherhead Center for International Affairs. Recent publications include, as editor and coauthor of two chapters with Byron J. Good, "Subjectivity in the Contemporary World" and "Subjective Experience and Interpretative Politics of Contemporary Indonesian Artists," in *Postcolonial Disorders* (2008); *Psychosocial Needs Assessment of Communities Affected by the Conflict in the Districts of Pidie, Bireuen, and Aceh Utara* (2006); *A Psychosocial Needs Assessment of Communities in 14 Conflict-Affected Districts in Aceh*, coauthored with Byron J. Good,

Jesse Grayman, and Matthew Lakoma (2007); and "Trauma in Postconflict Aceh and Psychopharmaceuticals as a Medium of Exchange" in Janis Jenkins (ed.), *We Are All Pharmaceutical Selves: Psychopharmacology in a Globalizing World* (2010).

**DIDIER FASSIN** is the James Wolfensohn Professor of Social Science at the Institute for Advanced Study in Princeton and director of studies in anthropology at the École des Hautes Études en Sciences Sociales in Paris. He was the founding director of the Interdisciplinary Research Institute for the Social Sciences (CNRS—INSER—EHESS—University Paris North). Trained as a medical doctor, he was previously vice president of Médecins Sans Frontières and is president of the Comité Médical pour les Exilés. His field of interest is political and moral anthropology, and he is currently conducting an ethnography of the state through a study of policing and the prison. His recent publications include: *De la question sociale à la question raciale?* (with Eric Fassin, 2006), *Les Politiques de l'enquête: Épreuves ethnographiques* (with Alban Bensa, 2008), *Les Nouvelles frontières de la société française* (2009) and *Moral Anthropology* (2012) as editor; *When Bodies Remember. Experience and Politics of AIDS in South Africa*, (2007), *The Empire of Trauma: An Inquiry into the Condition of Victimhood* (with Richard Rechtman,2009), *Humanitarian Reason: A Moral History of the Present* (2011) and *Enforcing Order. An Ethnography of Urban Policing* (2013).

**BYRON J. GOOD** is professor of medical anthropology and former chair (2000-2006), in the Department of Social Medicine, Harvard Medical School, and professor in the Department of Anthropology, Harvard University. He is director of programs in Global Mental Health in the Department of Social Medicine. His recent research has focused on early experiences of psychosis in Java and on the development of mental-health systems in Asia. His broader interests focus on studies of subjectivity in contemporary societies and the development of a "postcolonial" psychology. He has been actively involved in a program of postconflict mental-health work in Aceh, Indonesia, carried out by International Organization for Migration. His recent publications include *Subjectivity: Ethnographic Investigations*, edited with João Biehl and Arthur Kleinman (2007) and *Postcolonial Disorders*, edited with Mary-Jo DelVecchio Good, Sandra Teresa Hyde, and Sarah Pinto (2008), as well as *Clifford Geertz by His Colleagues*, edited with Richard A. Shweder (2004) and *Culture and Panic Disorder*, edited with Devon E. Hinton (2009).

**JESSE GRAYMAN** is a Ph.D. candidate in social and medical anthropology at the Harvard Graduate School of Arts and Sciences and the coordinator for the Center for Peace and Conflict Resolution Studies at Syiah Kuala University in Aceh, Indonesia. He also holds an M.P.H in epidemiology and an M.A. in Southeast Asian studies, both from the University of Michigan. His research on post-tsunami and postconflict recovery efforts in Aceh, Indonesia, is based on three years of field-work spent working with the International Organization for Migration (IOM) and other humanitarian groups working in Aceh. Publications include "Conflict Night-mares and Trauma in Aceh," in *Culture, Medicine, and Psychiatry* (2009) and *A Psy-chosocial Needs Assessment of Communities in 14 Conflict-Affected Districts in Aceh* (2007), both coauthored with Byron Good and Mary-Jo DelVecchio Good, along with Matthew Lakoma.

**DEIRDRE HOWARD-WAGNER** is a sociologist and senior lecturer in socio-legal stud-ies at the University of Sydney in Australia. Her area of research expertise is in indigenous people, law, and society. Her work has made a significant sociolegal and sociological contribution to the study of Australian federal Indigenous law and policy governing Indigenous affairs in the contemporary period, especially in the context of international human rights developments. Most recently, she has been writing on the "National Emergency Response" declared in the Northern Terri-tory in 2007, in particular: "The State's 'Intervention' in Indigenous Affairs in the Northern Territory: Governing the Indigenous Population through Violence, Abuse and Neglect," in Craig Browne and Justine McGill (eds.) *Violence and the Post-Colonial Welfare State in France and Australia* (2009) and "Whiteness, Power Rela-tions and Resistance and the 'Practical' Recognition of Indigenous Rights in New-castle," *Theory in Action* (2009).

**CHOWRA MAKAREMI** is a Ph.D. candidate in anthropology at the University of Montréal and member of the Research Group on Military and Humanitarian Interventions. She has a been a lecturer in human security at the graduate pro-gram in international studies at the University of Montréal (2006 and 2007). Her recent publications include: "Alien Exclusion: between Circulation and Confine-ment," special issue, *Cultures et Conflits* (2008), coedited with Carolina Kobelinsky; "Alien Confinement in Europe: Violence and the Law," in Colman Hogan and Marta Marín-Dòmine (eds.), *The Camp: Narratives of Internment and Exclusion* (2007) and "Zone of 'No-right' in Democracy: Emotions and the Law" in Mariella Pandolfi and Vincent Crapanzano (eds.), "Passions Politiques," special issue, *Anthropologie et Société* (2008).

**GEORGE E. MARCUS** was for twenty-five years chair of the Anthropology Depart-ment at Rice University. During that period, he coedited, with James Clifford, *Writing Culture: The Poetics and Politics of Ethnography* (1986), coauthored with Michael Fischer, *Anthropology as Cultural Critique: An Experimental Moment in the Human Sciences* (1986), inaugurated the journal *Cultural Anthropology*, and, through the 1990s, created and edited a fin-de-siècle series of annuals, *Late Editions*, eight volumes, intended to document the century's end by innovations in representing the ethnographic encounter. His most recent books are, with Fernando Mascarenhas, *Ocasiao: The Marquis and the Anthropologist, a Collaboration* (2005) and, conversations with Paul Rabinow, *Designs for an Anthropology of the Contemporary* (2008). In 2005, he moved to the University of California, Irvine, as Chancellor's Professor and founded a Center for Ethnography, dedicated to examining the vulnerabilities and possibilities of this venerable technology of knowledge making.

**UGO MATTEI** occupies the Alfred and Hanna Fromm Chair in International and Comparative Law at the University of California and is a professor of civil law at the University of Turin, Italy, where he is the academic coordinator of the International University College. The editor in chief of *Global Jurist*, he is a member of the editorial board of the *International Review of Law and Economics* and of the executive editorial board of the *American Journal of Comparative Law*. His most recent book in English, written with the anthropologist Laura Nader, is *Plunder: When the Rule of Law is Illegal* (2008).

**LAURENCE MCFALLS** is professor of political science at the University of Montréal, where he also directs the Canadian Centre for German and European Studies. His research and publications include work on French politics, post-Communist transitions, German reunification, humanitarian interventions, and Max Weber and the epistemology of the social sciences. He recently edited *Max Weber's 'Objectivity' Reconsidered* (2007) and authored *Construire le politique* (2006).

**ADI OPHIR** teaches continental philosophy and political theory at the Cohn Institute for the History and Philosophy of Science and Ideas, Tel Aviv University. He is also a fellow of the Hartman Institute for Advanced Jewish Studies. He was the founding editor of *Theory and Criticism*, the leading Israeli journal of critical theory and cultural studies. His recent books include *The Power of Inclusive Exclusion: Anatomy of Israeli Rule in the Occupied Palestinian Territories*, coedited with Michal Givoni and Sari Hanafi (2009), *The Order of Evils: Toward an Ontology of Morals* (2005), and *This Regime Which Is Not One: Occupation and Democracy between the Sea and the River*, coauthored with Ariella Azoulay (2008).

**ANNE ORFORD** is an Australian professorial fellow and the Michael D. Kirby Professor of International Law at the University of Melbourne, where she also directs the Institute for International Law and the Humanities. She researches in the areas of international law and legal theory with a particular focus on the legal legacies of European imperialism. Her publications include *Reading Humanitarian*

*Intervention: Human Rights and the Use of Force in International Law* (2003) and the edited volume *International Law and Its Others* (2006). She was awarded a five-year research fellowship by the Australian Research Council to undertake a project on cosmopolitanism and the future of international law from 2007 to 2011. The first book from that project, entitled *International Authority and the Responsibility to Protect*, will be published in 2010.

MARIELLA PANDOLFI is professor of anthropology at the University of Montréal and head of its research group on military and humanitarian interventions. Trained as a psychoanalyst, she received her Ph.D. in anthropology from École des Hautes Études en Sciences Sociales in Paris. As general secretary of Società Italiana di Psichiatria transculturale and vice president of Società Italiana di Antropologia Medica, her previous research developed political and psychoanalytical approaches to the anthropology of the body. Her recent interests have focused on the political and ethical legitimacy of humanitarian interventions and international aid in the post-conflict Balkans. She has been actively involved in a program of the international organization on migration (IOM) on psychosocial and trauma in response in Kosovo and Albania for the United Nations Office for Drug Control and Crime Prevention (UNODCCP). In 2004 she received Montréal's Woman of Distinction Award. Her recent publications include: *Sovranitete të lëvizshme: Kujtesa, konfliktet, dhuna në Ballkanin e erës globale* (2009); "Laboratory of Intervention: The Humanitarian Governance of the Postcommunist Balkan Territories" in *Postcolonial Disorders* (2008); and "La Zone grise des guerres humanitaires," in *Anthropologica* (2006). She co-edited, with Vincent Crapanzano, a special issue of *Anthropologie et Société* entitled "Passions politiques" (2008).

VANESSA PUPAVAC is a lecturer in the School of Politics and International Relations at the University of Nottingham. She trained as a lawyer and has previously worked for the United Nations. In 2003, she received the Otto Klineberg Intercultural and International Relations Award. She was appointed to the International Panel for the Programme of Strategic Cooperation between Irish Aid and Higher Education and Research Institutes for the period 2007 to 2011. Her publications on international aid and human rights include: "Human Security and the Rise of Global Therapeutic Governance," *Conflict, Security and Development* (2005), "The Politics of Emergency and the Demise of the Developing State: Problems for Humanitarian Advocacy," *Development in Practice* (2006), and "Refugee Advocacy, Traumatic Representations and Political Disenchantment," *Government and Opposition* (2008).

PETER REDFIELD is associate professor of anthropology at the University of North Carolina, Chapel Hill. Trained as a cultural anthropologist sympathetic to history, he concentrates on circulations of science and technology in colonial and postcolonial contexts. The author of *Space in the Tropics: From Convicts to Rockets in French Guiana* (2000), his current book project is an ethnographic study of Médecins Sans Frontières entitled *Life in Crisis: The Ethical Journey of Doctors Without Borders*. Related shorter works include "A Less Modest Witness: Collective Advocacy and Motivated Truth in a Medical Humanitarian Movement," *American Ethnologist* (2006) and "Doctors, Borders and Life in Crisis" *Cultural Anthropology* (2005), which won the Cultural Horizons Prize from the Society for Cultural Anthropology. Together with Erica Bornstein, he is editing a volume entitled *Forces of Compassion: Humanitarianism between Ethics and Politics* for the Advanced Seminar series of SAR Press.

PAULA VÁSQUEZ LEZAMA holds a doctorate in social anthropology and ethnology from the École des Hautes Études en Sciences Sociales in Paris and graduated in sociology from the Universidad Central de Venezuela. Her doctoral thesis is an ethnographic investigation into the humanitarian disaster generated by the massive mudslides of December 1999. She is the author, with Didier Fassin, of "De la tragédie collective à l'individuation du malheur: Normalisation de la violence et mise en cause morale des femmes sinistrées au Venezuela," *Anthropologie et sociétés* (2009) and of "Humanitarian Exception as the Rule: The Political Theology of the 1999 *Tragedia* in Venezuela," *American Ethnologist* (2005).

ALEX DE WAAL is director of the Social Science Research Council programs on emergencies and on AIDS and social transformation, a fellow of the Harvard Humanitarian Initiative, and a director of Justice Africa in London. He started his research career on the Horn of Africa in 1984 with a study of the famine in Darfur and subsequently studied the social, political, and health dimensions of famine, war, genocide, and the HIV-AIDS epidemic. In 2006, he served as advisor to the African Union mediation team for the Darfur conflict. He received his Ph.D. from Oxford University in 1988 and has written or edited thirteen books, most recently *AIDS and Power: Why There is No Political Crisis — Yet* (2006) and *War in Darfur and the Search for Peace* (2007). A completely revised and updated version of his book, coauthored with Julie Flint, *Darfur: A New History of a Long War* was published in 2008.

# Index

219; in World War II, 41. *See also* Humanitarianism, British; United Kingdom (UK).

British and Foreign Bible Society, 131.

Broome, Richard, 221, 235 n.24.

Brough, Mal, 227.

Brown, Gordon, 129.

Buddhism, 136–37, 145.

Bulgaria, 155.

Burciul, Barry, 275.

Bureaucracy, 326, 327, 331, 371.

Burger, Warren E., 98.

Burkina Faso, 178.

Burma (Myanmar), 9–10, 30, 41, 48–49, 178.

Burundi, 178.

Bush, George H. W., 295, 297, 304.

Bush, George W., 22, 57 n.21, 305, 307; catastrophization and, 76; Darfur crisis and, 308; Guantánamo Bay detention center and, 324; Iraq invasion and, 12; medical metaphor for intervention and, 319.

Butler, Judith, 263.

*CALCUTTA CHROMOSOME, THE* (GHOSH), 368.

Caldera, Rafael, 206, 215 n.27.

Cambodia, 50, 176, 178, 184, 368.

"Camp Justice," 324.

Canada, 93, 111, 112, 116, 219; Afghanistan intervention and, 114, 115, 117, 119; Hollow Water reserve, 229; ICISS and, 336; International Development Agency Program, 115, 118; psychological needs assessment (PNA) in Aceh and, 246, 254, 265 n.16; as "safe third country," 118.

*Candide* (Voltaire), 35.

Capitalism, global, 17, 48, 88 n.62, 317; Bretton Woods institutions and, 101; in colonial era, 40; consumer needs and, 90; corporate, 44; human security and, 117; predatory, 89, 90, 99, 104; progress and, 42; welfare state and, 100; zones of emergency and, 82.

CARE (Cooperative for Assistance and Relief Everywhere), 296, 300.

Carey, John, 134.

Carlsson, Ingvar, 107.

Carnegie, Andrew, 44.

Castro, Fidel, 93, 100.

Catastrophization, 17, 59, 67–72, 82–83; in Occupied PalestinianTerritories (OPT), 77–81; space and time in, 61, 77, 80; state of exception and, 70–71, 73–77; threshold of catastrophe, 70, 74, 75, 82; two-tier concept of, 59–67.

Catholic Agency for Overseas Development, 133.

Catholic Church, 34, 39.

Caucasus region, 115, 116.

Celebrities, relief and, 48.

Central Asia, 10.

Central Intelligence Agency (CIA), 73, 296–97.

Certeau, Michel de, 374.

Chad, 306.

Chaos, global, 115, 116, 121, 154, 156.

Charity, 34, 35–38, 42, 49.

Chatterjee, Partha, 39.

Chávez, Hugo, 19, 93, 124 n.9, 211; on "dignification," 198, 210; election of, 197, 212; failed coup against (2002), 214 n.15; fear of U.S.-backed coup d'état, 201; left-wing parties and, 206; Vargas mudslides and, 204; Venezuelan military and, 208.

Chechnya, 13, 15, 178, 285.

Chernobyl disaster, 87 n.46.

Chile, 93, 139.

China, imperial, 41.

China, People's Republic of: Beijing Olympic Games, 10; Confucian harmony promoted in, 98; Darfur crisis and, 312; floods in, 9, 10; material prosperity in, 145; rule of law and, 94; Sichuan earthquake (2008), 30, 31; Tibet occupied by, 31.

Chow, Rey, 335.

Christian Aid, 133, 145.

Christianity, 35, 37, 305.

Church Missionary Society, 131.

Cities, disasters and, 62.

Citizenship, 31, 129; Australian Aborigines and, 220, 221, 233; therapeutic, 331; world, 348.

Civilians, 36, 46, 337; documentation of abuses against, 277; international humanitarian law and, 338–43, 347; in Iraq, 14, 20; in Kosovo, 14; protection of, 111, 119, 126 n.70; as targets of violence, 29, 242, 250, 251, 254, 309; in World War II, 47.

Civilization, 43, 103–104; Buddhist view of, 136–37; "clash of civilizations," 21; Cold War and, 100; colonialism and, 39; *mission civilisatrice* (civilizing mission), 39, 41; rule of law and, 89, 93, 94; welfare state and, 99.

Civil society, 44, 107, 113, 161; in Aceh (Indonesia), 255; neocolonialism and, 175; NGOs and, 329; structure of exception and, 324.

Civil wars, 9, 85 n.20, 305, 325, 330, 337; as prototypical states of exception, 195 n.31; state authority as protection from, 343, 344. *See also* Wars.

Classes, social, 97, 326.

Clausewitz, Carl von, 274.

Cleland, J. B., 220.

Climate change, 145.

(2004) and, 244–46.

Germany, 99, 102; Kosovo security force (KFOR) and, 346, 347; Nazi regime, 221, 311.

Gesture, humanitarian, 17, 269.

Ghana, 129, 143.

Ghosh, Amitav, 367–68.

Giddings, Franklin H., 44.

*Gift Relationship, The* (Titmus), 135, 140.

Glasius, Marlies, 114.

*Glass Palace* (Ghosh), 368.

Globalization, 102, 113, 115, 159, 162.

Global warming, 29, 84 n.16, 87 n.44, 331.

Gluck, Kenny, 285.

Gluckman, Max, 357.

Good Samaritan, biblical parable of, 35, 317.

Gordon, Sue, 226.

Governance, good, 156, 157, 161–66, 166–68, 329.

Gramsci, Antonio, 100.

Gray zones, 163, 171 n.33, 189, 242.

Greece, 130, 155, 282–83.

Gros, Frédéric, 157.

Group therapy, 253.

Guantánamo Bay, 21, 324, 336.

Guatemala, 178, 369–70.

*Guernica* (Picasso), 20, 349–51.

Guevara, Che, 100.

*Guidelines on Mental Health and Psychosocial Support in Emergency Settings,* 262.

Guinea, 293 n.52.

Gulf War, First, 272, 316 n.40.

Gulf War, Second. *See* Iraq invasion [2003] (Second Gulf War).

Gypsies, 283, 292 n.50.

HABERMAS, JÜRGEN, 347–48.

Habibie, B. J., 245.

Habit, 323, 324.

Haiti, 9, 118, 141, 368.

Hamas, 67, 79, 81, 88 n.60.

Hamilton, Alexander, 91.

Hampson, Fen O., 116.

Hanis, Mark, 307.

Haraway, Donna, 377 n.29.

Harcourt, William Vernon, 22.

Hardt, Michael, 91.

Hardy, Thomas, 134.

Harrison, George, 48.

Haskell, Thomas, 42.

Hasluck, Paul, 222, 235 n.29.

Havel, Vaclav, 12, 273.

Havemann, Paul, 230.

Hazlitt, William, 131.

Health care/crises, 18, 63, 99; human security and, 112; immigrants' access to, 274; international destabilization and, 164; primary mission of MSF, 277; in Uganda, 184.

*Heart of Darkness* (Conrad), 269.

Hegel, G. W. F., 345–46.

Heyman, Josiah, 270, 287 n.5.

Hezbollah, 67.

Historicus, 9, 22.

History: end of, 21, 303; progressive view of, 41.

HIV (human immunodeficiency virus), 62, 177, 305, 330, 371.

Hobbes, Thomas, 122 n.17, 343–44, 345, 346, 351.

Hoffmann, Stanley, 273.

Hoggart, Richard, 134, 135, 140.

Holbrooke, Richard, 289 n.25.

Hollow Water reserve (Canada), 229.

Holocaust, 47, 178; Darfur crisis and, 306, 310; invocation of second Holocaust, 67; as perfect crime/disaster, 68, 85 n.19. *See also* Genocide.

Holzgrefe, J. L., 23 n.6.

*Homo Sacer: Sovereign Power and Bare Life* (Agamben), 324.

Honduras, 9.

Horkheimer, Max, 121.

Horton, Scott, 336.

Housing, 112.

Howard, John, 19, 217, 225–27.

Howson, Peter, 140.

Huber, Eugen, 96.

Hull House, 43.

Human, category of, 34, 38, 145–46.

Human Development Index, 109, 118.

*Human Development Report,* 108, 114.

Humanism, 38, 130, 136, 374.

Humanitarianism, 12, 173, 269–71, 286; charity and, 35–36; civilization and, 39; colonialism/imperialism and, 38–41, 53; economic assistance and, 52–53, 54; extralegal action justified by, 13; historical portrait of, 271–74; human rights advocacy and, 37; logistical capacities and, 45; managerial orientation, 44–45; progress and, 42–45, 53; prominence of, 29; reality principle and, 281–86; reciprocal dependency with military actions, 15; romantic subjects of, 133–36; as secular religion, 317; spread of humanitarian government, 17; therapeutic domination and, 318; witnessing as ideal, 36; worldview associated with, 275–80.

Investment, foreign, 93.

Iran, 13, 21, 67.

Iraq, 178, 270, 272, 295.

Iraq invasion [2003] (Second Gulf War), 12, 20, 21, 375 n.5; absence of postinvasion planning, 311; civilian and military casualties, 14, 24 n.10, 339; Darfur crisis and, 310–12; debates over decision to intervene, 13; humanitarian defense of, 15; medical metaphor for intervention and, 319; as neoimperial venture, 40; as "nonconsensual humanitarian intervention," 48; presented as humanitarian intervention, 30; Save Darfur movement and, 308; split among humanitarian organizations and, 278, 290 n.35; veiling of *Guernica* at UN and, 20, 349–51.

Ireland, 335.

Iron Fist (Uganda military offensive), 181.

Islam, 35, 92, 94, 251.

Israel, state of, 17, 30, 47, 67, 77–81, 87 n.45.

Italy, 93, 94, 102.

Ivory Coast (Côte d'Ivoire), 20, 330–31.

JAPAN, 33, 41, 98, 100, 111, 335.

Jeanpierre, Laurent, 165–66.

Jews, 221.

Jhabvala, Prawer, 136.

Johnson, Alan, 120.

Johnson-Sirleaf, Ellen, 330.

Jospin, Lionel, 273.

Journalists, 173, 282, 361, 364, 367.

Julliard, Jacques, 25 n.13.

Justice, 24 n.7, 120, 259, 286; alternative dispute regulation (ADR) and, 90, 94–99; economic, 248; international courts of, 20; silence of the court and, 348, 351.

KALDOR, MARY, 113, 114, 115–16, 117, 120, 124 n.44.

Kalla, Yusuf, 246.

Kant, Immanuel, 122–23 n.17, 345, 346, 348.

Kaplan, Robert D., 115.

Karadzic, Radovan, 158.

Katrina, Hurricane, 30, 31, 68, 87 n.46, 229–30.

Keen, David, 25 n.17.

Kennedy, David, 313.

Kenya, 85 n.25, 178, 180.

Keynes, J. M., 99.

Keynesianism, 138.

Khmer Rouge, 176.

Klein, Naomi, 93.

Knowledge workers, 361–66.

Korea, North, 9, 13.

Koselleck, Reinhardt, 191–92.

Koskenniemi, Martti, 348, 351.

Kosovo, 9, 155, 191, 270; Albanian Kosovars, 281–82, 289 n.25, 292 n.50; Dayton Accords and, 162; debates over decision to intervene, 13; emotional mobilization of public opinion and, 275; friend/enemy distinction in, 158–59; "good governance" in, 162–64; Havel's call for intervention in, 273; "humanitarian intervention" in, 12; human security concept and, 114; internationalized protectorate in, 154; international security force (KFOR) in, 346–47; landmark status in humanitarian discourse, 189; paradigmatic emergency in, 153; repatriation of refugees, 320; as sovereign nation-state, 161; therapeutic domination in, 328–29.

Kosovo, NATO air strikes in, 15, 16, 18, 20, 21, 281–83, 329; civilian deaths from, 14, 24 n.10; court cases related to, 346–47; doctrine of zero own-side casualties and, 302; as historical reference point, 311.

Kosovo Liberation Army (KLA), 283.

Kouchner, Bernard, 15, 23 n.3, 163, 193 n.10; Biafra crisis and, 176; as government minister, 189; Iraq (Second Gulf) War and, 290 n.35; Kosovo intervention and, 195 n.30; "right/duty to intervene" supported by, 275, 290 n.33; Somalia intervention and, 296.

Kurdistan, Iraqi, 12.

Kuwait, 272, 302.

LA FONTAINE, ANNIE, 320.

Laïdi, Zaki, 208.

Lake, Anthony, 311, 312.

Laksono, Karlina, 252–53.

Land mines, 111, 303–304.

Las Casas, Bartolomé de, 38–39.

Latin America, 10, 94, 209, 370, 372.

Lauterpacht, Hersch, 349.

Law, customary Aboriginal, 227, 228.

Law, international, 11, 31, 159, 321, 331; on cruel punishment, 338; Guantánamo Bay detention center and, 324; higher reasons set against, 13; humanitarian law, 335, 337, 338–43, 348; state power and, 342–43; U.S. sovereignty and, 351; war as vanishing point of, 349; world citizenship and, 348.

Law, rule of, 12, 17, 89, 90–94, 103; in Kosovo, 164; state of exception and, 324.

Leach, Edmund, 357.

Leavis, F. R., 133.

Lebanon war (2006), 153.

*Legality of the Threat or Use of Nuclear Weapons*, 341, 351.

Modernization, 94, 133, 161, 163, 230.

Montenegro, 282.

MONUSIL (United Nations Observer Mission in Sierra Leone), 14.

Moore, Sarah, 142.

Morales, Evo, 93.

Morality, 12, 18, 22, 51, 271. *See also* Ethics.

Mozambique, 48.

Mudslides, 9, 197.

Murphy, Deborah, 306, 311.

Museveni, Yoweri, 179, 181, 183.

Musharraf, Pervez, 86 n.39.

Myanmar. *See* Burma (Myanmar).

NADER, LAURA, 97.

Nafie, Nafie Ali, 312.

Nagorny-Karabakh region, 115.

Nargis, Cyclone, 48–49.

Nationalism, 16, 135, 344, 371.

National liberation, 33, 166.

National Society for the Prevention of Cruelty to Children, 140.

Nation-states, 12, 46, 47, 48, 166, 220.

NATO (North Atlantic Treaty Organization), 116, 154, 335; Albania in, 159, 161; calls for intervention in Darfur and, 308; peacekeeping and, 359; refugee camps and, 283; Yugoslavia bombed by, 339–41. *See also* Kosovo, NATO air strikes in.

Natural rights theory, 39.

Nature, state of, 324.

Nazis, 68, 130.

Necropolitics, 243.

*Negative Dialectics* (Adorno), 85 n.19.

Negri, Antonio, 91.

Nehru, Jawaharlal, 100, 136.

Neoconservatism, 313.

Neoliberalism, 77, 102, 154, 165, 166, 327.

Netherlands, 335.

Neutrality, 20, 33, 275; as autonomy from politics, 52; charity and, 37; difficulty of sustaining, 51–52; human rights in conflict with, 48, 376 n.6; human security and, 116–17; Kosovo conflict and, 282.

Neville, A. O., 220.

*New and Old Wars* (Kaldor), 116.

New International Economic Order (NIEO), 120, 126 n.75, 138.

New Orleans, inundation of, 30, 31, 229.

*New Wars and Human Security* (Kaldor and Johnson), 120.

New Zealand, 219.

Nguyen, Vinh-Kim, 330, 331.

Nicaragua, 178.

Nietzsche, Friedrich, 134, 323.

Nigeria, 175.

Nightingale, Florence, 36, 43.

Nobel Peace Prize: campaign to ban landmines and, 304; of MSF, 175, 177, 195 n.34, 279, 285.

Nongovernmental organizations (NGOs), 18, 19, 40, 45, 93, 165; in Aceh (Indonesia), 248, 250, 259, 260; anthropology and, 359, 361, 362; antipolitics and, 278; autonomy of, 52; Bosnia conflict and, 281; civil society and, 161, 329; Cold War and, 328; collaboration with occupying troops, 284; Darfur crisis and, 313; decline of communism and, 273; development integrated with security and, 352; emergency imaginary and, 31; humanitarian worldview and, 275; Human Security Response Force and, 117; images deployed by, 34; in Kosovo, 208; in Liberia, 330; mobile sovereignties and, 162, 321; in Occupied PalestinianTerritories (OPT), 80; political value-rationality and, 327; proliferation of, 69; scientific philanthropy and, 44; security discourse and, 167; Somalia intervention and, 295, 296, 300; therapeutic legitimacy and, 20; in Uganda, 179, 182.

Nordstrom, Carolyn, 190.

North, Global, 54, 166.

North America, 42, 314.

Norway, 111, 346, 347.

*Nouveau Cyné, Le* (Crucé), 120.

Nuclear energy, 138.

Nuclear weapons, 338, 341–42, 348–49.

Nussbaum, Martha, 272.

Nyerere, Julius, 100.

OAKLEY, ROBERT, 297.

Obama, Barack, 22, 307.

Occupied PalestinianTerritories (OPT), 9, 17, 20, 30, 87 n.45; asymmetry of suffering and, 24 n.9; catastrophization of, 59, 67; suspension of catastrophe in, 88 n.61; verge of humanitarian catastrophe in, 77–91. *See also* Gaza Strip; Palestinians.

Oil crisis (1970s), 100.

Omaar, Rakiya, 296.

Operation Allied Force, 339–41.

Operation Restore Hope, 12, 92, 295–99, 296, 311–12, 314. *See also* Somalia.

Operation Steel, 12.

Operation Turquoise, 12.

Organization for Security and Co-operation in Europe, 162, 165, 321.

Racism, 104, 222, 224, 232.
Rangel, José Vicente, 200, 214 n.9.
Rationality, instrumental, 49, 52, 323, 324, 325, 326.
Reagan, Ronald, 100, 101.
Recession, global, 22.
Rechtman, Richard, 259.
Red Crescent, 51, 56 n.8.
Red Cross, International Committee of the, 1, 37, 47, 56
    n.8, 376 n.6; founding of, 36, 42, 189, 273, 276–77;
    Holocaust and, 187; in Iraq, 14; MSF as alternative
    form of, 175; Somalia intervention and, 299.
Reformation, Protestant, 44.
Refugee camps, 52, 176, 186, 269, 276, 284; catastro-
    phization and, 75, 80; in Kosovo, 283; managerial
    rationalization and, 44; sexual abuses in Africa,
    293 n.52.
Refugees, 31, 50; from Afghanistan, 114; Albanian
    Kosovars, 14; anthropology and, 358, 361, 363; in
    Bangladesh war, 11; in Ethiopia, 33; human security
    and, 167; repatriation of Kosovo refugees, 320; from
    wars of Protestant Reformation, 44; in World War
    II, 47.
Regime change, 48, 309.
Rehn, Olli, 164, 172 n.34.
Reid, Anthony, 244.
Religion, 36, 37, 44, 345, 371.
Reportage, 362, 364, 367, 370.
Rereading Cultural Anthropology, 366.
Resources, allocation of, 49–50.
Responsibility, ethical and political, 16, 119, 337, 352.
Responsible Tourism Awards, 143.
Reterritorialization, 61, 68.
Ribbon culture, 142.
Rice, Condoleezza, 92.
Rice, Susan, 311, 312.
Rieff, David, 157–58, 178, 281.
Right to intervene (droit d'ingérence), 10, 11–12, 23
    nn.2–3, 120, 126 n.75; in Balkans, 162; Kouchner as
    supporter of, 195 n.30, 275, 290 n.33.
Robertson, Boni, 224.
Rodríguez, Isaías, 200.
Rogers, Nanette, 226.
"Rogue states," 32.
Romania, 155.
Romanies, 221.
Romantic movement, 35, 133–36.
Roosevelt, Franklin D., 110, 122 n.15.
Rosales, Manuel, 212.
Rose, Gen. Michael, 339.
Rosmarin, Sam, 316 n.34.

Roth, Kenneth, 24 n.10.
Russia, post-Soviet, 94, 163, 178, 285.
Rwanda, 9, 30, 54, 179, 191; call for military interven-
    tion in, 57–58 n.23; Darfur crisis compared to, 306;
    failure of Somalia intervention and, 301–302, 314;
    genocide in, 15, 21, 49, 57–58 n.23, 68, 173; Hutu
    refugees, 146; medical care of genocidaires, 49;
    Operation Turquoise, 12; testimonies of genocide
    survivors, 68; UN peacekeeping mission in, 368.

SADAQA, 35.
"Safe third country," 118.
Sahel drought, 32.
Said, Edward, 367.
Salamanca, School of, 39.
Salazar, Raul, 200–201, 214 n.15.
Salignon, Pierre, 278.
Salvation, discourse of, 159–61, 168.
Sands, Philippe, 336.
Sanitation, 42, 93.
Saramati, Ruzhdi, 347.
Saramati v. France, Germany and Norway, 346, 347.
Save Darfur Coalition, 295, 305–309, 313, 316 n.32,
    335–36.
Save the Children, 299–300.
Schmitt, Carl, 47, 73, 188, 318; friend/enemy distinction,
    158; on state of exception, 86 n.38, 189, 324.
Schumacher, E. F., 18, 136–37, 138, 139, 145.
Science, 42, 322, 331, 343.
Seattle protests (1999), 102.
Securitization, 107–108, 108–109, 116, 117–18.
Security, discourse of, 66, 168, 327.
Security, human, 107, 109, 119–21, 167–68; freedom from
    fear/want and, 110–11; friend/enemy distinction
    and, 158; legalizing/legitimating interventions and,
    118–19; network of, 114–16; policing of violence,
    116–18; remilitarization of, 112–14.
Sen, Amartya, 108.
September 11, 2001 (9/11), attacks, 21, 76, 114, 324, 371.
Sepúlveda, Juan Ginés de, 38.
Serbia/Serbians, 21, 163, 281, 282–83, 329.
Sexuality, 325, 331.
Shaftesbury, Lord (Anthony Ashley Cooper), 271.
Shelter, 55, 93.
Shining Path guerrillas, 367.
"Shock and awe" doctrine, 345, 354 n.42.
Siad Barre, Mohamed, 305, 315 n.21.
Sierra Leone, 14, 21, 30, 293 n.52.
Slavery and antislavery movements, 39, 42, 44, 112,
    129–30, 271; agency of slaves in Haiti, 141; defense

231; tripartite typology of rationality, 322, 323–24, 331.

Weber, Olivier, 273.

*We Did Nothing* (Polman), 368.

Weiss, Thomas, 275.

Welfare state, 44, 87 n.41, 135; Australian Aboriginal communities and, 231; Cold War and, 100; dismantling of, 95, 99, 218.

Welfarism, 39.

"We Must Defend the Union" (Brown), 129.

West Bank, 78, 79, 87 n.49.

Western world, 11, 34; Balkan policy, 153–56; "foreign policy ethics" and, 114; global recession and, 22; history of humanitarianism, 17; individualistic culture of, 98; legitimization of power in, 102; rule of law and, 89, 92, 93.

Westphalia, Treaty of (1648), 10, 120.

*We the Peoples: The Role of the United Nations in the 21st Century* (Annan), 118–19.

Whitaker, Ben, 137.

White Australia policy, 220.

Wilberforce, William, 18, 130, 137, 138, 139; contradictory humanitarian tradition of, 131–33; Corn Laws supported by, 131, 145; as evangelical reformer, 141–42; as pessimistic humanist, 136; reputation as progressive, 141.

Wild, Rex, 228.

Williams, Raymond, 134, 135, 140.

Williams, Rowan, 142.

Witnessing/bearing witness, 20, 36, 49, 55, 259–60, 282; anthropology and, 362, 363, 365, 366–74; law and, 365; *testimonio* genre, 370, 372.

Women, 53, 269; in Aceh (Indonesia), 241, 248, 249, 251, 257; in colonial Africa, 97–98; colonial civilizers and women's bodies, 39.

Wordsworth, William, 133.

Working classes, British, 134, 136, 138, 139, 140, 144.

World Bank, 92, 101, 102, 303; "fight against poverty," 127 n.81; Kosovo and, 164; Liberia and, 330; psychological needs assessment (PNA) in Aceh and, 255, 256, 261, 265 n.16; *Voices of the Poor* report, 139, 144.

World Bank Group, 99–100.

World Food Programme, 81, 86 n.36, 285.

World Health Organization, 279, 304, 337.

World Summit, 337.

World-system theory, 360.

World Trade Center, attack on, 76, 371.

World War I, 37.

World War II, 10, 44, 54, 69, 99, 108, 110, 130, 134, 156, 245, 221, 303.

*Writing Culture* initiative, 367.

YUDHOYONO, SUSILO BAMBANG, 245.

Yugoslavia, former, 24 n.10, 30, 320; breakup of, 48, 155; civil wars, 325; NATO bombing campaign against, 339–41.

Yusuf, Irwandi, 255.

*ZAKAT*, 35.

Zannier, Lamberto, 163.

Zarifian, Philippe, 156–57.

Ziegler, Jean, 78–79.

Series design by Julie Fry
Typesetting by Meighan Gale
Printed and bound by Maple Press